D0292225

Cash Flow and
Security Analysis

Cash Flow and Security Analysis

Kenneth S. Hackel, CFA
President, Systematic Financial Management, Inc.
and
Joshua Livnat, Ph.D., CPA
Leonard N. Stern School of Business, New York University

BUSINESS ONE IRWIN
Homewood, IL 60430

© KENNETH S. HACKEL and JOSHUA LIVNAT, 1992

All rights reserved. No part of this publication may be
reproduced, stored in a retrieval system, or transmitted,
in any form or by any means, electronic, mechanical,
photocopying, recording, or otherwise, without the prior
written permission of the publisher.

This publication is designed to provide accurate and
authoritative information in regard to the subject matter
covered. It is sold with the understanding that neither the
author nor the publisher is engaged in rendering legal, accounting,
or other professional service. If legal advice or other expert
assistance is required, the services of a competent
professional person should be sought.

*From a Declaration of Principles jointly adopted by a Committee
of the American Bar Association and a Committee of Publishers.*

Project editor: Jane Lightell
Production manager: Ann Cassady
Designer: Heidi J. Baughman
Production services: Elm Street Publishing Services, Inc.
Compositor: Carlisle Communications, Ltd.
Typeface: 10/12 Times Roman
Printer: Book Press, Inc.

Library of Congress Cataloging-in-Publication Data

Hackel, Kenneth S.
    Cash flow and security analysis / by Kenneth S. Hackel and Joshua
Livnat.
        p.   cm.
    ISBN 1-55623-387-6
    1. Investment analysis.   2. Cash flow.   I. Livnat, Joshua.
II. Title.
HG4529.H33   1992
658. 15′244 — dc20   92–13544

Printed in the United States of America
2 3 4 5 6 7 8 9 0 BP 9 8 7 6 5 4 3 2

*This Book Is Dedicated
to Our Families*

Preface

The world of money management and equity investment is changing at a pace not seen before. More sophisticated pension sponsors, new legal requirements, and the growth of quantitative techniques in risk measurement are forcing security analysts and investment advisors to improve their analysis and investment process. Central to this improvement is a better understanding of cash flow analysis.

At present, pension fund consultants classify money managers (and investors) as growth investors, market timers, sector rotators, and value investors. The latter category of investors focuses on a wide variety of investment criteria such as low price/earnings multiples, asset values, or private market values. However, given the severe measurement problems inherent in accounting, more and more professional investors are beginning to focus on entities' cash flows.

An entity's cash flows can be classified as cash flows from operating activities, financing activities, or investing activities. In this book, we show how these cash flows interact and how they are used to estimate the entity's free cash flow, which is used to identify firms that are consistent generators of cash flows and have the ability to easily pay down their debt. We will show how these firms are good values for investors.

Due to the growing integration of U.S. and foreign capital markets and the increasing difficulty of comparing reported earnings of U.S. and foreign firms, cash flow analysis is essential for successful portfolio selection.

Acknowledgments

We would like to thank many individuals and corporations who helped in the preparation of this book. We received great encouragement from our parents, Bernice (OB"M) and David Hackel, and Rachel and Meyer (OB"M) Livnat, to seek knowledge and better understanding of the world around us. We were lucky to have the support of our wives, Gail and Shoshana, and our children, Emily, Eli, and Betsy, and Orit, Ofer, and Shira, who never treated the book as a competitor for our time. We greatly benefited from our teachers, Professors Ronen, Schiff, and Sorter at New York University.

We gratefully acknowledge employees at Systematic Financial Management, Inc., Yvonne McNair at New York University, David Hill from Factset, and Ralph Rieves at Business One Irwin for their help. We also wish to thank Prudential Securities, the California Public Employees Retirement System, Smith Barney and Co., and Wheat First Securities, which have exhibited a strong commitment to investing on the basis of free cash flows. Special thanks are due to many pension consultants who took the time to understand and learn what cash flow analysis is all about.

Kenneth S. Hackel
Joshua Livnat

Contents

CHAPTER 1

Introduction

Everything flows and nothing stays

Heracleitus

People work, save, invest, and start businesses primarily to obtain cash. Their success in those endeavors is usually measured by the cash return on these activities, expressed as a percent increase of cash but discounted at an appropriate rate of interest. An important dimension of the cash return is how reliably an individual can continue to expect that return. Investors and creditors are therefore especially interested in future cash flows and, in particular, the amounts, timing, and uncertainty of cash flows. This book introduces the reader to the world of investments that uses these three dimensions of cash flows.

1.1 PURPOSE OF THE BOOK

This book is written with the underlying assumption that cash flow analysis is the most important tool at the investor's (or creditor's) disposal. While it is certainly recognized that there is a widespread arsenal of valuation techniques and procedures that have been developed by investors, academicians, and businesspeople throughout the years, eventually cash flow analysis must enter the picture. This is true whether the analyst evaluates a share of stock or a nonpublic business. Furthermore, even for asset-based sales, while appraisals may be an important determinant of the price, cash flow analysis becomes the most important variable because it is cash that eventually pays for the cost of the asset.

Unfortunately, the current corporate reporting system in the United States does not properly reflect how business decisions are made. For example, hiring decisions, purchasing decisions, capital decisions, and financing decisions, in essence all important corporate decisions, must be made only after considering the entity's ability to maximize its free cash flow and recover the cash invested in the firm.

The purpose of this book is to advocate a fundamental approach to investment in equity securities that is based on the analysis of free cash flows. Free cash flows can be loosely defined as the cash that a firm collects from its customers minus any expenditures that are necessary to sustain the current growth of the firm. Although this definition of free cash flows has been used before, its application varies considerably across users of financial statements. In this book, we describe in detail one procedure to estimate free cash flows, which we consider the most comprehensive estimation method. We further show how this definition of free cash flows can be used to select firms for a portfolio that earns abnormal returns.

We describe in this chapter the components we chose to highlight because we felt them to be attractive to money managers, security analysts, investors, creditors, financial statement users and preparers, and students of business.

1.2 THE MARKET SETTING

The U.S. capital market is characterized by three major markets in which equity securities trade: the New York Stock Exchange (NYSE), the American Stock Exchange (ASE), and the Over-the-Counter (OTC) market. Currently, there are about 1,900 securities that are traded on the NYSE, about 900 on the ASE, and an additional 8,000 or so securities are traded in the OTC market. Thus, there are about 10,800 securities that an investor can include in a portfolio. The major question facing an investor is how to select a subset of these securities for investment, because direct investment in all of these securities is prohibitively costly. The investor can invest in an index fund, which is a fund that holds a portfolio of securities that constitutes a widely accepted index such as the S&P 500. However, an investment in an index fund will not yield any abnormal returns (beyond the index) to the investor. Therefore, an investor who wishes to outperform the market has to invest in a subset of all available securities. This investor needs to decide how to focus on a subset of securities for investment.[1]

The first step in an investment process is to screen all potential investment candidates and select a subset of firms for a more detailed investigation. Screening is usually done by selecting one or more screening criteria. For example, one screening criterion that has attracted wide attention (but which we show in Chapter 7 has been an undesirable criterion in recent periods) is the price to earnings ratio (P/E). One can sort all firms according to their P/E ratios and then select the subset of firms with the lowest P/E ratios for further analysis. If the investor wants to ensure enough liquidity in the particular stocks, another criterion may be imposed on the selection process. For example, the investor may impose a minimum of $100 million market value for firms that are available for investment. The investor can also impose other screening criteria such as the exclusion of certain industries (e.g., financial services), or the exclusion of foreign firms.

Regardless of the specific screening criteria used, after screening all available securities, the investor obtains a list of firms that passed the screening criteria. This list constitutes likely candidates for investment purposes. The investor has to obtain more information about the firms on this list and determine which of these firms should be included in the final portfolio. The information that the investor needs depends on

---

[1]Some funds or portfolio managers have a very clearly defined, but narrow, investment focus. For example, some portfolios are concentrated in a specific industry. Others hold only small stocks or are designed to maximize dividend yield such as "tilt" funds. However, such investments may expose the investor to a greater risk.

factors that are considered important. For example, some investors may be interested in the market position of the firm; does it have any monopolistic advantages (such as patents or special licenses)? Some investors may be concerned about the management team of a particular firm, about its labor relationships, and so on. This information should be collected after the initial screening, but before the final investment decision is made.

Finally, the investor should decide what the desired investment goals are and their implications for selling decisions. The investor should determine *a priori* when a security is overpriced and should be sold. For example, an investor may decide that a security should be liquidated from the portfolio if the ratio of its price to free cash flow exceeds the median ratio of firms included in the S&P 500. It may decide to liquidate an investment in a security of a firm that engaged in a significant takeover of another firm, or if a significant legal suit has been brought against the firm. These selling criteria are an integral part of the investment strategy and should be decided upon when the investment is made. Figure 1–1 describes the three steps of the investment process.

1.3 "SOFT" AND "HARD" INFORMATION

Information about firms can be classified into two major types: quantitative or "hard" information and qualitative or "soft" information. In making investment decisions, investors use both types of information. For initial screening of firms, investors usually use quantitative information. This information is readily available in a machine-readable format, such as the S&P Compustat database. It is reasonably homogeneous across firms and it can be used with a computer program or a computer screening routine. However, an in-depth analysis of a firm will usually include some qualitative information as well. For example, the strength of management or the level of employee skills are two attributes that are based on "soft" information.

In Chapter 2 of this book, we develop a checklist of attributes that an investor may desire to examine before making an investment decision. From our long experience in financial statement analysis, we have compiled a list of attributes that most investors assess either formally or informally. Some investors make an effort to go through this list explicitly for every firm they analyze. Others implicitly or intuitively go over this

FIGURE 1–1   The Investment Process

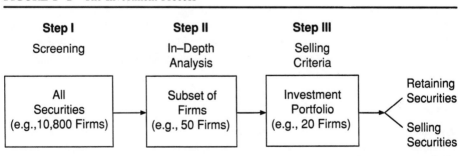

Step I	Step II	Step III	
Screening	In–Depth Analysis	Selling Criteria	
All Securities (e.g.,10,800 Firms)	Subset of Firms (e.g., 50 Firms)	Investment Portfolio (e.g., 20 Firms)	Retaining Securities / Selling Securities

FIGURE 1–2   Variables Used in Making Investment Decisions

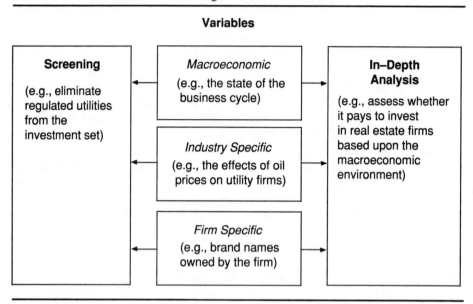

list of items. We believe that an organized checklist is a powerful tool for systematic investment decisions. Therefore, we begin this book by providing such a list.

The list of attributes that is provided in the next chapter includes items that relate to the macroeconomy in which the firm operates, the industries in which the firm does business, and some firm-specific attributes. For this checklist of items, we describe their possible effects on future cash flows, on free cash flows, and on the expected operating performance of the firm. We also provide the reader with a possible list of data sources, such as where one can find information about these attributes. Figure 1–2 illustrates the checklist of items and its potential use in the investment process.

We believe that the list of attributes we provide in the next chapter will enable the investor to construct not only a formal process of investment decision making *after* a subset of firms is identified, but also in setting up some screening variables. For example, in Chapter 2 we describe the diversification strategy that a firm may follow. Typically, a firm may diversify into related areas of business or into unrelated areas of business. When an investor sets up a screen for investment, the investor may include in the screen a desirable diversification strategy, such as a measure for unrelated diversification. Thus, some of the attributes on our list can be used for screening as well as for further in-depth analysis.

1.4 THE STATEMENT OF CASH FLOWS

The astute reader may wonder why we need to calculate or estimate free cash flows if a statement of cash flows is now routinely provided by firms on an annual and even a quarterly basis. To understand the limitations of the statement of cash flows for

FIGURE 1–3   Economic Decisions of a Firm

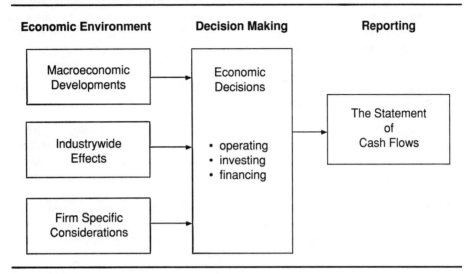

investment analysis, we devote Chapters 3 and 4 to a detailed discussion of this statement.

Chapters 3 and 4 explain the objectives of the statement of cash flows and describe the major components of this statement. Generally, the statement of cash flows is intended to provide investors with information about cash flows from operating, investing, and financing events. The chapters explain why these events are of paramount importance to investors and creditors of the firm. Chapter 3 illustrates in detail the construction of a statement of cash flows for one particular firm. Figure 1–3 describes how the underlying economic environment of a firm affects its decisions and how these decisions are captured by the statement of cash flows.

In Chapters 3 and 4 we also take a critical view of the way most firms report operating cash flows—the indirect method. This method provides substantially less information about components of cash flows from operations than the direct method, but is still used by most firms. We show how the components of cash flows from operating activities can be estimated, and in Chapter 5 we show how these components can be used to estimate free cash flows.

Chapter 4 provides a rich set of illustrations and examples of disclosures from real-world financial statements of firms. We illustrate the different components of cash flows that firms choose to report in the statement of cash flows. Our illustrations always begin with examples that are very common and proceed to describe some uncharacteristic disclosures by firms. In the latter cases, we evaluate the disclosure practices and speculate on the motives of firms for such disclosures.

Chapter 4 also contains a detailed analysis of factors that are related to the statement of cash flows. We describe the process that a careful investor may want to follow to analyze the major components of cash flows. For example, we show the importance of the components of cash flows from operations, the stability of net operating cash flows, and the relationships among the components of investing cash flows. We believe that such an analysis is important for most investors, even if they do not use free cash flows as the primary component in their investment decision.

1.5 EARNINGS, CASH FROM OPERATIONS, AND FREE CASH FLOWS

Chapter 5 is the focal chapter in this book. It is the chapter in which we provide detailed procedures to estimate free cash flows. We examine the limitations of earnings and net operating cash flows for investment analysis and provide the reasons for estimation of free cash flows. We show the superiority of free cash flows for investment purposes in Chapter 7.

Earnings of firms are highly publicized in the investment community, and sudden changes in earnings attract wide attention from analysts, investors, creditors, and the financial press. Prior academic studies showed that earnings changes are positively associated with security returns, so earnings increases are likely to be associated with price increases and decreases with earnings declines. Nevertheless, earnings is a number that is subject to some discretion by management, and is affected, in particular, by the accounting methods used to report earnings. We feel that investors would probably be better off using a number that is less subject to managerial discretion.

Net operating cash flow has been suggested as an alternative to earnings. In Chapter 5, we discuss the limitations of operating cash flows for investment purposes. In particular, net operating cash flows as currently reported by firms may contain elements that are nonrecurring, such as proceeds from a legal suit against a competitor for infringement of a patent. Also, net operating cash flows does not include any investments that the firm has to make in order to sustain the current level of growth. Thus, it is also of limited use for investors and creditors.

Free cash flows is subject to less managerial discretion; it is not affected by the choice of accounting methods and is unaffected by managerial discretion with respect to real cash expenditures. Free cash flows is estimated as net cash collected from customers minus all expenditures that are necessary to sustain the current level of growth. Figure 1–4 shows the financial statements that are used to derive free cash flows, net operating cash flows, and earnings of a firm.

In Chapter 5, we show two approaches to estimate free cash flows using real-world examples. We describe a process that can be used by investors and creditors and develop detailed procedures that can be used to construct a screen based on free cash flows. This screen is used in Chapter 7 to devise an investment strategy.

1.6 TOTAL DEBT OF A FIRM, INCLUDING OFF-BALANCE-SHEET LIABILITIES

The decade of the 1980s will be remembered by the large wave of acquisition activity that was financed mostly by debt, including management and leveraged buyouts (LBO). The underlying economic rationale had been that acquired firms were believed

FIGURE 1–4   Sources for Earnings, Net Cash from Operations, and Free Cash Flows

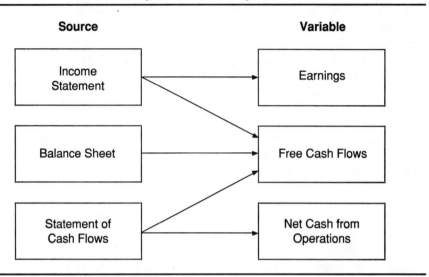

to have had strong and consistent cash flows that could have been used to pay off the assumed debt. As a result of the LBO boom, many firms found themselves with excess amounts of debt when they entered the 1990 recession.

We feel excess debt can be very dangerous to the viability of a firm and should be examined very closely by investors and creditors. Furthermore, we believe that investors and creditors should carefully scrutinize the financial statements to determine whether the firm has any other obligations that are not recorded on the balance sheet. The purpose of Chapter 6 is to discuss the relationship between free cash flows and debt, where debt consists not only of liabilities on the balance sheet, but also of off-balance-sheet liabilities.

Unlike prior literature on the relationship between debt and earnings or cash flows, we develop a measure that is based on the relationship between debt and free cash flows. Free cash flows represents an amount that a firm generates from its operations, but does not have to reinvest in the business in order to sustain the current growth. Thus, free cash flows can be either distributed entirely to shareholders without affecting future cash flows or used to pay down debt not due, again without affecting future cash flows. Therefore, we measure the debt capacity of a firm by the ratio of total debt (including off-balance-sheet liabilities) to free cash flows. The larger this ratio, the longer it will take the firm to pay off its debt.

Chapter 6 covers several areas that include potential off-balance-sheet liabilities, such as operating leases, pensions, and other postretirement benefits. It shows how investors and creditors should adjust total debt to include these obligations that are not recorded on the balance sheet. The importance of these adjustments and consideration of the debt capacity are discussed in Chapter 7.

1.7 PORTFOLIO SELECTION AND PERFORMANCE

Chapter 7 provides comparisons of the stock market performance of three portfolios—one that is based on P/E ratios, one that is based on net operating cash flows, and one that is based on free cash flows. It shows that the portfolio that is based on free cash flows performed the best among the three portfolios. It also shows that the performance of this portfolio is better at periods when the market as a whole declines.

To form portfolios, one can use several screening criteria that identify subsets of firms for investment purposes. One such screening variable is the P/E ratio, which is widely quoted in the financial press. It is typically believed that one should hold securities with low P/E ratios and sell short securities with high P/E ratios. Our results show that securities with low P/E ratios outperformed the market at the beginning of the 1980s, but have *not* outperformed the market in recent years. Thus, one cannot rely on P/E ratios for identifying investment candidates.

We also formed portfolios of firms based on the ratio of market value to net cash flow from operating activities. This ratio is similar to the P/E ratio in that it measures (roughly) the number of years it will take an investor to recapture the initial investment in the firm by the cash generated from operations. Similar to the portfolios that are based on P/E ratios, net operating cash flows cannot be used to identify a subset of firms that earn abnormal returns in recent years.

However, we find that a portfolio that is based on the ratio of market value to free cash flows has consistently earned abnormal returns over the most recent 11 years. This portfolio is selected based on several criteria; firms in this portfolio must have a low ratio of market value to average free cash flows over the past four years. These firms must also have a low ratio of debt to average free cash flows. They also have to show positive growth in their net operating cash flows over the most recent four- and eight-year periods. We find that very few firms fulfill all of these requirements. Those that do are firms with stable patterns of free cash flows that are underpriced by the market. The returns on holding this portfolio exceed the returns on holding the S&P 500. Figure 1–5 portrays three examples of screening criteria that are used in Chapter 7 to form portfolios for investment.

In Chapter 7, we provide results of back-testing the investment strategy that are based on free cash flows, as well as results of a live portfolio for the same periods. We explain that both types of evidence are needed to support the conclusions about the superiority of the investment strategy. The back-tests are artificial in terms of timing of investment or liquidation of a security; however, they ensure that no other considerations beyond the specified investment strategy are used for investment. Live portfolio results are deemed to be superior because these results adjust for transaction costs and information bias. However, results of a live portfolio cannot guarantee that other considerations were not responsible for investment or liquidation decisions. We feel the two approaches (live and back tests) are important complements to each other and we report the results for both.

1.8 SUMMARY

The purpose of this book is to educate the reader about what we believe is an important investment concept—free cash flows. We believe that one can use this concept to screen many candidates for investment and select a subset of firms for an in-depth

FIGURE 1–5   Examples of Screening Criteria for Portfolios Used in this Book

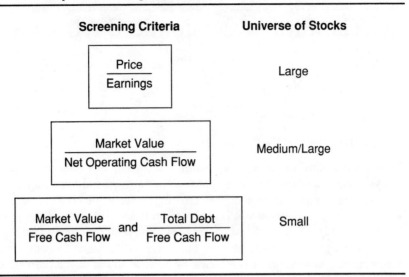

analysis. The estimation of free cash flows enables investors to use a reasonably sophisticated level of fundamental analysis on a computer screen that identifies a subset of firms for in-depth fundamental analysis. We hope the methods advocated in this book will help investors make better, and more informed, investment decisions.

CHAPTER 2

The Firm's Economic Environment

2.1 INTRODUCTION

Before one begins any analysis of a firm, whether it is a cash flow analysis, ratio analysis, credit analysis, investment analysis, or any general financial statement analysis, it is very important to understand the firm's economic environment. Familiarity with the economic environment is achieved on three levels — (1) macroeconomic developments, (2) industrywide events, and (3) firm-specific attributes (see Figure 2–1).

Generally, one wants to become familiar with the macroeconomy in which the firm operates, how the firm is affected by various stages of the business cycle, the firm's own life cycle, and the general forecasts of future economic developments. These macroeconomic developments will affect the firm's cash flows, and therefore, the firm's market value.

Example:

Firms that sell consumer goods may be directly affected by the general condition of the economy and the particular stage of the business cycle. Firms that sell consumer electronics expect their sales to decline when the economy contracts and increase when the econ-

FIGURE 2–1 Financial Analysis of a Firm

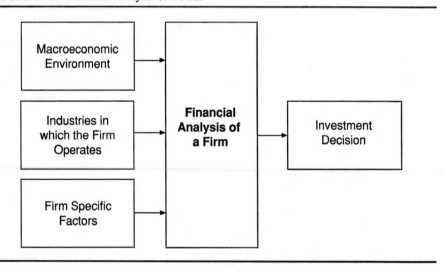

omy expands. In order to induce consumers to purchase goods, such firms reduce prices at an economic downturn, leading to lower operating cash flows for the firms. Many marketers of electronic goods offered deep discounts on their merchandise during November and December of 1990, in anticipation of bad holiday sales due to the economic recession.

Example:

A notable casualty of the 1980s was the banking industry, whose cash and deposits include amounts required to be maintained at the Federal Reserve, while loans, which make up the major share of its assets, are not "liquid" in the sense they are usually rolled over rather than paid. When rising interest rates caused wide negative spreads, cash flows of banks evaporated. When interest rates fell, cash flows soared.

The second level of analysis is the industry (or industries) in which a firm operates. Recognizing the peculiarities affecting the entity or industry under evaluation is vitally important. The analysis of cash flows can differ from one entity to another and from one industry to another, depending on the particular industries in which the firm operates. The analyst wishes to identify expected growth rates for the industry, expected operating capacity, expectations for technological advances, and so on. The analyst should also examine interrelationships among several industries in those cases where a firm operates in more than one industry or is dependent on another industry or on some other economic factor (e.g., the value of the dollar, or dependency of either revenues or supplies on other entities). The industrywide events are likely to affect the firm's own cash flows in a significant manner.

Example:

Tobacco firms generally enjoy a loyal brand clientele, although their potential market decreases with the decrease in the number of smokers in the population. Nevertheless, tobacco firms' cash flows are stable and predictable and are affected mostly by industry-specific events, such as the ability to increase selling prices, as opposed to economywide events. Such firms may be severely affected by an unfavorable decision in a legal case of product liability against them. Stock prices of tobacco firms are greatly affected by major court cases in these areas, and would see their operating cash flows soften if they were to lose such a case.

Example:

Banks and other financial intermediaries that do not maintain a good maturity balance (of assets and liabilities) have shown a high propensity for failure, as those institutions that borrowed "short term" and lent "long term" found out.

For manufacturing concerns, liquidity may appear to be in balance. However, if assets are more liquid than liabilities, there could be a surplus of short-term cash that can be used to repay interest-bearing debt; if the reverse is true, there could be a cash flow deficiency.

In the growing service sector, where the investment in fixed assets is typically low compared with liabilities, there is a greater need to estimate the *timing* of cash inflows.

It is the chief responsibility of the cash flow analyst to be cognizant of permissible industry/accounting methods, how they differ from other industries, and new accounting proposals and tax legislation that affect cash flows. For analysts who take pride in their earnings forecasts, assessing operating and free cash flows is invaluable in the determination of the "quality" of those earnings and to aid in setting an appropriate price/earnings multiple. Earnings quality is partially determined by the ease in which reported income is converted into cash.

Finally, the analyst should focus on firm-specific characteristics—any unique resources (or problems) that cannot be identified for other firms in the same industry. Some examples include a firm that has a monopoly in producing one product (e.g., a utility company) or a firm that relies on a single supplier of raw materials. Positive factors will increase cash flows for the particular firm and will result in higher stock prices, whereas firms with negative factors may have more volatile cash flows.

> **Example:**
>
> Drexel, Burnham and Lambert, a small security firm, became a large operation due to its development and large market share of the high-yield bond market ("junk bonds", as they were known). With the deterioration in this market (and the allegations of illegal trading), the firm lost its unique competitive advantage and was forced into bankruptcy.

In this chapter, we develop a checklist of items that should be considered in an analysis of the economic environment of a firm and provide examples of data sources that are available for this analysis.

2.2 THE MOTIVES FOR UNDERSTANDING THE ECONOMIC ENVIRONMENT

There are three main reasons why an analyst who is studying cash flows would like to understand the economic environment of a firm. Figure 2–2 illustrates these reasons, which are then explained in more detail.

1. *Evaluation of past performance*

   In many cases, an analyst wishes to evaluate a firm's historic operating cash flows, as reflected in its published financial reports. The analyst should have a good idea of the economic environment that prevailed during the period covered by the financial statements to better understand the reasons for success or failure of the firm.

> **Example:**
>
> Suppose the analysis is of a firm in the oil business during the years 1973–1974. The analyst who is familiar with the firm and its economic environment will expect to see a major increase in revenues and operating cash flows between these two years, or between 1974 and prior years, due solely to the oil embargo. Evaluation of past performance that ignores the effects of the oil embargo may erroneously conclude that management was able to substantially increase sales and operating cash flows due to greater market penetration or similar reasons.

FIGURE 2-2   Financial Statement Analysis

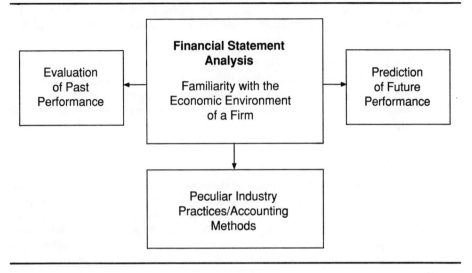

Example:

A tender offer for Revco Corporation, a large drug store chain, was made at the height of its operating cycle, a time when retail sales were higher than normal. Subsequent to the tender offer, retail sales and cash flow collapsed, forcing the firm into bankruptcy. The cash flow analyst should be familiar with the economic conditions so that an assessment can be made as to whether retail sales are expected to increase, decrease, or remain stable.

2. *Prediction of future performance*
   Often, the analyst examines published financial reports in order to make predictions about future performance of the firm. This is called *feedback*. In making these predictions, the analyst should have a good understanding of the economic environment a firm faces. The analyst should also consider any expectations of changes from the historical growth rates for the particular industry, as well as other microeconomic and macroeconomic factors.

Example:

Throughout the mid-1980s, computer manufacturers of mainframes or personal computers enjoyed a very high growth rate of revenues and cash flows. However, market expectations in the mid-1980s were such that the high growth rates achieved in the past would not be sustained in the future. Therefore, an analyst who bases predictions of future sales on historical growth rates may overstate future growth rates, given the pessimistic outlook for such firms.

Example:

Many entities that went private via leveraged buyout (LBO) ran into difficulties when the economy slowed during the 1990s. The retailing industry is a notable example where large companies enjoyed good growth during the 1982–1990 economic expansion, but where many companies either fell into bankruptcy or were faced with prospects of bankruptcy when demand fell and when high interest payments associated with the LBO eroded cash flows.

3. *Identification of particular business practices and accounting rules*
There are certain industries that follow different business practices and accounting rules than the majority of firms. When an analyst examines firms from these industries, it is important to understand the context of the business transactions as well as their accounting descriptions.

Example:

Firms in the broadcasting industry may invest resources in creating a program or a movie that is expected to generate future cash flows from future broadcasting or screening. In such cases, the original expenditures on the program or movie are capitalized and amortized over the expected life of the program. The analyst should be aware of that practice when analyzing financial statements of a firm in the broadcasting industry, and should be able to assess whether the amortization period that the firm chooses is adequate or too liberal, as well as its effects on estimating cash flows.

Example:

Headquartered in Des Moines, Iowa, Meredith Corp. is a Fortune 500 diversified media company involved in magazine and book publishing, television broadcasting, and residential real-estate marketing and franchising.
Note (1),(e),(f) of Meredith Co.'s 1989 annual report states:

e. *Unearned Subscription Revenue*
Unearned subscription revenue consists of gross unearned subscription revenue, net of acquisition costs, and is recorded and recognized pro rata as delivery of magazines is made, beginning with the month of initial delivery.

f. *Deferred Film Rental Costs*
Deferred film rental costs reflect the value of all films available for showing and are stated at cost less amortization. Film rental costs are charged to operations on an accelerated amortization basis over the contract period. The cost of broadcast film rental estimated to be charged to operations during the next fiscal year has been classified as a current asset.

2.3 THE FIRM'S BUSINESS SEGMENTS

In Statement No. 14 (1976), the Financial Accounting Standards Board (FASB) required firms to disclose information about their business segments. A business segment is any group of similar businesses that contributes at least 10 percent to revenues, operating profits, or identifiable assets of a firm (FASB, 1976, para. 15). The FASB required the disclosure of revenues, operating profits, and identifiable assets by segments. Many firms also disclose capital expenditures and depreciation by segments.

The FASB required firms to disclose geographical distribution of sales for firms that operate in more than just one part of the world and the disclosure of sales to major customers who purchase at least 10 percent of total revenues.

Example:

General Electric (GE) reports operations in 11 different segments during 1989. Although GE is well known for its electric appliances and light bulbs, it is less famous for its power-generating equipment or financial services. A firm may actually derive most of its revenues (or cash flows) from lines of business of which most people are unaware. In the case of GE, electric appliances constitute only slightly more than 10 percent of consolidated revenues.

Figure 2–3 on page 17 portrays the distribution of revenues across the 11 segments.

GE Industry Segment Details

Industry Segment Details

(In millions)	Revenues For the years ended December 31								
	Total revenues			Intersegment revenues			External revenues		
	1989	1988	1987	1989	1988	1987	1989	1988	1987
GE									
Aerospace	$ 5,282	$ 5,343	$ 5,262	$ 77	$ 166	$ 78	$ 5,205	$ 5,177	$ 5,184
Aircraft Engines	6,863	6,481	6,773	69	119	48	6,794	6,362	6,725
Broadcasting	3,392	3,638	3,241	1	—	—	3,391	3,638	3,241
Industrial	7,059	7,061	6,662	701	706	708	6,358	6,355	5,954
Major Appliances	5,620	5,289	4,721	—	—	—	5,620	5,289	4,721
Materials	4,929	3,539	2,751	33	40	32	4,896	3,499	2,719
Power Systems	5,129	4,805	4,995	128	126	125	5,001	4,679	4,870
Technical Products and Services	4,545	4,431	3,670	194	161	337	4,351	4,270	3,333
Earnings of GEFS	927	788	552	—	—	—	927	788	552
All Other	319	394	3,176	—	—	4	319	394	3,172
Corporate Items and Eliminations	(1,415)	(1,477)	(1,287)	(1,203)	(1,318)	(1,332)	(212)	(159)	45
Total GE	42,650	40,292	40,516	—	—	—	42,650	40,292	40,516
GEFS									
Financing	7,333	5,827	3,507	—	—	—	7,333	5,827	3,507
Insurance	2,710	2,478	2,217	—	—	—	2,710	2,478	2,217
Securities Broker-Dealer	2,897	2,316	2,491	—	—	—	2,897	2,316	2,491
All Other	5	34	10	—	—	—	5	34	10
Total GEFS	12,945	10,655	8,225	—	—	—	12,945	10,655	8,225
Eliminations	(1,021)	(858)	(583)	—	—	—	(1,021)	(858)	(583)
Consolidated revenues	$54,574	$50,089	$48,158	$ —	$ —	$ —	$54,574	$50,089	$48,158

source: General Electric, *Annual Report*, 1989.

Example:

Singer Co. is probably familiar to most people for its sewing machines. In fact, Singer had sold the division that produced sewing machines in 1986. In 1987 it operated in four segments, and was greatly dependent on the U.S. government for defense-related projects. Figure 2–4 on page 17 illustrates the composition of segment assets across the four segments.

Singer Company Financial Information for Business Segments

Revenues, operating income, assets, depreciation and amortization, and capital expenditures by major product areas and lines of business for each of the years in the three-year period ended December 31, 1987, are shown below. Amounts are in millions.

Year Ended December 31	Defense Electronics[1]	Training Systems[1]	Motor Products	Meter Products	Less General Corporate Expenses	Amounts Applicable to Corporate	Discontinued Operations	Total
Revenues								
1987	$783.4	$785.6	$230.1	$103.6	$—	$—	$—	$1,902.7
1986	719.8	710.9	181.9	112.6	—	—	—	1,725.2
1985	650.5	628.5	182.4	108.1	—	—	—	1,569.5
Operating income[2]								
1987	34.1	34.1	26.6	11.8	19.6	—	—	87.0
1986	72.5	23.7	15.6	17.3	15.0	—	—	114.1
1985	53.1	15.0	21.2	17.3	10.6	—	—	96.0
Assets								
1987	818.1	477.6	90.5	51.2	—	152.0	—	1,589.4
1986	644.8	402.6	85.9	50.8	—	103.8	—	1,287.9
1985	307.4	320.9	70.1	46.7	—	113.7	315.6	1,174.4
Depreciation and amortization								
1987	38.3	13.6	5.2	2.3	—	2.5	—	61.9
1986	31.1	28.4	4.6	2.2	—	2.6	—	68.9
1985	21.5	13.3	4.0	2.1	—	2.4	—	43.3
Capital expenditures								
1987	43.2	26.4	5.6	2.9	—	6	—	78.7
1986	62.5	18.2	5.2	4.1	—	.6	—	90.6
1985	41.1	32.1	6.6	5.4	—	2.6	—	87.8

[1]Amounts reported for the years prior to 1987 have been reclassified to conform to the 1987 presentation which reflects separately the Company's high-technology operations. For purposes of segment reporting under Statement of Financial Accounting Standards No. 14, Defense Electronics should be added to Training Systems.
[2]Operating results for 1987 include a $45 million charge for higher-than-anticipated costs required to complete the development phase of three technically complex Defense Electronics programs.

FIGURE 2–3   GE 1989 Revenues

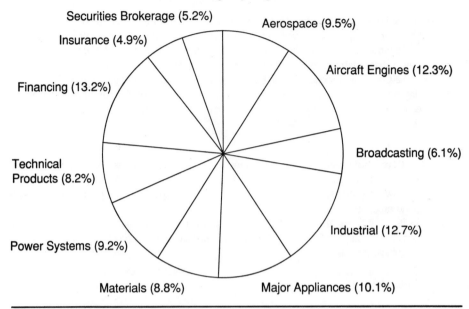

Percentage by Segment

Securities Brokerage (5.2%)

Insurance (4.9%)

Financing (13.2%)

Technical
Products (8.2%)

Power Systems (9.2%)

Materials (8.8%)

Aerospace (9.5%)

Aircraft Engines (12.3%)

Broadcasting (6.1%)

Industrial (12.7%)

Major Appliances (10.1%)

SOURCE: General Electric, *Annual Report*, 1989.

FIGURE 2–4   Singer 1987 Assets

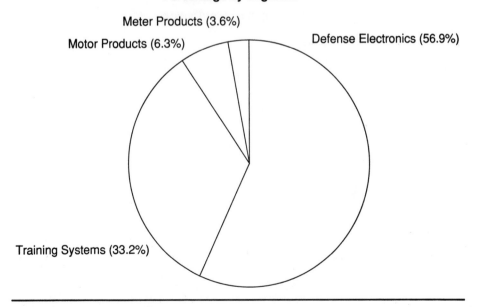

Percentage by Segment

Meter Products (3.6%)

Motor Products (6.3%)

Defense Electronics (56.9%)

Training Systems (33.2%)

SOURCE: Singer Co., *Annual Report*, 1987.

Example:

Black & Decker manufactures, markets, and services power tools, household products, and other labor-saving devices. Products include drills, saws, toaster ovens, coffee-makers, and electric mowers. However, in its financial statements, Black & Decker does not disclose segment data, claiming that it operates in just a single line of business:

"The Corporation operates in one business segment— the manufacturing, marketing and servicing of a wide range of power tools, household products and other labor-saving devices generally used in and around the home and by professional users." (1988 Annual Report, p. 32)

Example:

NCR Corp. (now part of AT&T) develops, manufactures, markets, installs, and services business information processing systems for worldwide markets. NCR's products include various work-stations, multi-user computer systems, communication processors, and synergistic products.

In its 1989 financial statements, NCR included a footnote on its international operations, which appears on page 19. Figure 2-5 portrays the distribution of revenues across the various geographical regions.

Example:

General Mills is a leading producer of consumer foods and operator of chain restaurants. The company also makes and sells food products in Canada, Europe, Japan, Korea, and Latin America. Products are distributed to retail food chains, co-ops, and wholesalers.

FIGURE 2–5   NCR 1989 Revenues

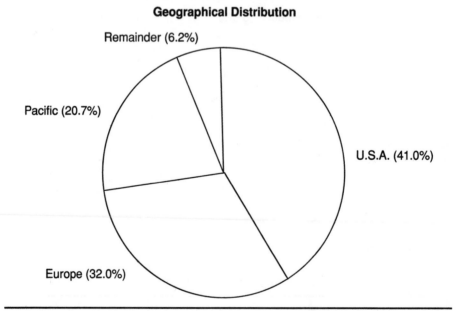

Geographical Distribution

Remainder (6.2%)

Pacific (20.7%)

U.S.A. (41.0%)

Europe (32.0%)

SOURCE: NCR Corp., *Annual Report*, 1989.

General Mills included a footnote on segments in its 1989 financial statements, presented on page 20.

In addition to a footnote about segments in the annual report, segment information is also available in the first section of Form 10-K, which must be filed with the Securities and Exchange Commission (SEC) once a year. The first section of this report contains general information about the business of the firm. It includes a description of the major products and areas of business in which the firm operates. It also includes

NCR 1989 Geographical Data

	1989	1988	1987
Revenue for the year ended December 31			
United States			
Customer	**$ 2,442**	$ 2,467	$ 2,559
Intercompany	**483**	453	411
	2,925	2,920	2,970
Europe			
Customer	**1,908**	1,978	1,797
Intercompany	**150**	155	163
	2,058	2,133	1,960
Pacific (Australasia, Far East and Canada)			
Customer	**1,235**	1,189	954
Intercompany	**138**	119	127
	1,373	1,308	1,081
Latin and South America, Middle East and Africa			
Customer	**371**	356	331
Intercompany	**3**	5	12
	374	361	343
Intercompany eliminations	**(774)**	(732)	(713)
Consolidated revenue	**$ 5,956**	$ 5,990	$ 5,641
Operating income for the year ended December 31			
United States	**$ 327**	$ 359	$ 386
Europe	**211**	241	215
Pacific	**173**	190	154
Latin and South America, Middle East and Africa	**10**	21	23
Consolidated operating income	**721**	811	778
Corporate items and intercompany eliminations	**18**	(24)	(12)
Consolidated income before income taxes	**$ 739**	$ 787	$ 766
Identifiable assets as of December 31			
United States	**$ 2,092**	$ 2,117	$ 2,067
Europe	**1,097**	1,114	1,079
Pacific	**550**	573	483
Latin and South America, Middle East and Africa	**177**	195	208
Consolidated identifiable assets	**3,916**	3,999	3,837
Corporate assets and intercompany eliminations	**584**	718	704
Consolidated total assets	**$ 4,500**	$ 4,717	$ 4,541

SOURCE: NCR Corp., *Annual Report*, 1989.

General Mills Segment Information

Note Fifteen: Segment Information

In Millions	Consumer Foods	Restaurants	Unallocated Corporate Items (a)	Consolidated Total
Sales				
1989	$3,998.7	$1,621.9		$5,620.6
1988	3,667.5	1,312.1		4,979.6
1987	3,397.6	1,112.5		4,510.1
Operating Profits				
1989	452.4	127.7	$(62.6)	517.5
1988	421.2	104.0	(54.8)	470.4
1987	382.8	91.8	(55.8)	418.8
Identifiable Assets (b)				
1989	1,571.6	862.2	454.3	2,888.1
1988	1,391.6	736.0	545.7	2,673.3
1987	1,171.6	557.9	632.7	2,362.2
Capital Expenditures				
1989	254.1	182.9	5.4	442.4
1988	184.2	157.3	69.2	410.7
1987	142.1	142.4	44.6	329.1
Depreciation Expense				
1989	96.0	51.3	1.5	148.8
1988	85.7	41.7	1.4	128.8
1987	77.8	33.4	1.6	112.8

(a) Corporate expenses reported here include net interest expense and general corporate expenses. Corporate capital expenditures include capital expenditures of discontinued operations through the date disposition was authorized.

(b) Identifiable assets for our segments consist mainly of receivables, inventories, prepaid expenses, net land, buildings and equipment, intangible assets and investments and miscellaneous assets. Corporate identifiable assets consist mainly of cash, short-term investments, deferred income taxes, marketable investments and net assets of discontinued operations.

SOURCE: General Mills, *Annual Report*, 1989.

other information that is relevant for other subsections of this chapter. One can use the description of products and lines of business to identify the industries in which the firm operates.

The Bureau of the Census has used a widely accepted system to classify firms into industries, which is known as the Standard Industrial Classification (SIC) system. Under this system, each broad industry is assigned a two-digit SIC code, such as #20 for the food and kindred products group. Within this broad industry, businesses are assigned to more specific industries with three- and four-digit SIC codes, such as 202 for dairy products, and 2024 that represents ice cream and frozen desserts. The Bureau of the Census has classified each business establishment of each surveyed firm into 1 of 214 4-digit SIC industries. When a firm has establishments in just one four-digit SIC industry, it is classified as a single-industry company. When it has establishments in more than one four-digit SIC industry, it is classified as a multi-industry company. The cash flow analyst may compare firms from the same four-digit SIC industry, and may attempt to forecast future cash flows within a particular industry.

Exhibit 2-1 reproduces summary statistics from the 1982 Census classification of firms. It shows that the vast majority of firms, about 99 percent of the surveyed companies, operated in just a single industry. However, the table also shows that the 39.1 million multi-industry companies employed about 42 percent of the 616 million American employees, and paid wages that amounted to about 54 percent of total wages. Moreover, sales and revenues of the multi-industry companies amounted to

EXHIBIT 2-1   Statistics about Single- and Multi-Industry Companies 1982 Census

	Single-Industry		Multi-Industry		Total	
Number of Firms (Mil.)	4217.1	99%	39.1	1%	4256.2	100%
Number of Employees (Mil.)	355.2	58%	261.4	42%	616.6	100%
Annual Payroll (Billion Dollars)	422.4	46%	491.5	54%	913.9	100%
Sales (Billion Dollars)	2551.7	48%	2810.3	52%	5362.0	100%

SOURCE: 1982 U.S. Census.

about 52 percent of total sales made by all U.S. companies. Thus, the statistics in the exhibit show that although multi-industry companies comprise less than 1 percent of the total number of U.S. companies, they are responsible for more than 50 percent of the U.S. employment, wages, and sales. This clearly indicates the importance of multi-industry firms within the U.S. economy. Most large publicly traded firms operate in more than one industry.

A very useful source of information about the SIC industries in which a firm operates can be found in Standard & Poor's *Registrar of Corporations*. In addition to data about the firm's address, telephone number, directors, and so on, this source lists the four-digit SIC codes.

Example:

Although Black & Decker indicated that it operated in a single line of business, Standard & Poor's shows that it operates in eight different four-digit SIC industries.

It is important to understand the type of businesses the firm is in before analyzing its financial statements. Traditionally, a firm is assigned to an industry according to its largest segment in terms of revenues. This may be misleading for a firm that operates in more than just one major line of business because the firm's highest cash flow generator may not be the same segment that contributes the largest amount of revenues. A convenient way of assessing the extent of operations in more than one industry is to construct a table that shows the percentage of total revenues, profits, or assets that each of the segments is responsible for. This gives an immediate indication about the diversity of operations across business segments.

Example:

In the case of General Mills, whose data are provided in a previous example, we find that in 1989 the consumer foods segment accounted for 71 percent of total sales, whereas the restaurants accounted for the remainder, or 29 percent. However, the consumer foods segment was more profitable, contributing 78 percent of operating profits, while accounting for only 65 percent of identifiable assets of General Mills. Also worth noting, General Mills has decided to expend a larger amount on capital assets in the consumer foods segment, but the proportion is much smaller than the proportion this segment contributes to either sales or operating profits. Thus, General Mills may have decided to invest more in its restaurants segment because it believed that this part of its business had greater opportunity for growth, which would eventually increase both operating and free cash flows.

It should be noted that current disclosure of segment data is insufficient to estimate the major components of cash flows from operating, financing, or investing activities. Most firms disclose data about sales, operating profits, and identifiable assets in each of their segments, but there is usually no disclosure of segment balance sheet, income statement, or cash flow statements. Thus, an analyst cannot estimate components of cash flows for each of a firm's segments—unless the segment discloses a complete set of financial statements— because it is required to do so by regulators or because of other reasons, such as a part of due diligence review that precedes a takeover process. However, in most cases the analyst is limited to segment information about revenues, operating profits, identifiable assets, depreciation, and capital expenditures. These data are available in the footnotes to the financial statements and can be accessed from computer data bases and easily analyzed.

Example:

National Service Industries is a diversified firm that has four major segments. Factset, an information service firm, provides an analysis of National Service Industries, shown on pages 23–27.

Note that National Service Industries, a firm with total sales of about $1.6 billion in 1990, has four major segments: lighting equipment, textile rental, other, and chemical segments. At the bottom of Factset's analysis, one can find the contribution of each segment to sales, operating profits, capital expenditures, and identifiable assets. In addition, for each of the segments, Factset estimates operating cash flows by adding back depreciation to operating profits of the segment. As we shall see in the next chapter, this is just a rough approximation of operating cash flows. For each segment, Factset reports the percentage change in sales and operating profits, and two profitability measures. The first profitability measure is based on multiplying asset turnover (sales divided by average identifiable assets in the most recent two years) by the operating margin (operating profit divided by sales times 100). The second is identical to the first, except that operating cash flow replaces operating profit in the margin ratio.

It should be noted that the segment analysis reported by Factset is not exhaustive; other analysts can add their own unique ratios or other types of analysis. However, with the limited data available on segments, there is not much broader analysis that can be applied.

Sometimes a firm will report that it operates in a single line of business. In such a case, the cash flow analyst will have little information about revenues, profits, or cash flows for various parts of the business, such as for different brands or important products.

Example:

H.J. Heinz Co. has the following footnote in its financial statements about its segment data:
"The company is engaged principally in one line of business—processed food products—which represents over 90% of consolidated sales."
However, the firm reports data about operations in various geographical regions.

In some cases, the assignment of firms into a particular four-digit SIC industry yields an industry that has very dissimilar firms.

NSI 63765710 National Service Industries Inc.

	8/90	8/89	8/88	8/87	8/86	8/85	8/84	Growth Rate or Mean Values	
								3 Years	5 Years
Lighting Equipment	(3646, 3645)								
Net sales	717.2	658.7	602.8	559.4	522.1	469.4	NA	8.7	8.6
COGS & SGA	638.0	590.7	540.9	502.3	460.7	415.3	NA	8.4	8.8
Depreciation and amortization	15.3	12.8	11.3	10.1	8.2	7.0	NA	14.8	16.5
Operating profits	63.9	55.2	50.6	47.0	53.1	47.1	NA	10.6	5.0
Operating cash flow	79.2	68.0	61.9	57.1	61.3	54.1	NA	11.4	6.8
Capital expenditures	30.0	20.3	14.0	16.1	22.9	13.8	NA	25.0	10.2
Identifiable assets	295.1	263.5	241.7	225.4	214.9	182.4	NA	9.4	9.2
Percent change analysis									
Net sales	8.9	9.3	7.8	7.2	11.2	0.0			
Operating profits	15.6	9.1	7.8	-11.5	12.7	0.0			
Profitability analysis									
Asset turnover	2.57	2.61	2.58	2.54	2.63	NA		2.59	2.59
× Operating margin	8.9	8.4	8.4	8.4	10.2	10.0	NA	8.6	8.9
= Operating ROA	22.9	21.9	21.7	21.3	26.7	NA		22.1	22.9
Operating cash ROA	28.4	26.9	26.5	25.9	30.9	NA		27.3	27.7
Textile rental	(7213, 7218)								
Net sales	397.0	355.8	321.0	294.5	282.4	271.0	NA	10.5	8.0
COGS & SGA	335.7	301.8	272.4	250.3	242.2	235.0	NA	10.3	7.5
Depreciation and amortization	17.8	15.5	12.9	11.5	10.1	9.0	NA	16.0	14.6
Operating profits	43.6	38.5	35.8	32.7	30.1	27.0	NA	9.8	9.7

continued

23

NSI   63765710 National Service Industries Inc. (continued)

	8/90	8/89	8/88	8/87	8/86	8/85	8/84	Growth Rate or Mean Values 3 Years	5 Years
Operating cash flow	61.3	54.1	48.7	44.2	40.2	36.0	NA	11.5	11.0
Capital expenditures	23.1	22.6	17.5	18.7	12.3	15.8	NA	9.4	11.1
Identifiable assets	251.6	213.8	189.3	184.4	168.5	170.4	NA	11.1	8.0
Percent change analysis									
Net sales	11.6	10.8	9.0	4.3	4.2	0.0			
Operating profits	13.1	7.7	9.5	8.4	11.8	0.0			
Profitability analysis									
Asset turnover	1.71	1.77	1.72	1.67	1.67	NA	NA	1.73	1.71
× Operating margin	11.0	10.8	11.1	11.1	10.7	10.0		11.0	10.9
= Operating ROA	18.7	19.1	19.2	18.5	17.8	NA		19.0	18.7
Operating cash ROA	26.4	26.8	26.0	25.0	23.7	NA		26.4	25.6
Other	(1742, 2677)								
Net sales	300.7	306.9	290.4	289.4	306.3	290.5	NA	1.7	0.5
COGS & SGA	276.8	275.9	269.1	258.3	278.9	268.9	NA	2.3	0.4
Depreciation and amortization	6.5	5.5	4.6	3.9	6.9	5.6	NA	18.6	0.7
Operating profits	17.4	25.5	16.6	27.2	20.5	16.1	NA	-8.6	1.7
Operating cash flow	23.9	31.1	21.3	31.1	27.4	21.6	NA	-4.0	1.4
Capital expenditures	9.8	12.1	8.9	8.3	11.0	15.2	NA	8.1	-5.1
Identifiable assets	131.6	124.4	123.8	110.8	120.0	124.2	NA	5.3	1.5

Insulation service	117.0	127.0	118.0	116.0	109.0	88.0	NA		
Mens' apparel	42.0	41.0	48.0	54.0	58.0	71.0	NA		
Envelopes	93.0	89.0	77.0	70.0	66.0	61.0	NA		
Marketing services	49.0	50.0	47.0	50.0	74.0	70.5	NA		
Percent change analysis									
Net sales	-2.0	5.7	0.3	-5.5	5.4	0.0			
Operating profits	-31.6	53.3	-38.7	32.6	27.6	0.0			
Profitability analysis									
Asset turnover	2.35	2.47	2.48	2.51	2.51	NA		2.43	2.46
× Operating margin	5.8	8.3	5.7	9.4	6.7	5.5	NA	6.6	7.2
= Operating ROA	13.6	20.6	14.2	23.6	16.8	NA		16.1	17.7
Operating cash ROA	18.7	25.0	18.1	26.9	22.4	NA		20.6	22.2
Chemical (2841, 2842)									
Net sales	232.9	218.1	200.0	183.6	172.2	160.3	NA	8.3	7.9
COGS & SGA	198.1	185.6	166.8	153.7	144.6	135.2	NA	9.1	8.1
Depreciation and amortization	2.4	2.1	2.0	1.6	1.3	1.1	NA	13.0	16.7
Operating profits	32.4	30.4	31.2	28.3	26.3	23.9	NA	3.9	6.0
Operating cash flow	34.8	32.5	33.2	29.9	27.6	25.0	NA	4.4	6.6
Capital expenditures	12.1	6.6	3.5	2.1	7.7	2.9	NA	79.9	22.8
Identifiable assets	90.4	81.6	72.0	66.1	61.5	53.5	NA	11.2	10.7
Percent change analysis									
Net sales	6.8	9.0	8.9	6.6	7.4	0.0			
Operating profits	6.6	-2.5	10.1	7.6	10.0	0.0			

continued

NSI 63765710 National Service Industries Inc. (continued)

	8/90	8/89	8/88	8/87	8/86	8/85	8/84	Growth Rate or Mean Values	
								3 Years	5 Years
Profitability analysis									
Asset turnover	2.71	2.84	2.90	2.88	3.00	NA	NA	2.81	2.86
× Operating margin	13.9	13.9	15.6	15.4	15.3	14.9		14.5	14.8
= Operating ROA	37.7	39.6	45.1	44.4	45.7	NA		40.8	42.5
Operating cash ROA	40.5	42.3	48.1	46.9	48.0	NA		43.6	45.2
Company totals									
Net sales	1647.8	1539.5	1414.2	1326.9	1282.9	1191.2	0.0	7.6	6.6
COGS & SGA	1448.5	1353.9	1249.2	1164.6	1126.4	1054.4	0.0	7.6	6.5
Depreciation and amortization	42.0	36.0	30.8	27.1	26.5	22.8	0.0	15.8	12.4
Operating profits	157.3	149.7	134.2	135.1	130.0	114.0	0.0	5.8	6.0
Operating cash flow	199.3	185.6	165.0	162.3	156.5	136.8	0.0	7.6	7.1
Capital expenditures	75.0	61.6	44.0	45.2	53.9	47.6	0.0	20.4	7.8
Identifiable assets	768.6	683.3	626.8	586.7	564.9	530.5	0.0	9.4	7.4
Percent change analysis									
Net sales	7.0	8.9	6.6	3.4	7.7	0.0			
Operating profits	5.1	11.5	-0.7	3.9	14.0	0.0			
Profitability analysis									
Asset turnover	2.27	2.35	2.33	2.30	2.34	4.49	NA	2.32	2.32
× Operating margin	9.5	9.7	9.5	10.2	10.1	9.6		9.6	9.8
= Operating ROA	21.7	22.8	22.1	23.5	23.7	43.0		22.2	22.8
Operating cash ROA	27.5	28.3	27.2	28.2	28.6	51.6		27.7	28.0

Percent of company totals

Net sales							
Lighting equipment	43.5	42.8	42.6	42.2	40.7	39.4	NA
Textile rental	24.1	23.1	22.7	22.2	22.0	22.8	NA
Other	18.2	19.9	20.5	21.8	23.9	24.4	NA
Chemical	14.1	14.2	14.1	13.8	13.4	13.5	NA
Operating profits							
Lighting equipment	40.6	36.9	37.7	34.8	40.8	41.3	NA
Textile rental	27.7	25.7	26.7	24.2	23.2	23.6	NA
Other	11.1	17.1	12.4	20.1	15.8	14.1	NA
Chemical	20.6	20.3	23.2	20.9	20.2	21.0	NA
Capital expenditures							
Lighting equipment	40.0	33.0	31.8	35.7	42.5	28.9	NA
Textile rental	30.8	36.7	39.9	41.2	22.8	33.1	NA
Other	13.1	19.6	20.3	18.4	20.3	31.9	NA
Chemical	16.1	10.7	8.0	4.7	14.4	6.1	NA
Identifiable assets							
Lighting equipment	38.4	38.6	38.6	38.4	38.0	34.4	NA
Textile rental	32.7	31.3	30.2	31.4	29.8	32.1	NA
Other	17.1	18.2	19.8	18.9	21.2	23.4	NA
Chemical	11.8	11.9	11.5	11.3	10.9	10.1	NA

SOURCE: © 1986, 1987, FACTSET DATA SYSTEMS

Example:

SIC industry code 1400 includes DeBeers Mines, which has interests primarily in diamond mining and distribution. It also includes Vulcan Materials, which sells construction materials and chemicals.

Evaluation of Diversification

An analysis of the business segments should include an assessment of the firm's diversification. There are two major types of corporate diversification—related and unrelated. In related diversification, the firm diversifies into areas of business that use similar input factors, similar manufacturing techniques, or similar distribution channels. Unrelated diversification is characterized by operations that have no commonalities. The advantage of related diversification is the synergies that are created from using similar inputs for various products. The disadvantage of related diversification is that most businesses tend to move together; downturns in the economy simultaneously affect all segments, and so one or more segments would not offset the poor operating cash flows of the down-cycle segments. The main advantage of unrelated diversification is the stability of operations and cash flows; not all segments are equally affected by the business cycle at the same time. The disadvantage of unrelated diversification is that economies of scale or economies of scope are likely to be suboptimal, because the firm may not be able to fully utilize its assets within the firm. Management of firms that diversified into unrelated areas of business may also not be able to apply the same priorities that made the core business successful, and troubles in one division can actually drag down cash flows of the entire firm.

Example:

Nashua Corporation began as a marketer of copiers and office supplies, and later expanded into manufacturing of discs for the computer industry. When the disc drives business collapsed in 1991, so did Nashua's cash flows and stock price, as can be seen in Figure 2–6.

The analyst should assess whether the firm followed a strategy to diversify into related or unrelated areas of business. The analyst should also determine the exposure of the firm to the business cycle and what one should expect to find in terms of the amount, growth, and stability of cash flows.

Example:

In the example of National Service Industries used above, the firm operated in the following segments: lighting equipment, textile rental, other, and chemical. The primary SIC codes for the segments were 3646, 7213, 1742, and 2841, respectively. It can be seen that there is very little similarity in operations among the four segments. They operate in four different SIC industries, even at the two-digit SIC level. Thus, the firm may be perceived to have diversified into unrelated areas of business.

In terms of the sensitivity of the firm to the business cycle, it should be noted that the four segments are probably not affected by the business cycle at the same time. Lighting

FIGURE 2–6   NSH: Nashua Corporation

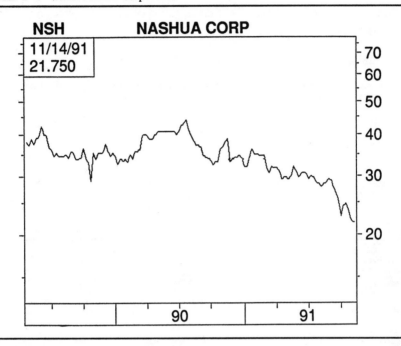

equipment and the insulation service (the major component of the "other" segment) are probably affected by the housing market, which tends to lead the business cycle. Textile rental and chemical either lag the business cycle or coincide with the business cycle. Thus, the firm seems to be less sensitive to the business cycle than firms that operate in a single sector of the economy.

Example:

In a previous example, we showed that General Mills operated in the consumer foods and the restaurants areas of business. One can immediately think about related areas of business in the two segments, including products, research and development efforts, marketing, sharing of technology, managerial expertise, and ability to test products. Thus, the firm may be perceived as a firm that chose to diversify into related areas of business. It should be noted that General Mills will be affected by the business cycle in a similar manner across both of its segments, with the restaurants segment affected by the business cycle to a greater degree. However, the food business is usually considered a very stable business in terms of operating cash flows.

Another area of investigation is the geographical distribution of revenues. When a firm has a seasonal product, it may be worthwhile to diversify into the other part of the hemisphere to take advantage of smoothing sales. It is also important to assess the risk of such seasonal operations as well as the risk of operating in specific countries. These risks can be driven by economic factors, such as interest rate changes, and by political risks, such as oil firms with investments in unstable parts of the world.

Another area that the cash flow analyst should examine is the firm's disclosure of cash flows by segment, or at least the disaggregation of cash flows from industrial and financial activities.

Example:

Ashland Oil Inc. reports segment cash flows from operations in its 1990 financial statements. These are as follows:

Ashland Oil: Information by Industry Segment

Ashland Oil, Inc. and Subsidiaries
Information by Industry Segment
Years Ended September 30

(In thousands)	1990	1989	1988	1987	1986
Sales and operating revenues					
Ashland Petroleum	$3,949,191	$3,176,818	$3,146,185	$2,918,812	$3,366,095
SuperAmerica Group	1,997,514	1,795,429	1,603,698	1,364,627	1,364,545
Valvoline	700,553	616,576	571,385	551,646	528,892
Chemical	2,245,252	2,229,578	2,089,777	1,643,040	1,477,311
Construction	1,083,117	1,065,710	1,064,127	760,471	720,909
Engineering	348,238	600,629	646,342	557,098	463,703
Exploration	399,278	253,049	198,803	247,818	232,234
Intersegment sales[1]					
Ashland Petroleum	(1,349,189)	(1,032,954)	(929,773)	(813,345)	(851,225)
Exploration	(346,009)	(202,588)	(167,637)	(212,729)	(184,409)
Other	(33,517)	(38,616)	(27,366)	(27,227)	(25,797)
	$8,994,428	$8,463,631	$8,195,541	$6,990,211	$7,092,258
Operating income (loss)					
Ashland Petroleum	$ 205,999	$ 141,931	$ 178,721	$ 9,970	$ 251,607
SuperAmerica Group	45,792	52,957	50,671	16,169	37,455
Valvoline	36,875	35,669	30,261	48,194	37,037
Chemical	69,732	128,468[2]	101,917	90,294[3]	70,645
Construction	52,783	39,840	68,271	61,901	69,366
Engineering	(27,377)[4]	(90,187)[5]	(18,544)[6]	10,190	16,554
Exploration	40,275	20,407	2,018	1,046	(22,760)
Other	—	—	—	—	(1,305)
General corporate expenses	(92,757)	(148,148)[7]	(124,419)[8]	(75,111)	(83,619)
	$ 331,322	$ 180,937	$ 288,896	$ 162,653	$ 374,980
Cash flows from operations					
Income adjusted for noncash charges[9]					
Ashland Petroleum	$ 207,058	$ 170,098	$ 184,417	$ 117,259	$ 246,141
SuperAmerica Group	53,878	64,057	55,667	27,170	35,670
Valvoline	38,956	36,514	29,120	35,296	20,555
Chemical	82,860	97,388	84,117	89,277	63,430
Construction	76,570	70,501	81,538	52,155	63,093
Engineering	(2,546)	(33,096)	(21,590)	20,498	13,708
Exploration	92,019	101,805	43,166	99,288	51,192
Other	—	—	—	—	1,687
Coal investments	12,106	11,536	17,421	15,610	13,208
Corporate	(142,209)	(121,326)	(116,729)	(14,091)	7,021
Change in operating assets and liabilities	(47,610)	(312,535)	39,596	(133,348)	(84,273)
	$ 371,082	$ 84,942	$ 396,723	$ 309,114	$ 431,432

SOURCE: Ashland Oil, *Annual Report*, 1990.

The cash flow analyst can assess the contribution of each segment to total cash flows from operating activities. Figure 2–7 shows the contribution of each of the segments in a graph.

Finally, the capital expenditures made in each of the segments may indicate where the firm decides to grow and in what areas it decides to shrink operations. A large and consistent stream of investments in one area of business may indicate that the firm decides to concentrate and develop that area, probably because it feels that area has the best future prospects. The analyst could compare the expectations of the firm, as evidenced by the relative investments in each of the segments, with market expectations about each of these industries.

2.4 RELIANCE ON MAJOR CUSTOMERS

The reliance on one or a few major customers exposes the firm to a greater business risk. If a major customer goes out of business, or if it is adversely affected by any external events, the firm's sales, and consequently its cash flows, may be badly hurt. Data about major customers is sometimes found in the footnote on segment reports or in the business description section of Form 10-K. The analyst should consider the

FIGURE 2–7   Ashland Oil Segment Cash Flows

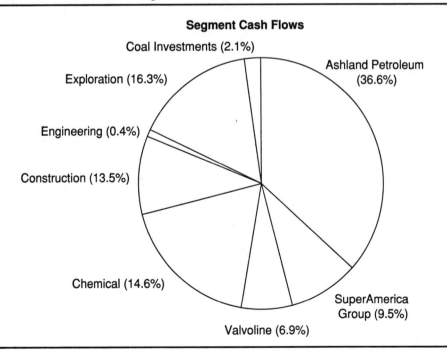

Segment Cash Flows

Coal Investments (2.1%)

Ashland Petroleum (36.6%)

Exploration (16.3%)

Engineering (0.4%)

Construction (13.5%)

Chemical (14.6%)

SuperAmerica Group (9.5%)

Valvoline (6.9%)

extent of additional risk that is imposed on the firm due to its reliance on a major or a few major customers.

Example:

Harsco manufactures military vehicles and defense systems, scaffolding and concrete-forming equipment, plastic piping, propane tanks, and seamless steel cylinders, and provides materials handling and engineering services to steel producers.

In 1989, Harsco's management outlined the outlook for the future as follows:

"The Company's performance over the next couple of years will depend, to a major extent, on just when and how the legal and contractual issues in the Defense Group's tracked and wheeled vehicle contracts, discussed in Note 10 of the financial statements, are resolved. Assuming the general industrial economy remains strong, Industrial Services and Building Products and Engineered Products should post solid performances in 1990. The key to the magnitude of increased profitability, however, rests with Defense."

With respect to defense spending, there are clear indications that the movement toward democracy in Eastern Bloc countries will result in cuts in the defense budget. The extent to which these cuts will impact on the company's defense operations is not clear. As to existing contracts, the preliminary budget request for 1991 provides no funding for the fifth program year for the five-ton trucks, but it does include funds for the exercise of the sixth option on the ACE contract. Management anticipates that cancellation of the fifth program year of the truck contract may have a slightly favorable impact on earnings and that the exercise of option six on the ACE contract will result in an additional loss of at least $21 million unless the claims, discussed in Note 10 of the financial statements, are favorably resolved beforehand.

Defense sales of Harsco in 1989 accounted for 25 percent of consolidated sales, as seen in the segment information on page 33.

2.5 RELIANCE ON MAJOR SUPPLIERS

Most firms rely on outside sources for their input factors such as raw materials, components used in production, labor force, and so on. An ideal situation for the manufacturing entity is when there are many suppliers of these input factors and when suppliers compete intensely for customers. In such cases, the firm is virtually guaranteed a steady source of supply at competitive prices. However, when a firm relies on one supplier, or just a few suppliers of important input factors, the firm is exposed to a greater risk or perhaps disruption of supply. The supplier may go out of business, may decide to halt the supply of a certain component, or may decide (or be forced) to raise prices. In all of these cases, production is likely to be interrupted and the firm is likely to be adversely affected. The analyst can find information about major suppliers in the business description section of Form 10-K, or in a recent prospectus.

Example:

Airlines are dependent on the price of oil for their profitability. When the supply of fuel is hampered, profitability of the airline is negatively affected, because prices of oil will reflect the short supply of oil. Although the airline is not dependent on any individual supplier of

Harsco: Information by Industry Group and Geographical Area

HARSCO CORPORATION
Notes to Consolidated Financial Statements

Information By Industry Group and Geographic Area:

Financial information by industry group and geographic area for the years 1989, 1988 and 1987 is as follows:

INDUSTRY GROUP

(In millions)	1989	1988	1987
Net Sales to Unaffiliated Customers			
Industrial Services and Building Products	$ 454.9	$ 447.8	$ 403.0
Engineered Products	555.3	492.4	398.9
Defense	341.0	338.8	367.3
Total	$1,351.2	$1,279.0	$1,169.2
Pre-Tax Income			
Group Operating Profit (Loss)			
Industrial Services and Building Products	$ 66.6	$ 78.5	$ 61.9
Engineered Products	48.5	37.3	27.0
Defense	(71.9)	(44.4)	29.5
Total Group Operating Profit	43.2	71.4	118.4
General corporate expense, net	(7.4)	(7.2)	(6.9)
Interest income, etc., net	5.5	5.2	1.6
Interest expense	(16.4)	(16.2)	(8.0)
Equity in net income (loss) of unconsolidated companies	(2.7)	1.2	2.7
Pre-tax income	$ 22.2	$ 54.4	$ 107.8
Identifiable Assets			
Industrial Services and Building Products	$ 254.7	$ 235.4	$ 221.7
Engineered Products	232.8	259.0	222.8
Defense	315.3	284.7	217.3
Subtotal	802.8	779.1	661.8
Corporate	172.2	111.3	139.5
Investments in unconsolidated companies	3.2	2.7	1.0
Total assets	$ 978.2	$ 893.1	$ 802.3
Depreciation			
Industrial Services and Building Products	$ 28.1	$ 26.7	$ 32.3
Engineered Products	16.0	15.5	15.2
Defense	10.7	10.0	7.0
Corporate	1.4	1.6	1.6
Total depreciation	$ 56.2	$ 53.8	$ 56.1
Capital Expenditures*			
Industrial Services and Building Products	$ 42.2	$ 40.6	$ 21.9
Engineered Products	11.1	14.4	9.9
Defense	13.9	12.6	25.9
Corporate	.4	1.4	2.9
Total capital expenditures	$ 67.6	$ 69.0	$ 60.6

* Excludes property, plant and equipment from acquired companies of $5.4, (principally Engineered Products) in 1988.

SOURCE: Harsco Corporation, *Annual Report*, 1989.

fuel, it is greatly dependent on the world supply of oil. The analyst should have some expectations of future prices of fuel to analyze the future prospects and cash flows of an airline.

Example:

Southwest Airlines provides air transportation services on routes between 29 cities in the Southwest and Midwest regions of the United States.

Southwest Airlines showed in its 1985 annual report that fuel costs comprised more than 27 percent of operating costs, and in some years as much as 40 percent of operating costs.

	Year Ended December 31, 1985			
	Consolidated	Southwest	Muse Air	1984
Fuel cost per gallon	80.49¢	80.52¢	79.80¢	80.53¢
Fuel's percent of operating costs	27%	27%	29%	31%

Southwest Airlines explicitly recognizes this in the discussion of operations in its 1989 report:

"We experienced significant operating cost increases throughout 1989, however, which served to dampen an otherwise very successful year. Fuel costs, in particular, escalated in the fourth quarter to a system average of 66 cents per gallon and then skyrocketed in January 1990 to 79 cents per gallon. As an energy-dependent Company, we are continually exploring ways to manage this risk more effectively, in addition to continually adding more fuel-efficient aircraft to the fleet (the 737-300 and -500). Even so, we are consistently among the lowest in the industry in terms of the average cost of fuel per gallon. Aircraft maintenance was the other cost category where larger increases were experienced in 1989 and are expected in 1990 due, in part, to the increase in the fleet of 737-300s which is more expensive to maintain than their 737-200 predecessor. Thus, the increased maintenance cost offsets, to an extent, the fuel savings obtained from these aircraft."

2.6 COMPETITION IN THE INDUSTRY

Economic theory suggests that the more competitive an industry is, the lower profit and cash flow margins are to any firm that operates in that industry. Thus, it is important to assess the degree of competition in each of the industries in which the firm sells its products. The analyst should assume that if the industry is very competitive, the firm is unlikely to obtain any abnormal cash flows. However, if the industry is not competitive, it can indicate that the major firms in the industry may earn abnormal cash flows and be characterized by a better ability to generate free cash flows. One can assess the competition in an industry by examining concentration ratios in the industry. For example, one can examine the percentage of industry sales made by the four (or eight) largest firms in the industry. The larger this ratio is, the more concentrated the industry, and the less competitive it is likely to be. The Bureau of the Census publishes concentration ratios for four-digit SIC industries. Alternatively, the analyst can construct this ratio from published sources, such as Standard & Poor's Compustat data base.

Example:

Checking the Standard & Poor's Compustat data base showed that two industries, pharmaceutical and computer makers, have largely different four-firm concentration ratios. In the pharmaceutical industry, denoted by SIC code 2834, the largest four firms sell about 37 percent of total sales of firms included in the Compustat data base. However, computer manufacturers, excluding IBM, denoted by Compustat industry 3571, had a four-firm concentration ratio of 63 percent. (Exhibit 2–2 provides a list of firms in these two industries and their sales during 1990.) This clearly shows that the pharmaceutical industry is less concentrated than the computer industry, corresponding with our intuition. Had IBM been included in the calculations of the computer industry, the results would have been even more accentuated.

EXHIBIT 2–2   Compustat Firms Industry 2834 — Pharmaceutical Industry

Ticker Symbol	Name	1990 Sales (in millions)
JNJ	JOHNSON & JOHNSON	11232.0
BMY	BRISTOL MYERS SQUIBB	10300.0
SBE	SMITHKLINE BEECHAM PLC -ADS	9195.0
BAX	BAXTER INTERNATIONAL INC	8100.0
MRK	MERCK & CO	7671.5
AHP	AMERICAN HOME PRODUCTS CORP	6775.2
PFE	PFIZER INC	6406.0
ABT	ABBOTT LABORATORIES	6158.7
LLY	LILLY (ELI) & CO	5191.6
GLX	GLAXO HOLDINGS PLC -ADR	4966.0
WLA	WARNER-LAMBERT CO	4686.9
SGP	SCHERING-PLOUGH	3322.9
UPJ	UPJOHN CO	3032.7
RPR	RHONE-POULENC RORER	2917.4
4655B	WELLCOME PLC -ADR	2779.2
MKC	MARION MERRELL DOW INC	2462.0
SYN	SYNTEX CORP	1521.0
NVO	NOVO-NORDISK A/S -ADR	1455.9
IMA	IMCERA GROUP INC	1424.6
AGN	ALLERGAN INC	883.9
CAR	CARTER-WALLACE INC	634.9
GNE	GENENTECH INC -RED	434.8
6243C	SCHERER (R.P.)	350.4
TEVIY	TEVA PHARM INDS -ADR	295.2
BMD	A.L. LABORATORIES INC -CL A	275.5
ICN	ICN PHARMACEUTICALS INC-DEL	272.0
FRX	FOREST LABORATORIES -CL A	176.3
6464B	LYPHOMED INC	159.0
IVX	IVAX CORP	141.5
SPI	SPI PHARMACEUTICALS INC	140.7
PLI	LEINER (P) NUTRITIONAL PRODS	135.3
AZA	ALZA CORP -CL A	99.3
MYL	MYLAN LABORATORIES	91.1
CHTT	CHATTEM INC	84.4
BCL	BIOCRAFT LABORATORIES INC	83.5
NBTY	NATURE'S BOUNTY INC	70.8
BRL	BARR LABORATORIES INC	70.3
ELN	ELAN CORP PLC -ADR	66.1
NATR	NATURES SUNSHINE PRODS INC	60.1
CGEN	COLLAGEN CORP	54.3
ZENL	ZENITH LABORATORIES	53.3
PRX	PHARMACEUTICAL RES INC	49.0
KV	K V PHARMACEUTICAL CO	34.5

continued

EXHIBIT 2–2   Compustat Firms Industry 2834 — Pharmaceutical Industry (*continued*)

Ticker Symbol	Name	1990 Sales (in millions)
NOVX	NOVA PHARMACEUTICAL CORP	32.9
HDG	HALSEY DRUG CO INC	26.4
DRMD	DURAMED PHARMACEUTICALS INC	25.7
3PHAR	PHARMACONTROL CORP	23.5
JMED	JONES MEDICAL INDS INC	19.7
EVGD	EVERGOOD PRODUCTS CORP	18.2
AKRN	AKORN INC	14.2
DBHI	HICKAM (DOW B.) INC	13.3
ATPH	ARMSTRONG PHARMACEUTICALS	12.6
COB	COLUMBIA LABORATORIES INC	12.1
MSAM	MARSAM PHARMACEUTICALS INC	12.0
NATA	NATURAL ALTERNATIVES	11.9
CARN	CARRINGTON LABS	11.6
SYGN	SYNERGEN INC	8.7
PDKL	PDK LABS INC	7.5
CYGN	CYGNUS THERAPEUTIC SYSTEMS	5.9
BPH	BIOPHARMACEUTICS INC	5.6
GRPI	GREENWICH PHARMACEUTICALS	5.6
VIRA	VIRATEK INC	4.9
DDIX	DDI PHARMACEUTICALS	4.8
UG	UNITED GUARDIAN INC	4.6
IMNR	IMMUNE RESPONSE CORP/DEL	4.3
VSTR	VESTAR INC	4.2
MOGN	MGI PHARMA INC	3.9
REGN	REGENERON PHARMACEUT	3.8
ANME	ANGIO MEDICAL CORP	3.6
ZILA	ZILA INCORPORATED	3.5
IMUL	IMMULOGIC PHARMACEUTICAL CP	3.3
MTNAE	MONTANA NATURALS INTL	3.1
POLXF	POLYDEX PHARMACEUTICALS LTD	2.2
CHMX	CHEMEX PHARMACEUTICALS INC	2.0
ISIP	ISIS PHARMACEUTICALS INC	1.8
RLAB	ROYCE LABORATORIES INC	1.5
3CHBAC	CHESAPEAKE BIOLOGICAL LABS	1.5
RPCX	ROBERTS PHARMACEUTICAL CORP	1.2
SMRX	SUMMA RX LABORATORIES INC	1.2
THRX	THERAGENICS CORP	1.1
PRCY	PROCYTE CORP	1.1
NOVN	NOVEN PHARMACEUTICALS INC	1.0
MRE	MEDCO RESEARCH INC	0.8
IVET	INNOVET INC	0.5
LDAKA	LIDAK PHARMACEUTICALS -CL A	0.3
ALBM	ALPHA 1 BIOMEDICALS INC	0.3
UBS	U S BIOSCIENCE INC	0.2

EXHIBIT 2–2   Compustat Firms Industry 2834 —Pharmaceutical Industry (*continued*)

Ticker Symbol	Name	1990 Sales (in millions)
IPIC	INTERNEURON PHARMACEUTICALS	0.1
CEPH	CEPHALON INC	0.1
HLIX	HELIX BIOCORE INC	0.0
GYNX	GYNEX INC	0.0
BLM	BELMAC CORPORATION	0.0
GNSA	GENSIA PHARMACEUTICALS INC	0.0
HMED	HIMEDICS INC	0.0
IMGN	IMMUNOGEN INC	0.0
IMNOC	IMMUNO THERAPEUTICS INC	0.0
MDRXA	MEDICIS PHARMACEUT CP -CL A	0.0
NRGN	NEUROGEN CORP	0.0
RECP	RECEPTECH CORP	0.0
SU	SUMMA MEDICAL CORP	0.0
TOCRZ	TOCOR INC	0.0
VMRX	VIMRX PHARMACEUTICALS INC	0.0

Compustat Firms Industry 3571 —Computer Industry (without IBM)

Ticker Symbol	Name	1990 Sales (in millions)
AAPL	APPLE COMPUTER INC	5558.4
TAN	TANDY CORP	4499.6
CPQ	COMPAQ COMPUTER CORP	3598.8
AMH	AMDAHL CORP	2158.8
TDM	TANDEM COMPUTERS INC	1865.9
CBU	COMMODORE INTL LTD	887.3
CYR	CRAY RESEARCH	804.4
DELL	DELL COMPUTER CORP	546.2
ASTA	AST RESEARCH INC	533.8
EVRX	EVEREX SYSTEMS INC	436.5
TCOR	TANDON CORP	421.8
SGI	SILICON GRAPHICS INC	419.8
ATC	ATARI CORP	411.5
SRA	STRATUS COMPUTER INC	403.8
NORKZ	NORSK DATA A S -ADR	374.5
CCURC	CONCURRENT COMPUTER CP	340.1
SQNT	SEQUENT COMPUTER SYSTEMS INC	248.8
TDAT	TERADATA CORP	224.2
ENCC	ENCORE COMPUTER CORP	215.2
CNX	CONVEX COMPUTER CORP	209.3

continued

EXHIBIT 2–2   Compustat Firms Industry 3571 — Computer Industry (without IBM) (*continued*)

Ticker Symbol	Name	*1990 Sales (in millions)*
PYRD	PYRAMID TECHNOLOGY	175.5
AALR	ADVANCED LOGIC RESEARCH INC	172.0
ALTO	ALTOS COMPUTER SYS	139.9
ZEOS	ZEOS INTL LTD	127.1
ALNTC	ALLIANT COMPUTER SYSTEMS CP	72.8
ARIX	ARIX CORP	56.6
ALMI	ALPHA MICROSYSTEMS	52.8
SEQS	SEQUOIA SYSTEMS INC	48.6
FLP	FLOATING POINT SYSTEMS INC	46.9
OSICE	OSICOM TECHNOLOGIES INC	46.3
BQC	QANTEL CORP	40.6
STRR	STAR TECHNOLOGIES INC	33.4
ZCAD	ZYCAD CORP	30.4
CRAY	CRAY COMPUTER CORP	13.0
TTOI	TEMPEST TECHNOLOGIES INC	6.4
3NDIC	NATIONAL DATACOMPUTER INC	5.4
SULC	SULCUS COMPUTER CORP	4.8
THEQE	HITECH ENGINEERING CO	1.7
SUPR	SUPERCOMPUTING SOLUTIONS	1.7

Additional discussion of the competition in the firm's industries may also be available in the business discussion of Form 10-K or a recent prospectus.

Example:

Nintendo is a semi-monopolistic manufacturer of video games. It constantly studies ways to diversify applications of its video games, such as electronic mail boxes.

Nintendo has managed to deter competition in its business by a proprietary system that cannot be copied without an express permission and by having exclusive arrangements with some retailers. It keeps tight control over its game software by manufacturing its own cartridges. As a result, it was able to retain the largest market share in the video game market, and it currently accounts for about 93 percent of sales in this market.

Example:

The communication industry is characterized by intense competition. For example, BBN states in its 1990 10-K Form:

"Competition in the field of wide-area communications is intense and is characterized by rapid technological advances. BBN's success in this market will depend upon its ability to market competitive products and services as an integrated communications offering to government agencies and commercial organizations.

BBN attempts to distinguish its products and services from those of its competitors by its 'system solution' approach. In particular, BBN provides its customers with a complete range of products and services, from consulting through implementation, the application of which yields a close fit with a customer's existing and expected communications requirements. The Company believes such an approach allows it to compete successfully against much larger organizations.''

2.7 RELATED FIRMS

One of the most noticeable differences between Japanese and American corporations is the extent of intercorporate investments. In Japan, many corporations are interlocked with other corporations through intercorporate investments. Many directors serve on the boards of more than one firm, and operations of firms are much more coordinated than would be the case without these special relationships. For example, one of the reasons it is easier to adopt just-in-time inventory systems in Japan than in the United States is the intercorporate investments, where a firm may own a significant equity holding in a supplier. In the United States, it is less frequent to see such strong relations among firms. However, when such relations exist, it may be useful to assess them and the potential benefits that may be obtained by both firms. In particular, such firms can obtain economies of scale, economies of scope, and ability to obtain financing at a cheaper rate.

Example:

Many firms find it beneficial to have a separate entity that operates as a finance subsidiary. The finance subsidiary usually purchases the receivables of the parent company and collects those receivables on its own. It also issues its own debt, which is secured by the accounts receivable which it purchased. The finance subsidiary can branch to its own operations which do not involve the parent's receivables. For example, it can factor receivables of other firms or engage in leasing transactions with other firms. Most of the automobile manufacturers have their own finance subsidiaries, such as GMAC with GM. Clearly, it is worthwhile to know about the relationship between GMAC and GM when analyzing the cash flows of GMAC or GM.

Example:

Westinghouse Electric Corp. took a $1.68 billion pretax charge in the third quarter of 1991 due to loan problems at its Westinghouse Financial Services division. The finance subsidiary of Westinghouse made bad real-estate loans and was forced to take a pretax charge against income of $975 million in the prior year, in addition to the $1.68 billion charge in 1991. The firm had to restructure its operations, reducing its work force by about 4,000 jobs. Due to these problems, Westinghouse had difficulties in placement of its commercial paper and its credit ratings were reduced.

To find out about related firms, one has to observe whether certain related transactions are reported in the financial statements. Further information can be obtained from the 10-K Form, which lists the firm's subsidiaries, and from the proxy statement, where major investors (with more than 5 percent of outstanding stock) in the firm are listed.

2.8 EXPERIENCE IN THE INDUSTRY

Experience in a particular business may aid managers in adapting to changes in business conditions, to changes in the political environment, and to changes in the microstructure of the firm. Experienced managers are more likely to be aware of changes that affect the business and are more likely to react faster to these changes. Furthermore, experience in an industry may enhance long-term planning and formulation of strategy, and, in particular, the ability to forecast future cash flows. Most business failures occur during the first three years of a business's life. Presumably, an older and more experienced business, one which has shown it can adapt to changes, is less prone to mistakes that are typical to new and inexperienced business managers. Good managers will adjust discretionary spending to maintain a certain level of free cash flows during business contractions. The analyst should attempt to assess whether the firm's management has sufficient experience in the business, whether it was able to survive a recession before, and whether or how it still incurs development-stage expenses. All these factors may either increase the business risk or increase the economic benefits to a firm. For these reasons, it is important to study the volatility of cash flows over several business cycles.

Example:

Dynatech Corp. designs, manufactures, and sells a diverse line of electronic and mechanical instruments and systems used in measurement, analysis, and control in the communications and scientific markets and by some government agencies.

Dynatech is a firm that started as a research and development (R&D) contract firm and, 31 years later, developed into a diversified high-technology firm. In its discussion of operations for 1989, Dynatech writes:

"Given the speed at which technology changes and the susceptibility of single-product companies to broad market swings, this recipe has spurred Dynatech's development from an R&D contract firm to a diversified, high-technology company which designs, manufactures, and markets more than 1,000 products through 40 well-focused operating subsidiaries to customers around the globe."

2.9 AGE OF THE BUSINESS

Related to experience in a business is the age of the business. However, age may also affect the financial statements of a firm because of the historical cost assumption embedded in Generally Accepted Accounting Principles. Under this assumption, the firm uses historical acquisition cost of assets as the carrying value on the balance sheet, without any adjustments to market values. Thus, older firms might have greater discrepancies between market value of assets and their book values. Obviously, the most likely assets to be affected by this bias are property, plant, and equipment, with a particular emphasis on properties and plant. Other assets include noncurrent investments that are carried at the lower cost or market value.

A direct way to find the age of a business is from the date of incorporation, which is available, for example, in Moody's guides. Alternatively, the analyst can consult the differences between book and current-cost values of assets for 1979–1983, when such data were required to be disclosed. The analyst can also examine Form 10-K, which provides information about additions and acquisitions of property, plant, and equipment (PPE). If the firm provided these data for a long-enough time period, the analyst can construct an estimate of current values of PPE.

Example:

An interesting example involves the air rights above Sealand Inc.'s terminal in Hong Kong. These are not included in the balance sheet, but are discussed in management's letter as follows.

"We put up the *air rights over our terminal plus $15 million cash*, as our 50 percent share of this investment. Our partner is putting up the balance of *$145 million* to earn his 50 percent interest.

Hong Kong is the busiest container port in all Asia. The six-story, highrise warehouse with 2.2 million square feet of floor space promises to be the largest building in all of Asia. It will increase our present capacity in Hong Kong four-fold . . . and offer significant opportunities for us to provide a unique service to our customers while generating substantial incremental revenues."

2.10 BRAND-NAME RECOGNITION

Some firms are fortunate to have a very high level of brand-name recognition, which can lead to high and constant operating cash flows. For example, Coca-Cola is well known for its Coke brand and enjoys a strong market share because of it. Xerox is famous for inventing and manufacturing the first photocopier and still obtains benefits from its position in this industry. Such brand-name recognition can be very important to the continuing success of a business, and, in particular, to the growth and stability of future cash flows. In analyzing financial statements of a firm, the analyst should attempt to assess whether the firm has a brand or brands of products that are recognized within that industry, or whether the firm occupies a market "niche." Alternatively, the analyst should determine whether other firms within the industry have leading brand names. This analysis should indicate whether the firm may reap future benefits from its leading position in the industry, or whether it needs to invest additional resources to gain market share.

Example:

Hillenbrand Industries writes in its first quarterly report for 1991:
"Our objective is to be the recognized leader in each of our markets. We will never be satisfied with second place. Leadership companies generate higher cash flows that can be used to strengthen leadership positions and invest in related niche markets."

Example:

The advertising industry is one in which the largest firms have grown through consolidation, penetrated the market that is held by other firms, and acquired brand-name recognition through aggressive worldwide diversification.

Example:

Foote, Cone & Belding (FCB) provides advertising, public relations, direct marketing, sales promotion, and related services to clients worldwide. It is the fourth largest communications agency company in North America, and the seventh largest worldwide. Its global network includes 153 offices in 40 countries, with 1989 billings (including the Publicis-FCB European network) of $4.6 billion.

FCB states in its 1989 management letter that product quality improved substantially. It attributes part of that to "the combination of multicultural global management and exceptional local talent . . . linked by strong operating systems, practices, passion, and understanding."

2.11 MANAGEMENT TEAM

A good management team is a valuable asset to a firm, because it will lead the firm to higher cash flows. Good managers steer the firm in the right direction, develop it properly, and increase the value of shareholders' investments in the firm. In contrast, bad managers waste cash through bad or unnecessary investments, thereby reducing cash flows that otherwise could have been transferred back to shareholders or channeled into higher-yielding investments.

Publicly held companies are characterized by a separation between owners and managers. The owners (or their representatives, the board of directors) monitor the actions and decisions of management, but management is responsible for the daily operations of the firm. In the evaluation of a firm, the analyst must assess the quality of management and the quality of directors in a firm. Information about managers and directors is available in the proxy statement of a firm. This information should be studied to determine whether managers and directors have experience in the industry or in the business, and whether managers have the required skills for their position. Also, the analyst should assess the degree of nepotism in the firm, whether the board is composed of cronies of the major stockholder, or whether the board is simply an anti-takeover tool. Are managers and directors related? Is it possible that members of a particular family accept the public's money, but manage it poorly and cover their mismanagement through some improprieties?

Example:

Tyco Toys designs, develops, manufactures, and distributes a variety of toy products. Tyco products are sold by more than 2,500 large retail chains, wholesalers, and independent retailers.

During 1990, Tyco Toys had on its board of directors the chairman of the firm and one of his sons. In addition, the attorney for Tyco Toys was on the board of directors. In the 1990 proxy statement, another son was nominated for the board of directors. After some pressure from stockholders, the chairman of the board and his sons agreed to remove themselves from the board of directors.

Example:

Carlo De Benedetti, an Italian executive, acquired a strong reputation as an excellent manager who can take over troubled firms and turn them around in a short time. When rumors spread throughout the Italian stock exchange that he had been interested in a listed Italian firm, its stock price shot up close to 40 percent. This was in anticipation of a good manager coming aboard that firm.

Example:

After Armand Hammer's death, the stock price of Occidental Petroleum rose by more than $2 per share. Apparently, investors felt that while he was alive the firm's progress was limited because of his reluctance to sell some of the firm's noncore businesses.

2.12 LABOR RELATIONS

When the contracts in the automobile industry are up for renewal, the financial press is usually full of rumors, speculations, and reports of recent developments in the contract negotiations. Indeed, the extent of unionization of employees in a firm has a material effect on its future production, wage demands, and flexibility. During an economic upswing, a firm with a strong union is likely to be less flexible in adapting to changes in the environment. It is more likely to have greater disruptions in production due to strikes, labor insistence on working according to the "book," and so on. The analyst should therefore attempt to assess the degree of unionization and the type of labor relations of that firm, including a history of wage increases and all other factors that may be important in analyzing both the cost of operations (through wages) and revenues (through potential work stoppage). Information about these items can be obtained from the business discussion in the beginning of Form 10-K, or from the examination of newspaper clippings about a firm. For example, one may consult *The Wall Street Journal Index,* trade publications, local newspapers where the firm is headquartered, or the *Index of Business Periodicals* for recent information about the firm. From these, one can determine the length of former union contracts, terms and length of contract, and historical relationship with the union.

The analyst should also investigate the extent of employees' ownership of a firm. When employees own a substantial portion of the firm, they have a greater incentive to make the firm more prosperous. For instance, Food Lion, a large Southeastern food chain, keeps a very tight control over its operating costs, including labor costs. However, its employees have done very well through stock ownership plans in the company. Recently, because of favorable tax treatments, many firms had experienced large investments by their employees through an Employee Stock Ownership Plan (ESOP). An ESOP aligns the interests of investors and employees to a greater extent and can improve the productivity of such firms. Information about ESOPs can be obtained in footnotes to the financial statements, in proxy statements, or from the ESOP Council in Washington.

Example:

Big B, Inc. operates a chain of retail drug stores and stores that sell and rent medical equipment for home use.

In its 1990 letter to shareholders, the chairman and the president of the firm wrote:

"The past year has been a most difficult one, resulting in the first annual net loss in the 23-year history of Big B. Despite the loss of $1,465,000, fiscal 1991 had more positives than negatives. The biggest positive is the way all of Big B's employees pulled together to correct gross margin and expense problems which became evident during the year, and in recognition of this tremendous effort we gratefully dedicate this annual report to them. The fruits of their efforts are evident in our fourth quarter earnings of $2,455,000, the highest fourth quarter net income from operations in the history of the Company."

Example:

McKesson's largest shareholder is its ESOP, which holds more than 17 percent of the firm's common stock in trust for its participating employees. The chairman and CEO, Alan Sleenfreund, explained the decision to form an ESOP by saying:

"We established our ESOP because we really believe in sharing with our employees value that they help create. We are in a business that is driven by customer service and the need to constantly improve productivity. That makes it critical that employees recognize and understand that they benefit financially when McKesson achieves improved financial performance." (*McKesson Today,* December 1990, p. 1).

2.13 SERVICE TO CUSTOMERS

In their book *In Search of Excellence,* Peters and Waterman (1983) document the importance of service to customers for the excellent firm. According to their research, the group of excellent firms became excellent partly through meticulous service to customers, sometimes when it was seemingly uneconomical to do so. For example, Frito-Lay services more than 99 percent of the vending machines in which it sells products on a daily basis, even though not all of its products are sold out on a daily basis. Frito-Lay believes that in the long run such a strategy pays off, because of consumer loyalty and good relationships with owners of the vending machines. Thus, the analyst should attempt to assess whether the firm is well known for good service to its customers. This can be deduced from trade magazines, consumer publications, and the number of service centers the firm has. Better service to the customer may have a negative effect on immediate cash flows, because larger amounts of cash are expended on providing quality service to customers. However, future cash flows are likely to grow due to customers' loyalty and increases in market share.

Example:

Toys R Us, the world's largest toy retailer, will return a customer's money—not credit—for any reason, within 90 days with a receipt. This is probably a more lenient return policy than its competitors', indicating that the firm wants to maintain better service to the customer.

2.14 PRODUCT QUALITY

It is well known that Japanese firms place a great deal of emphasis on product quality and quality control. The literature is abundant with examples of Japanese firms that invest great resources to slightly reduce the rate of defective units in their production process. Superficially, it seems that these Japanese firms are not getting a proper rate of return on their investment in product quality; the amount of resources needed to reduce the number of defective units beyond a certain threshold cannot be justified by the direct savings on the repairs of these units. Nevertheless, the Japanese firms make such huge investments in quality control because they expect greater consumer confidence and loyalty to their products, which are later manifested by the consistent growth of operating cash flows. Inevitably, higher quality may lead to a larger market share and greater operating cash flows, even in periods of declining markets.

The analyst should therefore assess the quality of the firm's products or services as an integral part of the analysis. Information about product quality can be obtained from consumers' rankings, industry publications, description of business in Form 10-K, and from assessing the extent of returns and expenses for repairs in the financial statements.

Example:

One of the important lessons U.S. firms learned from their Japanese counterparts is the cultivation of close relationships with suppliers. Japanese firms work very closely with a small number of suppliers, who promise to increase the quality of their products, and who promise to deliver their products on time. This enables the purchasing firms to reduce their inventories due to deliveries close to production time (just-in-time inventories), reduce expenses on quality control inspections, and reduce the need to rework defective units. As a result, pressures are mounting on firms that supply parts or raw materials to U.S. firms to substantially increase quality. A related article appeared in the *The Wall Street Journal*, August 16, 1991, p. B-1.

2.15 OWNERSHIP STRUCTURE

Previous academic studies as well as anecdotal evidence suggest that the ownership structure of a firm is important to its profitability and risk. It has been shown before that firms controlled by owners are more profitable and have a greater tendency to diversify into related areas of business than firms that are controlled by managers. Empirically, such studies adopt the definition that a firm that has a diffuse ownership structure, with no single shareholder holding more than 5 percent of the outstanding stock, is a management-controlled firm. An owner-controlled firm is one in which there exists a single investor or entity who holds at least 20 percent of the outstanding stock. As mentioned before, it is hypothesized (and verified empirically) that, *on the average,* owner-controlled firms are more profitable and less diversified into unrelated areas of business than management-controlled firms. The hypothesized explanation for these findings is that managers tend to divert corporate resources for their own personal gains. In management-controlled firms it is easier for managers to divert such resources because they are less likely to be closely supervised than in owner-controlled firms. Similarly, it is hypothesized that managers wish to diversify their large human-capital investments in their own firm by making their firm more diversified. This causes managers in management-controlled firms, who are subject to less scrutiny, to invest in unrelated areas of business, leading to a more diversified firm. However, the extent of diversification may be suboptimal from the shareholders' point of view. A recent survey of academic studies in this area can be found in Hunt, *Journal of Accounting Literature*, 1986.

The analyst should determine whether the firm under analysis is a management-controlled or an owner-controlled firm. Even if it is a management-controlled firm, the analyst should attempt to assess whether management seems to be diverting assets to its own personal use at the expense of stockholders. Data about ownership structure, as well as data about compensation and borrowing by officers, are available in the proxy statement of a firm, where shareholders with more than 5 percent of the out-

Brown/Forman Proxy

SECURITY OWNERSHIP OF CERTAIN BENEFICIAL OWNERS AND MANAGEMENT

Voting Security Ownership of Certain Beneficial Owners. At April 30, 1989, the following persons were known to the management of the Corporation to be the beneficial owners of more than five percent of Class A Common Stock of the Corporation, the only class of voting securities of the Corporation:

Name and Address of Beneficial Owner	Amount and Nature of Beneficial Ownership			Percent of Class
	Sole Voting and Investment Power	Shared Voting and Investment Power[1]	Total	
W. L. Lyons Brown, Jr. 850 Dixie Highway Louisville, Kentucky	441,420	4,354,170	4,795,590	45.4
Owsley Brown Frazier 850 Dixie Highway Louisville, Kentucky	262,896	3,712,260	3,975,156	37.6
Dace Brown Farrer Hillcrest Farm Prospect, Kentucky		2,996,187	2,996,187	28.3
Owsley Brown II 850 Dixie Highway Louisville, Kentucky	290,389	1,618,662	1,909,051	18.1
Ina Brown 5900 Burlington Avenue Louisville, Kentucky	326,383	1,116,127	1,442,510	13.6
Robinson S. Brown, Jr. 5208 Avish Lane Harrods Creek, Kentucky	95,939	906,906	1,002,845	9.5
Harry S. Frazier 4810 Cherry Valley Road Prospect, Kentucky	194,448	705,438	899,886	8.5
Laura Lee Brown Deters 7001 U.S. Highway 42 Louisville, Kentucky	262,730	477,867	740,597	7.0

(1) Shared voting and investment powers are held by the above named beneficial owners as members of advisory committees of certain trusts and estates of which First Kentucky Trust Company of Louisville, Kentucky, is trustee or executor, and in addition, W. L. Lyons Brown, Jr., Owsley Brown II and Ina Brown are three of the eight trustees of the W. L. Lyons Brown Foundation which owns 11,451 shares of Class A Common Stock and 126,625 shares of Class B Common Stock. **As a result of the shared voting and investment powers described above, several persons are shown as the beneficial owners of the same securities.** Counting such shares only once, the aggregate number of shares of Class A Common Stock beneficially owned by the above named persons is 7,406,825 shares, or 70.0% of the outstanding shares of such stock.

SOURCE: Brown/ Forman, Proxy Statement, 1989.

standing stock are listed. One can examine who the major shareholders are, whether they are represented on the board of directors, are on various subcommittees that run the firm, and so on.

Example:

Brown/Forman is a well-managed consumer goods company. It is an excellent generator of operating and free cash flows and is certainly an owner-controlled firm, as can be seen from the data in its proxy statement on the previous page.

Example:

In their book, *Barbarians at the Gate* (Harper & Row, 1990), Burrough and Helyar describe the extravagant lifestyle that professional managers enjoyed at RJR-Nabisco prior to its going private. At that time, RJR was not controlled by any individual stockholder, and management had to account only to the board of directors, some of whom enjoyed many personal benefits from the firm at the discretion of management.

CHAPTER 3

The Statement of Cash Flows

This chapter introduces the reader to the statement of cash flows. Understanding the role of this statement is crucial for a general analysis of cash flows, and, in particular, for an analysis that is based on free cash flows. In this chapter, we shall see how the statement of cash flows is constructed and discuss the important components of the statement. In the chapter, we introduce the motivation for the statement of cash flows, historical developments in the disclosure of fund flows, and a detailed example for the construction of the statement. Readers familiar with this material can skip to the next chapter for illustrations of the main sections of the statement from current disclosures and interpretation of cash flows by a cash flow analyst.

The purpose of the statement of cash flows is to disclose information about economic events that affect cash during the accounting period. Three general types of economic events or activities are described in the statement: (1) operating cash flows, (2) financing cash flows, and (3) investing cash flows. Operating cash flows are ongoing operations of a business entity that affect cash, such as collections from customers, payments to suppliers and employees, and so on.[1] Financing cash flows are events that affect the financial structure of a firm, such as borrowing cash and repurchasing common stock. Investing cash flows are those events that affect the long-term assets of a firm, such as purchases of property, plant, and equipment (PPE) or sale of investments in subsidiaries.

The statement of cash flows provides information about these types of events if they affect cash during the accounting period. Presumably, the events that affect cash during a period are very important to investors, suppliers, creditors, and employees. Information about operating cash flows indicates the business' ability to generate sufficient cash from its continuing operations. Information about investing cash flows indicates how the business plans to expand or merely survive downturns through such actions as selling of assets. Information about financing cash flows illustrates how the business plans to finance its expansion and partially reward shareholders. If a financing event, for example, does not involve cash (e.g., the conversion of preferred stock to common stock), the information is disclosed in a separate portion of the statement of cash flows. To understand the current status of firms' disclosure of this statement, it is useful to review the historical developments of the statement.

---

[1]We shall provide exact definitions for these three categories of cash flows in the next chapter.

3.1 HISTORICAL BACKGROUND

The use of cash flow analysis as an investment yardstick is not new. William Morse Cole's[2] 1908 accounting treatise includes flow of funds statements. Corporate treasurers have long used cash flow as the basis to invest in capital projects; that is, the net present value of the cash return on the project must be greater than the current outlay of cash.

In 1963, only about half a century after Morse's accounting text, the precursor of the Financial Accounting Standards Board (FASB), the Accounting Principles Board (APB), in Opinion No. 3, *The Statement of Source and Application of Funds*, recommended presentation of a statement in the annual report that would provide information on sources and uses of funds.

In 1969, the Securities and Exchange Commission (SEC) mandated a funds statement in annual filings. In 1971, the APB released Opinion No. 19, *Reporting Changes in Financial Position*, which, for the first time, required a flow of funds statement for each period in which an income statement was presented. In this opinion, the APB did not specify the definition of funds that firms should use, and the majority of firms used working capital as their definition of funds. Furthermore, the APB required firms to disclose information about sources and uses of funds, but left firms with a lot of room to define for themselves what were the sources and uses of funds and how they were to be presented in the statement.

On December 15, 1980, the FASB issued a discussion memorandum entitled "Reporting Fund Flows, Liquidity and Financial Flexibility," which explains the reasons the FASB became interested in a fund-flow statement.

1. *Income and funds are different.* A business often experiences significant differences between income and fund flows. These differences vary from business to business and from time to time. They are particularly important when large price changes occur. Investors, creditors, and others are likely to need information about fund flows for assessments of future cash flows. Managers are familiar with the importance of information about fund flows for the evaluation of investment opportunities and for other kinds of budgeting.

2. *Information about liquidity and financial flexibility is needed for making assessments of future cash flows.* Information about liquidity and financial flexibility is useful for assessments of the timing and uncertainty of future cash flows. Financial flexibility is a measure of the adaptability of a business. The need for adaptability may be offensive or defensive. A business may need financial flexibility to take advantage of an unexpected new investment opportunity or to survive a crisis resulting from a change in operating conditions. Financial flexibility comes from quick access to cash. A financially flexible business might have large inflows of cash from operations, large borrowing capacity, or assets that can be quickly real-

---

[2]W. M. Cole, *Accounts: Their Construction and Interpretation for Businessmen and Students of Affairs* (Boston, Mass.: Houghton Mifflin, 1908).

ized in significant amounts. Information about liquidity could help the assessment of financial flexibility. It is a measure of the nearness to cash of assets and liabilities—the time interval that will lapse before assets become cash and before liabilities have to be paid.

3. *There appears to be a problem with current practice.* People have criticized the current practice for reporting fund flows as confusing because it compresses too much information into one statement and does not focus on a specific definition of funds. The concepts of liquidity and financial flexibility have not yet been developed in the authoritative literature.

4. *It is needed as part of a conceptual framework for financial accounting and reporting.*

In November 1981, the FASB issued an Exposure Draft of a proposed Concepts Statement, *Reporting Income, Cash Flows, and Financial Position of Business Enterprises.* This Exposure Draft discussed the role of a funds statement and guidelines for reporting components of fund flows, concluding that reporting funds flows should focus on cash rather than on working capital.

During its deliberations on the 1981 Exposure Draft, the FASB decided that detailed cash flow reporting should be addressed only on the standards level, but deferred consideration of the standards project until the results of a voluntary initiative by the Financial Executives Institute (FEI) were assessed. In late 1981, the FEI encouraged its members to change the definition of funds in the statement of changes in financial position required by APB Opinion No. 19 to cash and short-term investments. It also encouraged enterprises to experiment with alternative formats, such as grouping items by operating, investing, and financing activities. That experimentation with cash flow reporting in statements of changes in financial position was consistent with Opinion 19, which allowed flexibility in the focus and form of the statement.

In December 1983, the Board issued another Exposure Draft of a Concepts Statement, *Recognition and Measurement in Financial Statements of Business Enterprises*, which also discussed the role of the cash flow statement.

In December 1984, the FASB issued Concepts Statement No. 5, *Recognition and Measurement in Financial Statements of Business Enterprises*, which includes general guidance on a statement of cash flows and concludes that, in concept, a cash flow statement should be part of a full set of financial statements.

In April 1985, the FASB added to its agenda a cash flow reporting project of limited scope to (1) establish the objectives of a statement of cash flows, (2) define the few major components of cash flows to be presented in the statement, and (3) decide whether to require a statement of cash flows as part of a full set of financial statements for all enterprises.

In May 1985, the FASB staff organized a Task Force on Cash Flow Reporting. In June 1985, the FASB staff met with the task force to discuss appropriate objectives for a statement of cash flows. In November 1985, the staff met again with the task force to discuss the identification and definition of major elements of cash flows, the classification of certain transactions, the reporting of noncash transactions, and the methods for presenting cash flow from operating activities.

In March 1986, an advisory group on cash flow reporting by financial institutions was organized. In April 1986, the FASB met with the advisory group to discuss whether a statement of cash flows should be included in a complete set of financial statements of a financial institution as well as other cash flow reporting issues related to financial institutions.

In July 1986, the Board issued an Exposure Draft, *Statement of Cash Flows*. It proposed standards for cash flow reporting that require a statement of cash flows as part of a full set of financial statements of all business enterprises in place of a statement of changes in financial position.

In November 1987, the Board issued Tenet No. 95, *Statement of Cash Flows*, which established standards for cash flow reporting and required a statement of cash flows as part of a full set of financial statements. FAS No. 95 superseded APB No. 19, *Reporting Changes in Financial Position*. FAS No. 95 requires companies to present a statement of cash flows that classifies cash receipts and cash payments according to whether they result from operating, investing, or financing activities and provides a definition of each category. With the introduction of FAS No. 95, the FASB has made an undeniable move toward emphasizing the important role of cash flow analysis for investors and creditors. In the years to come, we will certainly see a continued shift toward the use of cash flow security analysis and cash flow accounting.

In February 1989, the FASB issued Statement No. 102, *Statement of Cash Flows—Exemption of Certain Enterprises and Classification of Cash Flows from Certain Securities Acquired for Resale*. FAS No. 102 exempted from the Statement of Cash Flows defined benefit plans covered under FAS No. 35, *Accounting and Reporting by Defined Benefit Plans*, and certain other employee benefit plans and highly liquid investment companies that meet specified conditions. FAS No. 102 also required that certain cash receipts and cash payments resulting from acquisitions and sales of securities and other assets that are acquired specifically for resale and are carried at market value or the lower of cost or market value be classified as operating cash flows in a statement of cash flows.

In December 1989, the FASB issued Statement No. 104, *Statement of Cash Flows—Net Reporting of Certain Cash Receipts and Cash Payments and Classification of Cash Flows from Hedging Transactions*. Statement No. 104 amended FAS No. 95 to permit banks, savings institutions, and credit unions to report in a statement of cash flows certain net cash receipts and cash payments for (1) deposits placed with other financial institutions and withdrawals of deposits, (2) time deposits accepted and repayments of deposits, and (3) loans made to customers and principal collections of loans. FAS No. 104 also permitted cash flows resulting from futures contracts, option contracts, or swap contracts that are accounted for as hedges of identifiable transactions or events to be classified in the same category as the cash flows from the items being hedged, provided that this accounting policy is disclosed.

We now provide a detailed example to illustrate the construction of a statement of cash flows.

3.2 EXAMPLE

To construct the statement of cash flows we use information from the balance sheet at the beginning and at the end of the accounting period, information about some economic events from the income statement, and additional information about events that are not incorporated in the income statement. To illustrate the construction of the statement, we use information that is adapted from the financial statements of Tyco Toys Inc. The data were modified for ease of exposition, and additional assumptions were made when data were unavailable in the financial statements. The financial statements of Tyco Toys Inc. are available at the end of this chapter. We also provide additional real-life examples of the statement of cash flows at the end of this chapter.

We begin the construction of the statement of cash flows with the construction of operating cash flows, using information from the balance sheet and income statement. We proceed to explain changes in balance sheet accounts by using the events described in the income statement. Those changes we cannot explain by events in the income statement will have to be explained by using additional information.

XYZ Company   Balance Sheet

Account	1989	1988	Difference
Cash	$ 13,000	$ 7,000	$ 6,000
Accounts receivable	109,000	54,000	55,000
Inventory	49,000	32,000	17,000
Prepaid expenses	14,000	10,000	4,000
Property, plant, and equipment	38,000	25,000	13,000
Accumulated depreciation	(18,000)	(13,000)	(5,000)
Notes receivable	8,000	7,000	1,000
Investment in subsidiary	4,000	4,000	—
Goodwill	86,000	13,000	73,000
Other assets	10,000	4,000	6,000
Total assets	$313,000	$143,000	
Notes payable	$ 24,000	$ 20,000	$ (4,000)
Current portion (LTD)	—	1,000	1,000
Accounts payable	28,000	15,000	(13,000)
Accrued expenses	44,000	30,000	(14,000)
Long-term debt (LTD)	118,000	20,000	(98,000)
Deferred tax	2,000	1,000	(1,000)
Minority interest	6,000	5,000	(1,000)
Common stock and paid-in capital	50,000	25,000	(25,000)
Retained earnings	43,000	27,000	(16,000)
Treasury stock	(1,000)	(1,000)	—
Translation adjustment	(1,000)	—	1,000
Total liability and equity	$313,000	$143,000	
Sum of differences			$ —

XYZ Company Income Statement

	1989
Sales	$385,000
Cost of goods sold	227,000
Selling, general, and administrative	116,000
Interest expense	15,000
Tax	10,000
Minority income	1,000
Net income	$ 16,000

Operating Cash Flows

1. Collections from customers

Sales	$385,000
Minus change in accounts receivable	(55,000)
Collections from customers	**$330,000**

The collections from customers are estimated by assuming that all sales are on credit. Because annual sales are $385,000, we expect that accounts receivable would have increased by $385,000. In fact, accounts receivable increased only by $55,000, implying that the balance, or $330,000, had been collected from customers.

2. Payments to suppliers and employees

Cost of goods sold	$227,000
plus selling, general and administrative expenses	116,000
plus change in inventory	17,000
plus change in prepaid expenses	4,000
minus change in accounts payable	(13,000)
minus change in accrued expenses	(14,000)
minus depreciation expense	(7,000)
Payments to suppliers and employees	**$330,000**

To estimate the payments to suppliers and employees, we aggregate cost of goods sold and selling and general and administrative expenses. We assume for a moment that these expenses represent cash payments to suppliers for purchases of merchandise and to employees for their services within the period. We also assume that all other overhead expenses incurred during the period were in cash. We add to this amount the increases in inventory and prepaid expenses, which again are assumed to be made in cash. Now, we subtract the change in accounts payable and accrued expenses, because these represent credits that were received from suppliers and employees for expenses that have not yet been paid during the period and that would be paid in the following period. We further subtract the annual depreciation expense because it represents an accounting expense that does not require a cash outflow.

3. Payment for taxes

Tax expense	$10,000
minus change in deferred taxes	(1,000)
Tax payment	**$ 9,000**

To estimate tax payments during the period, we assume that all the tax expenses on the income statement were deferred to future periods. This should have increased the deferred tax liability on the balance sheet by $10,000. Instead, we observe that the deferred tax liability increased only by $1,000. Thus, $9,000 became current taxes, and because there are no current taxes payable on the balance sheet, we assume that $9,000 were paid to the tax authorities during 1989. As we mention again later, under FAS No. 95, the actual cash tax payment has to be disclosed.

4. Interest payments

Interest expense/payment	**$15,000**

To estimate the interest payments during the period, we begin with the interest expense during the year, which we assume is all cash. We then modify it if there are interest payable or receivable accounts on the balance sheet. In this case, there are no interest receivable or payable accounts, so we assume that the interest payment is identical to the interest expense. As is the case for tax payments, the actual payment of interest is disclosed under FAS No. 95.

5. Total operating cash flows

$330,000 - 330,000 - 9,000 - 15,000 =	**$ (24,000)**

Investing Cash Flows

To estimate investing cash flows, we use the changes in balance sheet accounts that we haven't used before. We begin with the property, plant, and equipment (PPE) accounts, which include the original cost of PPE, the accumulated depreciation of PPE, and goodwill. Here we require additional information about the transactions that affected those accounts. Let us assume that the following additional information is available:

1. Additional PPE acquired during the year for cash amounted to $10,000.
2. PPE with an original cost of $3,000 and accumulated depreciation of $2,000 was sold for $1,000, which was paid for using a note receivable in excess of one year.
3. The firm acquired another firm with PPE of $6,000 and an excess of acquisition cost over fair market value of assets acquired (goodwill) of $73,000. The acquisition was paid for by using $30,000 cash, issuance of common stock of $22,000, and issuance of long-term debt in the amount of $27,000.
4. The investment in other assets of $6,000 was made in cash.

To estimate the various components of cash flows, we use the above additional information in the following manner:

1. Capital expenditures (investments in PPE)
According to the previous notes, the firm invested $10,000 in additional PPE. Thus, we have

Capital expenditures	**$(10,000)**

2. Proceeds from sale of PPE
According to the preceding notes, sale of old PPE having a book value of $1,000 (original cost of $3,000 minus accumulated depreciation of $2,000) was made for $1,000. Normally, if the proceeds were received in cash, it would have been recorded as an investing cash inflow. In effect, the firm had a disinvesting event, because it sold a portion of its fixed assets. However, in the current example, the sale was for long-term note receivable of $1,000 and not for cash. Thus, the proceeds from the sale of PPE are *not* included in the body of the cash flow statement. It should be noted that the noncurrent account "notes receivable" increased by $1,000 during the period.

3. Acquisition
According to the information above, the firm has made an acquisition, in which the acquired firm had PPE with fair market value of $6,000. In addition, the acquired firm had economic assets in the amount of $73,000 that had not been recorded on its books (this is the amount of goodwill in the transaction). Let us further assume that the only assets of the acquired firm are its PPE. Thus, the total acquisition cost is $79,000 (6,000 + 73,000). This acquisition was financed by using cash of $30,000, issuance of common stock for $22,000, and issuance of long-term debt of $27,000.

On the statement of cash flows, we record the acquisition in one of two ways:

Cash payment for acquired firm	**$(30,000)**

or, alternatively;

PPE of acquired firm	**$ (6,000)**
Other assets of the acquired firm	**(24,000)**
Acquisitions	**$(30,000)**

The net result is the same using both approaches: a cash outflow of $30,000 for the acquisition of another firm. The second approach provides a little more detail about the assets/liabilities of the acquired firm. Note that although the acquisition cost was $79,000, only cash outflows of $30,000 are included on the statement of cash flows. The balance will be reported in the portion of the statement that is intended for events that do not involve cash. This portion of the statement will be described later.

4. Other investing cash flows

Investments in other assets amounted to $6,000. Thus, we have:

Other investing cash flows	**$(6,000)**

5. Total investing cash flows

Total investing cash flows will be found by summing up the individual items above:

Total investing cash flows = (10,000 + 30,000 + 6,000)= $(46,000)

Note that at this point all the changes in asset accounts on the balance sheet, except for cash, have been incorporated in our analysis. Exhibit 3–1 explains how the differences in the balance sheet accounts between 1988 and 1989 are incorporated by the various parts of the statement.

Accounts receivable, inventory, and prepaid expenses were used for various operating cash flows. PPE had an increase of $13,000, which consists of capital expenditures of $10,000, PPE of acquired firm of $6,000 minus the original cost of PPE sold of $3,000. The accumulated depreciation account increased by $5,000. This increase is explained by the depreciation expense for the period of $7,000 minus the accumulated depreciation on old PPE that was sold during the period in the amount of $2,000. Notes receivable increased by $1,000 due to the sale of old PPE. The investment in subsidiary has not changed during the period. Goodwill increased by $73,000 due to the acquisition, and other assets increased due to additional cash investments of $6,000. Thus, all the changes in the asset accounts are fully incorporated into our analysis of operating or investing cash flows.

EXHIBIT 3-1

Account	Difference	Events
Cash	$ 6,000	
Accounts receivable	55,000	Operating—collections from customers
Inventory	17,000	Operating—payments to suppliers
Prepaid expenses	4,000	Operating—payments to suppliers
Property, plant, and equipment	13,000	Capital expenditures $10,000 PPE of acquired firm 6,000 PPE sold (3,000)
Accumulated depreciation	(5,000)	Depreciation expense (7,000) Accumulated depreciation on PPE sold 2,000
Notes receivable	1,000	Note received for sale of old PPE 1,000
Investment in subsidiary	—	
Goodwill	73,000	Acquisition 73,000
Other assets	6,000	Investment in assets 6,000

Financing Cash Flows

To estimate the outcome of events that affect financing cash flows, we focus on the changes in the liability and equity accounts on the balance sheet. Once more, we need additional information about the events that affect these accounts. We use the following additional information:

1. Notes payable in the amount of $4,000 were issued during the period. The current portion of long-term debt of $1,000 was paid in cash during the period.

2. Long-term debt during the period increased by $98,000, out of which $27,000 were issued to acquire the other firm. The balance of $71,000 (98,000 − 27,000) was issued to raise cash.

3. New common stock issued during the period was in the amount of $25,000, out of which $22,000 were issued to acquire the other firm, and the balance of $3,000 (25,000 − 22,000) was issued for cash.

4. Losses on translation of foreign financial statements increased by $1,000 during the period.

To estimate the financing cash flows based on the above information, we go through the following steps:

1. Issuance of short-term debt

Issuance of notes payable	**$4,000**

2. Payment of short-term debt

Payment of the current portion of long-term debt	**$(1,000)**

3. Issuance of long-term debt

Issuance of long-term debt for cash	**$71,000**

Note that only the portion of the increase in long-term debt that was received in cash during the period is included as a financing cash flow. The remainder, $27,000, which were issued as part of the acquisition, will be presented as a noncash event in the statement of cash flows.

4. Issuance of common stock

Issuance of common stock for cash	**$3,000**

Once again, notice that the common stock issued for the acquisition, $22,000, will be disclosed as a noncash event in the statement of cash flows. It is not included as a financing cash flow.

5. Effects of foreign currency translation

Effects of foreign currency translation	**$(1,000)**

6. Total financing cash flows

Total financing cash flows = 4,000 − 1,000 + 71,000 + 3,000 − 1,000 = $76,000

At this point, we were able to explain or incorporate all the changes in the liability or equity accounts in our analysis. The accounts payable and accrued expenses were used in the estimate of payments to suppliers and employees. The different debt accounts (notes payable, current portion of long-term debt, and long-term debt) were used in financing cash flows. The deferred taxes were used in estimating tax cash payments in the operating cash flows. The increase in minority interest of $1,000 is explained by minority shareholders' share of the profits, which were equal to exactly $1,000 on the income statement. The change in common stock and paid-in capital is incorporated in the financing cash flows. The change in retained earnings of $16,000 is fully explained by the year's income of $16,000, that is, the firm has paid no cash dividends. Finally, treasury stock had not changed during the year and the translation adjustment was incorporated into the financing cash flows above.

The only account we have not yet incorporated in the analysis is the cash account. However, the change in the cash account should be equal to the aggregate of all the effects of the operating, investing, and financing events on cash. Specifically, the change in cash should be equal to:

Total operating cash flows	$(24,000)
Total investing cash flows	(46,000)
Total financing cash flows	76,000
Increase in cash	**$ 6,000**

We can see that the change in the cash account is exactly identical to the aggregate of the events that affect cash during the period. We are now ready to present the statement of cash flows for 1989.

XYZ Corp.   Statement of Cash Flows— 1989

Operating Cash Flows:		
Collections from customers	$ 330,000	
Payments to suppliers, employees, etc.	(330,000)	
Tax payments	(9,000)	
Interest payments	(15,000)	
Total operating cash flows		$(24,000)
Investing Cash Flows:		
Purchases of PPE	$(10,000)	
Acquisitions	(30,000)	
Other, net	(6,000)	
Total investing cash flows		$(46,000)
Financing Cash Flows:		
Issuance of short-term debt, net	$ 3,000	
Issuance of long-term debt	71,000	
Issuance of common stock	3,000	
Effects of foreign currency translation	(1,000)	
Total financing cash flows		$ 76,000
Total Change in Cash		$ 6,000

continued

XYZ Corp.   Statement of Cash Flows — 1989 (*continued*)

Supplemental Schedule of Noncash Investing and Financing Events:
Acquisition of other firm:

Fair value of assets acquired	$ 79,000
Cash paid in acquisition	(30,000)
Noncash investing events	$ 49,000
Issuance of common stock	$ 22,000
Issuance of long-term debt	27,000
Noncash financing events	$ 49,000

Reconciliation of Net Income to Cash from Operating Activities:

Net income		$ 16,000
Adjustments:		
Depreciation and amortization	$ 7,000	
Minority income	1,000	
Increase in inventory	(17,000)	
Increase in accounts receivable	(55,000)	
Increase in prepaid expenses	(4,000)	
Increase in accounts payable	13,000	
Increase in accrued expenses	14,000	
Increase in deferred taxes	1,000	
	$(40,000)	(40,000)
Net operating cash flows		$(24,000)

The last two schedules in the statement of cash flows are intended to supply additional information about events that do not affect cash, but are nevertheless significant economic events. The first schedule provides a more complete picture about the acquisition and its financing. The second schedule is intended to explain why net income and net operating cash flows differ. This is required whenever the statement of cash flows is prepared using the ''direct'' method. We now explain the differences between the ''direct'' and ''indirect'' methods of reporting cash flows from operations.

3.3 DIRECT AND INDIRECT METHODS FOR REPORTING OPERATING CASH FLOWS

The FASB has given firms the option of reporting cash flows from operations using either the direct or the indirect method. Under the direct method, the main categories of operating cash flows are directly estimated and reported on the statement in a way that is similar to what we did in the previous example. However, the FASB has also allowed firms to report the operating cash flows by using the indirect method. The basis for this method is the accounting identity:

$$\text{Net Income} = \text{Revenues} - \text{Expenses}.$$

We can examine the revenues and expenses and segregate those that are noncash revenues or expenses and also those that are nonoperating cash flows. For example, the firm might have recorded income from unconsolidated subsidiaries that are carried on the balance sheet using the equity method. This income is included in net income, but is a noncash event if cash dividends were not paid by the subsidiary. Similarly, suppose the firm sold some old PPE at a gain. This gain is included in net income, but it reflects an investing cash flow and not an operating cash flow. Examples of noncash expenses include depreciation and deferred taxes. Thus, we can rewrite the accounting identity as:

$$\text{Net Income} = (CR + NCR) - (CE + NCE).$$

where CR is defined as cash revenues from operating activities, NCR are revenues that are noncash revenues or that are nonoperating cash flows. Similarly, CE are defined as cash expenses from operating activities, and NCE as noncash expenses or nonoperating cash flows that are included among the expenses. Simple collection of terms and transfer of terms to the other side of the equation yields:

$$(CR - CE) = \text{Net Income} + NCE - NCR.$$

By definition, $(CR - CE)$ is identical to the cash from operating activities. It can be derived by beginning with the net income of the firm and making adjustments to revenue and expense events that are either noncash or nonoperating cash flows. In particular, we *add* noncash (or nonoperating) expenses because they were subtracted from income to derive net income, and *subtract* noncash (or nonoperating) revenues because they were added to income in deriving net income.

Let us illustrate this approach to the estimation of net operating cash flows in the previous example. In effect, we have done exactly that at the bottom of the statement of cash flows in the schedule that reconciles net income with net operating cash flows. Let us present this schedule again and explain its components:

Reconciliation of Net Income to Cash from Operating Activities:

Net income		$ 16,000
Adjustments:		
Depreciation and amortization	$ 7,000	
Minority income	1,000	
Increase in inventory	(17,000)	
Increase in accounts receivable	(55,000)	
Increase in prepaid expenses	(4,000)	
Increase in accounts payable	13,000	
Increase in accrued expenses	14,000	
Increase in deferred taxes	1,000	
	$(40,000)	(40,000)
Net operating cash flows		$(24,000)

This schedule begins with net income of $16,000. It adds to net income depreciation and amortization that are noncash expenses. It also adds back minority income, because minority stockholders' share of income was subtracted from income to derive net income, whereas no dividends were actually remitted to minority stockholders. The schedule then subtracts increases in assets that are affected by operating cash flows, and adds back increases in liabilities that are affected by operating cash flows. For example, the increase in inventory is subtracted from net income, because, presumably, additional cash outlays were made to purchase or produce this inventory. The net income figure includes only those cash outlays for inventory that was sold (cost of goods sold). Similarly, we subtract the increase in accounts receivable because a portion of the sales revenue that was included in net income was not received in cash, but reflects an increase in receivables. We also add back accounts payable, for example, because it reflects a portion of the expenses that were subtracted from income in deriving net income, but that have not yet been paid in cash during the period. Instead, this portion is shown as accounts to be paid in the future. The logic for the other accounts is very similar.

The FASB has encouraged firms to use the direct approach to report operating cash flows. However, it required firms that use the direct method to add a schedule that reconciles net income with net cash flows. Thus, a firm that adopts the direct method for reporting cash flows from operating activities has to supply *all* the information that is required from a firm that uses the indirect method, but, *in addition*, has to supply information about the major components of operating cash flows. Obviously, reasonable managers will opt to minimize their exposure to costly *additional* disclosure and will use the indirect method the most for reporting cash flows from operations. Indeed, most firms today use the indirect method.

In the next chapter, we provide exact definitions of cash flows from financing, investing, and operating activities. We also provide many examples of such activities as reported in publicly available statements and discuss how these cash flows should be interpreted. Let us now show examples of entire statements of cash flows from published financial statements of corporations.

Tyco Toys: Consolidated Balance Sheets, 1989

Tyco Toys, Inc. and Subsidiaries
Consolidated Balance Sheets

December 31, 1989 and 1988 (in thousands, except share amounts)

	1989	1988
Assets		
Current Assets		
Cash and cash equivalents	$ 12,975	6,744
Receivables, net (note 4)	108,628	53,930
Inventories (note 5)	49,353	32,025
Prepaid expenses and other current assets (note 13)	13,743	10,060
Total current assets	184,699	102,759
Property and equipment, net (note 6)	20,570	12,294
Other assets		
Notes receivable from affiliates, net of current portion (note 7)	8,145	7,143
Investment in discontinued unconsolidated subsidiary (note 8)	3,500	3,831
Goodwill, net of accumulated amortization of $1,414 and $201 in 1989 and 1988, respectively	86,366	13,005
Other assets	9,859	3,512
Total other assets	107,870	27,491
Total assets (note 10)	$313,139	142,544
Liabilities and Stockholders' Equity		
Current liabilities		
Notes and acceptances payable (note 10)	$ 23,506	19,869
Current portion of long-term debt (note 11)	110	1,447
Accounts payable	28,515	15,110
Accrued expenses and other current liabilities (note 9)	44,289	29,390
Total current liabilities	96,420	65,816
Long-term debt, net of current portion (note 11)	117,796	19,369
Deferred income taxes	1,560	977
Minority interest (note 3)	5,326	4,882
Commitments and contingencies (notes 14 and 15)		
Stockholders' equity (notes 10, 11 and 12)		
Preferred stock, $.10 par value, 1,000,000 shares authorized; none outstanding	—	—
Common stock, $.01 par value, 20,000,000 shares authorized; 6,666,369 and 5,830,030 shares issued in 1989 and 1988, respectively	67	58
Additional paid-in capital	50,085	24,841
Retained earnings	42,819	27,138
Treasury stock, 40,795 shares in 1989 and 1988, at cost	(537)	(537)
Cumulative translation adjustment	(397)	—
Total stockholders' equity	92,037	51,500
Total liabilities and stockholders' equity	$313,139	142,544

SOURCE: Tyco Toys, *Annual Report*, 1989.

Tyco Toys: Consolidated Statement of Operations, 1989

Tyco Toys, Inc. and Subsidiaries

Consolidated Statements of Operations

Years ended December 31, 1989, 1988 and 1987 (in thousands, except per share amounts)

	1989	1988	1987
Net sales	$384,499	263,764	163,456
Cost of goods sold	226,522	163,479	104,434
Gross profit	157,977	100,285	59,022
Selling and administrative expenses	116,416	77,695	46,487
Operating income	41,561	22,590	12,535
Interest and debt expense	15,165	8,243	3,989
Interest and other (income) expense, net	40	(2,048)	(1,250)
Gain on sale of stock held for investment	—	(697)	—
Interest expense and other (income) expense, net	15,205	5,498	2,739
Income before income taxes, minority interest and discontinued operation	26,356	17,092	9,796
Provision for income taxes (note 13)	9,700	4,630	2,561
Minority interest	642	1,599	358
Net income from continuing operations	16,014	10,863	6,877
Equity in earnings (loss) of discontinued unconsolidated subsidiary, net of reserve for loss and minority interest (notes 8 and 17)	(333)	837	—
Net income	$ 15,681	11,700	6,877
Net income per common share:			
Primary:			
Income from continuing operations	$ 2.37	1.87	1.58
Net income	$ 2.33	2.02	1.58
Fully diluted:			
Income from continuing operations	$ 2.28	1.81	1.35
Net income	$ 2.25	1.96	1.35
Weighted average number of common shares outstanding:			
Primary	8,534	5,801	4,354
Fully diluted	8,854	5,801	5,378

SOURCE: Tyco Toys, *Annual Report, 1989.*

Tyco Toys: Consolidated Statements of Stockholders Equity, 1989

Tyco Toys, Inc. and Subsidiaries

Consolidated Statements of Stockholders' Equity

Years ended December 31, 1989, 1988 and 1987 (in thousands)

	Preferred Stock		Common Stock		Additional Paid-in Capital	Retained Earnings	Treasury Stock		Cumulative Translation Adjustment
	Number of Shares	Amount	Number of Shares	Amount			Number of Shares	Amount	
Balance at December 31, 1986	—	$—	3,200	$32	$ 2,588	$ 8,561	—	$—	$—
Net income	—	—	—	—	—	6,877	—	—	—
Conversion of debentures	—	—	1,599	16	12,933	—	—	—	—
Exercise of:									
Warrants	—	—	41	—	—	—	—	—	—
Options	—	—	79	1	506	—	—	—	—
Treasury stock acquired	—	—	(13)	—	—	—	13	(172)	—
Stock issued to acquire Nasta International, Inc.	—	—	263	3	4,731	—	—	—	—
Balance at December 31, 1987	—	—	5,169	52	20,758	15,438	13	(172)	—
Net income	—	—	—	—	—	11,700	—	—	—
Exercise of stock options	—	—	286	3	1,820	—	—	—	—
Tax benefit from exercise of certain options	—	—	—	—	649	—	—	—	—
Treasury stock acquired	—	—	(28)	—	—	—	28	(365)	—
Stock issued to acquire Nasta International, Inc.	—	—	363	3	(3)	—	—	—	—
Warrants issued	—	—	—	—	1,740	—	—	—	—
Notes to officers (note 12)	—	—	—	—	(123)	—	—	—	—
Balance at December 31, 1988	—	—	5,790	58	24,841	27,138	41	(537)	—
Net income	—	—	—	—	—	15,681	—	—	—
Exercise of stock options	—	—	53	1	601	—	—	—	—
Tax benefit from exercise of certain options	—	—	—	—	889	—	—	—	—
Securities issued to acquire View-Master	—	—	782	8	19,571	—	—	—	—
Cumulative translation adjustment	—	—	—	—	—	—	—	—	(397)
Warrants issued	—	—	—	—	4,060	—	—	—	—
Notes to officers (note 12)	—	—	—	—	123	—	—	—	—
Balance at December 31, 1989	—	$—	6,625	$67	$50,085	$42,819	41	($537)	($397)

SOURCE: Tyco Toys, *Annual Report*, 1989.

Tyco Toys: Consolidated Statements of Cash Flows, 1989

Tyco Toys, Inc. and Subsidiaries

Consolidated Statements of Cash Flows

Years ended December 31, 1989, 1988 and 1987 (in thousands)

	1989	1988	1987
Cash Flows From Operating Activities:			
Net income	**$15,681**	11,700	6,877
Adjustments to reconcile net income to net cash provided by operating activities:			
Depreciation and amortization	**6,908**	4,640	2,605
Minority interest in net income of subsidiary	**642**	1,599	358
Deferred income tax provision (benefit)	**583**	(2,097)	(268)
Gain on sale of stock held for investment	—	(697)	—
Undistributed (earnings) loss of discontinued unconsolidated subsidiary, net of reserve for loss	**333**	(837)	—
Change in Assets and Liabilities, net of effects from purchase of View-Master:			
(Increase) in receivables, net	**(29,077)**	(9,439)	(20,674)
(Increase) decrease in inventories	**3,404**	(6,017)	(12,123)
(Increase) in prepaid expenses and other current assets	**(2,278)**	(1,949)	(1,870)
(Increase) decrease in other assets	**(217)**	125	389
Increase in accounts payable	**4,645**	1,060	8,237
Increase (decrease) in accrued expenses and other current liabilities	**(4,197)**	3,869	(1,575)
Total adjustments	**(19,254)**	(9,743)	(24,921)
Net cash provided (utilized) by operating activities	**(3,573)**	1,957	(18,044)
Cash Flows From Investing Activities:			
Purchase of short-term investment	—	—	(1,223)
Proceeds from the sale of short-term investment	—	1,920	—
Disposition of equipment and assets held for sale	**110**	3,793	1,287
Capital expenditures	**(10,750)**	(5,532)	(8,426)
Investment in subsidiaries	—	(2,684)	—
Cash payment for purchase of View-Master	**(35,228)**	—	—
Cash effect from the acquisition of View-Master	**6,357**	—	—
(Reduction) increase in minority interest in subsidiary	**(7)**	(15)	2,455
Acquisition of net non-current assets of subsidiary	—	—	(3,135)
Excess cost over fair market value of assets acquired	**(4,215)**	—	(3,111)
Payments by Nasta to its former shareholders	**(8,117)**	(998)	—
Repayment (issuance) of notes receivable	—	2,500	(2,500)
Net cash (utilized) by investing activities	**(51,850)**	(1,016)	(14,653)
Cash Flows From Financing Activities:			
Proceeds from issuance of long-term debt	**85,500**	14,500	7,067
(Repayment) of long-term debt	**(2,976)**	(888)	—
(Repayment) increase of current portion of long-term debt	**(1,456)**	(234)	1,469
Increase (repayment) in notes and acceptances payable	**(16,605)**	(15,264)	23,300
Proceeds from issuance of Common Stock	**601**	1,813	507
Purchase of treasury stock	—	(365)	(172)
Issuance of preferred stock of subsidiary	—	—	4,734
Repayment (issuance) of notes receivable	**(1,002)**	736	(199)
Debt issuance costs	**(2,408)**	—	—
Net cash flows from financing activities	**61,654**	298	36,706
Net Increase in Cash and Cash Equivalents	**6,231**	1,239	4,009
Cash and Cash Equivalents, Beginning of Year	**6,744**	5,505	1,496
Cash and Cash Equivalents, End of Year	**$12,975**	6,744	5,505

SOURCE: Tyco Toys, *Annual Report*, 1989.

Tyco Toys: Consolidated Statements of Cash Flows, 1989 (continued)

Tyco Toys, Inc. and Subsidiaries
Consolidated Statements of Cash Flows

Years ended December 31, 1989, 1988 and 1987 (in thousands)

	1989	1988	1987
Supplemental disclosures of cash flow information:			
Cash paid during the year for:			
Interest	$13,452	8,112	3,989
Taxes	2,562	3,636	1,866
Supplemental schedule of noncash operating activities:			
Reclass from prepaid expenses to other assets	415	—	—
Supplemental schedule of noncash investing activities:			
Excess cost over fair market value of assets acquired	—	8,117	—
Leased equipment	55	108	106
Supplemental schedule of noncash financing activities:			
Reclass from long-term debt to notes and acceptances payable	—	10,116	402
Reclass from long-term debt to current portion of long-term debt	6	—	—
Securities issued to acquire View-Master	19,579	—	—
Cumulative translation adjustment	397	—	—
Tax benefit from exercise of certain stock options	889	649	—
Warrants issued	4,060	1,740	—

SOURCE: Tyco Toys, *Annual Report*, 1989.

Times Mirror, Co.: Statements of Consolidated Cash Flows

The Times Mirror Company and Subsidiaries

STATEMENTS OF CONSOLIDATED CASH FLOWS

		Year Ended December 31	
(In thousands of dollars)	1990	1989	1988
CASH FLOWS FROM OPERATING ACTIVITIES			
Net Income	$180,477	$297,987	$331,854
Adjustments to reconcile net income to net cash provided by operating activities:			
Items included in net income not affecting cash:			
Depreciation and amortization	245,138	221,218	197,525
Provision for losses on accounts receivable	45,115	34,187	29,321
Provision for noncurrent deferred income taxes	18,917	13,547	34,846
Nonrecurring gains		(9,156)	(58,880)
Other noncurrent deferrals and accruals, net	(15,669)	(59,399)	(61,282)
Changes in working capital accounts:			
Trade accounts receivable	(42,819)	(73,635)	(37,414)
Inventories	(18,885)	14,864	(26,056)
Trade accounts payable	15,781	21,717	38,966
Income taxes payable	(13,298)	(21,084)	26,168
Other prepayments and accruals, net	(7,817)	5,137	(23,510)
Net cash provided by operating activities	406,940	445,383	451,538
CASH FLOWS FROM INVESTING ACTIVITIES			
Proceeds from sales of operating assets	9,131	15,512	145,330
Acquisitions, net of cash acquired	(79,272)	(119,141)	(157,277)
Capital expenditures	(334,493)	(416,074)	(301,608)
Other investing activities, net	3,443	(5,109)	(7,933)
Net cash used in investing activities	(401,191)	(524,812)	(321,488)
CASH FLOWS FROM FINANCING ACTIVITIES			
Proceeds from debt	327,179	317,081	201,211
Repayment of debt	(166,004)	(106,331)	(193,881)
Repayment of bank loans of Employee Stock Ownership Plan	(15,000)	(13,400)	(11,900)
Common stock issuance related to stock options and awards	10,041	14,693	12,339
Repurchase of common stock	(24,332)	(2,800)	(2,389)
Dividends paid	(138,779)	(129,144)	(118,336)
Net cash provided by (used in) financing activities	(6,895)	80,099	(112,956)
Increase (decrease) in cash and cash equivalents	(1,146)	670	17,094
Cash and cash equivalents at beginning of year	37,824	37,154	20,060
Cash and cash equivalents at end of year	$ 36,678	$ 37,824	$ 37,154
Cash paid during the year for:			
Interest (net of amount capitalized)	$ 80,665	$ 53,903	$ 49,233
Income taxes	120,992	203,139	149,218

SOURCE: Times Mirror Co., *Annual Report*, 1990.

Tandy Corp.: Consolidated Statements of Cash Flows

Consolidated Statements of Cash Flows
Tandy Corporation and Subsidiaries

In thousands.	Year Ended June 30,		
	1991	**1990**	**1989**
Cash flows from operating activities:			
Net income	**$195,444**	$290,347	$323,504
Adjustments to reconcile net income to net cash			
provided by operating activities:			
Cumulative effect on prior years of change in			
accounting for extended warranty and service			
contracts, net of taxes of $5,471,000	**10,619**	—	—
Depreciation and amortization	**99,698**	92,115	75,429
Deferred income taxes and other items	**(29,633)**	(3,206)	277
Provision for credit losses and bad debts	**60,643**	33,073	22,929
Changes in operating assets and liabilities, excluding			
the effect of businesses acquired:			
Sale of customer receivables	**350,000**	—	—
Receivables	**(256,445)**	(273,921)	(90,362)
Inventories	**151,339**	(110,336)	14,320
Other current assets	**(2,028)**	(15,110)	(8,504)
Accounts payable, accrued expenses and income taxes	**37,716**	45,445	15,326
Net cash provided by operating activities	**617,353**	58,407	352,919
Investing activities:			
Additions to property, plant and equipment,			
net of retirements	**(139,453)**	(112,515)	(122,497)
Acquisition of Victor Technologies	**—**	(112,856)	—
Payment received on InterTAN note	**—**	35,906	—
Other investing activities	**(1,046)**	7,853	(130)
Net cash used by investing activities	**(140,499)**	(181,612)	(122,627)
Financing activities:			
Purchases of treasury stock	**(83,086)**	(369,982)	(198,823)
Sales of treasury stock to employee			
stock purchase program	**50,383**	52,019	49,449
Issuance of preferred stock to TESOP	**100,000**	—	—
Dividends paid, net of taxes	**(51,478)**	(49,760)	(53,458)
Changes in short-term borrowings—net	**(598,763)**	479,325	(11,612)
Additions to long-term borrowings	**210,167**	133,751	10,188
Repayments of long-term borrowings	**(52,981)**	(45,349)	(155,862)
Net cash provided (used) by financing activities	**(425,758)**	200,004	(360,118)
Increase (decrease) in cash and			
short-term investments	**51,096**	76,799	(129,826)
Cash and short-term investments			
at the beginning of the year	**135,197**	58,398	188,224
Cash and short-term investments			
at the end of the year	**$186,293**	$135,197	$ 58,398

SOURCE: Tandy Corp., *Annual Report*, 1991.

Petrie Stores Corp.: Consolidated Cash Flows

PETRIE STORES CORPORATION AND SUBSIDIARIES

Consolidated Cash Flows

	For The Years Ended		
	February 2, 1991 (52 Weeks)	February 3, 1990 (53 Weeks)	January 28, 1989 (52 Weeks)
	(In thousands of dollars)		
Cash flows from operating activities:			
Net income	$ 2,996	$ 32,265	$ 92,182
Adjustments to reconcile net income to net cash provided by operating activities:			
Depreciation and amortization of property and equipment	57,027	54,970	56,791
Other amortization	3,107	3,194	3,133
Loss on disposal of property and equipment	4,927	8,703	9,596
Provision for doubtful accounts.	959	720	1,335
Fair market value of treasury stock issued as compensation.	307	315	200
(Earnings) loss from investments at equity	16,676	(282)	(3,036)
Deferred income taxes.	(9,486)	942	(16,372)
Extraordinary item—(gain) on extinguishment of long-term debt	—	—	(101,800)
Changes in assets and liabilities:			
Decrease (increase) in:			
Accounts receivable	(1,980)	161	(768)
Merchandise inventories.	(6,040)	(12,629)	7,306
Refundable federal income taxes	—	—	12,700
Prepaid expenses	(779)	(884)	1,734
Other assets	(714)	(134)	117
Increase (decrease) in:			
Accounts payable	12,493	(5,801)	5,442
Accrued expenses and other liabilities	2,494	1,329	2,988
Income taxes.	(9,477)	1,362	14,798
Net cash provided by operating activities.	72,510	84,231	86,346
Cash flows from investing activities:			
Additions to property and equipment - net	(58,943)	(33,171)	(37,778)
Investments in common stock	2,797	(36,782)	—
Net cash (used in) investing activities.	(56,146)	(69,953)	(37,778)
Cash flows from financing activities:			
Cash dividends	(9,353)	(9,353)	(9,353)
Payments in connection with extinguishment of long-term debt.	—	—	(2,326)
Acquisition of treasury stock	(194)	(452)	(199)
Repayment of long-term obligations.	(234)	(211)	(189)
Net cash (used in) financing activities	(9,781)	(10,016)	(12,067)
Net increase in cash and short-term investments.	6,583	4,262	36,501
Cash and short-term investments – beginning of year.	122,192	117,930	81,429
Cash and short-term investments – end of year	$ 128,775	$ 122,192	$ 117,930
Supplemental disclosures of cash flow information:			
Cash paid during the year for:			
Interest.	$ 11,835	$ 10,508	$ 11,011
Income taxes.	$ 20,147	$ 20,794	$ 66,532

Supplemental disclosure of noncash investing and financing activities:

(a) In March and July 1988, substantially all of the Company's 7½ and 8% Subordinated Exchangeable Debentures were exchanged for approximately 14,200,000 shares of common stock of Toys "R" Us, Inc. owned by the Company. The exchanges resulted in a gain, after taxes, of $57,100,000.

(b) $15,000 of Convertible Subordinated Debentures ("debentures") were exchanged for 677 shares of the Company's common stock ("shares") in January 1989, $6,000 of debentures were exchanged for 271 shares in May 1989 and $5,000 of debentures were exchanged for 225 shares in July 1990.

SOURCE: Petrie Stores Corp., *Annual Report*, 1990.

Chock Full O'Nuts: Consolidated Statement of Cash Flows

CONSOLIDATED STATEMENTS OF CASH FLOWS
Chock Full o'Nuts Corporation and Subsidiaries Years ended July 31, 1990, 1989 and 1988

	1990	1989	1988
Operating Activities			
Net income/(loss)	$ 4,407,247	$ 3,461,104	$(1,543,513)
Adjustments to reconcile net income/(loss) to net cash provided by operating activities:			
Depreciation and amortization of property, plant and equipment	3,995,408	4,000,251	3,650,856
Amortization of deferred compensation and deferred charges	1,957,643	2,315,352	1,480,680
Loss related to termination of real estate agreements	6,000,000		
Provision for loss on note receivable	900,000		
(Gain)/loss on marketable equity securities		(2,484,278)	2,298,610
(Gain) on redemption of convertible subordinated debentures	(1,848,095)		
Deferred income taxes	(1,070,000)	777,000	260,000
Other, net	334,197	244,515	(282,839)
Changes in operating assets and liabilities, net of effects from acquired companies:			
Decrease in accounts receivable	767,693	1,263,850	1,385,218
(Increase)/decrease in inventory	(1,570,425)	14,030,184	(566,252)
(Increase)/decrease in prepaid expenses	(1,427,425)	395,983	(39,724)
Increase/(decrease) in accounts payable, accrued expenses and income taxes	(3,689,180)	1,205,670	(4,436,680)
Net Cash Provided by Operating Activities	8,757,063	25,209,631	2,206,356
Investing Activities			
Purchase of Jimbo's Jumbos, Incorporated, net of cash acquired		(31,015,501)	
Purchase of instant coffee business of Tetley, Inc. and peanut business of Everfresh Products, Inc.	(7,908,368)		
Purchases of short- term investments	(27,109,479)	(24,119,298)	(29,827,574)
Proceeds from sale of marketable equity securities and collection of principal on other short-term investments	37,519,171	23,490,052	
Purchases of property, plant and equipment	(1,749,667)	(3,054,622)	(3,796,830)
Other			(700,000)
Net Cash Provided by/(Used in) Investing Activities	751,657	(34,699,369)	(34,324,404)
Financing Activities			
Loans to employees' stock ownership plan	(1,140,000)	(1,750,000)	
Borrowings under short-term bank notes, net	1,000,000		
Proceeds from long-term debt	3,147,505		1,535,531
Principal payments of assumed long-term debt of Jimbo's Jumbos, Incorporated		(11,132,693)	
Principal payments of other long-term debt	(9,517,303)	(5,670,465)	(3,049,360)
Redemption of convertible subordinated debentures	(2,998,905)		
Net Cash (Used in) Financing Activities	(9,508,703)	(18,553,158)	(1,513,829)
Increase/(Decrease) in Cash and Cash Equivalents	17	(28,042,896)	(33,631,877)
Cash and cash equivalents at beginning of year	8,387,760	36,430,656	70,062,533
Cash and Cash Equivalents at End of Year	$ 8,387,777	$ 8,387,760	$36,430,656
Supplemental Information			
Cash paid during the year:			
Interest	$ 9,989,000	$11,133,000	$10,638,000
Income taxes	5,662,000	871,000	160,000
The decrease in inventory in 1989 includes an $11,082,658 reduction in inventory of Jimbo's Jumbos, Incorporated from date of acquisition and cash generated from the reduction was used to repay its long-term debt.			

SOURCE: Chock Full O'Nuts, *Annual Report*, 1990.

Systems Software Association: Consolidated Statement of Cash Flows

CONSOLIDATED STATEMENTS OF CASH FLOWS

(in thousands)	Year Ended October 31,		
	1991	1990	1989
Cash Flows From Operating Activities:			
Net Income	$16,705	$16,370	$11,140
Adjustments to reconcile net income to net cash from operating activities:			
Depreciation and amortization of property and equipment	4,313	2,690	1,644
Amortization of other assets	3,401	2,589	1,802
Provision for doubtful accounts	2,044	1,335	2,959
Deferred income taxes	(273)	719	(1,340)
Deferred revenue	3,665	6,341	5,245
Other	(58)		
Changes in operating assets and liabilities:			
Accounts receivable	(23,072)	(12,217)	(10,690)
Prepaid expenses and other current assets	(1,292)	(2,333)	586
Accrued commissions and royalties	3,222	6,128	3,907
Accounts payable and other accrued liabilities	3,546	(3,606)	3,197
Accrued compensation and related benefits	(2,152)	4,362	692
Income taxes payable	2,666	685	2,128
Net cash provided by operating activities	12,715	23,063	21,270
Cash Flows From Investing Activities:			
Purchases of property and equipment	(4,980)	(8,525)	(1,994)
Software costs	(5,322)	(4,245)	(3,283)
Sale of minority interest in subsidiary	1,004		
Investment in consolidated subsidiary, net of cash aquired	(736)		
Other	(797)	(2,383)	123
Net cash flows used in investing activities	(10,831)	(15,153)	(5,154)
Cash Flows From Financing Activities:			
Principal payments under capital lease obligations	(822)	(754)	(367)
Proceeds from exercise of stock options	716	406	317
Purchase of treasury stock	(2,493)		
Dividends paid	(2,934)		
Net cash used in financing activities	(5,533)	(348)	(50)
Effect of exchange rate changes on cash	(1,578)	400	(805)
Net increase (decrease) in cash and equivalents	(5,227)	7,962	15,261
Cash and equivalents:			
Beginning of year	28,432	20,470	5,209
End of year	$23,205	$28,432	$20,470

SOURCE: Systems Software Association, *Annual Report*, 1991.

Murphy Oil Corp.: Consolidated Statements of Cash Flows

CONSOLIDATED STATEMENTS OF CASH FLOWS

(Thousands of dollars)

Years Ended December 31	1990	1989	1988
Operating Activities			
Net income	**$114,009**	46,551	38,752
Adjustments to net income to reconcile to net cash provided by operating activities			
Depreciation, depletion, amortization, etc.	**218,713**	219,301	223,704
Provisions for major repairs and dismantlement costs	**30,500**	22,742	16,358
Expenditures for major repairs and dismantlement costs	**(21,367)**	(15,277)	(13,371)
Exploratory expenditures charged against income	**50,181**	34,605	42,093
Deferred and noncurrent income tax credits	**(11,437)**	(6,211)	(25,975)
Minority interest in income (loss) of a subsidiary	**23,556**	(2,464)	(11,841)
Gains from disposition of assets	**(86,634)**	(1,901)	(12,289)
Other—net	**14,681**	15,691	2,344
	332,202	313,037	259,775
Working capital (increases) decreases related to operating activities			
Accounts receivable	**(62,484)**	(47,026)	3,984
Inventories	**(12,141)**	(21,382)	4,173
Accounts payable and accrued liabilities	**125,226**	54,215	31,666
Income taxes	**3,938**	13,198	(9,019)
Payment of income tax and interest assessments	**(83,540)**	—	—
Other adjustments related to operating activities	**(10,835)**	(6,331)	(575)
Net cash provided by operating activities	**292,366**	305,711	290,004
Investing Activities			
Capital expenditures requiring cash	**(237,570)**	(199,936)	(190,353)
Proceeds from disposition of assets	**117,197**	5,681	63,064
Other—net	**666**	(4,398)	(8,637)
Net cash required by investing activities	**(119,707)**	(198,653)	(135,926)
Financing Activities			
Additions to long-term debt	**234**	37,915	80,492
Reductions of long-term debt	**(108,935)**	(90,356)	(143,383)
Increase (decrease) in notes payable	**1,814**	(4,246)	(8,395)
Dividends paid			
Murphy shareholders	**(33,894)**	(33,878)	(33,867)
Minority shareholders	**(6,015)**	(6,013)	(6,011)
Net cash required by financing activities	**(146,796)**	(96,578)	(111,164)
Effect of exchange rate changes on cash and cash equivalents	**5,980**	(2,995)	(2,919)
Net increase in cash and cash equivalents	**31,843**	7,485	39,995
Cash and cash equivalents at beginning of year	**242,720**	235,235	195,240
Cash and cash equivalents at end of year	**$274,563**	242,720	235,235

SOURCE: Murphy Oil Corp., *Annual Report*, 1990.

Parker Hannifin Corp.: Consolidated Statements of Cash Flows

Consolidated Statement of Cash Flows

(Dollars in thousands) For the years ended June 30,	1991	1990	1989
Cash Flows From Operating Activities			
Income from continuing operations	$ 59,168	$110,447	$ 98,347
Cumulative effect of changes in accounting principles			21,698
Adjustments to reconcile net income to net cash provided by operating activities:			
Depreciation	98,919	92,286	86,829
Amortization	5,085	5,258	5,598
Deferred income taxes	4,200	12,787	13,711
Foreign currency transaction loss	4,252	6,870	4,706
Loss (gain) on sale of plant and equipment	2,970	1,902	(258)
Provision for restructuring (excluding cash payments of $11,194 in 1991)	3,156		5,535
Changes in assets and liabilities, net of effects from acquisitions and discontinued operations:			
Accounts receivable	27,093	(52,620)	(42,857)
Inventories	72,211	(42,061)	(142,769)
Prepaid expenses	521	(1,986)	6,693
Other assets	3,956	(1,402)	677
Accounts payable, trade	(14,159)	(900)	8,580
Accrued payrolls and other compensation	(2,853)	7,159	4,962
Accrued domestic and foreign taxes	(2,599)	14,446	870
Other accrued liabilities	(380)	(19,441)	28,066
Other liabilities	9,167	(4,388)	28,819
Other discontinued operations		(524)	3,054
Net cash provided by operating activities	270,707	127,833	132,261
Cash Flows From Investing Activities			
Acquisitions (excluding cash of $163 in 1991 and $904 in 1990)	(2,036)	(21,000)	(4,297)
Capital expenditures	(112,047)	(125,680)	(149,414)
Proceeds from sale of plant and equipment	2,916	12,351	8,224
Proceeds from sale of discontinued operations		80,498	
Other	(2,958)	(13,279)	(1,651)
Net cash (used in) investing activities	(114,125)	(67,110)	(147,138)
Cash Flows From Financing Activities			
Exercise of stock options	1,925	1,668	1,937
(Payments of) proceeds from notes payable, net	(50,420)	5,796	60,373
Proceeds from long-term borrowings	119,364	64,371	30,149
Payments of long-term borrowings	(143,005)	(93,403)	(25,329)
Extraordinary loss on early retirement of debt		(6,065)	
Dividends paid, net of tax benefit of ESOP shares in 1991 and 1990	(43,415)	(41,995)	(40,967)
Purchase of treasury shares	(22,985)		
Net cash (used in) provided by financing activities	(138,536)	(69,628)	26,163
Effect of exchange rate changes on cash	(983)	1,830	(2,158)
Net increase (decrease) in cash and cash equivalents	17,063	(7,075)	9,128
Cash and cash equivalents at beginning of year	21,780	28,855	19,727
Cash and cash equivalents at end of year	$ 38,843	$ 21,780	$ 28,855

SOURCE: Parker Hannifin Corp., *Annual Report*, 1991.

Bass PLC: Consolidated Statements of Cash Flows

BASS PLC AND SUBSIDIARY COMPANIES

CONSOLIDATED STATEMENT OF CASH FLOWS

	Year ended September 30		
	1991	**1990**	**1989**
		(£ million)	
Net cash inflow from operating activities — (Note 25(i))	676	782	648
Returns on investments and servicing of finance			
Interest paid	(151)	(182)	(78)
Dividends paid to shareholders...................................	(115)	(101)	(80)
Interest received...	44	44	17
Dividends paid to minority shareholders	(3)	(2)	(2)
Net cash outflow from returns on investments and servicing of finance	(225)	(241)	(143)
Taxation			
UK corporation tax paid	(144)	(231)	(132)
Overseas tax paid (net)	(1)	—	—
Tax paid	(145)	(231)	(132)
Investing activities			
Purchase of subsidiaries (net of cash and cash equivalents purchased) ..	(139)	(65)	(188)
Purchase of tangible fixed assets	(334)	(366)	(397)
Trade loans made and purchase of other investments	(63)	(119)	(133)
Purchase of short-term investments..............................	(143)	—	—
Sale of short-term investments...................................	40	—	—
Trade loans repaid and sale of other investments....................	130	66	145
Sale of tangible fixed assets	193	465	87
Sale of subsidiaries (net of cash and cash equivalents sold)	45	12	10
Net cash outflow from investing activities	(271)	(7)	(476)
Net cash inflow/(outflow) before financing	35	303	(103)
Financing			
Issue of Ordinary Share capital	596	16	17
Rights issue costs..	(12)	—	—
Debenture issue costs	—	—	(2)
New borrowings during year(i)	1,277	924	687
Borrowings repaid during year	(1,183)	(1,662)	(390)
Net cash inflow/(outflow) from financing	678	(722)	312
Increase/(decrease) in cash and cash equivalents — (Note 25(ii))	713	(419)	209

(i) The net movement of commercial paper issued and repaid is included in new borrowings.

SOURCE: Bass PLC, *Annual Report*, 1991.

CHAPTER 4

Cash Flows from Investing, Financing, and Operating Activities

In the previous chapter, we described the preparation of the statement of cash flows, but did not define exactly the major components of the statement, that is, cash flows from investing, financing, and operating activities. In this chapter, we provide detailed explanations of the components of cash flows, as well as real-life examples from published financial statements. We show common examples of these components, but also some peculiar examples that we encountered when reviewing many sets of financial statements. Finally, we discuss how the cash flow analyst should interpret the cash flows from investing, financing, and operating activities.

4.1 CASH FLOWS FROM INVESTING ACTIVITIES

The FASB defines cash flows from investing activities as follows:

> Investing activities include making and collecting loans and acquiring and disposing of debt or equity instruments and property, plant, and equipment and other productive assets, that is, assets held for or used in the production of goods or services by the enterprise (other than materials that are part of the enterprise's inventory). (FASB, 1987, para. 15)

Thus, the definition of investing cash flows includes cash outflows used as investments in financial or fixed assets, but also cash receipts from disposition of such investments. Furthermore, investing cash flows are for investments in financial instruments as well as investments in real assets (PPE). The FASB further describes cash inflows and outflows from investing activities as:

Inflows

a. Receipts from collections or sales of loans made by the enterprise and of other entity's debt instruments (other than cash equivalents) that were purchased by the enterprise.

b. Receipts from sales of equity instruments of other enterprises and from returns of investment in those instruments.

c. Receipts from sales of property, plant, and equipment and other productive assets. (FASB, 1987, para. 16)

Outflows

a. Disbursements for loans made by the enterprise and payments to acquire debt instruments of other entities (other than cash equivalents).

b. Payments to acquire equity instruments of other enterprises.

c. Payments at the time of purchase or soon before or after purchase to acquire property, plant, and equipment and other productive assets. (FASB, 1987, para. 17)

It is more natural to first discuss the cash outflows for investing activities. The statement requires the classification of investments in PPE and other productive assets as investing activities. It further restricts the inclusion of these investments on the statement of cash flows to those amounts that were paid at the time of purchase, soon before, or soon after the time of purchase. Thus, an advance payment for PPE, or a down payment, will be included. However, a loan provided by the seller of the PPE will not be included as a cash flow from investing activity, because the buyer had not paid for the asset in cash.

The FASB includes in investing cash flows those investments in equity instruments of *other* enterprises (repurchases of the firm's own securities are classified as financing events), or investments in debt instruments of other enterprises, or loans made to other enterprises. The FASB notes that investments in debt instruments of other entities should be "other than cash equivalents." This is an important distinction because the statement of cash flows can be prepared using "cash and cash equivalents." Cash equivalents are short-term, highly liquid investments that are both:

a. readily convertible to known amounts of cash

b. so near their maturity that they present insignificant risk of changes in value because of changes in interest rates. (FASB, 1987, para. 8)

The FASB states that, generally, only investments with original maturities of three months or less qualify under the definition of a cash equivalent. Thus, when a treasurer purchases a Treasury note that has 60 days to maturity by using cash, cash and cash equivalents are unchanged.[1] However, if the treasurer purchased a 120-day Treasury note, an investing cash flow is recorded on the statement of cash flows with an offsetting decrease in cash and cash equivalents. Clearly, these rules leave management some room for manipulation close to the end of the accounting period. It should be noted that the FASB ruled that if a seven-year note, for example, is *purchased* less than 90 days before maturity, it can be classified as a cash equivalent. However, if it had been purchased more than 90 days before maturity, it does *not* get reclassified as cash equivalent when the balance sheet date falls within 90 days before its maturity.

Example:

Amax Inc. explores for, mines, refines, and sells aluminum, coal, gold, and molybdenum. The company also explores for and produces oil and natural gas, tungsten, magnesium, specialty metals, and zinc.

---

[1]The decrease in cash is exactly offset by the increase in cash equivalents (the Treasury note) because the maturity of the note is less than 90 days.

Amax Inc. states in its 1989 annual report that "cash and equivalent includes all unrestricted cash and liquid debt instruments purchased with a maturity of three months or less."

Example:

Petrie Stores operates a chain of approximately 1,600 (as of January 1990) women's specialty stores in 48 states. Stores specialize in the retail sale of a full selection of women's apparel at moderate prices to teen, junior, and contemporary miss customers.

Petrie Stores Co. shows on the balance sheet and the statement of cash flows "cash and short term investments." It states that "short term investments consist of commercial paper, repurchase agreements and other income producing securities of less than sixty days maturity. These investments are carried at cost plus accrued interest and dividends."

It seems reasonable that cash and cash equivalents will include only those items that could be readily converted to cash and also immediately used by the business entity. In some cases, a portion of the available cash is restricted by compensating balance agreements or by other agreements. It seems that restricted cash should not be included in "cash and cash equivalents" for purposes of the statement of cash flows. However, in some cases, firms deviate from this line of reasoning.

Example:

Foundation Health administers the delivery of managed health-care services through its HMO and government contracting subsidiaries.

In a footnote to the financial statements of Foundation Health Co. that were provided as part of its prospectus, it was stated that "cash equivalents include investments with maturities of three months or less. Included in cash and cash equivalents at June 30, 1989 was $4,000,000 on deposit at The Bank of New York as a compensating balance in connection with the Company's term loan agreement. During the nine month period ended March 31, 1990, the compensating balance restriction on these funds was removed." It should be noted that cash and cash equivalents on June 30, 1989, were shown on the balance sheet at about $34 million. Thus, the $4 million of compensating balances were a significant portion of that amount.

These examples show that we should examine what the firm classifies as cash and cash equivalents. Also, the firm may affect its investing activities by purchases of short-term investments with maturities of less than 90 days. Such investments may be shown as cash equivalents and may be omitted from investing activities.

It should be noted that cash flows from investing activities include both cash outflows and cash inflows. The inflows occur when a firm disposes of its investments in financial instruments or fixed assets.[2] The cash proceeds from such sales are included among the cash flows from investing activities and represent disinvesting activities by the firm. Can a firm net cash inflows against cash outflows? For example, can a firm net the proceeds from sales of PPE against additions to PPE? Usually, accountants are against offsetting any type of inflows with outflows, assets against

---

[2]Capital payments on debt instruments in which the firm invested are also considered cash inflows from investing activities; these are, in effect, disinvesting activities. However, interest payments on such debt are classified as operating cash inflows.

liabilities, or revenues against expenses. However, if the amount of the proceeds is immaterial, the firm may report the "net purchases of PPE."

Let us now examine several examples of investing activities.

Example:

ITT manufactures automotive products, electronic components, defense technology, and wood products. ITT also offers insurance and financial services, operates hotels, and has an interest in a telecommunications company.

ITT reports on its 1989 statement of cash flows the following investing activities:

Additions to plant, property, and equipment	(604)
Proceeds from divestments	206
Purchase of insurance and finance investments	(14,075)
Sale and maturity of insurance and finance investments	11,782
Finance receivables originated or purchased	(14,437)
Finance receivables repaid or sold	13,061
Change in temporary investments	305
Other	(77)

The first two items are self-explanatory: additional investments in PPE and sales of fixed assets or investments in other firms. The next two items represent an important facet of ITT's operations: additional purchases of investments in its insurance and finance divisions. Normally, an insurance company will invest the premiums paid on its policies and will use the proceeds from these investments to pay out claims. The two items represent purchases of such investments as well as sales (or maturity) of these investments. The next two items relate to financing ITT's own customers or financing other firms' customers. This is, in essence, a loan made to other entities or to other entities' customers. Thus, these loans constitute investing events. Finally, the change in temporary investments reflects either an increase in the market value of these investments or a liquidation of some temporary investments.

Example:

Sunshine Mining is a holding company, whose subsidiaries produce silver, gold, crude oil, and natural gas. Sunshine's principal subsidiaries are Sunshine Precious Metals Inc. and Sunshine Oil & Gas Inc.

Sunshine Mining Co. discloses the following cash flows from investing activities in its 1989 financial statements:

Additions to property, plant, and equipment	(17,308)
Proceeds from the disposal of property, plant, and equipment	3,460
Purchases of futures, forward, and option contracts	(19,221)
Sales of futures, forward, and option contracts	19,534
Investment in PT corporation	3,290
Other, principally investments	(8,188)

There are two interesting items in this section of the statement of cash flows. First, the purchases and sales of futures, forward, and option contracts are investments in financial instruments by Sunshine Mining Co. The firm states in its annual report that it "periodically enters into forward and option contracts to hedge its exposure to price fluctuations on oil and precious metals transactions." The firm mostly hedges its silver operations and its future oil production, although it is active in the forward market as an investor too. Note that these hedge transactions represent investments in financial instruments, and although they may actually hedge current or future inventories, they are accounted as investing activities. These contracts cover about 18 percent of current, or 5 percent of total, assets of Sunshine Mining Co. as of the balance sheet date.

The second interesting item is the investment in PT Corporation, which is shown as an increase in cash flows from investing activities of about $3.3 million. Thus, it may represent the cash proceeds from sale of this investment, or an increase in the value of this investment. To clarify which of these explanations is correct, we need to consult the footnotes to the annual report. The annual report shows that PT had unrealized losses on its own investments, which were large enough to wipe out stockholders' equity. Thus, the investment in PT on the books of Sunshine Mining was put at a value of zero on 12/31/89. However, PT had transferred dividends and other cash distributions to Sunshine of about $4.9 million, and income that was included from PT for the year on Sunshine's books amounted to $1.7 million, or net proceeds of about $3.2 million. It seems odd, though, that not all of the $4.9 million were shown as cash flows from *investing* activities, that is, Sunshine had not subtracted the $1.7 million of income from net income when it derived cash flows from operations. Thus, cash flows from operating activities are overstated by $1.7 million (Sunshine reported net operating cash flow of about $0.2 million for 1989).

Example:

When a firm acquires or disposes of entire businesses, one has to be careful in interpreting the relevant items on the statement of cash flows, because the amounts that are shown on the statement represent only the portion of the transaction that involved cash payments or receipts. The entire transaction may have been for a much larger amount.

Halliburton is one of the world's largest diversified oil field service engineering and construction companies. It also provides insurance services.

Halliburton reports in its 1989 financial statements:

Payments for the acquisitions of businesses, net of cash acquired	(42.4)
Receipts from dispositions of businesses, net of cash disposed	88.2

The supplemental schedule provides the following additional information:

Liabilities assumed in acquisitions of businesses	51.2
Liabilities disposed of in dispositions of businesses	663.9

During 1989, Halliburton effected two acquisitions and two dispositions. For stockholder reporting purposes, Halliburton recorded a $3.6 million pretax gain. The cash effect was dramatically different due to cash received as payment on the transactions. However, the balance sheet effect was not as large as the amount shown in the table. For instance, the $72 million cash receipt for The Life Insurance Company of the Southwest excludes the $40 million in cash the company had on its balance sheet.

Halliburton, 1989
Cash Effect Due to Business Transactions

Name of Co.	Type of Transaction	Cash Effect*	Income Effect
Sierra Geophysics	Acquisition	$ 0	—
C.F. Braun	Acquisition	($39 mil.)	—
Life Insurance Co. of the Southwest	Disposal	$72.0 mil.	$5.5 mil.
Zapata Gulf Marine	Disposal	$31.5 mil.	($1.9 mil.)
Total		$64.5 mil.	$3.6 mil.

*Cash effect is cash outlay or receipt of cash only.

Thus, it seems that the acquisitions of businesses were for $42.4 million cash plus assumed obligations of the acquired firms of $51.2 million, or a total consideration of $93.6 million. Similarly, the cash proceeds from the dispositions of businesses amounted to $88.2 million, plus liabilities that were assumed by the buyers of 663.9, or a total consideration of $752.1 million. In footnotes 8 and 13 to the financial statements, the firm discloses that cash used for one acquisition from internal sources was approximately $39 million, and the total goodwill in the acquisitions amounted to approximately $33.5 million. Thus, the net assets of the two acquired firms were approximately $60.1 million (93.6 − 33.5). The firm also reports total cash receipts for the two firms disposed during 1989 of approximately $103.5 million (31.5 + 72). Thus, cash on hand in the two disposed subsidiaries was about $15.3 million (103.5 − 88.2).

Example:

M.A. Hanna Co. is a leading international specialty-chemicals producer with interests in natural resources business.

M.A. Hanna Co. provided the following data about its acquisitions in its 1989 statement of cash flows:

Acquisitions of companies:	
Property, plant, and equipment and other assets	(20,933)
Long-term liabilities, excluding debt	165
Goodwill and other intangibles	(45,589)
Working capital	(21,129)

In its annual report, the firm discloses the cost of acquisitions during 1989 at $82.3 million, which is slightly lower than the net amount shown in the statement of cash flows. However, the section of financing cash flows shows "debt of companies acquired" of $9.5 million, leading to a net cash flow on the acquisition of about $77.9 million (20.9 − .2 + 45.6 + 21.1 − 9.5). Thus, it is likely that the cash in the firms acquired amounted to about $4.4 million (82.3 − 77.9).

Example:

Figgie International is a diversified firm with six operating groups serving consumer, technical, industrial, and service markets worldwide.

In its 1989 statement of cash flows, Figgie International reports a cash inflow of $12.1 million as the "changes in net assets of discontinued operation." Normally, when a firm intends to discontinue some of its operations, it will segregate the assets and liabilities that are attributed to these operations and will show them as "net assets of discontinued operations" or "net assets of businesses held for sale." When these assets are sold, the firm realizes a cash flow and simultaneously reduces the net assets of businesses held for sale.

Example:

The Travelers Corporation, an insurance firm, shows in 1989 the following items on its statement of cash flows:

Investment repayments	
Fixed maturities	2,022
Mortgage loans	1,309
Carrying value of investments sold	
Fixed maturities	5,153
Equity securities	732
Mortgage loans	—
Investment real estate	328
Investments in	
Fixed maturities	(9,153)
Equity securities	(1,013)
Mortgage loans	(1,308)
Investment real estate	(109)
Policy loans, net	(110)
Short-term securities purchased, net	(340)
Other investments	(179)
Securities transactions in course of settlement	(360)
Proceeds from disposition of subsidiaries and operations	124
Other	(75)

As an insurance firm, the Travelers makes investments in financial assets, out of which it pays claims later on. The financial assets include securities with fixed maturities, mortgage loans, equity securities, and investments in real estate. The items on the portion of the cash flow statement that relate to investing activities usually describe these financial investments or collections of principal on these investments. However, one of the items in the above list is "securities transactions in course of settlement," which represents additional investments in securities where cash was used to purchase certain financial instruments, but where the financial instruments were not yet the property of the firm on the balance sheet date. It also represents financial instruments that were loaned to other business entities and were not available for use by the Travelers as of the balance sheet date. Thus, it properly represents a cash flow from investing activity, and not cash flows from operating activity.

Example:

In some cases, investing activities represent payments for investments in intangible assets of firms.

Measurex Co. manufactures and services computer-integrated manufacturing systems that control continuous-batch manufacturing processes serving such industries as paper, plastics, and metals.

Measurex Co. shows as part of its investing activities "capitalized software" of about $3 million for 1989. The firm had cash expenditures of about $3 million on developing software, after the technical feasibility of the software products had been established (costs prior to this point cannot be capitalized). These expenditures are capitalized as an asset and are subsequently amortized over three years.

Similarly, Bic Corp., North America's leading ball-point pen producer (which also produces disposable butane lighters, disposable pencils, disposable razors, sailboards, and car racks), shows in its 1989 statement of cash flows a cash purchase of "trademarks and patents" for about $440,000. These are intangible assets, although they will probably help the firm generate greater cash flows in the future.

4.2 CASH FLOWS FROM FINANCING ACTIVITIES

The FASB broadly defines financing activities as follows:

Financing activities include obtaining resources from owners and providing them with a return on, and a return of, their investment; borrowing money and repaying amounts borrowed, or otherwise settling the obligation; and obtaining and paying for other resources obtained from creditors on long-term credit. (FASB, 1987, para. 18)

It further clarifies the nature of cash inflows or cash outflows from financing activities in the following manner:

Cash inflows from financing activities are:

a. proceeds from issuing equity instruments

b. proceeds from issuing bonds, mortgages, notes, and from other short- or long-term borrowing.

Cash outflows for financing activities are:

a. payments of dividends or other distributions to owners, including outlays to reacquire the enterprise's equity instruments

b. repayments of amounts borrowed

c. other principal payments to creditors who have extended long-term credit. (FASB, 1987, para. 19–20)

The logic underlying the definition of financing activities seems clear; all the events that represent increases of internal or external capital are financing cash flows, whereas those events that represent decreases of internal or external capital are disfinancing cash flows. Loosely speaking, internal capital is capital invested by shareholders in the firm, whereas external capital represents investment of creditors in the firm.

One important asymmetry in the treatment of internal and external capital under FAS No. 95 should be highlighted at this point: dividends paid to shareholders are classified as financing cash outflows, because they represent disfinancing events. However, payments of interest on a loan do not represent cash outflows from financing activities; instead, as we shall see in the next subsection, they represent an operating cash outflow. This is an asymmetric treatment, because both represent a return on capital to providers, and there should not be any distinction between a return to creditors and return to shareholders. The inclusion of interest payments among operating cash flows will bias the concept of cash flows generated from ongoing operations and the concept of free cash flows, as it is generally defined.

Let us now provide examples of financing cash flows from financial statements of firms.

Example:

Dominion Resources Inc. is a Virginia-based utility holding company. It derives its power from coal and nuclear sources.

Dominion Resources Inc. reports the following cash flows from financing activities on its 1989 statement of cash flows:

Issuance of common stock	108.8
Issuance of preferred stock	75.0
Issuance of long-term debt:	
Nonrecourse—nonregulated	134.7
Other	612.6
Issuance of short-term debt	205.5
Repayment of long-term debt and preferred stock	(545.1)
Principal payments of capital lease obligations	(5.6)
Common dividend payments	(320.5)
Other	(2.5)

The first four items represent issuance of additional stock (internal capital) and debt (external capital). The fifth item represents payments on long-term debt and preferred stock. Note that one cannot offset the new issuance of long-term debt and preferred stock against payments to retire older debt or preferred stock. Payments of dividends are included as an outflow (or a disfinancing event). The only item that is not immediately apparent is the payments on the principal of capital lease obligations. To explain it, recall that under FAS No. 13, assets under capital leases are included on the balance sheet as assets and liabilities. The asset/liability is the present value of future payments on the lease. Future payments under the lease agreement consist of interest payments on the loan, which is implicit in the lease, and also of a reduction in the principal obligation (or loan). The interest payment is included under operating cash flows, whereas the reduction of the principal is included among the financing cash flows, as a disfinancing event.

Example:

General Instrument Corp. is a diversified manufacturer of electronic components and systems, which was acquired via a leveraged buyout.

General Instrument Corp. reports the following items as financing cash flows on its 1989 statement of cash flows:

Proceeds from long-term debt	7,800
Stock repurchase	(242,181)
Debt repayments	(10,000)
Proceeds from stock options and employee stock plans including related tax benefits	12,701
Cash dividends	(14,629)

Note the large cash outflow on repurchasing the common stock. This is a disfinancing event; the equity of the firm is reduced because of the repurchase. Also note the proceeds to the firm from the exercising of stock options; the firm received additional cash from employees for stock that were issued to them (and in addition some tax savings for these items).

Example:

Standard Motors Products Inc. is a manufacturer of replacement parts for the electrical, fuel, brake, and temperature control systems of motor vehicles. Parts are used by cars, trucks, and marine and industrial engines.

Standard Motor Products Inc. includes the following items in its 1989 statement of cash flows among the financing activities:

Net borrowings under line-of-credit agreements	13,600
Proceeds from issuance of long-term debt	49,229
Principal payments of long-term debt	(4,436)
Reduction of loan to ESOP	1,676
Proceeds from exercise of employee stock options	567
Tax benefits applicable to ESOP	82
Loan to ESOP	(16,779)
Dividends paid	(4,191)

Among the items that should be noted are those related to the Employee Stock Ownership Plan (ESOP). Under the plan, employees are induced to purchase stock in the firm, because there are tax benefits to all parties. The firm may lend money to the plan, so that the plan can purchase additional shares. In this case, the firm loaned about $16.8 million to the plan in 1989. Notice that it is shown as a financing cash outflow, and not as an investing cash outflow. The reason is that funds loaned to the ESOP are used to purchase shares in the firm. Thus, the economic substance of the transaction is similar to the repurchase of common stock, which is shown as a disfinancing cash flow.

Example:

Southwest Airlines Co. is a scheduled air carrier operating in Texas and several southwestern and midwestern states.

Southwest Airlines Co. includes the following item as a financing cash inflow in its 1989 statement of cash flows:

Proceeds from sale and leaseback transactions	91,180

This transaction involves the purchase of a plane (or other equipment) by Southwest, sale of the asset to another party, receipt of cash for the asset, and then leasing the asset back from the buyer. The benefit to the buyer (lessor) is mostly through the utilization of tax advantages of owning the asset, which Southwest cannot utilize itself. The economic substance of the transaction, then, is very similar to a loan, in which an asset is placed as collateral, but is continued to be used by the borrower. Thus, Southwest chose to show the sale and leaseback as a financing event, acknowledging the transaction not as a sale (because then it would have been classified as a disinvesting event), but as a loan.

Example:

Amax Inc. explores for, mines, refines, and sells aluminum, coal, gold, and molybdenum. The company also explores for and produces oil and natural gas, tungsten, magnesium, specialty metals, and zinc.

Amax Inc. includes the following items as financing cash flows on its 1989 statement of cash flows:

Repayments of long-term debt	(124,900)
Share repurchase payment	(60,600)
Repayments of sales of future production	(52,100)
Dividends paid on common and preferred stock	(51,900)
Decrease in unearned revenue	(25,900)
Decrease in capital lease obligation	(4,800)
Issuance of common shares	48,800
Issuance of long-term debt	44,000
Increase in short-term borrowings	1,000

Among the items that are uncommon are the repayments of sales of future production and the decrease in unearned revenue. The firm shows a balance sheet liability entitled "proceeds from sales of future production," which represents a loan to the firm that is guaranteed by future sale of coal. During 1989, the loan had been reduced by approximately $52.1 million, and is shown as a disfinancing event on the statement of cash flows. Similarly, unearned revenue represents loan facilities that are satisfied by future delivery of gold and silver. Upon such delivery, the firm records sales, cost of goods sold, and a reduction of the liability "unearned revenue." During 1989, the firm paid about $26 million of loan facilities, mostly by the delivery of gold.

Example:

Bethlehem Steel Corp. is the second largest domestic steel producer, although it has fabricating and other operations as well. Its products are used largely in heavy construction and capital goods markets.

Bethlehem Steel Corp. includes two interesting items among its financing activities for 1988:

Pension financing (funding)	(514.3)
Discontinued assets and facilities payments	(63.2)

The first item represents payments to the pension fund to reduce the pension obligation of the firm. Can this be shown as a financing cash flow? Normally, payments made to the pension fund are included as an operating cash flow, like all other payments made to employees. In this case, a substantial portion of the firm's obligation for postretirement benefits are to former employees in its discontinued facilities. The firm may have decided to show the funding of this obligation as a repayment of a loan, because the obligation was accrued on the balance sheet before, as part of the expected future costs of the discontinued operations.

The second item seems to represent payments that are made on discontinued assets, probably to cover retirement benefits to employees in discontinued facilities. The firm uses proceeds from sales of assets to reduce these payments. It probably shows the proceeds from the sale of assets as an investing cash flow.

Example:

Ethyl Corp. is a producer of specialty industrial and petroleum chemicals, also has interests in insurance. It is the largest domestic supplier of lead antiknock additives.

The 1989 statement of cash flows for Ethyl Corp. includes a financing cash inflow of $100 million, which is represented as dividend received from Tredegar Industries. Normally, the receipt of dividends is included as an operating cash inflow, and not as a financing cash flow. However, in the case of Ethyl, the firm combined some of its aluminum, plastics, and energy businesses into Tredegar. The shares of the new firm were distributed to shareholders of Ethyl, except for $100 million, which were transferred as a dividend from Tredegar to Ethyl. Ethyl used this dividend, together with other cash, to pay off about $152.5 million of maturing notes. Thus, Ethyl classified this special dividend as a financing activity, because it deemed this special dividend to be related to the retirement of debt. This interpretation seems to be at odds with FAS No. 95, which would probably require the dividend to be shown as a cash inflow from operating activities, or as a disinvesting activity.

Example:

MNC Financial Co. is a holding company that owns Maryland National Bank (the largest bank in that state), American Security Bank in Washington, D.C., Virginia Federal S&L, and MBNA America, which conducts extensive credit card operations. The company is also engaged in providing services for smaller corporations, real-estate lending, and retail banking.

MNC Financial reports the following financing activities for the three months ending on 3/31/1990:

Net decrease in noninterest-bearing demand deposits, interest-bearing transactions, and savings accounts	(74,369)
Net decrease in short-term borrowings	(1,180,536)
Net increase in certificates of deposit	1,234,702
Proceeds from issuance of long-term borrowings	2,705
Maturities of long-term borrowings	(12,087)
Proceeds from the issuance of common stock	3,042
Dividends paid	(26,479)
Decrease in other financing activities	(275)

The first item represents a decline in deposits, which are, in effect, loans made to MNC Financial. It should also be noted that MNC had an inflow of cash through issuance of certificates of deposit, which helped the firm bridge the payback in short-term borrowings.

4.3 CASH FLOWS FROM OPERATING ACTIVITIES

The FASB defined cash flows from operating activities as ''all transactions and other events that are not defined as investing or financing activities.'' It broadly explained that ''operating activities generally involve producing and delivering goods and providing services. Cash flows from operating activities are generally the cash effects of transactions and other events that enter into the determination of net income.'' (FASB, 1987, para. 21)

The FASB provided a list of specific cash flows from operations:

a. Cash receipts from sales of goods or services, including receipts from collection or sale of accounts and both short- and long-term notes receivable from customers arising from those sales

b. Cash receipts from returns *on* loans, other debt instruments of other entities, and equity securities interest and dividends

c. All other cash receipts that do not stem from transactions defined as investing or financing activities, such as amounts received to settle lawsuits; proceeds of insurance settlements except for those that are directly related to investing or financing activities, such as from destruction of a building; and refunds from suppliers. (FASB, 1987, para. 22)

It further described cash outflows for operating activities as:

a. Cash payments to acquire materials for manufacture or goods for resale, including principal payments on accounts and both short- and long-term notes payable to suppliers for those materials or goods

b. Cash payments to other suppliers and employees for other goods or services

c. Cash payments to governments for taxes, duties, fines, and other fees or penalties

d. Cash payments to lenders and other creditors for interest

e. All other cash payments that do not stem from transactions defined as investing or financing activities, such as payments to settle lawsuits, cash contributions to charities, and cash refunds to customers. (FASB, 1987, para. 23)

As seen from the above, the FASB treated cash flows from operations as the "residual" cash flow; it comprises all events that are *not* classified as investing or financing activities. This means that, for many firms, the cash flow from operating activities is likely to contain special items that are not easily assignable to investing or financing cash flows. Furthermore, it is likely to contain activities that will not recur in the future, such as settlements of law suits. Thus, the analyst should ideally separate those nonrecurring and special items from other operating cash flows. However, this is not easily done in practice, because most firms follow the indirect approach to disclose the cash flows from operating activities.

Indeed, the FASB states:

In reporting cash flows from operating activities, enterprises are encouraged to report major classes of gross cash payments and their arithmetic sum—the net cash flow from operating activities (the direct method). Enterprises that do so should, at minimum, separately report the following classes of operating cash receipts and payments:

a. Cash collected from customers, including lessees, licensees, and the like

b. Interest and dividends received

c. Other operating cash receipts, if any

d. Cash paid to employees and other suppliers of goods or services, including suppliers of insurance, advertising, and the like

e. Interest paid

f. Income taxes paid

g. Other operating cash payments, if any.

Enterprises are encouraged to provide further breakdowns of operating cash receipts and payments that they consider meaningful and feasible. For example, a retailer or manufacturer might decide to further divide cash paid to employees and suppliers (category [d] above) into payments for costs of inventory and payments for selling, general, and administrative expenses. (FASB, 1987, para. 27)

Let us examine several disclosures of operating cash flows using the direct method.

Example:

Great Northern Iron Ore Properties owns mineral and nonmineral lands in the Mesabi Range in Minnesota. It derives income from taconite production and from royalties.

Great Northern Iron Ore Properties reports the following cash flows from operating activities on its 1989 financial statements:

Cash received from royalties and rents	$11,381,352
Cash paid to suppliers and employees	(1,200,626)
Interest received	833,811
Income taxes paid	—

Example:

Commerce Clearing House Inc. publishes current information, primarily in the fields of tax and business law.

Detailed information about operating cash flows can be found in Commerce Clearing House Inc.'s 1989 financial statements:

Receipts from customers	$ 674,356
Interest income	12,821
Miscellaneous	2,861
Payments to suppliers	(308,039)
Payments to employees	(266,482)
Payments for pensions and profit sharing plans	(12,610)
Income taxes paid	(36,795)
Interest paid on long-term obligations	(3,217)

In this financial report there is substantially more disclosure; payments to suppliers and employees are separated into two items, and payments for fringe benefits such as pensions and profit sharing plans are segregated from direct payments to employees. Note also that CCH is a net creditor, as is evidenced by interest income (interest received in cash) exceeding interest payments.

Example:

Manitowoc Company Inc. designs, manufactures, and markets commercial ice cube machines, shipbuilding equipment, cranes, and excavators.

Manitowoc Co. reports the following cash flows from operating activities in its 1989 financial statements:

Cash received from customers	$ 186,283,043
Cash paid to suppliers and employees	(189,686,352)
Interest and dividends received	4,120,622
Income taxes paid	(1,527,514)
Restructuring costs paid	(4,679,097)
Miscellaneous cash receipts	211,343
Net cash used in operating activities	$ (5,277,955)

As can be seen in the disclosure, Manitowoc had more cash payments than cash receipts in its operations. Normally, this is not a favorable signal, because a business entity is expected to generate cash inflows from its operations. However, in this case, note that restructuring costs amounted to about $4.7 million, most of the $5.3 million of net cash outflows on operating activities. It is hoped that these restructuring costs are nonrecurring, or else management changes may be indicated. Thus, an analyst who wishes to predict future cash flows should not concentrate on net cash flows from operating activities, but on those cash flows that are expected to recur in the future.

Example:

Lubrizol Corp. engages primarily in the development, manufacturing, and marketing of automotive chemical additives, fuel additives, lubricants, and specialty oils.

Lubrizol reports the following cash flows from operating activities in its 1988 financial statements:

Received from customers	$1,109,333
Paid to suppliers and employees	(957,945)
Received from patent litigation settlement	80,000
Income taxes paid	(44,566)
Received from the sale of investments	16,529
Interest and dividends received	11,640
Interest paid	(5,447)
Other, net	2,238
Cash provided from operating activities	$ 211,782

Note that here net operating cash flow is positive (inflow), and amounts to about $212 million. However, a careful examination of the individual items reveals that almost one-half of the net operating cash inflow comes from a patent litigation settlement ($80 million), a cash inflow that is usually nonrecurring. Furthermore, the firm reports about $17 million that were received from sales of investments. This item is classified as an operating cash flow, although proceeds from disposal of investments should be classified as a cash inflow from investing activity.

Example:

Comdisco Inc. is the largest independent lessor and marketer of computer and high-technology equipment. It leases, places, and remarkets IBM computer equipment, as well as other high-tech equipment. It also operates data centers and telecommunication sites and offers alternative data processing and telecommunication centers of customers in cases of power outages or other disasters (such as the 1988 earthquake in San Francisco).

In 1989, Comdisco disclosed the following information about its major types of cash receipts in its financial statements:

Leasing receipts, primarily rentals	$ 607
Leasing costs, primarily rentals paid	(113)
Sales	339
Sales costs	(244)
Disaster recovery receipts	85
Disaster recovery operating costs	(40)
Other revenue	36
Selling, general, and administrative expenses	(189)
Interest	(100)
Income taxes	(1)

The firm reports the cash receipts (and cash outlays) from three major sources—leasing of equipment, sales of equipment, and the disaster recovery services. It also provides information about other components of cash flows.

The FASB allowed firms to disclose information about operating cash flows using the indirect method. In particular, it stated:

> Enterprises that choose not to provide information about major classes of operating cash receipts and payments by the direct method as encouraged in paragraph 27 shall determine and report the same amount for net cash flow from operating activities indirectly by adjusting net income to reconcile it to net cash flow from operating activities (the indirect or reconciliation method). That requires adjusting net income to remove (a) the effects of all deferrals of past operating cash receipts and payments, such as changes during the period in inventory, deferred income, and the like, and all accruals of expected future operating cash receipts and payments, such as depreciation, amortization of goodwill, and gains and losses on sales of property, plant, and equipment and discontinued operations (which relate to investing activities), and gains or losses on extinguishment of debt (which is a financing activity). (FASB, 1987, para. 28)

Let us examine several examples of disclosure according to the indirect method.

Example:

General Instrument Corp. reports the following information on its statement of cash flows for 1990:

Income from continuing operations	$ 88,402
Adjustments to reconcile income to net cash provided by operating activities:	
Depreciation and amortization	91,336
Deferred income taxes	7,112
Long-term liabilities	17,050
Receivables and inventories	3,146
Accounts payable, accrued liabilities, and income taxes	(41,731)
Other	1,893
Cash provided by operations	$167,208

This statement of cash flows begins with net income. It adds to net income depreciation and amortization which is a noncash expense that was subtracted to derive net income. It also adds back deferred income taxes, because a portion of the tax expense was deferred to the future and was not paid during the period. Normally, we do not find long-term liabilities added back to net income in deriving net cash flows from operating activities. The increase in long-term debt is usually classified as a financing event. However, if the increase in long-term liabilities is due to operating activities, such as for pension expenses that were not paid in cash, a liability is recorded on the balance sheet. It also adds back the change in receivables and inventories, because the increase in receivables implies that not all sales were collected during the period. It also adds back the change in inventory, because the increase in inventory implies that the firm not only incurred expenditures for the goods that were sold, but also for goods that were purchased (or manufactured) for inventory. It subtracts the net increase in accounts payable, accrued liabilities, and income taxes, because these items represent future cash outflows whose offsetting effects were included in expenses (such as tax expense or labor expenses).

Example:

Standard Motor Products Inc. manufactures replacement parts for automotive systems, such as ignition, brakes, and temperature control.

Standard Motor Products discloses cash flows from operating activities for 1989 as shown on the next page.

Note that the gain on sale of marketable securities is *subtracted* from net income, because the gain plus the book value of the marketable securities represent the proceeds received from the sale of these investments. However, the proceeds from the sale of investments should be included in investing cash flows, and because the gain was added in deriving net income, it should be subtracted here.

Note that there are three adjustments that relate to taxes. The first relates to prepaid taxes, the second to the current taxes payable, and the third to deferred taxes. All of them are necessary to derive the payment of taxes during the period, because the tax expense on the income statement includes deferred and current taxes. The current taxes may not be identical to cash payments for taxes due to prepayments of taxes on certain items, or the accrual of taxes that will be paid in the next period.

	1989
Net income	$ 13,143
Adjustments to reconcile net income to net cash provided by operating activities:	
Depreciation and amortization	7,344
Loss on disposal of property, plant, and equipment	466
(Gain) loss on sale of marketable securities	(179)
Change in assets and liabilities:	
(Increase) in accounts receivable, net	(17,009)
(Increase) in inventories	(20,940)
(Increase) decrease in prepaid taxes based on earnings	2,568
(Increase) decrease in other assets	(5,563)
Increase (decrease) in accounts payable	(92)
Increase (decrease) in taxes based on earnings	(431)
(Decrease) in deferred income taxes	(2,384)
Increase (decrease) in other current assets and liabilities	(3,095)
Increase (decrease) in sundry payables and accrued expenses	(260)
Total adjustments	(39,575)
Net cash provided by (used in) operating activities	(26,432)

Example:

Meredith Corp. is a Fortune 500 diversified media firm that is engaged in magazine and book publishing, television broadcasting, and residential real-estate marketing.

Meredith Corp. reports its 1989 cash from operating activities as follows:

Cash flows from operating activities:	
Net earnings	$33,154
Adjustments to reconcile net earnings to net cash	
provided by operating activities:	
Depreciation and amortization	22,341
Amortization of film contract rights	34,922
Deferred income taxes	5,016
Equity in earnings of printing operations, net of distribution received	(9,125)
Decrease in receivables	513
(Increase) in inventories	(7,913)
(Increase) in supplies and prepayments	(3,575)
(Decrease) in accounts payable and accruals	(4,850)
Additions to unearned subscription revenue and other deferred items	9,489
Net cash provided by operating activities	79,972

As can be seen, Meredith amortizes its film contract rights. This amortization does not involve cash, and is similar to the depreciation of tangible assets. Thus, it adds this charge back, since it was subtracted in deriving net income. Note that Meredith subtracts equity earnings in the derivation of cash from operations. The reason is that equity earnings represent the share of Meredith in income of other firms that are not consolidated in the financial statements of Meredith. These earnings are added to Meredith's income when deriving net income, but they do not represent cash receipts, except for the cash dividends that are distributed by the investees back to Meredith. Thus, Meredith subtracts the earnings, net of cash distributions, in computation of net operating cash flow. Note further the last item in the preceding schedule—the addition to unearned subscription revenue, which is added to net income in computing net cash flow from operations. This item is added, because it was not included in net income since Meredith has not provided all the services required under the subscription agreement. Nevertheless, the firm has already received payment for the subscription, so its cash flows from operating activities should increase.

Example:

A.T. Cross manufactures and markets high-quality writing instruments, such as ball point and fountain pens and mechanical pencils. It also markets luggage, leather goods, and various gift items.

A.T. Cross Co. reports the following items on its 1989 statement of cash flows:

Net income	$36,001,500
Adjustments to reconcile net income to net cash provided by operating activities:	
Depreciation	5,185,348
Amortization	2,986,762
Provision for losses on accounts receivable	702,552
Deferred income taxes	(1,456,126)
Provision for warranty costs	1,760,927
Changes in operating assets and liabilities, net of effects from acquisitions—Note G:	
Accounts receivable	(3,585,809)
Inventories	(8,924,315)
Other assets—net	(2,434,214)
Accounts payable	(3,881,963)
Other liabilities—net	5,069,781
Warranty costs paid	(1,560,927)
Foreign currency transaction (gain) loss	670,817
Net cash provided by operating activities	30,534,333

A.T. Cross adds back to net income the provision for losses on accounts receivable because the provision is a noncash expense that was subtracted in deriving net income. Note that A.T. Cross also adds back the provision for warranty costs for the same reason. However, unlike the provision for losses on accounts receivable, it subtracts actual payments made under its warranty. This is not necessary with accounts receivable that are written off, because no cash is involved when accounts receivables are written off; it is just an accounting entry.

Example:

Harsco Corp. manufactures military vehicles and defense systems, scaffoldings, concrete-forming equipment, plastic piping, propane tanks, and various steel products.
   Harsco reports the following items in its 1989 disclosure of operating cash flows:

Net income	$ 11,362
Adjustments to reconcile net income to net cash provided by operating activities:	
Depreciation	56,229
Other, net	3,324
Changes in assets and liabilities, net of the effect of businesses acquired:	
Notes and accounts receivable	8,457
Inventories	(59,719)
Other current assets	(16,313)
Accounts payable	4,158
Accrued long-term contract costs	56,689
Other current liabilities	5,164
Advance deposits on long-term contracts	63,296
Other noncurrent assets and liabilities	(3,100)
Net cash provided by operating activities	$129,547

Note that Harsco subtracts about $60 million from net income because of the increase in inventory. However, it then adds back to net income about $57 million for the decrease in accrued long-term costs and about $63 million for advance deposits on long-term contracts. The first of these latter two items represents costs that are recognized for the production of inventory (i.e., work performed on long-term contracts), although they have not been paid during the accounting period. The second of the two items represents payments that were made by the customers for the long-term contracts. These payments qualify as cash flows from customers and should be added to operating cash flows, as Harsco did.

Example:

Sonat Inc. is a diversified firm that operates in the oil and gas fields. It is active in the transmission and sale of natural gas, contract drilling, and exploration and production of oil and gas.
   Sonat Inc. reports the following items on its 1989 operating cash flows:

Cash flows from operating activities:

Net income (loss)	$ 108,978
Adjustments to reconcile net income to net cash provided by operating activities:	
Depreciation, depletion, amortization, and valuation adjustments	163,120
Deferred income taxes and investment tax credits	37,523
Equity in (earnings) of joint ventures, less distributions	(9,021)
(Gain) on sale of assets	(11,004)
Reserves for regulatory matters	(334,074)
Natural gas purchase contract settlement costs	210,986
Other	17,791
Change in working capital	60,566
Net cash provided by operating activities	244,865

Two items stand out in this schedule: the reserves for regulatory matters and natural gas purchase contract settlement costs. The first is subtracted from income, because in 1989 the regulating body approved prior rate increases for one of the firm's subsidiaries. Thus, additional revenue was recognized in 1989, although the cash inflows representing these revenues were actually received by the firm much earlier. Instead of recognizing these revenues immediately, the firm created reserves for fear that future refunds to customers were needed if the regulating body would not approve the rate increases. When the rate increases were approved, revenues and income increased, but cash flows in 1989 were unaffected. Thus, the firm had to subtract this item from income to derive cash from operating activities. The second item, natural gas purchase contract settlement costs, reflects reserves for future potential losses on contracts to purchase natural gas. Because no cash is involved yet, it represents a noncash accounting entry similar to depreciation expense or reserves for future repairs under warranty, and it is added back to income to derive cash from operating activities. These two items together account for about one-half of the cash from operations. Still, as we emphasized, these items do *not* represent current cash flows.

Example:

Sunshine Mining Company is engaged in the production of gold, silver, crude oil, and natural gas.

Sunshine Mining Co. reports the items shown on page 98 on its 1989 statement of cash flows.

As can be seen, Sunshine added the common stock that was issued for services provided of $791,000 to net income in computing cash from operations. To understand this item, it can be assumed that some other entity provided services to Sunshine, for which the other entity was compensated with common stock. The services were recorded as operating expenses, and were subtracted in deriving net income. However, these services did not necessitate an outflow of cash, and therefore, they are added back to net income in deriving cash from operations. This item does *not* appear in the section of financing cash flows, because no cash was received for the issued shares. However, if the amount was material, it should have been disclosed in the schedule of noncash financing events.

	1989
Cash provided (used) by operations:	
Net loss	$(38,345)
Adjustments to reconcile net loss to net cash provided (used) by operations:	
Depreciation, depletion, amortization, and impairment provisions	37,134
Amortization of discount on Silver Indexed Bonds	1,916
Gain on the sale of fixed assets	(828)
Common stock issuances for:	
Interest on Silver Indexed Bonds	—
Services provided and other	791
Net (increase) decrease in:	
Accounts receivable	(1,800)
Inventories	2,374
Other current assets	1,341
Other assets and deferred charges	(657)
Net increase (decrease) in:	
Accounts payable—trade	578
Oil and gas proceeds payable	1,947
Accrued expenses	(3,435)
Other liabilities and deferred credits	(784)
Other, net	(10)
Net cash provided (used) by operations	222

Example:

MNC Financial reports the following items in its statement of cash flows for the first three quarters of 1990:

Net income	$ 6,189
Adjustments to reconcile net income to net cash provided by operating activities:	
Provision for possible credit losses	134,939
Provision for depreciation, amortization, and other	15,772
Deferred income taxes	690
(Gain) loss on sale of investment securities	(1,077)
Decrease in interest receivables	27,060
Increase in interest payables	4,436
(Increase) decrease in trading accounts	17,075
(Increase) in other operating activities	(58,823)
Net cash provided by (used for) operating activities	146,261

Note that the most significant item here is the provision for credit losses; these are expected losses on loans or other lines of credit that were extended to customers. When deriving net income, these losses were subtracted from operating income. However, because they do not involve cash outflows, they are added back when computing cash from operations. Note how the change in estimating future credit losses affects net income, but has no effect on cash from operations.

4.4 ESTIMATING COMPONENTS OF OPERATING CASH FLOWS

To estimate the components of cash flows from operating activities, we use the information in the income statement and the schedule that reconciles net income to cash flows from operating activities. Let us illustrate this technique using the 1989 annual report from Sara Lee Corp. These statements provide the following information (in millions of dollars):

	Year Ended 7/1/89
Net sales	$11,717.67
Cost of sales	(8,040.44)
Selling, general, and administrative	(2,936.14)
Interest expense	(153.78)
Interest income	20.58
Unusual items, net	31.59
Income taxes	(228.98)
Net income	$ 410.50
Net income	$ 410.50
Adjustments for noncash items:	
Depreciation and amortization	279.95
Unusual items, net	(31.59)
Increase in deferred taxes	42.51
Other noncash credits, net	(102.13)
Changes in current assets and liabilities, net of businesses acquired	
and sold	(105.83)
Net cash from operating activities	$ 493.41
Components of the changes in current assets and liabilities:	
Increase in trade accounts receivable	$ (14.68)
Increase in inventories	(181.36)
Increase in other current assets	(37.78)
Increase in accounts payable	209.13
Decrease in accrued liabilities	(49.32)
Decrease in accrued income taxes	(31.82)
Change in current assets and liabilities	$ (105.83)

From these data, we can estimate the individual components of operating cash flows by using the information on operating events from the income statement and information about changes in account balances from the schedule that reconciles net income to net operating cash flows. Note that increases in inventories and trade accounts receivable are not identical to the changes in the balance sheet accounts from 1988 to 1989. The reasons for these differences are explained in the following Lotus Development Corporation example.

Sara Lee Corp.: Consolidated Statements of Income

CONSOLIDATED STATEMENTS OF INCOME

(in thousands except per share data)	Years ended		
	July 1, 1989	July 2, 1988	June 27, 1987
Net Sales	$11,717,678	$10,423,816	$9,154,588
Cost of sales	8,040,447	7,096,756	6,309,565
Selling, general and administrative expenses	2,936,149	2,717,504	2,328,704
Interest expense	153,781	119,925	105,632
Interest income	(20,588)	(23,705)	(37,159)
Unusual items, net	(31,592)	—	—
	11,078,197	9,910,480	8,706,742
Income before income taxes	639,481	513,336	447,846
Income taxes	228,989	188,261	180,787
Net Income	410,492	325,075	267,059
Preferred dividend requirements	(14,358)	(9,394)	(4,125)
Earnings available for common stockholders	$ 396,134	$ 315,681	$ 262,934
Net Income per Common Share	$ 3.50	$ 2.83	$ 2.35
Average shares outstanding	113,395	111,670	111,687

SOURCE: Sara Lee Corp., *Annual Report*, 1989.

1. Cash collections from customers:

	Year Ended 7/1/89
Net sales	$11,717.67
Increase in trade accounts receivable	(14.68)
Cash collections from customers	**$11,702.99**

2. Cash payments to suppliers and employees:

Cost of sales	$ (8,040.44)
Selling, general, and administrative	(2,936.14)
Depreciation and amortization	279.95
Other noncash credits, net	(102.13)
Increase in inventories	(181.36)
Increase in other current assets	(37.78)
Increase in accounts payable	209.13
Decrease in accrued liabilities	(49.32)
Cash payments to suppliers and employees	**$(10,858.09)**

Sara Lee Corp.: Consolidated Balance Sheets

CONSOLIDATED BALANCE SHEETS

(dollars in thousands except share data)	July 1, 1989	July 2, 1988	June 27, 1987
Cash and equivalents.	$ 117,498	$ 178,552	$ 302,862
Trade accounts receivable, less allowances of $63,862 in 1989, $54,850 in 1988 and $47,084 in 1987	813,672	717,532	609,998
Inventories			
Finished goods	830,340	674,186	640,723
Work in process	171,560	109,213	86,382
Materials and supplies	450,064	344,054	284,614
	1,451,964	1,127,453	1,011,719
Other current assets.	116,587	65,335	35,827
Total current assets	2,499,721	2,088,872	1,960,406
Investments in associated companies	188,989	88,763	116,320
Trademarks and other assets	265,867	258,053	230,133
Property, at cost			
Land	68,988	64,203	51,023
Buildings and improvements	965,215	822,594	720,741
Machinery and equipment	1,607,377	1,345,120	1,356,151
Construction in progress	221,840	210,043	100,354
Assets under capital leases	23,823	42,599	38,700
	2,887,243	2,484,559	2,266,969
Accumulated depreciation	1,114,227	1,067,855	1,026,399
Property, net.	1,773,016	1,416,704	1,240,570
Intangible assets.	1,795,139	1,159,678	644,246
	$6,522,732	$5,012,070	$4,191,675

SOURCE: Sara Lee Corp., *Annual Report*, 1989.

3. Cash payment for taxes:

Income taxes	(228.98)
Increase in deferred taxes	42.51
Decrease in accrued income taxes	(31.82)
Cash payment for taxes	**$(218.29)**

Sara Lee Corp.: Consolidated Balance Sheets (continued)

CONSOLIDATED BALANCE SHEETS

	July 1, 1989	July 2, 1988	June 27, 1987
Notes payable	$ 279,026	$ 94,599	$ 219,354
Accounts payable	966,508	769,733	510,580
Accrued liabilities	988,084	905,180	766,322
Accrued income taxes	10,143	11,813	20,892
Current maturities of long-term debt	31,665	24,836	78,114
Total current liabilities	2,275,426	1,806,161	1,595,262
Long-term debt	1,488,230	893,434	632,624
Deferred income taxes	346,470	298,952	280,527
Other liabilities	315,243	213,426	192,307
Preferred stock (authorized 13,500,000 shares; no par value)			
Convertible adjustable: Issued and outstanding—607,000 in			
1989 and 1,500,000 in 1988 and 1987; redeemable at			
$50 per share	30,350	75,000	75,000
Auction: 1,500 shares issued and outstanding in 1989 and			
1988; redeemable at $100,000 per share	150,000	150,000	—
Convertible ESOP: 4,827,586 shares issued in 1989	350,000	—	—
Unearned deferred compensation	(347,903)	—	—
Common stockholders' equity			
Common stock: (authorized 300,000,000 shares; $1.33 1/3 par value)			
113,667,303 shares issued in 1989 and			
119,596,068 in 1988 and 1987	151,556	159,461	159,461
Capital surplus	18,779	24,212	3,667
Retained earnings	1,750,961	1,597,259	1,408,504
Foreign currency translation adjustments	(6,380)	15,337	20,048
Treasury stock, at cost: None in 1989, 9,037,505 shares			
in 1988 and 8,872,115 shares in 1987	—	(221,172)	(175,725)
Total common stockholders' equity	1,914,916	1,575,097	1,415,955
	$6,522,732	$5,012,070	$4,191,675

SOURCE: Sara Lee Corp., *Annual Report*, 1989.

4. Cash payment for interest:

Interest expense	$(153.78)
Interest income	20.58
Cash payment for interest	**$(133.20)**

Sara Lee Corp.: Consolidated Statements of Common Stockholders' Equity

CONSOLIDATED STATEMENTS OF COMMON STOCKHOLDERS' EQUITY

(dollars in thousands except per share data)	Total	Common Stock	Capital Surplus	Retained Earnings	Foreign Currency Translation Adjustments	Treasury Stock
Balances at June 28, 1986	$1,154,678	$ 79,730	$ 6,965	$1,320,475	$(42,350)	$(210,142)
Net income	267,059	—	—	267,059	—	—
Cash dividends						
Common ($.95 per share)	(102,148)	—	—	(102,148)	—	—
Convertible adjustable preferred ($2.75 per share)	(4,125)	—	—	(4,125)	—	—
Stock issuances						
Two-for-one stock split	—	79,731	(28,426)	(51,305)	—	—
Public offering	21,893	—	10,919	—	—	10,974
Business acquisitions	39,538	—	18,698	—	—	20,840
Stock option and purchase plans	27,633	—	375	—	—	27,258
Company acquired under pooling-of-interests	41,073	—	(16,167)	(21,452)	—	78,692
Treasury stock purchases	(100,003)	—	—	—	—	(100,003)
Translation adjustments	62,398	—	—	—	62,398	—
Other	7,959	—	11,303	—	—	(3,344)
Balances at June 27, 1987	1,415,955	159,461	3,667	1,408,504	20,048	(175,725)
Net income	325,075	—	—	325,075	—	—
Cash dividends						
Common ($1.15 per share)	(126,926)	—	—	(126,926)	—	—
Convertible adjustable preferred ($3.03 per share)	(4,547)	—	—	(4,547)	—	—
Auction preferred ($3,231.13 per share)	(4,847)	—	—	(4,847)	—	—
Stock issuances						
Business acquisitions	18,000	—	8,990	—	—	9,010
Stock option and purchase plans	34,028	—	(5,203)	—	—	39,231
Treasury stock purchases	(91,653)	—	—	—	—	(91,653)
Translation adjustments	(4,711)	—	—	—	(4,711)	—
Other	14,723	—	16,758	—	—	(2,035)
Balances at July 2, 1988	1,575,097	159,461	24,212	1,597,259	15,337	(221,172)
Net income	410,492	—	—	410,492	—	—
Cash dividends						
Common ($1.38 per share)	(155,304)	—	—	(155,304)	—	—
Convertible adjustable preferred ($3.70 per share)	(3,714)	—	—	(3,714)	—	—
Auction preferred ($7,096.00 per share)	(10,644)	—	—	(10,644)	—	—
Stock issuances						
Business acquisitions	80,140	—	34,430	—	—	45,710
Stock option and purchase plans	33,066	716	11,956	—	—	20,394
Conversion of convertible adjustable preferred stock	44,650	—	16,299	—	—	28,351
Treasury stock purchases	(37,388)	—	—	—	—	(37,388)
Retirement of treasury stock	—	(8,606)	(72,067)	(87,128)	—	167,801
Translation adjustments	(21,717)	—	—	—	(21,717)	—
Other	238	(15)	3,949	—	—	(3,696)
Balances at July 1, 1989	$1,914,916	$151,556	$ 18,779	$1,750,961	$ (6,380)	$ —

SOURCE: Sara Lee Corp., *Annual Report*, 1989.

5. Other cash flows:

Unusual items, net	$ 31.59
Unusual items, net (adjusted to show it is a nonoperating cash item)	(31.59)
Other cash flows	**$ 0.00**
Total Operating Cash Flow	**$493.41**

Sara Lee Corp.: Consolidated Statements of Cash Flows

CONSOLIDATED STATEMENTS OF CASH FLOWS

	Years ended		
(dollars in thousands)	July 1, 1989	July 2, 1988	June 27, 1987
Cash Flows from Operating Activities			
Net income	$ 410,492	$325,075	$267,059
Adjustments for non-cash items included in net income:			
Depreciation and amortization of intangibles	279,945	250,920	201,607
Unusual items, net	(31,592)	—	—
Increase (decrease) in deferred income taxes	42,509	15,102	(10,629)
Other non-cash credits, net	(102,134)	(10,897)	(28,945)
Changes in current assets and liabilities, net of			
businesses acquired and sold	(105,827)	152,080	227,536
Net cash flows from operating activities	493,393	732,280	656,628
Cash Flows from Investing Activities			
Purchases of property and equipment	(541,483)	(448,974)	(286,547)
Acquisitions of businesses	(910,147)	(881,442)	(236,293)
Investments in associated companies	(176,107)	(6,019)	(86,216)
Dispositions of businesses	484,668	227,243	70,870
Sales of property	21,377	157,235	32,237
Other	1,095	10,665	2,211
Net cash flows used in investing activities	(1,120,597)	(941,292)	(503,738)
Cash Flows from Financing Activities			
Issuance of convertible ESOP stock in 1989 and			
auction preferred stock in 1988	350,000	150,000	—
Issuances of common stock	33,066	34,028	49,526
Purchases of common stock	(37,388)	(91,653)	(100,003)
Borrowings of long-term debt	257,273	393,092	10,916
Repayments of long-term debt	(44,813)	(125,860)	(41,516)
Short-term borrowings (repayments), net	184,427	(124,755)	123,743
Payments of dividends	(169,662)	(136,320)	(106,273)
Net cash flows from financing activities	572,903	98,532	(63,607)
Effect of changes in foreign exchange rates on cash	(6,753)	(13,830)	57,420
Increase (decrease) in cash and equivalents	(61,054)	(124,310)	146,703
Cash and equivalents at beginning of year	178,552	302,862	156,159
Cash and equivalents at end of year	$ 117,498	$178,552	$302,862
Components of the Changes in Current Assets and Liabilities			
(Increase) decrease in trade accounts receivable	$ (14,682)	$ 49,199	$104,865
(Increase) in inventories	(181,359)	(38,207)	(31,556)
(Increase) decrease in other current assets	(37,777)	(25,127)	2,961
Increase in accounts payable	209,126	109,482	67,570
(Decrease) increase in accrued liabilities	(49,318)	91,996	111,063
(Decrease) in accrued income taxes	(31,817)	(35,263)	(27,367)
Changes in current assets and liabilities	$(105,827)	$152,080	$227,536
Supplemental Disclosures of Cash Flow Information			
Cash paid during the year for:			
Interest	$ 129,877	$110,474	$ 94,286
Income taxes	233,343	215,661	222,048

SOURCE: Sara Lee Corp., *Annual Report*, 1989.

In the above estimation, we have used all the information on the income statement and the information in the reconciliation schedule. Thus, the net operating cash flow is identical to that reported by the firm. Still, there are two important differences that should be highlighted; the estimates for tax and interest payments are not identical to those reported by the firm. Under FAS No. 95, firms have to disclose payments for taxes and interest, *even* if they use the indirect method to report cash flows from operating activities. Accordingly, Sara Lee Corp. reports the following data:

	Year Ended 7/1/89
Tax payments as reported	$(233.34)
Estimated payments for taxes	(218.29)
Error in estimation	$ (15.05)
Interest payments as reported	$(129.88)
Estimated payments for interest	(133.20)
Error in estimation	$ 3.32
Total (underestimation) error	$ (11.73)

In the above estimation, we can use the actual numbers reported by the firm, and because the underestimation error is small enough, we can assign it to "other" cash flows from operating activities. Thus, our estimates will be:

Cash collections from customers	$ 11,702.99
Cash payments to suppliers and employees	(10,858.09)
Tax payments as reported	(233.34)
Interest payments as reported	(129.88)
Other operating cash flows	11.73
Net operating cash flow	$ 493.41

Let us perform the same procedure for Lotus Development Corp., which reports operating cash flows using the direct method. Initially, we will use the same procedures as those above to estimate the components of cash flows from operating activities and then compare the results with the actual components reported by the firm.

Lotus Development Corporation

The company's financial statements provide the following information (in thousands of dollars):

	Year Ended 12/31/89
Net sales	$ 556,033.00
Cost of sales	(104,949.00)
R&D	(94,343.00)
Sales and marketing	(221,745.00)
General and administrative	(61,078.00)
Interest income, net	5,644.00
Other income, net	5,389.00
Provision for income taxes	(16,990.00)
Net income	$ 67,961.00
Net income	$ 67,961.00
Depreciation and amortization	33,827.00
Increase in accounts receivable	(10,028.00)
Increase in inventory	(6,095.00)
Increase in accounts payable and accrued expenses	16,569.00
Net change in other working capital items	23,201.00
Net cash provided by operations	$ 125,435.00

Lotus Development Corporation: Consolidated Statements of Operations

LOTUS DEVELOPMENT CORPORATION
CONSOLIDATED STATEMENTS OF OPERATIONS
Years ended December 31,

(In thousands, except per share data)	1989	1988	1987
Net sales	$556,033	$468,547	$395,595
Cost of sales	104,949	90,825	68,676
Gross margin	451,084	377,722	326,919
Operating expenses:			
Research and development (Note B)	94,343	83,837	58,420
Sales and marketing	221,745	170,750	126,848
General and administrative	61,078	54,124	46,546
Total operating expenses	377,166	308,711	231,814
Operating income	73,918	69,011	95,105
Interest income, net (Note J)	5,644	9,568	3,960
Other income, net (Note K)	5,389	1,295	3,853
Income before provision for income taxes	84,951	79,874	102,918
Provision for income taxes (Note H)	16,990	20,949	30,875
Net income	$ 67,961	$ 58,925	$ 72,043
Net income per share	$1.61	$1.29	$1.58
Weighted average common and common equivalent shares outstanding	42,301	45,551	45,720

SOURCE: Lotus Development Corporation, *Annual Report*, 1989.

Lotus Development Corporation: Consolidated Balance Sheets

LOTUS DEVELOPMENT CORPORATION
CONSOLIDATED BALANCE SHEETS

(In thousands)	December 31, 1989	December 31, 1988
Assets		
Current assets:		
Cash and short-term investments	$274,977	$192,433
Accounts receivable, less allowances for doubtful accounts of $4,200 and $3,936	97,712	92,035
Inventory (Note C)	23,171	18,088
Other current assets	13,937	7,430
Total current assets	409,797	309,986
Property and equipment, net of accumulated depreciation and amortization of $75,418 and $55,482 (Note D)	129,702	86,953
Software and other intangibles, net of accumulated amortization of $36,972 and $35,802 (Note B)	27,100	16,026
Investments and other assets (Note E)	37,678	9,157
Total assets	$604,277	$422,122

SOURCE: Lotus Development Corporation, *Annual Report,* 1989.

It should be noted that the reconciliation schedule here (and in the previous Sara Lee example) reports different increases in accounts receivable and inventories than those calculated by subtracting the balances on the balance sheet. For example, the increase in accounts receivable on the balance sheet amounts to $5.677 million, whereas the increase reported in the reconciliation schedule is $10.028 million. The difference between these two figures stems from accounts receivable that are not due to trade receivables. For example, if some of these receivables are caused by sale of fixed assets, these receivables should *not* be considered for the change in operating cash flows, because these receivables are related to disinvesting cash flows. Similarly, the increase in inventories according to the balance sheet is of $5.083 million, whereas the reconciliation schedule reports an increase of $6.095 million. Obviously, the firm has carefully examined the change in inventories and excluded those items that do not represent operating cash flows. Normally, it is a good procedure to compare the changes in the reconciliation schedule with those reported on the balance sheet to identify any material differences and their possible sources. In many cases, these differences arise because of acquisitions or divestitures, where the balance sheet differences are likely to include the effects of the acquisition, but the reconciliation schedule in the cash flow statement does not. These differences are likely to be included as part of the acquisition costs in the investing activities section of the statement of cash flows.

Estimating operating cash flows using the information above:

Lotus Development Corporation: Consolidated Balance Sheets (continued)

(In thousands)	December 31, 1989	December 31, 1988
Liabilities and Stockholders' Equity		
Current liabilities:		
Notes payable to banks (Note I)	$ 2,975	$ 9,441
Accrued employee compensation	17,688	11,771
Accounts payable and accrued expenses	63,125	45,491
Deferred revenue (Note B)	15,798	16,592
Income taxes payable (Note H)	10,253	1,231
Total current liabilities	109,839	84,526
Deferred income taxes (Note H)	13,693	10,400
Long-term debt (Note I)	202,440	95,000
Commitments and contingencies (Notes E and F)		
Stockholders' equity (Note G):		
Preferred stock, $1.00 par value, 5,000,000 shares authorized, none issued	–	–
Common stock, $.01 par value, 100,000,000 shares authorized; 57,940,650 and 55,561,312 issued; and 41,607,816 and 41,666,344 outstanding	579	556
Additional paid-in capital	139,762	109,429
Retained earnings	334,246	266,285
Treasury stock, 16,332,834 and 13,894,968 shares at an average cost of $11.94 and $10.37 per share	(194,937)	(144,030)
Translation adjustment	(1,345)	3
Deferred employee compensation	–	(47)
Total stockholders' equity	278,305	232,196
Total liabilities and stockholders' equity	$604,277	$422,122

SOURCE: Lotus Development Corporation, *Annual Report*, 1989.

1. Cash collections from customers:

	Year Ended 12/31/89
Net sales	$556,033.00
Increase in accounts receivable	(10,028.00)
Decrease in deferred revenue	794.00
Cash collections from customers	**$546,799.00**

Lotus Development Corporation: Consolidated Statements of Cash Flows

LOTUS DEVELOPMENT CORPORATION
CONSOLIDATED STATEMENTS OF CASH FLOWS
Years ended December 31,

(In thousands)	1989	1988	1987
Cash flows from operations:			
Cash received from customers	$545,997	$425,601	$394,300
Cash paid to suppliers and employees	(429,245)	(359,693)	(270,600)
Interest received	18,153	11,980	7,560
Interest paid	(14,884)	(3,614)	(3,258)
Income taxes recovered (paid)	9,270	(12,438)	(20,371)
Other, net	(3,856)	258	1,127
Net cash provided by operations	125,435	62,094	108,758
Cash flows from investments:			
Payments for purchase of property and equipment	(68,906)	(55,161)	(25,258)
Payments for investments	(24,513)	(1,004)	(4,800)
Payments for software and other intangibles	(23,197)	–	(17,624)
Net cash used for investments	(116,616)	(56,165)	(47,682)
Cash flows from financing activities:			
Proceeds from issuance of long-term debt	107,440	65,000	–
Purchase of common stock for treasury	(43,552)	(56,205)	(1,279)
Issuance of common stock	15,916	10,649	8,042
Net short-term borrowings under credit facilities	(6,079)	2,151	3,913
Net cash provided by financing activities	73,725	21,595	10,676
Net increase in cash and short-term investments	82,544	27,524	71,752
Cash and short-term investments at beginning of year	192,433	164,909	93,157
Cash and short-term investments at end of year	$274,977	$192,433	$164,909

(In thousands)	1989	1988	1987
Reconciliation of net income to net cash provided by operations:			
Net income	$67,961	$58,925	$72,043
Depreciation and amortization	33,827	37,253	27,984
(Increase) in accounts receivable	(10,028)	(49,359)	(5,652)
(Increase) in inventory	(6,095)	(9,163)	(1,633)
Increase (decrease) in accounts payable and accrued expenses	16,569	13,837	(3,116)
Net change in other working capital items	23,201	10,601	19,132
Net cash provided by operations	$125,435	$62,094	$108,758

SOURCE: Lotus Development Corporation, *Annual Report*, 1989.

Lotus Development Corporation: Consolidated Statements of Stockholders' Equity

LOTUS DEVELOPMENT CORPORATION
CONSOLIDATED STATEMENTS OF STOCKHOLDERS' EQUITY

Years ended December 31, 1987, 1988 and 1989. (Note G) (In thousands)	Common Stock	Additional Paid-In Capital	Retained Earnings	Translation Adjustment	Treasury Stock	Deferred Employee Compensation	Total
Balance, December 31, 1986	$526	$66,624	$135,317	($776)	($83,135)	($3,963)	$114,593
Acquisition of 174,375 shares of common stock	–	(184)	–	–	(4,608)	184	(4,608)
Exercise of 461,695 incentive stock options	5	2,886	–	–	–	–	2,891
Exercise of 1,406,119 non-qualified stock options	14	7,566	–	–	–	–	7,580
Income tax benefit related to exercise of stock options	–	5,483	–	–	–	–	5,483
Issuance of 63,002 shares of common stock under employee stock purchase plan	1	899	–	–	–	–	900
Amortization of deferred employee compensation	–	–	–	–	–	2,145	2,145
Currency translation effect	–	–	–	1,019	–	–	1,019
Net income	–	–	72,043	–	–	–	72,043
Balance, December 31, 1987	546	83,274	207,360	243	(87,743)	(1,634)	202,046
Acquisition of 3,282,087 shares of common stock	–	–	–	–	(56,287)	–	(56,287)
Exercise of 377,060 incentive stock options	4	2,904	–	–	–	–	2,908
Exercise of 490,839 non-qualified stock options	5	4,833	–	–	–	–	4,838
Income tax benefit related to exercise of stock options	–	15,434	–	–	–	–	15,434
Issuance of 136,858 shares of common stock under employee stock purchase plan	1	2,984	–	–	–	–	2,985
Amortization of deferred employee compensation	–	–	–	–	–	1,587	1,587
Currency translation effect	–	–	–	(240)	–	–	(240)
Net income	–	–	58,925	–	–	–	58,925
Balance, December 31, 1988	556	109,429	266,285	3	(144,030)	(47)	232,196
Acquisition of 2,437,866 shares of common stock	–	–	–	–	(50,907)	–	(50,907)
Exercise of 407,864 incentive stock options	4	3,471	–	–	–	–	3,475
Exercise of 1,750,513 non-qualified stock options	17	16,354	–	–	–	–	16,371
Income tax benefit related to exercise of stock options	–	7,083	–	–	–	–	7,083
Issuance of 220,961 shares of common stock under employee stock purchase plan	2	3,425	–	–	–	–	3,427
Amortization of deferred employee compensation	–	–	–	–	–	47	47
Currency translation effect	–	–	–	(1,348)	–	–	(1,348)
Net income	–	–	67,961	–	–	–	67,961
Balance, December 31, 1989	$579	$139,762	$334,246	($1,345)	($194,937)	$–	$278,305

SOURCE: Lotus Development Corporation, *Annual Report*, 1989.

2. Cash payments to suppliers and employees:

Cost of sales	$(104,949.00)
R&D	(94,343.00)
Sales and marketing	(221,745.00)
General and administrative	(61,078.00)
Depreciation and amortization	33,827.00
Increase in inventory	(6,095.00)
Increase in accounts payable and accrued expenses	16,569.00
Net change in other working capital items (without taxes and deferred revenue)	13,385.00
Cash payments to suppliers and employees	**$(424,429.00)**

3. Cash receipts from taxes:

Provision for income taxes	$(16,990.00)
Increase in deferred taxes	3,293.00
Increase in accrued income taxes	$ 9,022.00
Income tax paid	**$ (4,675.00)**

4. Cash payment and receipt of interest:

Interest expense	$(15,494.00)
Capitalized interest	(1,808.00)
Cash payment for interest	**$(17,302.00)**
Interest income	$ 19,330.00
Cash receipt from interest	**$ 19,330.00**

5. Other cash flows:

Other income, net	$ 5,389.00
Cash receipt from other income	**$ 5,389.00**
Total Operating Cash Flow (1. through 5.)	**$ 125,112.00**
Total operating cash flow	$ 125,112
As reported	(125,435)
Difference	$ (323)
Difference explained by:	
Increase in deferred taxes	3,293
Interest capitalized (twice)	(3,616)
Total	$ (323)

(Both items were not included specifically in the company's reconciliation schedule.)

Comparison of Estimated to Reported Components

	As Reported	Estimated	Percent Error
Cash received from customers	545,997	546,799	(1)
Cash paid to suppliers and employees	(429,245)	(424,429)	1
Interest received	18,153	19,330	(6)
Interest paid	(14,884)	(17,302)	(16)
Income tax recovered	9,270	(4,675)	150
Other, net	(3,856)	5,389	(240)
Total	$ 125,435	125,112	1

As can be seen from the previous table, estimating net cash flows from operations can be done fairly accurately. Furthermore, given the information available in the reconciliation schedule, estimates of the cash received from customers and cash paid to suppliers and employees are reasonably close to the amounts that the firm would have reported had it used the direct method. Significant differences occur for interest received or paid, because, for most firms, only the income statement interest expense/income are available, but not changes in balance sheet amounts. Obviously, these amounts are available to the firm, which uses them to report the actual cash received or paid for interest. It should be noted that the FASB required firms to disclose the amount of cash paid for interest if they used the indirect method for deriving cash from operating activities.

Another item with large differences between reported and estimated amounts for Lotus is the taxes paid. Normally, large differences occur when not all tax-related balance sheet accounts are separately disclosed on the balance sheet. For example, some prepaid taxes or deferred taxes that represent an asset may be included with prepaid and other assets on the balance sheet. Some deferred tax liabilities may be included with other liabilities. Thus, in these cases, it is impossible to estimate the taxes paid during a period in a reasonable manner. Again, it should be emphasized that the actual cash paid for taxes should be separately disclosed in the statement of cash flows (or in footnotes) for firms that use the indirect method to derive cash from operating activities.

Finally, by definition, very little information will be available to estimate the "other operating cash flows." More than anything else, it would probably be a "plug" figure and is likely to contain the largest estimation error. However, one should not be too concerned about these errors, because most of these "other" operating cash flows would not recur and therefore would not have any important consequences for future cash flows.

4.5 INTERPRETATION OF OPERATING CASH FLOWS

Net cash flow from operating activities indicates the amount of cash that the firm was able to generate from (or needed to spend on) its ongoing business activities. Ideally, a firm should be able to generate cash from its business activities in every period.

However, in reality, financially healthy firms generate cash from their business activities in most periods, but spend more cash on their business activities than they receive from customers in some periods. Also, a firm may be in the development stage of its business. It may invest in developing its products or in setting production facilities and distribution channels (investment activities), while larger cash receipts from customers are expected to occur only in the future. Another example is a seasonal business that invests in setting up inventories during one or two quarters, while most sales are made during other quarters (such as during the holiday season). Operating cash flows are likely to be negative during the quarters when inventories are built, but positive in quarters when inventories are sold.

For some periods, and for some firms, a negative net cash flow from operations is acceptable, such as a manufacturer who works on long-term contracts and must build inventories during the initial stages of production. However, in the majority of cases, a positive net cash flow from business activities is expected. A business that spends more cash on its ongoing activities than it generates has to finance these activities somehow. It can just use up its cash reserves, borrow additional cash, raise additional equity, or liquidate investments or fixed assets. All of these options cannot be sustained for prolonged periods. For example, it is unlikely that creditors will keep lending to a business that continuously does not generate an acceptable level of cash from its operations. Similarly, liquidation of assets might reduce the chances of generating cash flows from operations in the future. Thus, continuous negative cash flows from operating activities (that are unrelated to a seasonal business or the operating cycle of the business) should be carefully examined by the cash flow analyst.

In addition to net cash flows from operating activities, one should examine the components of cash flows. Actual cash inflows begin with the collection of cash from accounts receivable. The ease in which the entity collects its accounts receivables is an important determinant of its financial flexibility. Improvements in the collection period begin at the credit approval. For small, unknown, or start-up entities, a greater degree of due diligence by the credit analyst is needed.

Reduction in accounts receivable, next to planned reduction in inventory, is the most sought-after way to increase operating cash flow. Faster collection periods, made possible by vastly improved credit analysis computer software that enables the credit analyst to review prospective and existing accounts, have upgraded and abetted operating cash flow. Additionally, the conservative use of customer credits and discounts, along with great strides in accounts receivable software packages, have helped improve the flow of collections.

Because of the growth in and ease of software programs, credit department analysts today have at their fingertips, among other Treasury department schedules, an aging schedule of the entity's accounts receivable. Although some analysts like to look at the average collection period[3] in days, the formula does not provide them with the more important collection and credit information such as (1) which clients pay their

---

[3]The average collection period is defined as 360/average accounts receivable turnover. In turn the accounts receivable turnover is defined as net sales/average accounts receivable.

bills on time and might be accorded credits, and (2) which clients have run into severe payment problems so that further delivery of goods to these clients is unjustified and that they should probably be classified as bad debt.

Computer software has made the credit manager's job much easier. With the push of a button, most credit managers can check the payment history of their clients over many years, thereby making the credit approval process much quicker, simpler, and more accurate. Credit managers still use time-honored techniques to reduce their bad debt expense and aid the accounts receivable process, that is, minimize the nominal amount of receivables outstanding. Credit service agency reports, such as Dun & Bradstreet (D&B) credit reports, are still widely used, although many credit managers feel the data in such reports are, to a great extent, outdated. D&B reports can be helpful if they show lawsuits against the company, show the company's financial statement, or show the employment and educational backgrounds of key employees.

Trade references, which also help the credit analyst gather information about potential clients, come in a variety of sources. The new-account customer application designates areas for both trade and bank referrals. Sales professionals, who visit the prospective new account's offices and facilities, are likely to spot the products of companies that can be called for references, even though these firms might not be listed on the credit application. The credit application itself usually provides useful information to the credit analyst.

Good credit analysis is vitally important to helping the enterprise's cash flow, as errors by credit department analysts can be very costly to the entity. Trade shows and reference checks of the client's competitors are also useful as are telephone leads resulting from the questioning of competitors. Analyzing financial statements for trends in operating cash flow, free cash flow, and leverage are essential to the credit analyst because cash flow trends are leading indicators of financial failure. Newspapers and magazines are also likely to bring a flow of financial information to the credit department, especially for the larger customer. Some credit managers take a careful approach to rumored takeover candidates because credit downgrades often result after a takeover.

If one observes a pattern of declining receipts from customers, it may indicate a maturing product, softening of demand, lenient credit policy toward customers, and so on. The cash flow analyst may be interested to find out the reasons for this development, and may ascertain the reasons by examining other firms in the industry, management discussion of activities (and liquidity) in the reports, or direct inquiry of the firm's management.

Similarly, if a significant increase in cash payments to employees or suppliers that is beyond the proportionate increase in cash receipts from customers is observed, the cash flow analyst should examine whether the firm experienced unfavorable business conditions. For example, the firm might have problems marketing its products and therefore be caught with an unwanted build-up of inventories. It may spend more cash on selling and general and administrative expenses than is warranted by its level of activities. Again, sometimes a firm may incur greater administrative costs in one period because it makes substantial changes in its operations (such as computerizing its operations). However, one should not observe continuous increases in cash payments to suppliers and employees beyond those called for by increases in demand.

While "involuntary" increases in the current asset accounts do occur, with advances in computer software programs for inventory control and accounts receivable/payable, such involuntary build-ups are not as frequent as was the case prior to the 1980s and can now be controlled more easily. Such software improvement is one of the reasons for the longevity of the business expansion that began in 1982. Even the recession that started at the end of the 1980s did not find most businesses with excess inventories.

Example:

In its discussion of cash flows during 1990, Ashland Oil Inc. comments on an increase in its cost of crude oil:

"However, as long as product prices move reasonably in tandem with crude oil prices, there is little impact on working capital from higher crude oil costs because the payment terms on our crude oil purchases are longer than the terms for our receivables."

This indicates the importance of examining the relationships between costs of the product and the ability of the firm to roll these costs over to the customer. Furthermore, it indicates the importance of assessing the credit terms of the firm from its suppliers and the credit terms it grants to its own customers.

In order to determine the quality of inventories, one has to measure the inventory turnover for the different products the entity sells, because almost all firms have products that are "hot" sellers and products that do not sell well. Unfortunately, this is impossible to do with published information. If the inventory turnover for an individual entity is showing a slowing trend, the analyst should ask management which product lines are contributing to the inventory build-up.

If the entity's products are not what its customers are demanding, operating and free cash flow will be affected and perhaps signal that management should be taking the appropriate measures to correct the problems. The solution may not lie with the product itself but how it is being promoted (analyze advertising expenditures compared to the industry), or its cost of manufacture, which may be too high relative to the industry.

When management decides to reduce prices of slow-moving inventory, operating cash flows increase, although profit margins and earnings are decreased as compared to what it would have otherwise been. Nevertheless, this strategy is probably superior to a strategy that lets the inventory remain on the shelves.

Inventory bulges can be expensive and there is no guarantee inventory can be sold at a profit. Cash tied up in inventory could be otherwise used to reduce interest-bearing debt or earn a money market rate of return.

Example:

Federal-Mogul, in its 1990 first quarter report to shareholders, writes:

"The (warehouse) facility has also implemented a new computer system that provides better order and inventory management, and freight consolidation. It tracks a product from the time an order is placed with a supplier, to the moment it is shipped, then received by a customer.

This new system allows us to forecast and manage inventory more accurately, and at the same time serve our customers better and save the company money.''

Not surprisingly, many advances in the production process are directly related to minimizing inventory, such as just-in-time (JIT) inventory control techniques, process mapping, reducing cycle time, and total quality management. Advances such as ''cell'' manufacturing, in which the production process divides the work force into groups, or ''cells,'' has improved both the quality of the product and the level of inventories. In cell manufacturing, raw material is ordered and inspected by the same group that is also responsible for its portion of the production process. Levels of work-in-process inventory are controlled by the continuous passage of goods from one cell to the next and by the elimination of space for storing work-in-process inventory within a cell.

Example:

Martin Marietta Corp. practices ''total quality management'' (TQM), a team approach to the productive process. The company defines TQM as follows:

1. TQM recognizes workers as experts and gives them the freedom and decision-making authority they need if they are to develop new and better ways of performing their jobs.
2. TQM advocates the goal of zero defects for every employee throughout the company.
3. TQM provides quantification, measurement, and feedback about quality to employees.
4. TQM is teamwork. Workers and managers work as a team. It has been proven time and time again that if management shares the decision-making process authority with workers, the very things managers are supposed to manage—cost, quality, and production schedules—begin to improve automatically.

Another area that has recently received a lot of attention is the cycle time in a manufacturing process. Cycle time is defined as the length of time from the receipt of a customer's order until it is shipped to the customer. Firms have a clear incentive to reduce cycle time because short delivery periods constitute a strategic advantage. Furthermore, many manufacturers' experience shows that short cycle times lead to smaller inventories, reduce inventory costs, and lead to fewer defects.

The reduction of cycle time can be caused by emphasis on quality improvement. Firms that invest in quality improvement find that improvements can occur by simplifying the design and then the production process for any specific product. It is found that setup costs and switchover costs can be substantially reduced by simpler designs of the product or by greater investment in the production process. These investments may cause a lower utilization rate of the firm's capacity, but greater quality, reduced cycle time, and greater customer satisfaction. In the long run, reductions in cycle time and increases in quality pay off handsomely.

The cash flow analyst should investigate whether the firm needs to improve the quality of its products and reduce its cycle time. Information about these items can be found in the management discussion and analysis or in press releases from the firm. The analyst may ask management if the firm intends to apply for the Baldrige National Quality Award. The analyst can also examine the turnover ratios of the firm; these should increase if the firm is able to conduct its operations with smaller inventories, fewer assets, or with more efficient credit policy.

Payment of taxes is another area that the cash flow analyst should investigate in detail. In some cases, a firm may defer its tax payments to the future. The analyst should examine the tax expense and its relationship to actual cash payments for taxes. When the two differ significantly, the analyst should investigate the reasons for these differences. Are they expected to reverse in the near future? In the distant future? What are the causes for these differences? Do they result from tax loss carryforwards? If so, what is the amount that is still available to be used in the future for both tax and financial reporting purposes? The answers to these questions should affect the projections for future cash payments to the tax authorities and financial reporting. Of course, tax loss carryforwards can be a valuable asset if the company is expected to utilize the credits in future periods.

Example:

Inter-Regional Financial Group (a broker–dealer) has been able to take advantage of tax-loss carryforwards. As shown in its 1990 annual report, IFG was able to generate $4.8 million in operating cash flow from utilizing tax-loss carryforwards.

Example:

In a meeting with analysts, Marathon Oil Co. discussed its tax outlook in detail. Among the comments made at the meeting are:

"We believe that the U.K. tax regime is politically stable. Our confidence in the U.K. tax regime is evidenced by our aggressive capital investment program. Future changes in the tax regime are generally expected to be neutral or beneficial and not detrimental."

"In Tunisia, the tax system is based on variable royalty and tax rates. The system is similar in philosophy with the PRT in that the investor is allowed to recover his investment plus a return before being burdened with tax and royalty. We expect to pay tax and royalty in 1991 for the Ezzaouia Concession on the Zarzis Permit."

"Unlike the U.K., where exploration and production incentives enacted by the government have resulted in a substantial increase in exploration and production activity in the U.K., the United States has enacted tax law changes that act as disincentives to production and exploration activity in the States. As a result, exploration and production in the States has steadily declined throughout the '80s and early '90s."

Such information is important to the cash flow analyst because it not only helps predict future tax payments, it also helps predict future capital expenditures and revenues.

Other operating cash flows should probably receive close scrutiny by the cash flow analyst who is interested in forecasting future cash flows. The analyst should investigate whether these cash flows are expected to persist in the future. For example, cash payments or receipts from settlement of legal cases may not persist in the future. Thus, the analyst might choose to exclude these from predictions of future cash flows from operating activities.

Finally, operating cash flows include payments for interest. As discussed previously, the cash flow analyst may be interested in examining the cash flows generated from operations before interest payments are subtracted. The analyst can then make necessary adjustments to different levels of debt, consider floating new debt, or assume that it will do so in the future. Focusing on the current level of interest payments or interest received may also be misleading when comparing firms within the same industry. Presumably, net operating cash flows can differ across firms because of different levels of financial leverage in firms' capital structure. Thus, it seems more reasonable to exclude interest from operating cash flows in the initial stages of the analysis and include it again when focusing on the free cash flows.

The analyst should also examine the growth rate and stability of the enterprise's operating cash flows. For companies like Food Lion and Wal-Mart, which have a high rate of growth due to rapid store expansion, one should also see a rapid rate of growth in operating cash flow, but not necessarily free cash flow, as we shall see in the next chapter.

4.6 INTERPRETING CASH FLOWS FROM FINANCING ACTIVITIES

Cash flows from financing activities should first be segregated to cash inflows and cash outflows from financing activities. The net cash flows from financing activities will be determined by the net cash generated from operating activities minus net cash used for investing activities minus the increase in cash balance. Thus, once the cash flow analyst examines the cash generated from operations and cash investments, net cash financing is of little relevance. However, the composition of net cash from financing activities is of great relevance.

The most significant source of financing for most firms is debt borrowing. The academic literature is unclear about the implications of debt financing, but it is considered favorable because interest on debt is tax deductible. However, a firm that is highly levered has a greater risk of bankruptcy and with it the expected costs of bankruptcy to shareholders. Thus, a firm should have some "optimal" level of debt; increases beyond this level are undesirable for the firm, whereas increases up to that point are favorable. The cash flow analyst may wish to consider whether the firm's increase in debt financing is favorable or not, depending on the analyst's assessments of the optimal level of debt for the firm. One way of assessing the optimal level of debt is to assess the pro-forma ability of the firm to meet scheduled debt payments from free cash flows (we provide a more detailed discussion of this point in Chapter 6).

Another implication of debt financing is that current owners/shareholders of the firm indicate they wish to retain full ownership of the firm, possibly because they perceive a high probability that the value of the firm will grow in the future. Thus, increases in debt financing, or at least increases in debt financing that are not accompanied by increases in equity financing, may be perceived as favorable signals about the future prospects of a firm. However, increases in debt financing can cause conflicts of interest between stockholders and bondholders, which, in turn, can lead management to invest in suboptimal projects. These conflicts may lead to undesirable consequences or to wasted resources that are dedicated to reduce this conflict. Thus, issuance of debt may sometimes be viewed negatively by the cash flow analyst.

Another aspect of debt financing is the composition of debt. Is it short- or long-term debt? What are the interest rates on the debt? What does the principal payment schedule look like? Traditionally, it is recommended that short-term debt be used to finance short-term assets, whereas long-term debt should be used to finance investment in long-term projects. The logic behind this recommendation can be seen by a firm that invests in a long-term project that is expected to yield 12 percent annually, and finances it with a short-term loan carrying an interest rate of 10 percent. Suppose that after three years, short-term interest rates increase to 14 percent and the firm still needs to finance its project. The project will be cash flow negative, although it could have been cash flow positive had the firm financed the project with long-term debt, even if that debt had carried interest of 10.5 percent. This is evident in banks that borrowed funds at the short-term rate and loaned these funds at the long-term rate. Such banks went into financial difficulties and had to be bailed out by the government. Thus, the analyst should assess the composition of debt and relate it to investments by the firm. In particular, the analyst should examine whether debt is being refinanced, retired, if net new debt is issued, what it is used for, and whether the firm's creditworthiness is such that it cannot borrow long-term funds at reasonable interest rates.

Turning to equity financing, the cash flow analyst should examine whether the issued equity causes the debt to equity ratio to move away or toward the optimal level. Also, the analyst should examine the type of securities issued, whether they are common stock, preferred stock, other securities, or financial instruments, and their potential conversion to common stock. Some theories in finance posit that issuance of equity provides a positive signal about future prospects of a firm, because a greater proportion of the firm will be owned by owners rather than creditors. However, a contrary view is that current owners of a firm will invite others to invest in their firm only if they expect future prospects to be worse, and, in effect, invite others to share the burden.

A symmetric argument can be made for repurchases of a firm's common stock. It can be argued that the firm probably has no better investment opportunities, and, therefore, decides to invest in "identical" risk–return tradeoff—its own securities. However, a diametric argument is that management possesses inside information that future prospects are very favorable and the stock market does not share these expectations; management decides to repurchase stocks at these low prices.

Finally, the payment of a cash dividend is considered an important signalling mechanism by most; management will signal its expectations about the future by increases or decreases of cash dividends. When cash dividends are increased, management signals that it expects future cash flows to be favorable, so that a higher level of dividends can be sustained. When a firm reduces its cash dividend, the market interprets it as a negative signal about future cash flows, which are expected to decrease or remain low, and will be insufficient to sustain the current level of cash dividends.

It may be useful to examine the stability of operating cash flows that generally relates to the level of cash dividends. Firms that are consistent operating-cash-flow generators, such as Philip Morris, the tobacco and food company, and regulated companies, such as public utilities, usually have a higher payout ratio than firms with large swings in operating cash flows. Cyclical companies usually pay lower cash dividends, since they can maintain a lower level of cash dividend payments from their operations. For example, Boeing Co. experienced large swings in its cash from operations whereas Pfizer Inc. has realized consistent operating cash flows. Pfizer pays out about 40–50 percent of its operating cash flows in dividends to shareholders, whereas Boeing has a rate of 10–20 percent. Thus, stability of operating cash flows is an important factor for the cash flow and credit analyst.

4.7 INTERPRETING CASH FLOWS ON INVESTING ACTIVITIES

As we saw earlier, most firms disclose in this section cash outlays on capital expenditures, acquisitions, investments in financial instruments, investments in unconsolidated subsidiaries, and purchases of additional shares from minority shareholders. Clearly, each of these investing activities has an opposite counterpart of a disinvesting activity; for example, the sale of investments.

The cash flow analyst should investigate the capital expenditures of a firm and the retirement of PPE during the accounting period. Capital expenditures should be sufficient to at least sustain the current levels of operations. They can be compared to past capital expenditures, levels of investments by competitors, improvements in technology, current levels of PPE, and the firm's unit growth rates. A significant increase in sale of PPE might indicate that the firm is suffering from cash shortage and should generate cash by selling fixed assets. This strategy means that the firm is reducing the scale of operations or that it is gradually liquidating. The cash flow analyst should carefully examine these events because of the implications for future cash flows.

The firm has two major options in its future expansion—to expand internally through further investments in capital expenditures or to invest in existing operations of other firms through acquisitions. Most studies to date show that, on the average, it is detrimental for a firm to expand through acquisition of other firms; most such acquisitions do not work as originally intended. Thus, the cash flow analyst might want to assess the chances of success for the firm's acquisitions and the related costs of these acquisitions in terms of additional debt that is assumed or issued. The analyst should also assess the potential synergies that can be created from the acquisitions. These could have favorable effects on future cash flows by eliminating redundant operations.

Finally, the cash flow analyst should examine additional investments in unconsolidated subsidiaries, that is, those subsidiaries in which the firm has less than 50 percent of the stock, investments in joint ventures, and investments in other financial instruments. These investments should be carefully assessed in terms of their potential future cash flow consequences. Usually, investments in other entities, where the investing firm does not control the investee, are considered less desirable than investments in entities where a firm has full control. Similarly, the cash flow analyst should examine the reasons for investments in financial instruments: are these made to "park" cash that will be needed in the near future for investments or are these investments made because the firm has no superior investment opportunities?

Sometimes the distinction between investing or operating cash flows is not clear-cut. For example, a cash payment might pertain to an item that could be considered either inventory or a productive asset. If so, the appropriate classification shall depend on the activity that is likely to be the predominant source of cash flows for the item. For example, the acquisition and sale of equipment to be used by the enterprise or rented to others is generally considered to be an investing activity. However, equipment sometimes is acquired or produced to be used by the enterprise or rented to others for a short time period and then sold. In these circumstances, the acquisition or production and subsequent sale of those assets can be considered an operating activity.

Needless to say, this ambiguity in reporting requirements leads to different interpretations. Some leasing companies include the collections of principal on their capital leases as cash flows from operating activities on the grounds that the equipment leased is, in fact, inventory. Other leasing entities include such payments in investing activities on the grounds that the leases represent investments in the traditional sense. Thus, the cash flow analyst needs to examine the accounting treatment of capital leases and their classification as investing or operating cash flows.

Similarly, the analyst should examine the implications of disinvesting events as carefully as investing events. Also, the cash flow analyst should note that the current requirements of FAS No. 95 are that only the cash portion of these events is disclosed in the statement of cash flows. In most cases, it is reasonable to focus not only on the cash portion of the transaction but on the noncash portion because of its future consequences. For example, the sale of a division for cash, notes receivable, and stocks is likely to yield future cash inflows. These inflows should be incorporated by the cash flow analyst as well as the current inflow of cash from the sale of the division, which is reported in the statement of cash flows. Such information is usually disclosed as supplemental information to the statement. This leads us to a discussion of the supplemental information to the statement of cash flows.

4.8 SUPPLEMENTAL INFORMATION

FAS No. 95 requires firms to disclose additional information about their important economic events during the period beyond the direct cash flow implications of these events. For example, when a firm engages in a transaction that is, in effect, a financing or an investing event, but the entire consideration is not cash, the firm should report the transaction in a separate schedule, usually at the bottom of the statement of cash flows. The reason for this supplemental disclosure is that most financing and investing events are significant economic events—they affect the long-run viability of the firm and should be disclosed to investors and creditors regardless of whether they are cash alone or a combination of cash and other consideration.

The FASB also required firms that report net operating cash flows using the indirect approach to report the tax payments and the interest payments during the period. Let us examine several disclosures of these items.

Example:

In its 1989 annual report, Ingersoll Rand reports the following items:

Noncash activity:	
Notes receivable from asset disposals	$ 2,325
Cash paid during the year for:	
Interest, net of amount capitalized	37,150
Income taxes	102,944

Ingersoll Rand reports proceeds from sales of property, plant, and equipment of $8,194 in its cash flows from investing activities. However, part of the consideration received for these asset disposals was in the form of a note, so the firm reported an additional noncash consideration for disposal of assets in the amount of $2,325.

The firm also provides information about payments for interest and taxes during the period, although these are included as part of the net operating cash flows. However, this information is required to be disclosed separately by FAS No. 95.

Example:

Hercules Inc. reports the following items at the bottom of its 1989 statement of cash flows:

Supplemental disclosure of cash flow information:	
Cash paid during the year for:	
Interest (net of amount capitalized)	$40,659
Income taxes	59,332
Noncash investing and financing activities:	
Conversion of notes and debentures	17,494
Common stock issued for purchase acquisitions	613
Contribution of net assets to joint ventures	—

As before, Hercules reports its payments for interest and taxes. It also reports additional items about events that did not affect cash, the first of which is the conversion of notes and debentures into other items that did not involve cash. Also, the firm reports that it issued common stock to acquire other firms, so the acquisitions were not affected through cash payments alone. The last item, although not applicable in 1989 (but a large amount in 1987), represents an investment in a joint venture that is effected through transfer of noncash items into a joint venture with another entity. Because it is done without using any cash, the firm reports it in the supplemental schedule as an investment event that did not require cash.

Example:

ADC Telecommunications Inc. reports in its 1989 statement of cash flows the following item:

Supplemental disclosure:	
Long-term debt assumed in acquisition of Kentrox	$2,200

Since a portion of ADC's consideration for the acquisition was in the form of assumption of debt, and not cash, a supplemental disclosure is required.

4.9 FINANCIAL SUBSIDIARIES

The free cash flow analyst must take into account the cash flow implications of financial subsidiaries, and, in particular, finance subsidiaries of a firm. Finance subsidiaries are large cash borrowers when the parent entity is in the growth stage and large cash providers when the parent firm is in the mature stage of growth or during economic downturns. Bad debts of finance subsidiaries can prove to be a terrible bane for the parent if the parent is holding the paper itself instead of selling it without recourse.

Example:

Inter-Regional Financial Corp., the parent company of two regional brokerage firms, saw its stock price tumble from $27.125 to $12.5 the year its leasing division ran into trouble.

For entities with finance divisions, it is necessary to analyze the leasing component separately from the operating company. The leasing entity represents a separate and distinct asset with separate and distinct operating and free cash flow characteristics. The leasing affiliate is dependent, to a large extent, on the financial health of the parent for its own success, including the parent's ability to meet its fixed income obligations. When analyzing the operating cash flows of an entity with a finance and insurance subsidiary, such as Unisys Corp., it is appropriate to adjust for the cash transfers into and out of the financial subsidiaries.

Example:

Trinity Industries, Inc. is a large manufacturer of heavy metal products such as railcars, marine products, and containers. It also has a leasing subsidiary.

In its statement of cash flows, Trinity separates its depreciation expense and capital spending for its leasing operation. It is imperative to review and analyze the statement of cash flows for Trinity's leasing operation for which it files separate 10-K and 10Qs. The investment activities sections for Trinity and its leasing division are closely intertwined. For example, Trinity has entered into an agreement (the "Fixed Charges Coverage Agreement") with the leasing subsidiary whereby Trinity is obligated to make such payments to the subsidiary as may be required to maintain the registrant's net earnings available for fixed charges (as defined) at amounts equal to, and not less than, one and one-half times the fixed charges (as defined) of the subsidiary. The Fixed Charges Coverage Agreement will terminate in accordance with its terms at such time as (1) all amounts payable by the subsidiary under the 10 5/8 percent Equipment Trust Certificates due January 31, 1995, have been paid in full and (2) the subsidiary shall have delivered a certificate of its certified public accountants demonstrating that net earnings available for fixed charges, without considering any payments by Trinity, have not been less than one and one-half times fixed charges in each of the five most recently completed fiscal years, provided that the subsidiary and Trinity agree in connection with "Future Financing Agreements" to maintain the Fixed Charges Coverage Agreement in force and effect during the term of such "Future Financing Agreements."

Source: March 31, 1990 10-K, Trinity Industries Leasing Company.

Trinity Industries: Consolidated Statement of Cash Flows

CONSOLIDATED STATEMENT OF CASH FLOWS

(in millions)

	Year Ended March 31		
	1990	1989	1988
Cash flows from operating activities:			
Net income...	**$38.2**	$30.3	$13.0
Adjustments to reconcile net income to net cash provided by operating activities: Depreciation:			
Excluding Leasing Subsidiaries	**21.6**	17.8	15.3
Leasing Subsidiaries..	**12.4**	13.1	13.9
Deferred provision for income taxes..	**15.0**	14.9	6.7
(Gain) loss on sale of property, plant and equipment	**(1.9)**	0.4	(0.9)
Accretion of discount on long-term debt	**6.2**	6.1	6.2
Payment of prepayment premium..	**–**	–	(2.2)
Other...	**1.4**	(0.6)	–
Change in assets and liabilities:			
Increase in receivables...	**(17.1)**	(30.1)	(16.8)
(Increase) decrease in inventories..	**37.4**	(68.5)	(36.7)
(Increase) decrease in other assets......................................	**(1.9)**	0.6	0.2
Increase (decrease) in accounts payable and accrued expenses...	**(7.6)**	10.8	(3.4)
Increase (decrease) in other liabilities....................................	**(9.7)**	16.7	8.6
Total adjustments	**55.8**	(18.8)	(9.1)
Net cash provided by operating activities...................................	**94.0**	11.5	3.9
Cash flows from investing activities:			
Proceeds from sale of property, plant and equipment..........................	**4.8**	9.0	14.9
Capital expenditures:			
Excluding Leasing Subsidiaries	**(28.1)**	(21.9)	(10.3)
Leasing Subsidiaries..	**(10.0)**	(18.0)	(41.9)
Payment for purchase of acquisitions, net of cash acquired...	**(16.8)**	(36.0)	(5.5)
Net cash required by investing activities	**(50.1)**	(66.9)	(42.8)
Cash flows from financing activities:			
Issuance of common stock	**2.0**	1.8	1.7
Net borrowings under short-term debt	**(2.5)**	17.0	15.0
Proceeds from issuance of long-term debt..	**0.2**	62.7	95.6
Payments to retire long-term debt	**(30.8)**	(18.4)	(78.9)
Dividends paid	**(11.8)**	(8.9)	(8.6)
Net cash (required) provided by financing activities..........................	**(42.9)**	54.2	24.8
Net increase (decrease) in cash and cash equivalents.............................	**1.0**	(1.2)	(14.1)
Cash and cash equivalents at beginning of period................................	**6.4**	7.6	21.7
Cash and cash equivalents at end of period.......................................	**$ 7.4**	$ 6.4	$ 7.6

Excluding Leasing Subsidiaries, interest paid in fiscal 1990, 1989, and 1988 was $11.4, $7.6, and $5.1, respectively. Leasing Subsidiaries' interest paid in fiscal 1990, 1989, and 1988 was $25.6, $22.0, and $20.8, respectively.

SOURCE: Trinity Industries, *Annual Report*, 1990.

Trinity Industries Leasing Company Statement of Cash Flows (in millions)

	Year Ended March 31		
	1990	1989	1988
Cash flows from operating activities:			
Net income	$ 10.6	$ 10.6	$ 9.4
Adjustments to reconcile net income			
to net cash provided by operating activities:			
Depreciation	13.7	13.3	12.7
Deferred provision for federal income tax	3.0	5.5	5.5
(Gain) loss on retirement of equipment	(0.4)	0.4	—
Payment of prepayment premium	—	—	(2.2)
Other	0.1	0.2	0.2
Changes in assets and liabilities:			
(Increase) decrease in other assets	1.3	(0.5)	2.3
Decrease in accounts payable and			
accrued liabilities	(0.6)	(0.1)	(3.1)
Increase in other liabilities	1.0	2.3	1.6
Total adjustments	18.1	21.1	17.0
Net cash provided by operating activities	28.7	31.7	26.4
Cash flows from investing activities:			
Proceeds from retirement of equipment	3.3	8.7	12.5
Capital expenditures	(10.0)	(18.0)	(41.9)
Net cash required by investing activities	(6.7)	(9.3)	(29.4)
Cash flows from financing activities:			
Increase in notes receivable from Trinity	(8.5)	(74.0)	(33.4)
Proceeds from issuance of long-term debt	—	61.6	95.6
Payments to retire long-term debt	(13.0)	(9.6)	(68.5)
Decrease in long-term obligation under capital lease	(0.5)	(0.4)	(0.5)
Transfer from Trinity of deferred tax liability	—	—	3.8
Net cash required by financing activities	(22.0)	(22.4)	(3.0)

SOURCE: Trinity Industries Leasing Co., *Annual Report*, 1989.

4.10 OTHER EXAMPLES AND DISCLOSURE REQUIREMENTS

The statement of cash flows for Sunshine Mining Company, a natural resource holding company for silver and gold, is quite interesting on several counts. To begin, Sunshine pays interest on its "Silver Indexed Bonds" and contributions to employees' retirement plans with stock in the company, an operating expense. Sunshine is also an active participant in the futures markets, taking both hedging and speculative positions. Option premiums and gains or losses related to these contracts are included in revenues (operating activities). Proceeds on its hedged positions are shown under investing activities. Gains on unhedged positions are included as part of "other—net" under operating activities.

FASB statement 104 permitted hedged transactions to be classified in the same category as the cash flows being hedged, provided that the accounting policy is disclosed, as is the case with Sunshine in its notes to the 10-K. However, it is impossible, based solely on a review of Sunshine's investment activity section in its statement of cash flows, to determine the profitability of the forward contracts, because the investment activities include only closed-out positions. Profitability is listed in the footnote to the 10-K. Except for 1987, speculative trading has been unrewarding.

Under Sunshine's operating activities, an "extraordinary gain on settlement of pension obligations" is debited because the cash was actually received a year earlier, in 1986, but a book gain was not recorded until a year later. The company deferred recognition of the gain until it could determine whether any significant future benefits were due to its employees other than what was known and accounted for. This information is found in Sunshine's Form 10-K for 1989.

The Charles Schwab Corporation, a large brokerage firm, splits its operating activities into two major areas. It differentiates between operating cash flows and operating cash flows that result from changes in customer-related balances. This simplifies the analytical process because a brokerage firm can easily create operating cash flows through the short-term investments account. Furthermore, transactions taken specifically for customers can obscure the firm's own transactions.

Ethyl Corporation breaks down its cash flows from various activities in its major operating segments—chemicals and insurance. Entities can be as creative in their reporting as they would like. The type of reporting in which the statement of cash flows is broken down by various operating groups is extremely helpful to the cash flow analyst.

In fact, the most helpful cash flow statement for the typical public corporation would not be by major categories of business as Ethyl does, but by business segments that the parent entity controls. Because most large public entities and every major company included in the S&P Industrials operate in more than one line of business, investment decisions can be improved if the cash flow analyst has access to that closely held data.

Sunshine Mining: Notes to Consolidated Financial Statements Showing Unhedged Position

---

SUNSHINE MINING COMPANY

NOTES TO CONSOLIDATED FINANCIAL STATEMENTS

The Company periodically enters into forward and option contracts to hedge its exposure to price fluctuations on oil and precious metals transactions. At December 31, 1989, the Company had entered into contracts designated as hedges which included forward sales contracts covering 750,000 ounces of silver at prices ranging from $5.50 to $6.45 per ounce. The Company also had forward sales contracts covering 100,000 barrels of oil at prices ranging from $20.50 to $21.41 per barrel, and sold call option contracts covering 550,000 barrels of oil at prices ranging from $19.40 to $21.00 per barrel. Option premiums, and gains and losses related to changes in values of these contracts, which are deferred and included in revenues when the related products are sold, increased revenues by approximately $2.0 million in 1989 and $563,000 in 1988.

SOURCE: Sunshine Mining Company, *Annual Report*, 1989.

Sunshine Mining Company: Consolidated Statements of Cash Flows

SUNSHINE MINING COMPANY

CONSOLIDATED STATEMENTS OF CASH FLOWS
For the Years Ended December 31, 1989, 1988 and 1987
(In Thousands)

	1989	1988	1987
Cash provided (used) by operations:			
Net loss	$(38,345)	$(54,017)	$(51,771)
Adjustments to reconcile net loss to net cash provided (used) by operations:			
Depreciation, depletion, amortization and impairment provisions	37,134	38,166	46,446
Amortization of discount on Silver Indexed Bonds	1,916	1,617	1,365
Extraordinary loss on extinguishment of debt	—	—	3,393
Extraordinary gain on settlement of pension obligations	—	—	(4,007)
Gain on the sale of fixed assets	(828)	—	—
Common stock issuances for:			
Interest on Silver Indexed Bonds	—	6,183	6,180
Services provided and other	791	616	2,089
Net (increase) decrease in:			
Accounts receivable	(1,800)	9,494	3,430
Inventories	2,374	(2,445)	1,290
Other current assets	1,341	(5,301)	(814)
Other assets and deferred charges	(657)	(556)	(3,864)
Net increase (decrease) in:			
Accounts payable — trade	578	(15,686)	2,373
Oil and gas proceeds payable	1,947	(793)	(1,462)
Accrued expenses	(3,435)	2,755	(4,865)
Other liabilities and deferred credits	(784)	(425)	(5,945)
Other, net	(10)	(2,098)	(5,646)
Net cash provided (used) by operations	222	(22,490)	(11,808)
Cash provided (used) by investing activities:			
Additions to property, plant and equipment	(17,308)	(17,170)	(8,894)
Proceeds from the disposal of property, plant and equipment	3,460	5,430	8,912
Purchases of futures, forward and option contracts	(19,221)	(8,786)	(12,851)
Sales of futures, forward and option contracts	19,534	9,656	18,834
Investment in PT Corporation	3,290	(3,400)	—
Other, principally investments	(8,188)	527	(2,758)
Net cash provided (used) by investing activities	(18,433)	(13,743)	3,243
Cash provided (used) by financing activities:			
Issuance of long-term debt	—	153,583	122,549
Principal repayments and retirements of long-term debt	(4,598)	(86,295)	(183,625)
Issuance of common stock	—	355	89,921
Exercise of warrants and stock options	—	339	2,959
Net cash provided (used) by financing activities	(4,598)	67,982	31,804
Increase (decrease) in cash and cash investments	(22,809)	31,749	23,239
Cash and cash investments, January 1	82,839	51,090	27,851
Cash and cash investments, December 31	$ 60,030	$ 82,839	$ 51,090
Supplemental cash flow information — interest paid in cash	$ 21,814	$ 13,798	$ 13,318

SOURCE: Sunshine Mining Company, *Annual Report*, 1989.

Charles Schwab Corporation: Consolidated Statement of Cash Flows

THE CHARLES SCHWAB CORPORATION
Consolidated Statement of Cash Flows
(IN THOUSANDS)

	Year Ended December 31, 1989	Year Ended December 31, 1988	Nine Months Ended December 31, 1987	Three Months Ended March 31, 1987
				(Predecessor)
Cash flows from operating activities				
Net income	$ 18,919	$ 7,390	$ 8,235	$ 17,445
Noncash items included in net income:				
Depreciation and amortization	52,535	43,775	34,844	3,429
Debentures issued in lieu of interest	2,845	5,381	2,502	
Deferred income taxes	1,369	1,601	(5,271)	8,137
Other	260	427	(1,358)	398
Change in accounts payable and accrued expenses	11,002	(22,211)	10,022	(4,610)
Increase in other assets	(901)	(3,647)	(7,786)	(8,000)
Cash provided before change in customer-related balances	86,029	32,716	41,188	16,799
Change in customer-related balances (excluding the effects of the 1989 acquisition of Rose & Company Investment Brokers, Inc.):				
Payable to customers	750,610	635,867	53,472	208,331
Receivable from customers	(134,076)	35,754	101,511	(82,482)
Drafts payable	(514)	6,048	(17,677)	(68,722)
Payable to brokers and dealers	24,211	(46,629)	(11,861)	59,636
Receivable from brokers and dealers	5,454	2,772	2,555	3,386
Short-term investments required to be segregated under Federal or other regulations	(648,611)	(632,844)	(127,944)	(125,578)
Net change in customer-related balances	(2,926)	968	56	(5,429)
Cash provided by operating activities	83,103	33,684	41,244	11,370
Cash flows from investing activities				
Cash payments for businesses acquired, net of cash received	(23,305)		(92,516)	
Purchase of office facilities and equipment	(11,048)	(8,141)	(17,151)	(4,552)
Proceeds from sale of equipment	818	663	8,578	559
Collection on note receivable from Profit Sharing Plan	494	1,729		
Cash used by investing activities	(33,041)	(5,749)	(101,089)	(3,993)
Cash flows from financing activities				
Long-term borrowings			150,000	
Repayment of long-term borrowings	(6,365)	(69,756)	(96,610)	(1,191)
Proceeds from issuance of redeemable preferred stock			6,000	
Preferred stock redeemed			(6,000)	
Payment for surrendered contingent payment rights	(14,505)	(14,451)		
Repurchase of stock appreciation rights	(3,150)			
Dividends paid	(2,287)			
Purchase of treasury stock	(1,829)	(156)		
Net proceeds from sale of common stock	238	298	144,013	
Other			(306)	(2,830)
Cash provided (used) by financing activities	(27,898)	(84,065)	197,097	(4,021)
Increase (decrease) in cash and equivalents	22,164	(56,130)	137,252	3,356
Cash and equivalents at beginning of period	81,262	137,392	140	79,128
Cash and equivalents at end of period	$103,426	$ 81,262	$137,392	$ 82,484

SOURCE: Charles Schwab Corporation, *Annual Report*, 1989.

Ethyl Corp.: Consolidated Statement of Cash Flows

CONSOLIDATED

STATEMENTS OF CASH FLOWS Ethyl Corporation & Subsidiaries

(In Thousands of Dollars)

Years ended December 31	1991	1990	1989
Cash and cash equivalents at beginning of year	**$ 38,998**	$ 79,835	$112,084
Cash flows from operating activities:			
Chemicals and Corporate:			
Income from continuing operations	**206,668**	232,189	219,468
Adjustments to reconcile to cash flows from operating activities:			
Undistributed earnings of Insurance segment	**(99,199)**	(70,208)	(61,519)
Depreciation and amortization	**89,879**	88,522	81,683
Special charges	**11,185**	48,710	—
Gain on sale of subsidiary	**—**	(78,993)	—
Deferred income taxes	**6,469**	5,644	11,692
Change in assets and liabilities, net of effects from acquisitions and sale of subsidiary:			
(Increase) in accounts receivable	**(4,390)**	(8,626)	(11,286)
(Increase) decrease in inventories	**(31,619)**	(37,142)	5,045
Increase (decrease) in accounts payable and accrued expenses	**20,083**	5,012	(20,599)
(Decrease) increase in income taxes payable	**(32,485)**	24,601	(3,010)
Other, net	**(20,206)**	(21,609)	(14,275)
Total Chemicals and Corporate	**146,385**	188,100	207,199
Total Insurance (see Note 18 on page 41)	**181,025**	278,989	328,751
Net cash provided from continuing operating activities	**327,410**	467,089	535,950
Income from discontinued operations	**—**	—	11,864
Net cash provided from total operating activities	**327,410**	467,089	547,814
Cash flows from investing activities:			
Chemicals and Corporate:			
Capital expenditures	**(166,148)**	(151,822)	(119,082)
Acquisitions of businesses (net of $993 cash acquired in 1989)	**(24,035)**	(61,575)	(33,563)
Proceeds from sale of subsidiary	**—**	108,003	—
Other, net	**(17,350)**	(5,614)	3,850
Total Chemicals and Corporate	**(207,533)**	(111,008)	(148,795)
Total Insurance (principally changes in investments, net) (see Note 18 on page 41)	**(760,901)**	(752,057)	(556,919)
Net cash (used in) investing activities of continuing operations	**(968,434)**	(863,065)	(705,714)
(Increase) in net assets of discontinued operations	**—**	—	(6,429)
Net cash (used in) total investing activities	**(968,434)**	(863,065)	(712,143)
Cash flows from financing activities:			
Chemicals and Corporate:			
Additional long-term debt	**138,400**	291,250	42,000
Repayments of long-term debt	**(2,260)**	(108,500)	(152,822)
Regular dividends paid	**(71,008)**	(71,670)	(57,746)
Special dividend paid	**—**	(179,108)	—
Repurchases of capital stock	**(1,838)**	(31,836)	(45,660)
Dividend received from Tredegar Industries, Inc.	**—**	—	100,000
Other, net	**1,253**	233	2,441
Total Chemicals and Corporate	**64,547**	(99,631)	(111,787)
Total Insurance (principally net increase in investment and universal life contract liabilities) (see Note 18 on page 41)	**578,854**	454,770	243,867
Net cash provided from total financing activities	**643,401**	355,139	132,080
Increase (decrease) in cash and cash equivalents:			
Chemicals and Corporate	**3,399**	(22,539)	(47,948)
Insurance (see Note 18 on page 41)	**(1,022)**	(18,298)	15,699
	2,377	(40,837)	(32,249)
Cash and cash equivalents at end of year	**$ 41,375**	$ 38,998	$ 79,835

SOURCE: Ethyl Corp., *Annual Report*, 1991.

Since entities already compile cash flow statements as part of a full set of financial statements on the individual companies they own and control, the added cost of releasing such information to the public would be small. Of even greater help would be the release of the entity's budgets for all its affiliated companies. Through such information, the analyst could prepare and evaluate a free cash flow prediction in a much more detailed manner, including which affiliates and business segments are truly free cash flow generators, which are cash users, and which are not meeting expectations. Through the release of the budgets, the cash flow analyst can have a clearer understanding of where management is placing its priorities and the cash effects a divestiture of a company or segment would have on the cash needs of the remaining entity. It might be expected that merger and acquisition activity as well as reorganizations would step up dramatically if such information was in the public domain. Investors would force management of an entity with poor cash-generating divisions to divest such underachievers if the entity as a whole is a high producer of operating and free cash flow.

Example:

Utility firms provide to investors and the public information not only about the most recent years, but also forecasts for the next five years. This information can be used by the cash flow analyst to predict future financial results and is useful in a firm's valuation. We include here the information made public by Minnesota Power.

Minnesota Power—Core Utility Operations: Sales, Sources and Financial Requirements

Minnesota Power – Core Utility Operations
Sales, Sources and Financial Requirements

	Actual	Forecast				
	1990	1991	1992	1993	1994	1995
Electric Sales and Capability						
Electric Sales – Million kWh						
Retail	8,173	8,195	8,031	8,298	8,083	7,886
Resale	1,043	968	878	985	877	942
Industrial Economy	1,160	637	565	415	415	415
Electric Generating Capability – MW	1,461	1,473	1,473	1,473	1,473	1,473
Net Participation Purchases – MW	107	78	40	40	40	40
System Peak Demand – MW	1,248	1,265	1,295	1,334	1,308	1,283
Net Firm Capacity Sales – MW	10	150	155	0	0	0
Reserve Margin	24.6%	9.6%	4.3%	13.4%	15.7%	17.9%
Load Factor	85%	83%	80%	80%	80%	79%
Electric Generation Sources						
Steam (Coal)	58%	54%	57%	61%	59%	62%
Hydro	5%	5%	6%	6%	6%	6%
Purchases						
Square Butte (Lignite)	20%	19%	22%	20%	23%	21%
Other	17%	22%	15%	13%	12%	11%
Capital Expenditures – Millions						
Minnesota Power	$41	$40	$44	$54	$46	$44
SWL&P	2	3	2	1	2	2
Rainy River Energy	24	4	0	0	0	0
Total Capital Expenditures	$67	$47	$46	$55	$48	$46

SOURCE: Minnesota Power, *Annual Report*, 1990.

Minnesota Power—Consolidated: Financial Forecast

Minnesota Power – Consolidated
Financial Forecast
(Dollars in Millions)

	Actual	Forecast				
	1990	**1991**	**1992**	**1993**	**1994**	**1995**
Capital Requirements						
Capital Expenditures						
Core Utility	67	47	46	55	48	46
Core Support	1	2	15	62	57	57
Water Resources	27	45	31	25	19	19
Total Capital Expenditures	95	94	92	142	124	122
Maturities and Sinking Funds	18	8	21	9	76	12
Total Capital Requirements	113	102	113	151	200	134
Sources of Capital						
Internal Cash Flow						
Depreciation	36	37	41	45	53	58
Deferred Taxes and Deferred ITC	(9)	0	0	7	7	9
Plant and Subsidiary Sales	75	0	0	0	0	0
AFDC	(1)	(1)	(1)	(1)	(1)	(1)
Other	16	23	18	7	10	10
Total Internal Sources	117	59	58	58	69	76
Percent of Capital Expenditures	123%	63%	63%	41%	56%	62%
External Sources						
Short-Term Debt	32	8	(29)	0	0	0
Long-Term Debt	19	47	46	43	102	34
Preferred Stock	0	0	0	0	0	0
Common Stock	0	(73)	3	4	4	4
Total External Sources	51	(18)	20	47	106	38
Total Sources of Capital	168	41	78	105	175	114
Cash For (From) Investments and Other	55	(61)	(35)	(46)	(25)	(20)

SOURCE: Minnesota Power, *Annual Report*, 1990.

CPI Corp. begins its cash flow statement with a single-line entry of its operating activities and then immediately goes into financing and investment activities. With net income and depreciation such an important part of CPI's cash flow, it is surprising it has relegated the operating activities to the bottom of the statement.

CPI's 1989 statement of cash flows is also interesting because it shows net additions to property and equipment of $21,109,188 in 1989 and $19,271,091 in 1988. In the management discussion and analysis section, these expenditures are broken down by lines of business, but the amounts are $25,616,000 and $29,736,000, respectively. Examination of the relevant schedules in Form 10-K, V and IV, show that additions were $25,615,968 and $29,736,454 for 1989 and 1988, respectively. However, retirements were $11,159,031 in 1989 and $10,393,852 in 1988. The net additions to PPE in 1989, that is, additions minus retirements, comes to about $21,325,000 (additions of $25,616,000 minus net book value of assets retired that had original cost of $11,159,000 and accumulated depreciation of $6,868,000 from Schedule VI). This is very close to the amount reported in the statement of cash flows, indicating that cash proceeds were close to net book value of assets retired. In 1988, the net additions are equal to about $25,502,000 (additions of $29,736,000 minus net book value of $10,394,000 less $6,160,000). From the cash flows from investing activities section we see net additions to PPE of only $19,271,091 for 1988. However, under acquisitions for 1988 we find that PPE of businesses purchased during 1988 was about $6,231,655. Thus, it is likely that CPI included the PPE of businesses acquired in its capital expenditures (and additions to PPE in Schedule V). This shows that the cash flow analyst should attempt to reconcile amounts in the statement of cash flows with amounts and other information that are available in footnotes, other disclosures in the financial statements, and disclosures in the management discussion and analysis section.

Changes in the value of a foreign currency do not, by themselves, produce operating or free cash flows as they do not produce cash until converted to U.S. dollars. This belief is reflected in the statement of cash flows for most entities, where the effects of changes in currency exchange rates are segregated into one line item, which is typically shown immediately before the change in cash balance.

CPI Corp.: Schedule V, Consolidated Property and Equipment

CPI CORP.

CONSOLIDATED PROPERTY AND EQUIPMENT

Fiscal Years Ended February 3, 1990, February 4, 1989 and February 6, 1988

	Balance at Beginning of Year	Additions Charged to Costs and Expenses	Retirements	Balance at End of Year
52 Weeks Ended February 3, 1990:				
Land	$ 1,456,366	$ 6,923	$ 21,912	$ 1,441,377
Building and improvements	30,190,542	8,122,947	3,832,661	34,480,828
Machinery and equipment	80,920,780	11,596,336	4,951,270	87,565,846
Furniture and Fixtures	20,804,091	5,889,762	2,353,188	24,340,665
	$133,371,779	$ 25,615,968	$ 11,159,031	$ 147,828,716
52 Weeks Ended February 4, 1989:				
Land	$ 630,681	$ 840,535	$ 14,850	$ 1,456,366
Building and improvements ...	27,270,896	4,302,969	1,383,323	30,190,542
Machinery and equipment	69,541,673	19,610,391	8,231,284	80,920,780
Furniture and fixtures	16,585,927	4,982,559	764,395	20,804,091
	$114,029,177	$ 29,736,454	$ 10,393,852	$ 133,371,779
52 Weeks Ended February 6, 1988:				
Land	$ 630,681	$ -	$ -	$ 630,681
Building and improvements ...	23,544,778	4,436,182	710,064	27,270,896
Machinery and equipment	63,109,634	10,765,860	4,333,821	69,541,673
Furniture and fixtures	13,753,047	3,289,707	456,827	16,585,927
	$101,038,140	$ 18,491,749	$ 5,500,712	$ 114,029,177

SOURCE: CPI Corp., *Form 10-K*, 1989.

CPI Corp.: Schedule IV, Consolidated Accumulated Depreciation of Property and Equipment

CPI CORP.

CONSOLIDATED ACCUMULATED DEPRECIATION OF PROPERTY AND EQUIPMENT

Fiscal Years Ended February 3, 1990 February 4, 1989 and February 6, 1988

	Balance at Beginning of Year	Additions Charged to Costs and Expenses	Retirements	Balance at End of Year
52 Weeks Ended February 3, 1990:				
Building and improvements	$ 13,394,096	$ 3,144,437	$ 2,337,961	$ 14,200,572
Machinery and equipment	32,312,212	11,244,063	3,235,579	40,320,696
Furniture and Fixtures	9,662,873	3,511,588	1,294,771	11,879,690
	$ 55,369,181	$ 17,900,088	$ 6,868,311	$ 66,400,958
52 Weeks Ended February 4, 1989:				
Building and improvements ...	$ 10,995,899	$ 3,179,499	$ 781,302	$ 13,394,096
Machinery and equipment	27,097,655	10,074,016	4,859,459	32,312,212
Furniture and fixtures	7,154,835	3,027,421	519,383	9,662,873
	$ 45,248,389	$ 16,280,936	$ 6,160,144	$ 55,369,181
52 Weeks Ended February 6, 1988:				
Building and improvements ...	$ 8,204,766	$ 3,002,094	$ 210,961	$ 10,995,899
Machinery and equipment	19,959,205	9,029,164	1,890,714	27,097,655
Furniture and fixtures	4,870,228	2,615,326	330,719	7,154,835
	$ 33,034,199	$ 14,646,584	$ 2,432,394	$ 45,248,389

SOURCE: CPI Corp., *Form 10-K*, 1989.

Most investors believe the value of a foreign investment is enhanced if it is situated in a relatively stable country with a stable currency, but this is a matter of business decision and asset valuation, not cash flow analysis. Therefore, although the statement of cash flow calls for a separate line entry for the effect of exchange rate changes on cash, the effects are in no way cash flows in U.S. dollars. In fact, prior to FAS No. 95, many companies did not obtain cash flow information from their subsidiaries, but rather prepared a separate statement of changes in financial condition from the subsidiaries' balance sheets and income statements.

The new standards call for the financial statement to reflect the reporting currency equivalent of cash receipts and payments that occur in a foreign currency. Because the change in exchange rate affects the change in an enterprise's cash balance during a period, but is not a cash receipt of payment, the FASB decided that the effect of exchange rate changes on cash should be reported as a separate item on the reconciliation of beginning and ending changes of cash. Under the statement, the company must use the exchange rates in effect at the time of the cash flows to translate the foreign cash flows on the subsidiaries' statement of cash flows. A weighted-average exchange rate for the period may be used for translation if the result is essentially the same as if the exchange rates at the dates of the cash flows were used. However, after translating the foreign cash flows from operating, investing, and financing activities using the (weighted-average)

CPI Corp.: Consolidated Statement of Cash Flows

C P I   C O R P

CONSOLIDATED STATEMENTS OF CASH FLOWS

		Fiscal Year		
		1989	1988	1987
FISCAL YEARS ENDED FEBRUARY 3, 1990, FEBRUARY 4, 1989 AND FEBRUARY 6, 1988	Cash flows from operating activities	$55,875,733	$50,147,351	$47,530,746
	Financing and capital activities:			
	Net increase (decrease) in debt	(175,344)	474,122	(337,364)
	Issuance of common stock to employee stock plans	1,135,225	1,992,885	871,835
	Investments by minority interests in LBP Partnership	441,440		1,471,432
	Cash dividends	(6,573,188)	(4,138,497)	(2,732,940)
	Purchase of treasury stock	(26,892,827)	(8,097,469)	-
	Cash flows from financing and capital activities	(32,064,694)	(9,768,959)	(727,037)
	Cash flows before investing activities	23,811,039	40,378,392	46,803,709
	Investing activities:			
	Additions to property and equipment, net	(21,109,188)	(19,271,091)	(13,562,147)
	Acquisitions:			
	Property and equipment	(216,060)	(6,231,655)	(1,861,284)
	Intangible assets	(534,634)	(4,729,019)	(1,366,216)
	Long-term investments	2,521,671	(3,148,316)	-
	Restricted stock	(8,581)	(1,030,973)	-
	Cash flows from investing activities	(19,346,792)	(34,411,054)	(16,789,647)
	Net cash and short-term investments generated	4,464,247	5,967,338	30,014,062
	Cash and short-term investments at beginning of period	65,523,321	59,555,983	29,541,921
	Cash and short-term investments at end of period	$69,987,568	$65,523,321	$59,555,983
RECONCILIATION OF NET EARNINGS TO CASH FLOWS FROM RESULTS OF OPERATIONS	Net earnings from continuing operations	$30,916,066	$31,918,771	$25,770,706
	Adjustments for items not requiring cash:			
	Depreciation and amortization	22,170,876	19,549,090	18,010,576
	Deferred income taxes	(448,000)	169,000	1,287,000
	Deferred compensation	3,060,793	1,411,402	1,266,230
	Minority interest in losses of consolidated subsidiaries	(439,364)	(577,020)	(1,143,961)
	Other	(1,160,949)	(323,320)	(247,915)
	Decrease (increase) in current assets:			
	Receivables and inventories	2,666,855	(5,989,902)	1,513,853
	Deferred costs applicable to unsold portraits	(579,637)	(349,505)	(475,959)
	Prepaid expenses and other current assets	(138,064)	(1,184,689)	(1,044,171)
	Increase (decrease) in current liabilities:			
	Accounts payable, accrued expenses and other liabilities	(18,012)	3,969,824	3,065,656
	Income taxes	998,219	880,349	1,431,253
	Deferred income taxes	40,000	2,202,000	(588,000)
	Net cash flows from continuing operations	57,068,783	51,676,000	48,845,268
	Net losses from discontinued operations	(2,245,587)	(1,602,235)	(1,282,600)
	Depreciation and amortization	62,413	399,174	301,919
	Write-off of intangible assets	946,303		
	Decrease (increase) in receivables and inventories	577,354	(523,505)	(303,343)
	Increase (decrease) in accounts payable, accrued expenses and other liabilities	(533,533)	197,917	(30,498)
	Net cash flows from discontinued operations	(1,193,050)	(1,528,649)	(1,314,522)
	Cash flows from operating activities	$55,875,733	$50,147,351	$47,530,746
	Supplemental information:			
	Interest paid	$114,627	$83,039	$80,263
	Taxes paid.	$15,448,019	$17,053,753	$17,526,405

SOURCE: CPI Corp., *Annual Report*, 1989.

CPI Corp.: Capital Expenditures

C P I C O R P	1989	1988	1987
Capital expenditures:			
Portrait studios	$ 5,391	$ 4,364	$ 4,477
One-hour photofinishing..............	10,517	13,161	11,771
Other products and services.	2,716	7,224	913
Corporate..........................	6,730	4,142	888
Discontinued Tender Sender operations. .	262	845	443
	$ 25,616	$ 29,736	$ 18,492

SOURCE: CPI Corp., *Annual Report,* 1989.

exchange rate at the time of the transaction, foreign cash flows can also be translated using the exchange rate at the end of the period. The differences are aggregated and reported, together with the effect of the exchange rate on the beginning cash balance, as "the effect of exchange rate changes on cash" in a single-line item on the statement of cash flows of the parent firm. This item is likely to be small for most firms, even for those with major operations outside the United States.

Example:

PepsiCo is a worldwide food company, as shown by the geographic industry segment breakdown. In 1989, PepsiCo had non-U.S. sales of $2.7 billion and non-U.S. assets of over $3 billion. Its foreign currency effect has been minimal, as shown in its statement of cash flows. Therefore, unless the entity keeps large amounts of cash on hand in a currency that depreciates rapidly during a period, the foreign currency effect in the statement of cash flows is bound to be minimal.

4.11 SUMMARY

This chapter dealt with cash flows from investing, financing, and operating activities— the three most important areas of business activities. It also described estimation procedures for the components of cash generated by operating activities, which will be used to estimate free cash flows in Chapter 5.

PepsiCo.: Industry Segments

Consolidated Statement of Cash Flows

(in millions)
PepsiCo, Inc. and Subsidiaries
Fifty-two weeks ended December 30, 1989, fifty-three weeks ended December 31, 1988 and fifty-two weeks ended
December 26, 1987

	1989	1988	1987
Cash Flows from Continuing Operations:			
Income from continuing operations	$ 901.4	$ 762.2	$ 605.1
Adjustments to reconcile income from continuing operations to net cash generated by continuing operations:			
Depreciation and amortization	772.0	629.3	563.0
Deferred income taxes	71.2	20.1	59.0
Other noncash charges and credits–net	128.4	213.4	105.4
Changes in operating working capital:			
Notes and accounts receivable	(149.9)	(50.1)	(95.6)
Inventories	(50.1)	13.8	4.1
Prepaid expenses, taxes and other current assets	6.5	37.8	39.7
Accounts payable	134.9	138.2	(76.9)
Income taxes payable	80.9	55.1	23.3
Other current liabilities	(9.4)	74.7	107.4
Net change in operating working capital	12.9	269.5	2.0
Net Cash Generated by Continuing Operations	1,885.9	1,894.5	1,334.5
Cash Flows from Investing Activities:			
Acquisitions and equity investments	(3,296.6)	(1,415.5)	(371.5)
Purchases of property, plant and equipment	(943.8)	(725.8)	(770.5)
Proceeds from sales of property, plant and equipment	69.7	67.4	98.6
Proceeds from sales of businesses	–	283.2	161.6
Other short-term investments–by original maturity:			
Three months or less–net	667.0	(411.1)	(736.1)
More than three months–purchases	(2,131.1)	(692.6)	(1,311.8)
More than three months–sales	1,476.4	902.0	1,526.2
Other, net	(97.9)	(58.7)	(72.9)
Net Cash Used for Investing Activities	(4,256.3)	(2,051.1)	(1,476.4)
Cash Flows from Financing Activities:			
Proceeds from issuances of long-term debt	71.7	475.3	598.3
Payments of long-term debt	(405.4)	(190.0)	(113.4)
Short-term borrowings–by original maturity:			
Three months or less–net	2,292.2	306.7	114.7
More than three months–proceeds	1,109.5	292.0	547.9
More than three months–payments	(476.2)	(367.4)	(1,157.0)
Proceeds from nonrecourse obligation	–	0.1	299.3
Cash dividends paid	(241.9)	(199.0)	(172.0)
Purchases of treasury stock	–	(71.8)	(18.6)
Other, net	(28.9)	(24.5)	(38.8)
Net Cash Generated by Financing Activities	2,321.0	221.4	60.4
Effect of Exchange Rate Changes on Cash and Cash Equivalents	(17.1)	(1.4)	(8.0)
Net Increase (Decrease) in Cash and Cash Equivalents	(66.5)	63.4	(89.5)
Cash and Cash Equivalents–Beginning of Year	142.7	79.3	168.8
Cash and Cash Equivalents–End of Year	$ 76.2	$ 142.7	$ 79.3

SOURCE: PepsiCo., *Annual Report*, 1989.

PepsiCo.: Consolidated Statement of Cash Flows

Industry Segments:		Net Sales			Operating Profits[a]			Identifiable Assets[b]		
		1989	1988	1987	1989	1988	1987	1989	1988	1987
Soft Drinks:	U.S.	$ 4,623.3	$ 3,667.0	$ 3,112.9	$ 586.9	$ 409.5	$ 363.1			
	Foreign	1,153.4	971.2	862.7	103.2	53.4	46.5			
		5,776.7	4,638.2	3,975.6	690.1	462.9	409.6	$ 6,241.9	$ 4,074.4	$2,779.8
Snack Foods:	U.S.	3,211.3	2,933.3	2,782.8	668.3	587.3	520.0			
	Foreign	1,003.7	581.0	419.2	152.6	49.0	27.6			
		4,215.0	3,514.3	3,202.0	820.9	636.3	547.6	3,366.4	1,641.2	1,632.5
Restaurants:	U.S.	4,684.8	3,950.3	3,499.5	361.8	307.0	281.6			
	Foreign	565.9	430.4	341.0	59.4	44.4	37.8			
		5,250.7	4,380.7	3,840.5	421.2	351.4	319.4	3,095.2	3,105.1	2,782.9
Total:	U.S.	12,519.4	10,550.6	9,395.2	1,617.0	1,303.8	1,164.7			
	Foreign	2,723.0	1,982.6	1,622.9	315.2	146.8	111.9			
		$15,242.4	$12,533.2	$11,018.1	$1,932.2	$1,450.6	$1,276.6	$12,703.5	$ 8,820.7	$7,195.2

Geographic Areas:[a], [b], [c]									
United States	$12,519.4	$10,550.6	$ 9,395.2	$1,617.0	$1,303.8	$1,164.7	$ 9,633.2	$ 7,264.6	$5,699.4
Western Europe	739.0	390.8	308.0	55.5	13.0	6.7	1,754.8	187.7	169.1
Canada and Mexico	899.0	726.3	501.5	126.3	55.0	39.9	460.6	348.0	359.8
Other	1,085.0	865.5	813.4	133.4	78.8	65.3	854.9	1,020.4	966.9
							12,703.5	8,820.7	7,195.2
Corporate Assets[c]							2,423.2	2,314.6	1,827.5
Total	$15,242.4	$12,533.2	$11,018.1	1,932.2	1,450.6	1,276.6	$15,126.7	$11,135.3	$9,022.7
Interest and Other Corporate Expenses, Net				(581.7)	(323.4)	(331.0)			
Income from Continuing Operations Before Income Taxes				$1,350.5	$1,127.2	$ 945.6			

	Capital Spending			Depreciation and Amortization Expense		
	1989	1988	1987	1989	1988	1987
Soft Drinks	$ 267.8	$ 198.4	$ 202.0	$306.3	$195.7	$166.5
Snack Foods	257.9	172.6	195.6	189.3	156.8	154.1
Restaurants	424.6	344.2	370.8	269.9	271.3	237.1
Corporate	9.2	14.9	6.6	6.5	5.5	5.3
	$ 959.5	$ 730.1	$ 775.0	$772.0	$629.3	$563.0

Supplementary Restaurants Data:						
	Net Sales			Operating Profits[a]		
Pizza Hut	$2,453.5	$2,014.2	$1,753.2	$208.6	$153.3	$138.0
Taco Bell	1,465.9	1,157.3	1,004.4	112.6	81.6	91.4
KFC	1,331.3	1,209.2	1,082.9	100.0	116.5	90.0
	$5,250.7	$4,380.7	$3,840.5	$421.2	$351.4	$319.4

SOURCE: PepsiCo., *Annual Report*, 1989.

CHAPTER 5

Operating Income, Operating Cash Flow, and Free Cash Flow

5.1 INTRODUCTION

This chapter discusses three variables that can be used to analyze and computer-screen a large set of firms, so that a subset of firms that are potentially good investment candidates can be investigated in depth. Three variables we discuss in this section are operating income, net operating cash flow, and free cash flow. Operating profit is a widely used criterion for investment purposes. It is used, for example, in earnings multiples, mostly because earnings is readily available from financial statements. Net operating cash flow is used less frequently for investment purposes, primarily because, prior to FAS No. 95, which required the disclosure of an entire statement of cash flows, net operating cash flow had to be estimated from other financial statements. Finally, free cash flow is hardly used at all for investment purposes, because it is fairly complex to estimate, although, intuitively, it seems the most reasonable criterion for investment.[1]

We begin this chapter with a discussion of the limitations of earnings reports in general and their specific shortcomings for investment purposes. We then review the potential usefulness of net operating cash flow and its pitfalls as an investment criterion. Finally, we introduce the concept of free cash flow, show how it can be estimated, and how it can be used for portfolio selection.

5.2 EARNINGS AND ITS LIMITATIONS

Security analysts, portfolio managers, and most investment services highlight earnings as one of the most important financial indicators.[2] For example, most research reports prepared by analysts and newspapers publish, in addition to stock price and dividend information, the price/earnings ratio of a firm. Financial news services vary in the earnings number they report; some use the most recent (known) annual earnings per share, others use the running sum of the last four quarterly earnings per share, whereas

---

[1]There are several simplistic definitions of free cash flows that security analysts and firms use. The most common of these is pretax profit plus depreciation, minus capital spending. As we show later on, this definition excludes many important elements of free cash flows.

[2]See, for example, the debate between Kenneth S. Hackel and David Dreman about stock valuation theories in *The Wall Street Journal*, July 17, 1989. David Breman advocates an investment strategy that is based on low price/earnings ratios.

others use a combination of forecasted and historical earnings. Some services use primary earnings per share, others use fully diluted earnings per share. Some use earnings before extraordinary items, whereas others use net income. In short, earnings figures are not uniform across various sources of information.

Example:

In a press release to analysts and portfolio managers, PepsiCo, the large soft-drinks manufacturer, wrote the following comments on its third quarterly report for 1991:

"As you know we have been very aggressive in disclosing items that we believe are of an unusual nature so that you can make whatever adjustments you deem necessary to understand the quality and underlying trend of our earnings growth. In the third quarter of 1990, there were quite a few such unusual items and, as we recall, some of you found it confusing. Now, to make it even more challenging we are asking you to compare that quarter to the third quarter of 1991 which also has unusual items.

To help in this task, we have added two schedules to the package this quarter. These schedules are designed to make it a little clearer what constitutes an 'apples to apples' comparison. One schedule analyzes the impact of unusual items on net income and earnings per share, and the second schedule presents segment operating profits and growth excluding the unusual items. We hope you find them helpful. Of course, if you need any further clarification, we would be happy to assist you."

As can be seen, the selling, administrative, and other expenses in 1990 *and* in 1991 contain unusual items. In 1991, the unusual items include a $91 million restructuring charge, whereas in 1990 there is a gain of $118 million on stock offering. Should the analyst include the entire amounts of selling, administrative, and other expenses in income as reported? Should the analyst exclude these items because they are not expected to recur? How about amounts that relate to discontinued operations? The example shows how crucial it is to use the same definition of earnings for all firms in any comparison of firms based on earnings or earnings components. It also shows the danger of using net earnings for comparisons of earnings across time.

To compound the problem, firms are required under Generally Accepted Accounting Principles (GAAP) to follow accrual accounting, which introduces many estimates into the financial statements and which allows firms to account for the same economic transaction in differential manners. For example, consider the "corner" retail store that keeps its books on a cash basis, that is, revenues match cash taken in and pretax profits are very close to cash receipts minus cash spent. In contrast, earnings and cash increases are not identical for public companies that use accrual instead of cash accounting. With accrual accounting, the entity may record revenues before cash is actually collected, and it may record expenses that do not require an outlay of cash, such as recording an accrued liability. Thus, reported income for the public company almost never matches net cash receipts from operations.

When preparing its financial statements, a firm has to make assumptions about future developments so that it can estimate future values that are necessary for current recordkeeping. For example, accrual accounting requires estimation of depreciation expense for a period. Most firms estimate the depreciation expense by predicting the useful lives of depreciable assets and the salvage (residual) values of these assets.

PepsiCo, Inc. and Subsidiaries
Condensed Consolidated Statement of Income
(in millions except per share amounts, unaudited)

PepsiCo, Inc. and Subsidiaries
Condensed Consolidated Statement of Income
(in millions except per share amounts, unaudited)

	12 Weeks Ended		
	9/7/91	9/8/90 (a)	% Change
Net Sales	$ 4,881.3	$ 4,475.7	9
Costs and Expenses, net			
Cost of sales	2,349.4	2,152.2	9
Selling, administrative and other expenses	1,949.0 (b)	1,714.7 (c)	14
Amortization of goodwill and other intangibles	47.6	45.2	5
Gain on joint venture stock offering	-	(118.2) (c)	-
Interest expense	137.4	158.9	(14)
Interest income	(35.5)	(43.1)	(18)
	4,447.9	3,909.7	14
Income from Continuing Operations Before Income Taxes	433.4 (b)	566.0 (c)	(23)
Provision for Income Taxes (e)	148.0	215.7	(31)
Income from Continuing Operations	285.4 (b)	350.3 (c)	(19)
Discontinued Operation Charge	-	(13.7) (d)	-
Net Income	$ 285.4	$ 336.6	(15)
Per Share:			
Continuing Operations	$ 0.36 (b)	$ 0.44 (c)	(18)
Discontinued Operation	-	(0.02) (d)	-
Net Income Per Share	$ 0.36	$ 0.42	(14)
Average shares outstanding	802.2	799.6	

NOTES:
(a) Certain amounts have been reclassified to conform with the 1991 presentation.
(b) Includes an unusual charge of $100.4 million ($62.4 after-tax or $0.08 per share) consisting of a $91.4 million restructuring charge at domestic snack foods and a $9.0 million charge at domestic KFC related to a delayed national roll-out of the new skinless chicken product.
(c) Includes an unusual net credit of $70.6 million ($23.8 after-tax or $0.03 per share) consisting of the $118.2 million gain on joint venture stock offering partially offset by $47.6 million in unusual charges (described in the attachments) included in selling, administrative and other expenses.
(d) Represents $14.0 million pre-tax in additional amounts provided for various pending lawsuits and claims relating to a business sold in a prior year.
(e) The effective tax rates were 34.1% in 1991, 38.1% in 1990, and 33.6% in 1990 excluding the unusual tax effects of the gain on joint venture stock offering.

Clearly, these estimates can be expected to contain errors, which may affect accounting earnings. Indeed, firms update their estimates of useful lives of fixed assets, causing income for the period to increase or decrease, sometimes substantially.

Example:

Sometimes firms revise their earnings figures due to new reporting requirements. An extreme case occurred when the SEC changed a reporting requirement for oil and gas firms after they issued preliminary earnings reports to investors.

OIL FIRMS SCRAMBLE TO RESTATE EARNINGS IN WAKE OF SEC RULING IN WRITE-DOWNS

A growing number of oil companies are reporting first-quarter write-downs on their reserves, including some that didn't foresee doing so.

Several large, independent oil companies recently reported results that didn't include substantial write-downs to reflect the sharp drop in oil prices. They had assumed that the SEC would approve a staff proposal to postpone such write-downs until year's end.

But on Tuesday, to everyone's surprise, the SEC decided to retain rules that require oil companies using full-cost accounting to take quarterly write-downs if the book value of oil and natural gas reserves exceeds current market value. As a result, the companies are scrambling to restate earlier, less grim earnings reports.

Houston-based Pennzoil Co., for instance, had posted profit of $43.3 million without explaining in its news release that the results were based on what proved to be a poor prediction of the SEC ruling. Just as it was poised to mail out shareholder reports, Pennzoil had to slip a disclaimer into the envelopes saying that ''the first quarterly earnings and financial results that appear herein will have to be restated.'' Pennzoil accountants were busy Friday recalculating the numbers.

On Thursday, Mesa Limited Partnership, based in Amarillo, Texas, restated its results to a $169 million loss, compared with the $31 million profit it posted a few days earlier.[3]

Furthermore, a firm can, in many cases, choose the accounting method it applies for a specific type of transaction. For example, purchases of inventory might be identical for two firms, but accounting earnings and inventories on the balance sheet might be different because one firm uses LIFO for inventories, whereas the other uses methods such as FIFO or weighted average.

Example:

When leaf tobacco prices declined during the second half of 1982, it benefitted such companies as Philip Morris and R.J. Reynolds, which used LIFO, as opposed to such companies as American Brands, which used weighted average in accounting for its large leaf tobacco inventories. When prices declined, companies that used LIFO for inventory purposes showed higher accounting income than firms that used other methods.

Not only do firms have some latitude in choosing different accounting methods under GAAP, they also have some latitude in applying accounting standards to their

---

[3]*The Wall Street Journal*, May 12, 1986.

specific situations. Thus, firms may have different approaches to revenue recognition, expense recognition, and allocation of costs across periods. This flexibility in applying accounting standards can be desirable, because in reality no two businesses are identical. It allows managers of firms that consider their firms unique in some respect to signal it through the selection of accounting methods. However, this flexibility makes comparability of earnings across firms, and sometimes even for the same firm across different periods, extremely difficult. Thus, the great focus on earnings in making investment and valuation decisions may not be warranted.

Example—Revenue Recognition:

Are the two methods listed below liberal or conservative accounting practices?

1. "Sales revenue is generally recorded upon shipment of product in the case of sales contracts and upon installation in the case of sales-type leases. Revenue from service and rental agreements is recorded as earned over the lives of the respective contracts.

   Revenue under cost-type contracts is recognized when costs are incurred, and under fixed-price contracts when products or services are accepted and billings can be made. General and administrative expenses are charged to income as incurred. Cost of revenue under long-term contracts is charged based on current estimated total costs. When estimates indicate a loss under a contract, cost of revenue is charged with a provision for such loss."[4]

2. "The Corporation reports profits on long-term contracts on a percentage-of-completion basis determined on the ratio of earned billings to total contract price, after considering accumulated costs and estimated costs to complete each contract. Contracts in progress are valued at cost plus accrued profits less earned billings and progress payments on uncompleted contracts."[5]

Both entities use liberal accounting practices; Unisys recognizes revenues when its products are shipped, and Foster Wheeler records profits on long-term contracts using the percentage-of-completion method. Cash accounting has strong merits when such transactions occur, because cash collected from customers is the same regardless of the particular method that is used for revenue recognition. As a matter of fact, the first element in the debate between accrual accounting and cash accounting revolves around the issue of revenue recognition. The cash flow analyst believes in revenue recognition when collection is made on accounts receivable and cash is deposited in the bank. Under accrual accounting, there is a wide latitude for revenue recognition from progress payments to time of shipment. As seen for the Unisys Corporation, income recognition is subject to much leeway and is certainly different for most industries and entities.

Example—Revenue Recognition:

Warrantech Corp. changed its accounting method for recognizing revenue in the second quarter of 1991, retroactively from the first quarter. This change caused the company to

---

[4]Unisys Corporation, *1988 Annual Report.*
[5]Foster Wheeler Corporation, *1989 Annual Report.*

recognize revenues from service contracts on consumer electronic products mostly in the first year of the contract, instead of deferring the recognition of revenues to later years. The firm said that this change substantially reduced its reported net loss for the quarter.

Example—Expense Recognition:

The deferred asset account, which appears at the bottom of the assets list on the balance sheet, represents expenditures on items such as advertising expenses, rents paid in advance, and intangible assets such as goodwill that it is hoped will benefit the firm in future periods. This account should be closely inspected by the cash flow analyst. Changes in deferred assets could be attributed to changes in policy regarding payment of expenditures for such items as insurance, maintenance, and the costs to redesign and improve existing products, which the firm *hopes* will result in future cash flows. However, the addition to deferred assets usually requires an outlay of cash, whose expense recognition for accounting purposes is deferred for later periods. Advocates of cash flow analysis would disagree with the accounting convention of recording an asset of this kind for cash already spent and would consider it an immediate cash outflow in their analysis.

Example—Expense Recognition:

Accounting methods for allocation of the cost of purchases between cost of goods sold and ending inventory are another example of expense recognition, which cash flow analysts may find a problem. While the purchase of inventory for cash is a cash outflow, the cost assigned to cost of goods sold may not be a cash outflow and may depend on the particular accounting method chosen for cost allocation. In particular, the inflationary spirals during the 1970s taught security analysts to pay close attention to inventory accounting and its effect on reported profits due to changes in price levels. Investors, for example, realized that if an entity is in a commodity-type industry subject to swift price movements, LIFO accounting could increase reported profits during disinflationary periods. Furthermore, changes in price levels have a more discriminatory effect on reported earnings than on cash flows. When price levels change quickly, comparisons of earnings across firms are hampered by the amount of inventory held in relation to the company's peers and the inventory method practiced (LIFO versus FIFO). Free cash flow analysis, by essentially placing all companies on a cash basis and comparing firms according to their cash outlays on purchases or production of inventories, avoids much of the accounting skullduggery.

During inflationary periods, asset replacement may bear little resemblance to the historical cost represented on the balance sheet and, hence, earnings are grossly misstated. As an example, consider the LIFO reserve, which has grown substantially for many entities and is relegated to an off-balance-sheet asset. The LIFO reserve is not adequately treated by generally accepted accounting practices because it is not incorporated in the body of financial statements.

Example—Write-offs:

On November 11, 1983, when Union Carbide Corp. announced it was closing certain facilities resulting in a $140 million charge to net income, the company also pointed out the write-off would have no effect on cash flow. Union Carbide also pointed out that future cash flows would be enhanced as a result of the closing of the inefficient facilities. Carbide's stock reacted positively to the announcement, as it should have, ignoring the earnings implication of the charge. Write-offs, like those undergone by Union Carbide, are not uncommon and can cause large discrepancies between accounting earnings and cash flows.

Setting up reserves has a negative effect on accounting earnings, yet has no effect on cash flows.

In the third quarter of 1982, Clark Manufacturing Co. established a reserve of $214.5 million to cover plant shutdown costs at four U.S. and one European location, excess costs during the phase-down period, pension expense, and certain relocation costs. Charges to the reserve amounted to $33.4 million in 1982 and $130.6 million in 1983. In the third quarter of 1983, Clark reversed $7.7 million of excess reserves to income.

Accountants, bankers, business operators, economists, and security analysts have long debated the role and definition of earnings. Critics of GAAP have recognized that, because of the multitude of acceptable accounting methods available, financial reports across industry lines are usually vastly different, due primarily to peculiarities for the industry. Furthermore, it is difficult for trained security analysts to have a thorough understanding of the accounting methods within the industries of their specialty (and almost impossible outside their specialty), so they cannot discern accounting issues of rival industries and comment on matters concerning relative valuation. Without having a thorough knowledge of accounting standards for all industries, it is impossible to conclude how attractive any particular industry is simply because accounting practices are not uniform. For example, one cannot say with certainty that a particular industry is undervalued because it sells at a discount to the market, as measured by its P/E ratio, if the industry uses liberal accounting practices relative to the market. Because there is no market accounting practice, one must thoroughly understand the accounting practices and conventions used by all major industries before one is able to identify an attractive industry on the basis of its earnings.

Many stock analysts attempt to forecast earnings per share of firms that they follow. There is a lot of academic evidence that shows that, although the consensus (median) forecast of earnings per share by analysts is reasonably accurate, analysts usually overestimate earnings per share. To understand how difficult the task of predicting earnings per share is, one should consider not only the prediction of future economic events that affect earnings, but also the effects of managerial decisions about investments, financing, and accounting methods.

Example:

To illustrate the complexity of forecasting corporate earnings, we show five schedules from the 1989 United Telecommunications, Inc. Form 10-K. The analyst attempting to forecast expenses using accrual accounting will be confronted with estimating the variables in the expense tables on United Telecommunications, Inc.

The company's consolidated account of "property, plant and equipment" represents a maze of credits and debits to the balance sheet account as a result of acquisitions, exchanges, purchases, retirements, and other charges or credits. United Telecom's schedule of "accumulated depreciation" is also difficult to forecast because it includes retirements of property and property sold and write-offs of fully depreciated assets. Reclassification between other property, plant, and equipment accounts will also affect the depreciation schedules as will acquisitions. Because depreciation is often a very large expense item, its estimate is crucial for an accurate earnings forecast.

United Telecom's schedule of "valuation and qualifying accounts" and schedule of "supplementary tax information," which include maintenance and repairs and advertising expenses, are also important when estimating earnings. Many entities will not present a schedule of supplementary information if they deem it to be immaterial. United Telecom's "consolidated valuation and qualifying accounts" shows a large increase during 1988 in the provision for doubtful accounts due to the consolidation of U.S. Sprint. The following year, the account is reduced by almost $34 million, but it increases again in 1990.

United Telecom's computation of earnings (loss) per share is not difficult to approximate if the earnings applicable to common stock are known, especially given the large number of shares outstanding. Needed, however, are the common stock equivalent shares applicable to options and the employees stock purchase plan.

United Telecommunications, Inc.: Schedule V, Consolidated Property, Plant and Equipment

---

United Telecommunications, Inc.
Form 10-K

SCHEDULE V -- CONSOLIDATED PROPERTY, PLANT AND EQUIPMENT
Year Ended December 31, 1989
(Millions of Dollars)

	Balance beginning of year	Additions — Business acquisitions	Additions — Property exchanges	Additions, at cost	Retirements or sales	Other charges (credits)	Balance end of year
LONG DISTANCE COMMUNICATIONS SERVICES							
Digital fiber-optic network	$ 2,814.5	$ 83.1		$ 373.4	$ 18.9	$(39.6) (1)	$ 3,212.5
Data communications equipment	192.8			85.1	24.2	8.4 (2)	262.1
Administrative assets	309.4	145.8		209.1	53.8	(17.4) (3)	593.1
Construction-in-progress	176.3			37.4			213.7
	3,493.0	228.9		705.0	96.9	(48.6)	4,281.4
LOCAL COMMUNICATIONS SERVICES							
Land and buildings	404.4		$ 6.1	31.7	10.4	0.7	432.5
Other general support assets	321.4		3.6	41.9	30.8	0.9	337.0
Central office assets	2,372.1		31.4	332.8	250.0	(0.7)	2,485.6
Information origination/ termination assets	471.2		5.6	19.3	58.7	(3.2)	434.2
Cable and wire facility assets	3,156.7		76.5	254.4	105.3	(0.3)	3,382.0
Telephone plant under construction	133.8			(28.9)			104.9
Other	41.2		(10.9)	7.4	2.6	2.6	37.7
	6,900.8		112.3	658.6	457.8		7,213.9
COMPLEMENTARY AND OTHER	275.4			25.4	17.9	(23.3) (4)	259.6
	$10,669.2	$228.9	$112.3	$1,389.0	$572.6	$(71.9)	$11,754.9

SOURCE: United Telecommunications, Inc., Form 10-K, 1989.

United Telecommunications, Inc.: Schedule VI, Consolidated Accumulated Depreciation

United Telecommunications, Inc.
Form 10-K

SCHEDULE VI -- CONSOLIDATED ACCUMULATED DEPRECIATION
Years Ended December 31, 1990, 1989 and 1988
(Millions of Dollars)

Year ended Dec. 31	Balance beginning of year	Consolidation of US Sprint	Current year provisions Charged to income	Charged to clearing accounts	Retirements, renewals and replacements	Other	Balance end of Year
1990	$3,870.0		$1,022.7 (1)		$432.8 (2)	$ 7.1 (3) $ 11.7 (4)	$4,478.7
1989	$3,339.4		$ 923.7 (1)		$522.0 (2)	$ 26.0 (3) $114.8 (5) $(11.9) (6)	$3,870.0
1988	$2,625.5	$266.2	$ 876.8 (1)	$(1.6)	$410.9 (2)	$ 18.7 (3) $ (5.6) (7) $(29.7) (8)	$3,339.4

	1990	1989	1988
(1) Charged to income as depreciation expense. Reconciliation of depreciation expense to amount disclosed in the Annual Report to Shareholders - Consolidated Statements of Cash Flows:			
Amount charged to income above	$1,022.7	$923.7	$876.8
Amortization of intangibles, plant acquisition adjustment and extraordinary plant retirement credited to amount deferred on balance sheet	60.5	38.2	29.8
Depreciation and amortization expense included in income statement	$1,083.2	$961.9	$906.6
(2) Reconciliation of retirements or sales included in Schedule V -- Consolidated Property, Plant and Equipment:			
Amount charged to reserve above	$432.8	$522.0	$410.9
Net book value of long distance division retirements and other	75.2	50.6	220.8
Net property, plant and equipment sold or traded			
United TeleSpectrum, Inc.			72.4
United TeleSentinel, Inc.			5.4
Total Schedule V retirements and sales	$508.0	$572.6	$709.5

(3) Net salvage.
(4) Adjustment primarily represents reclassification of a valuation reserve from plant.
(5) Adjustment resulting from exchange of certain telephone properties in Iowa and Arkansas for similar assets owned by Contel of Kansas and The Kansas State Telephone Company, both Contel Corporation subsidiaries.
(6) Adjustment resulting primarily from the retirement of capital leases prior to full amortization.
(7) Reduction of accumulated depreciation per commission order.
(8) Long-distance communications services' accumulated depreciation reclassified to related property, plant and equipment accounts to record microwave network at estimated net residual value and data communications equipment net balances reclassified for initial contributed assets.

SOURCE: United Telecommunications, Inc., Form 10-K, 1989.

United Telecommunications, Inc.: Schedule VIII, Consolidated Valuation
and Qualifying Accounts

United Telecommunications, Inc.
Form 10-K

SCHEDULE VIII -- CONSOLIDATED VALUATION AND QUALIFYING ACCOUNTS
Years Ended December 31, 1990, 1989 and 1988
(Millions of Dollars)

	Balance beginning of year	Consol- dation of US Sprint	Additions		Other additions (deductions)	Balance end of year
			Charged to income	Charged to other accounts		
1990						
Allowance for doubtful accounts	$168.8		$361.5	$ 3.6	$(323.4) (1)	$210.5
1989						
Allowance for doubtful accounts	$202.5		$294.7	$16.7	$(345.1) (1)	$168.8
1988						
Allowance for doubtful accounts	$ 11.9	$305.5	$475.5	$ 1.6	$(592.0) (1)	$202.5

(1) Accounts charged off, net of collections.

SOURCE: United Telecommunications, Inc., Form 10-K, 1990.

Because it is difficult to accurately predict earnings given the vast number of
variables that is needed to formulate the estimate, it is not surprising to find earnings
surprises a daily event during corporate reporting periods. As many academic articles
document, there is a strong correlation (relationship) between earnings surprises and
stock reaction. That is, negative earnings surprises tend to be quickly followed by
drops in the price of the announcing company's stock, and vice versa. We believe that
this relationship is true only because there *generally* exists a positive relationship
between long-term growth in accounting earnings and cash flows (both cash flow from
operations and free cash flow). However, a careful analysis is needed to distinguish
these cases in which the direction of price changes should not follow the direction of
the earnings surprise.

Example:

Earnings surprises became so popular that the financial press pays close attention to them.
The Wall Street Journal published the following list on July 18, 1990.

Quarterly Earnings Surprises

Companies listed below reported quarterly profit substantially different from the average of analysts' estimates. The companies are followed by at least three analysts. Results in parentheses are losses.

The percent difference compares actual profit with the 30-day estimate where at least three analysts have issued forecasts in the past 30 days. Otherwise, actual profit is compared with the 120-day estimate.

Company Name	Actual EPS	Estimate [# of analysts] 30-Day	Estimate [# of analysts] 120-Day	Percent Diff.
Positive				
Upjohn	$ .62	$ .56 [4]	$ .57 [12]	10.71
Tosco	2.62	—	1.38 [3]	89.86
Augat	.27	—	.21 [4]	28.57
Envirosafe Svc	.47	—	.38 [3]	23.68
Adolph Coors	.68	—	.57 [4]	19.30
Fruit of the Loom	.60	—	.52 [4]	15.38
Huffy	.79	—	.70 [4]	12.86
Chemical Banking	1.02	—	.91 [8]	12.09
Intel	.84	—	.76 [24]	10.53
Reynolds Metals	1.75	—	1.59 [9]	10.06
Negative				
FMC Gold	$ .14	$ .16 [3]	$ .16 [3]	12.50
Diceon Electron	(.47)	—	(.08) [3]	—
United Telecom	.18	—	.58 [14]	68.97
Colorado Nat Bkshr	.11	—	.23 [4]	52.17
VF Corp	.37	—	.59 [6]	37.29
Oregon Metallur	.22	—	.30 [4]	26.67
Sundstrand	.57	—	.77 [6]	25.97
Rollins Environ	.12	—	.14 [5]	14.29
Diebold	.58	—	.67 [4]	13.43
Dominion Bkshr	.53	—	.61 [8]	13.11

SOURCE: Zacks Investment Research

As can be seen in this list, there were some wide variations with analysts' estimates for earnings that were announced on July 17, 1990. Interestingly, two of the entities that reported large negative surprises, United Telecom and VF Corp., had experienced very different market reactions.

United Telecom stock reacted by dropping 22.9 percent on 12 million shares, almost 17 times its normal trading volume. VF Corp. reacted by rising a quarter point on normal trading volume on a day when the S&P 500 declined slightly.

We believe that the difference in fortunes between the two entities is not their earnings but rather their free cash flow. United Telecom was generating negative free cash flow, despite positive earnings, mostly because of its large investment in U.S. Sprint. V.F. Corp. generated positive free cash flow for the quarter, and despite an increase in leverage during the year as a result of a large share buyback, Moody's Investors Service Inc. confirmed the

United Telecommunications, Inc.: Schedule X, Consolidated Supplementary Income
Statement Information

United Telecommunications, Inc.
Form 10-K

**SCHEDULE X -- CONSOLIDATED SUPPLEMENTARY
INCOME STATEMENT INFORMATION
Years Ended December 31, 1990, 1989 and 1988
(Millions of Dollars)**

The following table presents supplementary consolidated income statement information for United:

	1990	1989	1988
Maintenance and repairs (1)	$115.5	$103.6	$ 89.1
Taxes, other than payroll and income taxes:			
Property taxes	$115.5	$114.1	$117.3
Gross receipts and other	52.2	64.0	67.6
	$167.7	$178.1	$184.9
Advertising expense	$185.8	$144.8	$127.3

(1) Amount represents maintenance and repairs for long distance communications services. Maintenance and repairs is the primary component of plant operations expense for local communications services companies which totaled $848.1 million, $811.7 million and $737.5 million in 1990, 1989 and 1988, respectively. Complementary and Other businesses had no significant maintenance and repairs expense.

On a consolidated basis, United had no significant depreciation and amortization of intangibles expense or royalty expense during 1990, 1989 and 1988.

SOURCE: United Telecommunications, Inc., Form 10-K, 1990.

company's Single-A2 senior debt rating and Prime-1 rating for commercial paper. Moody's said that "despite facing a difficult retail environment, VF continues to generate strong cash flow and should continue to reduce debt levels."

5.3 NET OPERATING CASH FLOW

Because firms' earnings can vary widely depending on their accounting methods, accounting estimates, and applications of specific revenue and expense recognition rules to their own situation, one has to rely on some other measure to compare the performance of firms. Ideally, this measure should be free of the effects of as many accounting methods as possible. This leads investors and creditors to forge a measure that is based on cash flows.

United Telecommunications, Inc.: Exhibit 11, Computation of Earnings (Loss) per Common Share

United Telecommunications, Inc.
Form 10-K

EXHIBIT 11

COMPUTATION OF EARNINGS PER COMMON SHARE *
(In Millions Except Per Share Data)

	Year Ended December 31,		
	1990	1989	1988
Earnings applicable to common stock	$306.0	$359.9	$505.6
Add back			
Convertible preferred stock dividends	0.8	1.0	1.2
Interest, net of related income taxes, of			
5-percent convertible subordinated debentures	0.1	0.1	0.2
Earnings as adjusted for purposes of computing earnings per share assuming full dilution	$306.9	$361.0	$507.0
Weighted average number of common shares outstanding during the year	211.8	206.2	203.0
Common stock equivalent shares applicable to options and the employees stock purchase plan	2.1	2.9	1.4
Total number of shares for computing earnings per share assuming no dilution	213.9	209.1	204.4
Incremental common shares attributable to			
Additional dilutive effect of common stock options and employees stock purchase plan		0.2	0.8
Conversion of preferred stock			
First series	0.2	0.2	0.2
Second series	1.2	1.6	1.8
Conversion of 5-percent convertible subordinated debentures	0.2	0.2	0.6
Total number of shares as adjusted for purposes of computing earnings per share assuming full dilution	215.5	211.3	207.8
Earnings per common share			
Assuming no dilution	$ 1.43	$ 1.72	$ 2.48
Assuming full dilution	$ 1.42	$ 1.71	$ 2.44

* Common share data reflects the two-for-one stock split effective during 1989.

source: United Telecommunications, Inc., Form 10-K, 1990.

Cash flow analysis is an outgrowth of what is known as examining the quality of an entity's earnings. The reason for the growing popularity of cash flow analysis is the expanded use of liberal accounting practices by firms, and investors' concurrent inability to adequately interpret much of the reported financial statement jargon. For example, the average public investor wonders how an entity selling at a below-market price/earnings ratio could ever find itself in a financial predicament.

Example:

Integrated Resources was selling at 50 percent below the price/earnings multiple on the Standard & Poor's 500 when it was forced into a bankruptcy filing by its creditors.

Let us review some of the accounting areas that need to be investigated to assess the quality of earnings:

1. The deferred asset account, which appears as the last asset on the balance sheet, should always, to the extent possible, be closely inspected. Changes in deferred assets could be due to prepayment of expenditures for advertising, insurance, and maintenance, or other expenditures such as developmental costs, which the company *hopes* will result in future income. But isn't an addition to the deferred asset account, which is really an outlay of cash, an expense? Advocates of cash flow analysis would differ with the accounting convention of booking an asset of this kind for cash already spent.

2. The purchase of inventory, which is an outlay of cash, is not recorded by the accountant as an expense unless the inventory is sold. One should attempt to assess the likelihood that inventory will be sold and whether the firm has excess inventories. The inflationary spirals during the 1970s conditioned security analysts to pay strict attention to inventory accounting and its effect on reported profits of changes in price levels. Investors learned that if an entity is in a commodity-type industry, subject to swift price movements, LIFO accounting could increase reported profits during disinflationary periods.

   Changes in price levels have a more discriminatory effect on reported earnings than cash flows. When price levels change quickly, depending on the amount of inventory held in relation to the company's peers and the inventory method used (LIFO versus FIFO), earnings comparisons could be difficult to make. Free cash flow analysis, by essentially placing all companies on a cash basis, avoids much of the accounting skullduggery.

3. Asset replacement may bear little resemblance to the historical cost represented on the balance sheet and, hence, true earnings are understated.

4. The cost method versus the equity method of accounting for investments is another area of importance in determining earnings quality. While the cost method does not permit an entity to record its pro-rata earnings in the investee, it does include dividend income on the investor's income statement. The equity method allows the investor company to record its pro-rata share of net profits, even if these profits were not received in cash.

Example:

The 1989 statement of cash flows for John Deere Co., which uses the equity method for affiliates in Brazil and Mexico, includes $6.9 million under the heading "undistributed earnings of unconsolidated subsidiaries and affiliates." These earnings are included in determining net income, but because they had not been obtained in cash, John Deere subtracts them in its derivation of cash flows from operating activities.

5. Another factor affecting earnings quality is the ratio of profits from operations as opposed to interest or dividend income. It has been argued that a high ratio of dividend income to operating profits lowers earnings quality because it is not a result of operations and is therefore unpredictable. It is also argued that firms with a high ratio of interest and dividend income to total income from operations should be accorded a lower price/earnings multiple.

6. Contributing corporate stock or other assets such as real estate to the corporate pension fund in lieu of a cash contribution should be examined by the cash flow analyst or the analyst who is concerned about earnings quality.

7. The analyst should examine when and how revenues are recognized. Is it when the product is shipped, as installment payments are received, or when the contract is signed? Because services are becoming such an important part of revenue growth for many companies (including manufacturing entities), it is important to look at how revenues are recognized for the service portion of the business.

Because of the problems associated with earnings quality, a natural alternative to analyzing earnings of a firm is to look at net operating cash flow, which is subject to fewer accounting manipulations. Operating cash flows are insensitive to the firm's choice of an inventory accounting method because operating cash flows focus on *payments* for inventory purchases, which are the same regardless of the accounting method used for inventories. Another example is the choice of a depreciation policy. Whereas the choice of a depreciation method, for example, straight-line or accelerated depreciation, can affect earnings of a firm, it does not affect cash from operations at all. Thus, net operating cash flow is a figure that is less affected by the particular accounting methods that the firm selects. Furthermore, with the issuance of FAS No. 95, net operating cash flow is more uniformly reported across firms because the FASB has provided specific definitions for operating, as distinguished from investing or financing, cash flows.[6]

Example:

An increasing number of firms discuss not only the change in earnings from one period to another, but also the change in cash flows from operations. For example, Commercial

---

[6]Nevertheless, firms can still classify transactions in a way that will increase cash from operations rather than investing or financing cash flows, as we showed in the previous chapter. For example, Tandy Corp. sold its receivables and increased operating cash flows.

Metals Company, a steel manufacturing firm, discusses in its press release the changes in earnings and operating cash flows:

COMMERCIAL METALS COMPANY REPORTS EARNINGS
OF $12 MILLION

Dallas—October 22, 1991 — Commercial Metals Company (NYSE) today reported net earnings of $12.0 million or $1.12 per share on sales of $1.2 billion for the year ended August 31, 1991. This compares with earnings of $25.9 million or $2.27 per share, on sales of $1.1 billion for the same period last year. Cash flow from operations was $38.0 million compared to $48.7 million last year.

CMC President and Chief Executive Officer Stanley A. Rabin said, "Following 3½ consecutive years of strong earnings and excellent cash flow from operations, fiscal 1991 results were lower because of the recession."

The U.S. Department of Commerce's Bureau of Economic Analysis (B.E.A.) issues macroeconomic data on its version of cash flow. The B.E.A. compiles data based on its two definitions of cash flow. *Net cash flow* is defined by the B.E.A. as undistributed profits—profits after the deduction of taxes and dividends plus the capital consumption allowance, that is, depreciation charges and accidental damage to fixed capital.

The B.E.A. defines *current production cash flow*, or *net cash flow with inventory valuation adjustment (IVA) and capital consumption adjustment (CCA)*, as the sum of undistributed profits with IVA and CCA plus capital consumption allowances with CCA. The IVA converts inventory costs as reported by businesses to replacement cost valuation, and the CCA converts capital consumption allowances, based on tax returns, to a replacement cost valuation and to uniform service lives and depreciation formulas. Current production cash flow differs from net cash flow in that inventory profits have been deducted from current production cash flow but not from net cash flow. The data for the most recent years is provided in the following table:

Year	*Profits before Taxes Inventory Valuation Adjustment and Capital Consumption Allowance Adjustment*	*Net Cash Flow and Inventory Valuation Adjustment*
1980	177,189	219,083
1981	187,958	253,957
1982	149,985	255,002
1983	213,745	307,697
1984	266,908	348,505
1985	282,323	371,314
1986	282,129	370,393
1987	298,704	378,370
1988	328,620	401,958
1989	299,234	392,840

SOURCE: Department of Commerce.

Since the B.E.A. focuses only on current production, financing enhancements such as debt and stock offerings, capital gains and losses, and other capital transfers are not included. Likewise, cash outflows such as capital expenditures, affiliate advances, and debt repayments are not included.

The B.E.A.'s current production definition of cash flow may be useful during inflationary periods because the IVA will turn negative during periods of rising inventory profits; expenses are understated, assuming such inventory will be replaced.

The "break" seen in 1981 when cash flow begins to exceed profits by a widening margin resulted from the stepped-up tax (over book) depreciation permitted as a result of the 1981 tax code. The capital consumption allowance, of course, has no effect on cash flow.

The B.E.A estimates actual tax payments as part of its quarterly gross national product and corporate profit announcements; with information supplied by the Internal Revenue Service, the B.E.A. estimates year-end actual tax payments from quarterly tax payments using extrapolation models. The B.E.A.'s tax estimates implicitly assume the previous year's tax rate and are modified to reflect changes in tax law.

The estimates of the B.E.A. can be used as guidelines when analyzing macroeconomic data. However, they are of little use when analyzing a particular firm or a specific group of firms.

To understand the limitations of the net operating cash flows for investment purposes, consider the following scenario. Security analysts tell us that a particular security is selling at just three times cash flow, and, therefore, must be a bargain. However, low cash flow multiples being quoted by either corporate officers or security analysts are almost always based on operating cash flow, not free cash flow, a concept we introduce later. It is implausible that firms in this era can sell at anything near three times their consistent free cash flow and not be subject to takeover bids, unless the entity is in de-facto liquidation. As a matter of fact, companies that sell at less than four times operating cash flow are typically net borrowers, as shown in Exhibit 5–1.

Example:

Forbes magazine ran the following headline in its January 8, 1990, issue.

AT TWO TIMES CASH FLOW, BETHLEHEM STEEL IS ONE OF THE CHEAPEST STOCKS ON THE BIG BOARD

Forbes did not specify whether Bethlehem Steel's low cash flow multiple was based on its net operating cash flow, but a review of the firm's statement of cash flows indicated that, indeed, net cash from operations was the denominator for the cash flow multiple. However, even a cursory review of Bethlehem Steel's statement of cash flows revealed three pertinent points:

1. A large portion of its high operating cash flow was consumed by its underfunded pension fund payment (about $170 million out of about $700 million in 1989, and about $515 million out of total operating cash flow of $890 million in 1988).

2. Its operating cash flow was probably near a cyclical peak, given Bethlehem's operating cash flow was just $186 million three years earlier.

Exhibit 5-1   Compustat Firms with Low Operating Cash Flow Multiples but High Rate of Financing— 1990 (Millions of Dollars)

The first column in the exhibit is the operating cash flow multiple, or the market value (column 3) divided by net operating cash flow (column 2). Column 4 reports net debt financing as a percentage of market value. Column 5 reports net equity financing as a percentage of market value. Column 6 is the sum of columns 4 and 5, and indicates total financing required by the firm as a percentage of market value. Averages for columns 4-6 are reported at the bottom of the exhibit.

Ticker Symbol	Name	OCF Multiple	Operating Cash Flow	Market Value $ Mil.	Percent Net Debt Financing	Percent Net Equity Financing	Total Financing/ Market Value
AGNC	AGENCY RENT-A-CAR INC	2.9	102.4	293.5	-4	-1	-5
AKZOY	AKZO NV -ADR	2.4	1138.6	2754.1	-12	0	-12
ALK	ALASKA AIRGROUP INC	2.9	103.2	298.4	46	5	51
ABSB	ALEX BROWN INC	3.3	88.4	290.3	-2	-6	-8
AA	ALUMINUM CO OF AMERICA	3.7	1586.7	5889.2	-3	-8	-11
AMX	AMAX INC	3.4	534.3	1816.0	25	-1	24
AHC	AMERADA HESS CORP	3.6	1326.4	4719.4	5	0	5
AXP	AMERICAN EXPRESS	2.7	4584.0	12452.8	6	43	49
AMI	AMERICAN MEDICAL HOLDINGS	1.9	247.3	481.0	202	41	243
BZR	BEAZER PLC -ADR	1.3	328.6	430.7	-34	11	-23
BS	BETHLEHEM STEEL CORP	3.8	354.4	1361.4	-4	-8	-12
BRO	BROAD INC	1.2	341.1	411.4	18	0	18
C	CHRYSLER CORP	1.1	2579.0	2755.0	-170	-2	-172
CDO	COMDISCO INC	0.5	1495.0	782.4	70	-8	62
CMC	COMMERCIAL METALS CO	3.4	60.9	207.5	-12	-7	-19
CQ	COMMUNICATIONS SATELLITE	3.9	155.3	610.9	0	0	0
CNF	CONSOLIDATED FREIGHTWAYS INC	2.9	194.8	573.3	7	0	7
ACCOB	COORS (ADOLPH) -CL B	3.2	231.0	743.9	15	1	16
CNP.A	CROWN CENTRAL PETROL -CL A	2.1	123.3	260.6	-16	0	-16
CYM	CYPRUS MINERALS CO	4.0	199.3	794.4	17	-11	6
DCN	DANA CORP	3.4	362.0	1232.5	15	-2	13
DAL	DELTA AIR LINES INC	3.5	803.8	2813.4	37	-8	29
DSP	DIAMOND SHAMRCK OFFSHOR -LP	3.3	84.0	273.6	0	0	0
DRM	DIAMOND SHAMROCK INC	3.5	179.3	622.3	-8	0	-8
DSL	DOWNEY SAVINGS & LOAN ASSC	3.5	70.3	246.5	71	-47	24
ELRNF	ELRON ELECTRONIC INDS -ORD	3.9	56.9	223.5	-11	16	5
ENE	ENRON CORP	3.0	1106.8	3274.2	7	-15	-9
FMC	FMC CORP	3.8	445.3	1692.1	-10	0	-10
FRE	FED HOME LOAN MTG CO	2.7	2103.0	5665.9	82	-2	80
FI	FINA INC -CL A	4.0	282.2	1117.6	10	0	10
F	FORD MOTOR CO	2.0	7413.8	14734.6	63	-1	62
GY	GENCORP INC	1.7	195.0	340.8	-51	15	-36
GD	GENERAL DYNAMICS CORP	2.9	609.0	1780.6	-12	3	-9
GM	GENERAL MOTORS CORP	3.5	6781.6	23467.0	8	-1	7
GMH	GENERAL MOTORS CL H	1.4	951.5	1334.8	4	0	4
GP	GEORGIA-PACIFIC CORP	2.4	2073.0	4892.3	50	-2	48
GT	GOODYEAR TIRE & RUBBER CO	3.9	574.3	2238.8	6	1	7
GEG	GRACE ENERGY CORP	3.9	104.3	411.5	6	0	6
GQ	GRUMMAN CORP	2.4	253.3	611.5	-27	-7	-34
GOU	GULF CANADA RES LTD -ORD	3.3	367.1	1208.0	35	0	35
HI	HOUSEHOLD INTERNATIONAL INC	2.9	766.9	2217.6	13	42	55
ITT	ITT CORP	3.5	1939.0	6859.6	12	10	23
IAD	INLAND STEEL INDUSTRIES INC	3.6	189.2	680.8	18	-19	-1
IRC	INSPIRATION RESOURCE	2.6	97.7	256.9	-4	0	-4
INEL	INTELLIGENT ELECTRONICS INC	2.5	147.1	368.5	-8	0	-7
IMC	INTL MULTIFOODS CORP	3.7	154.9	576.3	-21	0	-21
IPPIF	INTERPROVINCIAL PIPE LINE	3.6	287.5	1045.4	-1	0	0

Exhibit 5–1 *(continued)*

Ticker Symbol	Name	OCF Multiple	Operating Cash Flow	Market Value $ Mil.	Percent Net Debt Financing	Percent Net Equity Financing	Total Financing/ Market Value
ITL	ITEL CORP	1.0	592.9	599.7	-42	-34	-75
JCI	JOHNSON CONTROLS INC	4.0	327.9	1307.4	5	0	5
KLM	KLM ROYAL DUTCH AIR -NY REG	4.0	205.4	818.7	83	-3	80
KMG	KERR-MCGEE CORP	3.6	579.0	2070.9	-2	-5	-7
KR	KROGER CO	3.1	497.8	1529.6	-25	1	-24
LSI	LSI LOGIC CORP	3.7	81.2	304.3	-9	2	-6
LIT	LITTON INDUSTRIES INC	3.8	490.4	1861.7	-4	-8	-12
LTR	LOEWS CORP	3.1	2310.1	7218.9	2	-6	-5
MAGAF	MAGNA INTERNATIONAL -CL A	2.2	160.3	354.7	16	-2	14
MAG	MAGNETEK INC	3.6	86.0	310.4	8	-7	1
MVL	MANVILLE CORP	1.9	180.4	336.5	-24	0	-23
MXM	MAXXAM INC	2.2	163.4	354.4	-56	-11	-67
NER	NERCO INC	3.6	226.6	809.2	23	-1	22
NWS	NEWS CORP LTD -ADR	2.9	715.7	2080.6	55	-17	38
OCENY	OCE VAN DER GRINTEN NV -ADR	1.9	238.4	446.9	-6	-2	-9
ORX	ORYX ENERGY CO	3.5	825.0	2867.6	49	-34	15
OCF	OWENS CORNING FIBRGLAS	3.9	361.0	1411.0	-17	0	-17
PHH	PHH CORP	0.8	635.7	483.2	-47	0	-47
PHM	PHM CORP	2.0	169.8	346.9	-96	1	-95
PWJ	PAINE WEBBER GROUP	0.3	1893.9	616.2	-262	-2	-264
PCC	PATHE COMMUNICATIONS CP	0.3	786.5	204.3	232	172	404
PD	PHELPS DODGE CORP	3.7	641.9	2402.9	-3	-1	-4
PHG	PHILIPS N V -NY SHARE	2.2	2520.0	5535.8	9	3	13
PHX	PHLCORP	3.8	54.1	203.5	0	0	0
PDG	PLACER DOME INC	3.4	763.6	2601.5	3	-1	3
NX	QUANEX CORP	3.7	55.5	204.4	19	-5	13
RN	RJR NABISCO HLDGS CORP	3.8	2716.0	10417.0	-55	14	-41
RPU	RHONE-POULENC SA -SPON ADR	1.3	1577.2	1977.4	75	45	119
RLC	ROLLINS TRUCK LEASING	2.4	120.3	286.7	2	0	2
R	RYDER SYSTEM INC	1.4	934.5	1298.2	-26	-4	-31
RYL	RYLAND GROUP INC	3.4	74.2	255.5	-114	-6	-120
SCR	SEA CONTAINERS LTD	3.4	70.0	241.3	43	-198	-156
SGAT	SEAGATE TECHNOLOGY	2.9	228.0	656.1	32	1	33
S	SEARS ROEBUCK & CO	2.7	5362.8	14276.0	39	-11	29
SQA.A	SEQUA CORP -CL A	3.5	158.7	554.2	27	-7	20
STX	STERLING CHEMICALS INC	3.4	85.4	289.0	-1	-2	-3
STO	STONE CONTAINER CORP	2.8	468.6	1316.9	12	0	12
TPP	TEPPCO PARTNERS -LP	3.8	68.8	263.3	139	85	223
TRW	TRW INC	3.4	775.0	2650.2	1	0	1
TWFS	TW HOLDINGS INC	1.3	219.0	281.9	-33	-11	-44
TXN	TEXAS INSTRUMENTS INC	3.7	694.0	2591.9	3	0	3
TXT	TEXTRON INC	3.7	777.2	2848.7	22	-3	19
TKC	THIOKOL CP	2.8	132.5	370.1	0	0	0
COMS	3COM CORP	3.4	67.5	228.8	-1	2	2
TOS	TOSCO CORP	3.2	206.6	665.0	-13	-6	-19
TPN	TOTAL PETROLEUM OF N AMERICA	3.4	149.3	511.9	-6	3	-3
TA	TRANSAMERICA CORP	1.5	1800.6	2748.8	-34	26	-8
E	TRANSCO ENERGY CO	3.8	224.0	858.1	63	0	62
TNV	TRINOVA CORP	3.8	189.0	709.1	4	-16	-12
X	USX-U S STEEL GROUP	3.5	428.0	1487.6	-6	-6	-12
UK	UNION CARBIDE CORP	3.1	868.0	2719.7	18	-20	-3
UIS	UNISYS CORP	0.7	1340.4	930.1	-24	20	-4
WY	WEYERHAEUSER CO	3.5	1590.1	5558.1	0	4	4
YELL	YELLOW FREIGHT SYSTEM-DEL	4.0	219.5	870.8	-2	-2	-3
	AVERAGE				5	0	5

3. Bethlehem was operating with the benefit of a very low tax rate due to losses in prior years. This is verified by examining the tax footnote, which reveals a $1.3 billion tax loss carryforward for tax purposes, and $850 million for alternative minimum tax purposes. The $105.3 million actual tax payment for 1988, as revealed in the tax footnote, is comprised mostly of a $99.6 million settlement of audit adjustments and interest related to their federal income tax returns for the years 1971 through 1978.

In fact, Bethlehem Steel's operating cash flow dried up in its first quarter of 1990. During this quarter, operating cash flow fell to $6 million from $119 million in the prior year. This illustrates well why it is preferable to average (or normalize) operating cash flows over four years as well as analyze its growth rate during both the past four- and eight-year periods.

While Bethlehem Steel was, in fact, selling at twice its last year's operating cash flow, it was, more importantly, selling at 45 times free cash flow, which is the concept we introduce next. At that time, Bethlehem Steel's free cash flow multiple was *twice* the market average.

Example:

In its December 25, 1989, issue, *Business Week* showed a table that included companies with low cash flow multiples. For example, Universal Health was selling at 2.4 times cash flow and Inland Steel at 2.6 times cash flow. This implies a 42 percent annual return on cash invested for Inland Steel and 38 percent for Universal Health, an obviously exaggerated rate. This, again, is due to the focus on net operating cash flow, a measure that does not take into account needs for further investments by the firm nor retirement of debt.

When corporate officers speak of their firm's cash flow, they are typically alluding to operating cash flow—but not always. CPI Corporation, in a September 15, 1989, report, defined cash flow as operating earnings plus depreciation and amortization. However, with the disclosure of the statement of cash flows according to FAS No. 95, many analysts, investors, and creditors have a better-defined measure of net operating cash flow. For investment purposes, investors can follow a rule of thumb; for example, if management has been unable to show positive operating cash flows for even a single year, one should not recommend purchase of the stock, because a firm should be able to generate cash from its basic businesses in a consistent manner. In stable industries such as consumer nondurable goods, firms should be able to show positive operating cash flows every year and exhibit growth of operating cash flows that exceeds the rate of inflation over a four- and eight-year period. However, this rule is probably too strict for more cyclical industries, and one may wish to relax it somewhat, perhaps excluding only entities that have not produced positive operating cash flows in at least six out of the past eight years.

Example:

Sometimes entities such as Boeing and other long-term contractors would be possible investment opportunities for which the analyst should allow some flexibility in applying the previous investment rule. Such entities, which operate under very long lead times, must operate with large amounts of inventory on hand when beginning projects, and may have negative operating cash flows in the beginning of the operating cycle. One can

Bethlehem Steel: Consolidated Statements of Cash Flows

Consolidated Statements of Cash Flows

		Year ended December 31	
(dollars in millions)	1989	1988	1987
Operating Activities:			
Net Income	$ 245.7	$ 403.0	$ 174.3
Extraordinary gains	—	11.4	70.4
Income before extraordinary gains	245.7	391.6	103.9
Adjustments for items not affecting cash from operating activities:			
Depreciation	325.3	333.6	338.9
Estimated restructuring losses — net (Note C)	105.0	113.0	75.0
Deferred taxes, etc.	12.6	19.7	(3.0)
Working Capital*:			
Receivables	61.6	(89.0)	(99.3)
Inventories	(43.9)	(61.4)	9.8
Accounts payable	29.8	50.3	47.3
Accrued employment costs	(33.6)	81.7	15.0
Accrued taxes	(.1)	(1.7)	5.6
Investment tax credit refund receivable (Note E)	—	130.0	(130.0)
Federal income tax payment (Note E)	—	(99.6)	—
Other — net	4.1	20.5	(1.7)
Cash Provided from Operating Activities	706.5	888.7	361.5
Investing Activities:			
Capital expenditures	(421.3)	(303.9)	(152.7)
Cash proceeds from sales of businesses and assets	38.4	47.2	87.8
Collateral investments	10.1	208.4	(84.2)
Other — net	23.6	18.4	14.3
Cash Used for Investing Activities	(349.2)	(29.9)	(134.8)
Financing Activities:			
Pension financing (funding) — net (Note I)	(172.7)	(514.3)	56.6
Revolving credit payments	—	(240.0)	(120.0)
Long-term debt payments (Note F)	(63.5)	(72.6)	(205.5)
Capital lease payments (Note G)	(34.8)	(155.7)	(52.4)
Restructured facilities payments	(27.5)	(63.2)	(34.9)
Cash dividends paid (Note L)	(37.5)	(45.0)	(11.2)
Common Stock issued (Note L)	1.0	185.4	188.0
Accrued employee investment plan stock	.8	2.0	41.6
Cash Used for Financing Activities	(334.2)	(903.4)	(137.8)
Net Increase (Decrease) in Cash and Cash Equivalents	23.1	(44.6)	88.9
Cash and Cash Equivalents — Beginning of Period	507.4	552.0	463.1
— End of Period	$ 530.5	$ 507.4	$ 552.0
Supplemental Cash Payment Information:			
Interest, net of amount capitalized	$ 65.0	$ 86.0	$ 142.6
Income taxes (Note E)	$ 9.0	$ 105.7	$ 2.6

*Excludes Financing Activities, Investing Activities, Investment tax credit refund receivable and Federal income tax payment.
The accompanying Notes are an integral part of the Consolidated Financial Statements.

Source: Bethlehem Steel Corp., *Annual Report*, 1989.

Bethlehem Steel Corporation: Consolidated Statements of Cash Flows

Bethlehem Steel Corporation

CONSOLIDATED STATEMENTS OF CASH FLOWS
(dollars in millions)

	Three Months Ended March 31	
	1991 (unaudited)	1990 (unaudited)
Operating Activities:		
Net Income (Loss)	$ (39.2)	$ 21.3
Adjustments for items not affecting cash from operating activities:		
Depreciation	58.3	75.8
Other - net (including deferred taxes)	17.3	-
Working capital (excluding financing and investing activities):		
Receivables	(17.7)	(37.3)
Inventories	(41.4)	(2.9)
Accounts payable	(27.7)	(23.9)
Accrued taxes and employment costs	(5.1)	(41.7)
Other - net	(1.3)	14.7
Cash Provided from (Used for) Operating Activities	(56.8)	6.0
Investing Activities:		
Capital expenditures	(102.6)	(100.2)
Cash proceeds from sales of businesses and assets	2.8	3.5
Collateral investments	-	(0.1)
Other - net	(2.0)	3.6
Cash Used for Investing Activities	(101.8)	(93.2)
Financing Activities:		
Pension financing (funding) - net	13.0	(45.5)
Revolving credit borrowings	80.0	-
Long-term debt borrowings	19.8	-
Long-term debt and capital lease payments	(10.8)	(10.2)
Restructured facilities payments	(5.0)	(7.2)
Cash dividends paid	(13.2)	(13.2)
Stock issued	-	0.5
Cash Provided from (Used for) Financing Activities	83.8	(75.6)
Net Decrease in Cash and Cash Equivalents	(74.8)	(162.8)
Cash and Cash Equivalents - Beginning of Period	273.5	530.5
- End of Period	$ 198.7	$ 367.7
Supplemental Cash Payment Information:		
Interest, net of amount capitalized	$ 18.3	$ 17.8
Income taxes	$ 1.8	$ 0.6

SOURCE: Bethlehem Steel Corp., First Quarter Report, Form 10-Q, 1991.

then modify the rule to preclude investment in entities that have two successive years of negative operating cash flows regardless of their industry.

Negative operating cash flows indicates that management has been unable to employ the assets of the entity properly or that the entity has encountered economic difficulties in producing cash flows. However, the financial services industry is an exception to the negative operating cash flows rule, because the purchase of investments—a use of cash—could cause negative operating cash flows.

5.4 CAN NET OPERATING CASH FLOW BE USED FOR PORTFOLIO SELECTION?

As is well known, many investors consider the P/E ratio their chief investment criterion when making portfolio selections. Fewer investors consider measures that are based on cash flows, particularly net cash flows from operating activities. Can this variable be used to identify investment candidates? This section examines the availability of firms with increasing cash flows from operating activities. In Chapter 7, we compare the performance of portfolios that are based on P/E ratios, net operating cash flow, and free cash flows.

A casual examination of the data shows that there is no shortage of entities that consistently generate positive operating cash flows each year, and it is easy to construct a diversified portfolio of such entities. For example, limiting ourselves to firms with a market capitalization above $200 million, positive reported net cash flow from operating activities in 1989, and estimated positive net operating cash flow for 1981, we find that 456 out of 606 available firms included in the Compustat Industrial File have shown positive growth rates in operating cash flows during the period 1981–1989.

It should be noted that firms with high net income growth are not necessarily firms with high operating cash flows growth, or vice versa.

Example:

During 1989, Borden, Inc. reported a $60.6 million loss but generated $212 million in operating cash flow. The major difference was a write-off of $571 million, which the company called a "reconfiguration charge," which was actually a noncash charge. A natural question is, of course, which measure is a better indicator of the company's financial success that year—the earnings report or the operating cash flow? Given that the write-off of older manufacturing facilities located in nongrowth areas and the consolidation and expansion of other facilities can be expected to enhance future operating cash flow, one can conclude that Borden's operating cash flow provided better "feedback", that is, gave the investor better predictive information than earnings for the year.

Exhibits 5–2 through 5–5 show large entities (with a market value of $200 million or more) whose operating cash flow is dramatically different from reported income. Exhibit 5–2 shows entities that had an operating profit for the most recent year, yet were characterized by negative operating cash flow. Exhibit 5–3 shows entities with an operating loss for the most recent year, yet had positive net operating cash flow. Exhibit 5–4 shows entities with average negative operating cash flow during the most recent four fiscal years, but with a positive average operating profit over the same period.

Exhibit 5–2 Firms with Positive Earnings and Negative Operating Cash Flow—1990 (Millions of Dollars)

Ticker	Name	Earnings	Net OCF	Market Value
AHM	AHMANSON (H.F.) & CO	191.0	-31.5	2121.7
AWT	AIR & WATER TECH -CL A	6.5	-7.8	516.1
AC	ALLIANCE CAPITAL MGMT -LP	33.9	-4.0	1047.5
APCC	AMERICAN PWR CNVRSION	9.3	-0.4	783.0
ACCMA	ASSOCIATED COMMUN -CL A	10.6	-2.9	709.3
BHC	BHC COMMUNICATIONS -CL A	481.2	-128.6	1525.6
BSC	BEAR STEARNS COMPANIES INC	119.4	-392.9	1974.4
BRAN	BRAND COMPANIES INC	11.2	-10.9	500.0
CML	C M L GROUP	14.0	-1.3	588.5
CDIC	CARDINAL DISTRIBUTION INC	17.4	-23.4	624.2
CCN	CHRIS-CRAFT INDS	291.7	-132.3	677.7
CCON	CIRCON CORP	0.3	0.0	222.4
CGRP	COASTAL HEALTHCARE GROUP INC	3.3	-0.2	365.6
CBU	COMMODORE INTL LTD	1.5	-2.9	486.0
CLIX	COMPRESSION LABS	2.6	-3.1	272.3
CDA	CONTROL DATA CORP	2.7	-85.8	489.0
CCR	COUNTRYWIDE CREDIT IND INC	22.3	-124.5	1224.2
DIA	DIASONICS INC	16.4	-17.2	205.8
DBRL	DIBRELL BROTHERS INC	14.6	-44.0	419.9
DUFM	DURR-FILLAUER MEDICAL	17.1	-3.5	288.3
FHT	FINGERHUT COMPANIES INC	47.7	-39.4	807.7
GLN	GLENFED INC	114.9	-140.7	256.7
GOT	GOTTSCHALKS INC	6.4	-5.1	231.5
GNT	GREEN TREE ACCEPTANCE INC	36.5	-17.6	510.2
HDYN	HEALTHDYNE INC	8.0	-3.9	394.3
HMY	HEILIG-MEYERS CO	20.9	-18.0	615.6
IRIC	INFORMATION RESOURCES INC	4.8	-2.5	765.2
IHSI	INTEGRATED HEALTH SVCS INC	1.4	-2.3	206.6
ITN	INTERTAN INC	27.7	-9.2	208.7
JSTN	JUSTIN INDUSTRIES	7.3	-3.7	209.1
KBH	KAUFMAN & BROAD HOME CORP	39.9	-43.3	670.3
KMATY	KOMATSU LTD -ADR	221.7	-174.4	5571.3
KUB	KUBOTA CORP -ADR	51.3	-62.9	7148.8
LA	L.A. GEAR INC	31.3	-40.3	300.4
LM	LEGG MASON INC	12.9	-2.5	229.7
LES	LESLIE FAY COMPANIES INC	29.1	-12.3	395.6
MAIL	MAIL BOXES ETC	4.0	-1.5	238.8
IV	MARK IV INDUSTRIES INC	24.9	-0.7	533.2
MCAWA	MCCAW CELLULAR COMM -CL A	371.4	-150.0	6377.0
MDV	MEDEVA PLC -SPON ADR	7.7	-1.5	639.9
MSEL	MERISEL INC	0.6	-15.7	279.4
MER	MERRILL LYNCH & CO	191.9	-182.5	5939.6
MIPS	MIPS COMPUTER SYSTEMS INC	7.1	-17.1	271.1
MS	MORGAN STANLEY GROUP INC	270.4	-4679.3	4247.6

Exhibit 5-2   (*continued*)

Ticker	Name	Earnings	Net OCF	Market Value
NLN	NEW LINE CINEMA CORP	6.3	-1.6	212.5
ODP	OFFICE DEPOT INC	9.7	-1.6	1358.1
OS	OREGON STEEL MILLS INC	28.5	-4.0	427.2
PIPR	PIPER JAFFRAY INC	10.3	-23.8	256.0
QHRI	QUANTUM HEALTH RESOURCES INC	1.2	-5.2	303.5
BQR	QUICK & REILLY GROUP INC	11.8	-6.7	260.2
RHR	ROHR INC	0.0	-155.7	353.0
RVAC	ROYAL APPLIANCE MFG CO	11.7	-5.4	564.0
RUS	RUSS BERRIE & CO INC	17.4	-7.5	385.8
SPW	SPX CORP	17.7	-31.4	214.3
SB	SALOMON INC	303.0	-174.0	3375.2
SQNT	SEQUENT COMPUTER SYSTEMS INC	18.8	-9.0	359.6
SDW	SOUTHDOWN INC	13.4	-22.2	245.1
SP	SPELLING ENTMT INC -CL A	6.5	-6.7	210.5
SPGLA	SPIEGEL INC -CL A	61.5	-130.9	805.7
SPLS	STAPLES INC	3.7	-3.9	578.8
SSSS	STEWART & STEVENSON SERVICES	29.4	-54.8	820.8
TRMB	TRIMBLE NAVIGATION LTD	2.1	-6.1	230.5
UTVI	UNITED TELEVISION INC	48.5	-7.2	269.6
VLMR	VALUE MERCHANTS INC	5.3	-8.2	259.3
VC	VENCOR INC	3.3	-5.9	529.6
VIRA	VIRATEK INC	1.3	-2.4	288.9

Exhibit 5-5 shows entities whose growth rates of operating cash flow are in excess of 10 percent per year during the most recent eight years, with an additional criterion that they can repay their debt from their operating cash flows (before interest payments) within five years. The growth rate in operating cash flow is important for investment purposes because entities that cannot show sufficient growth in operating cash flow, in effect, cannibalize themselves.

One can also select firms for a portfolio based on their operating cash flow multiples, as opposed to their price/earnings multiples. However, because some nonrecurring cash flows might be included in net operating cash flows, it is more judicious to average the net operating cash flows in the most recent four years. By calculating the average net operating cash flow multiple, we make adjustments for material changes affecting the entity, such as changes in financial leverage or changes in the nature of the business as a result of a business combination. For the majority of entities, it is preferable to study the four- and eight-year operating cash flow history. An eight-year period will almost assuredly contain at least one industry downturn or other major event (i.e., large acquisition, reorganization). Four- and eight-year periods represent suitable time periods for studying operating cash flows over a typical business cycle; it is important to study how management reacts or anticipates major turns of the business cycle. This examination offers the cash flow analyst important clues about how assets and cash flows are managed in the firm.

Exhibit 5–3 Firms with Negative Earnings and Positive Cash Flow— 1990 (Millions of Dollars)

Ticker	Name	Earnings	Net OCF	Market Value
AMR	AMR CORP-DEL	-39.6	685.8	5054.2
ADLAC	ADELPHIA COMMUN -CL A	-141.4	31.8	260.8
AMD	ADVANCED MICRO DEVICES	-53.6	108.0	1625.6
AMI	AMERICAN MEDICAL HOLDINGS	-82.3	247.3	842.8
APS	AMERICAN PRESIDENT COS LTD	-59.6	106.5	466.2
ADI	ANALOG DEVICES	-12.9	82.2	448.7
AZTR	AZTAR CORP	-15.9	15.7	250.4
BLY	BALLY MFG CORP	-292.3	105.8	274.3
BS	BETHLEHEM STEEL CORP	-463.5	354.4	1105.2
CTEX	C TEC CORP	-9.6	52.8	251.5
CVC	CABLEVISION SYSTEMS -CL A	-271.4	51.6	729.9
CACOA	CATO CORP -CL A	-10.0	6.2	232.6
CTY	CENTURY COMMUN -CL A	-80.3	21.7	797.8
CHR	CHARTER CO	-0.4	27.2	328.4
CMZ	CINCINNATI MILACRON INC	-22.1	32.7	451.5
CMCSA	COMCAST CORP -CL A	-178.4	97.6	2027.2
CQ	COMMUNICATIONS SATELLITE	-16.3	155.3	735.1
CNF	CONSOLIDATED FREIGHTWAYS INC	-28.0	194.8	574.2
CUM	CUMMINS ENGINE	-165.1	32.4	892.1
DGN	DATA GENERAL CORP	-139.8	46.0	354.9
DTC	DOMTAR INC	-286.9	66.4	457.6
ECO	ECHO BAY MINES LTD	-59.7	100.1	780.6
ENQ	ENQUIRER/STAR GROUP -CL A	-6.3	63.6	849.7
FPP	FISHER-PRICE INC	-37.3	88.0	523.0
FQA	FUQUA INDUSTRIES INC	-1.2	4.3	241.5
GD	GENERAL DYNAMICS CORP	-639.0	609.0	2436.1
GM	GENERAL MOTORS CORP	-1985.7	6781.6	23560.9
GSX	GENERAL SIGNAL CORP	-13.3	63.0	1076.0
GLM	GLOBAL MARINE INC	-35.8	42.7	226.4
GT	GOODYEAR TIRE & RUBBER CO	-38.3	574.3	3662.7
GFD	GUILFORD MILLS INC	-8.0	49.3	338.5
GOU	GULF CANADA RES LTD -ORD	-12.9	367.1	759.9
HTI	HEALTHTRUST INC-THE HSPTL CO	-53.2	348.6	1257.8
HENG	HENLEY GROUP INC/DEL	-101.0	41.0	569.9
HLN	HOLNAM INC	-28.0	28.0	606.6
HOME	HOMEDCO GROUP INC	-2.2	12.2	344.4
HM	HOMESTAKE MINING	-19.0	53.9	1565.3
ICN	ICN PHARMACEUTICALS INC-DEL	-26.7	22.5	240.2
5146B	INFINITY BROADCASTING -CL B	-39.7	8.9	217.7
IFMX	INFORMIX CORP	-23.1	2.7	420.5
IAD	INLAND STEEL INDUSTRIES INC	-20.6	189.2	746.9
IRC	INSPIRATION RESOURCE	-24.9	97.7	335.9
INMT	INTERMET CORP	-10.4	20.4	224.6
ISLI	INTERSOLV	-23.3	8.6	212.3

Exhibit 5–3   (*continued*)

Ticker	Name	Earnings	Net OCF	Market Value
IBCC	INTERSTATE BAKERIES CP	-8.2	59.9	350.3
ITL	ITEL CORP	-32.8	592.9	549.1
IVX	IVAX CORP	-0.8	5.8	2212.2
KLM	KLM ROYAL DUTCH AIR -NY REG	-184.7	205.4	1122.4
LSI	LSI LOGIC CORP	-33.9	81.2	399.4
LAC	LAC MINERALS LTD	-64.3	110.4	1001.7
LFC	LOMAS FINANCIAL CP	-452.4	284.6	320.6
MAGAF	MAGNA INTERNATIONAL -CL A	-194.6	160.3	661.4
MAN	MANPOWER INC/WI	-82.2	85.8	1118.1
MASX	MASCO INDUSTRIES INC	-24.4	72.1	497.9
MXTR	MAXTOR CORP	-45.4	13.2	208.8
MDR	MCDERMOTT INTL INC	-86.3	5.6	936.6
MCCS	MEDCO CONTAINMENT SVCS INC	-8.0	66.0	4434.6
MEDI	MEDIMMUNE INC	-4.1	0.4	432.0
MDP	MEREDITH CORP	-1.4	45.5	458.0
NEC	NATIONAL EDUCATION CORP	-14.9	26.9	282.4
NSM	NATIONAL SEMICONDUCTOR CORP	-150.3	125.9	1065.4
NAV	NAVISTAR INTERNATIONAL	-11.0	108.0	937.9
NWK	NETWORK EQUIPMENT TECH INC	-49.6	5.2	245.3
NNCXF	NEWBRIDGE NETWORKS CORP	-10.3	7.8	481.0
OXY	OCCIDENTAL PETROLEUM CORP	-1688.0	1526.0	6059.2
ORCL	ORACLE SYSTEMS CORP	-12.4	89.4	2800.9
OM	OUTBOARD MARINE CORP	-77.3	42.6	494.7
OI	OWENS-ILLINOIS INC	-56.2	248.2	475.6
PAGE	PAGING NETWORK INC	-0.8	9.3	609.9
PWJ	PAINE WEBBER GROUP	-57.4	1893.9	916.6
PKD	PARKER DRILLING CO	-18.8	8.7	275.8
PCC	PATHE COMMUNICATIONS CP	-120.9	786.5	335.6
PGU	PEGASUS GOLD INC	-38.2	30.2	379.4
PNF	PENN TRAFFIC CO	-27.5	59.1	255.0
PHG	PHILIPS N V -NY SHARE	-2679.8	2520.0	5461.5
PL	PINELANDS INC	-5.0	28.2	264.4
QVCN	QVC NETWORK INC	-17.0	21.5	446.9
RN	RJR NABISCO HLDGS CORP	-462.0	2716.0	8904.8
RB	READING & BATES CORP	-53.3	22.8	356.1
REPH	REPUBLIC HEALTH CP/DEL	-101.2	11.2	205.3
ROUS	ROUSE CO	-1.2	35.1	752.6
SHKIF	SHL SYSTEMHOUSE INC	-35.2	15.8	510.9
SFP	SANTA FE ENERGY PRTNRS -LP	-7.7	76.4	201.9
SFX	SANTA FE PACIFIC CORP	-101.2	230.5	2125.4
SHR	SCHERER (R.P.)/DE	-6.7	22.8	242.2
SFLD	SEAFIELD CAPITAL CORP	-21.3	31.5	229.0
SMI	SPRINGS INDUSTRIES -CL A	-6.8	115.6	645.5
SYBS	SYBASE INC	-6.0	1.9	548.0
TWFS	TW HOLDINGS INC	-67.8	219.0	405.5

Exhibit 5-3   (*continued*)

Ticker	Name	Earnings	Net OCF	Market Value
TCOMA	TELE-COMMUNICATIONS -CL A	-287.0	474.0	5663.9
TER	TERADYNE INC	-21.3	40.9	605.8
TXN	TEXAS INSTRUMENTS INC	-39.0	694.0	3097.8
COMS	3COM CORP	-27.7	53.8	396.8
TWX	TIME WARNER INC	-227.0	649.0	9314.5
TRB	TRIBUNE CO	-63.5	273.4	2821.6
TAM	TUBOS DE ACERO DE MEX -ADR	-8.6	46.8	435.9
TBS.A	TURNER BROADCASTING -CL A	-15.6	412.5	4094.2
UIS	UNISYS CORP	436.7	1340.4	1738.7
U	USAIR GROUP	-454.4	90.8	796.4
USR	U S SHOE CORP	-27.7	73.0	662.4
VLSI	VLSI TECHNOLOGY INC	-12.7	17.6	256.5
VANS	VANS INC	-0.2	5.7	222.5
VIA	VIACOM INC	-89.8	99.0	4162.8
WMS	WMS INDUSTRIES INC	-10.3	3.0	447.0
WAN.B	WANG LABORATORIES -CL B	-628.6	46.2	846.6
WATFZ	WATERFORD WEDGWOOD PLC -ADR	-48.1	23.4	734.9
WH	WHITMAN CORP	-31.3	141.6	1655.4

Typically, corporate managers and directors who have confidence in their entity's products and long-run outlook will continue to make necessary expenditures to ensure that operating cash flows will grow in the future. However, some corporate officers may panic at the first sign of a business downturn and "prune" the entity's balance sheet (primarily receivables, inventories, payables, and fixes assets). Others prudently adjust their level of discretionary spending to match a lower rate of expected growth. Sales of assets during a period of business weakness may be suboptimal, because assets would probably be sold at distressed prices. Thus, examination of net operating cash flows over an entire business cycle is important for the cash flow analyst.

Although net operating cash flows may be a better indicator of financial health and valuation than operating profits, it also suffers weaknesses. For example, net operating cash flows as reported by firms may include nonrecurring items. Such items as payments or receipts from settlements of legal suits are included in net operating cash flows, as are proceeds from insurance policies in excess of property book values destroyed by fire. However, such items will probably not recur in the near future, and should, therefore, be excluded from predictions of future cash flows. Because most firms use the indirect method to derive net operating cash flows (see Chapters 3 and 4 for a detailed discussion), the cash flow analyst cannot accurately derive these amounts that are not expected to recur in the future.

Another problem associated with operating cash flows is the classification of certain events as either operating cash flows or investing cash flows. For example, some real-estate firms classify mortgages as operating cash flows and some as investment

Exhibit 5–4   Firms with Average Positive Earnings and Average Negative Operating Cash Flow— 1990 (Millions of Dollars)

Ticker	Name	Average Earnings	Average Net OCF	Market Value
ARW	ARROW ELECTRONICS INC	1.8	-1.8	300.4
ACCMA	ASSOCIATED COMMUN -CL A	6.0	-13.8	709.3
BHC	BHC COMMUNICATIONS -CL A	435.8	-159.6	1525.6
BSC	BEAR STEARNS COMPANIES INC	144.9	-227.1	1974.4
BRAN	BRAND COMPANIES INC	5.3	-2.9	500.0
CCFR	CCC FRANCHISING CORP	0.0	0.0	208.2
CDIC	CARDINAL DISTRIBUTION INC	10.9	-10.3	624.2
FUN	CEDAR FAIR -LP	25.0	-2.4	417.9
CCN	CHRIS-CRAFT INDS	199.2	-117.0	677.7
CLCDF	CLEARLY CDN BEVERAGE CP	0.2	-2.2	293.0
CGRP	COASTAL HEALTHCARE GROUP INC	3.3	-0.2	365.6
CNM	CONTINENTAL MEDICAL SYSTEMS	7.3	-2.6	743.5
DEPLF	DEPRENYL RESEARCH LTD	2.0	-0.4	260.6
DIA	DIASONICS INC	5.0	-4.7	205.8
DBRL	DIBRELL BROTHERS INC	15.8	-0.2	419.9
EMC	EMC CORP-MASS	2.7	-0.4	389.1
EGGS	EGGHEAD INC/WA	0.2	-9.8	406.3
GIT	GITANO GROUP INC	20.6	-23.5	301.8
GLN	GLENFED INC	40.7	-3.1	256.7
GGUY	GOOD GUYS INC	6.4	-0.2	263.8
GOT	GOTTSCHALKS INC	5.0	-2.7	231.5
HDYN	HEALTHDYNE INC	6.5	-4.1	394.3
HMY	HEILIG-MEYERS CO	18.0	-7.2	615.6
IHSI	INTEGRATED HEALTH SVCS INC	1.4	-0.8	206.6
JBM	JAN BELL MARKETING INC	9.1	-20.1	421.5
KBH	KAUFMAN & BROAD HOME CORP	51.2	-36.9	670.3
LA	L.A. GEAR INC	28.2	-35.3	300.4
LES	LESLIE FAY COMPANIES INC	24.2	-9.8	395.6
MAIL	MAIL BOXES ETC	2.4	-1.1	238.8
IV	MARK IV INDUSTRIES INC	23.0	-9.2	533.2
MDV	MEDEVA PLC -SPON ADR	1.8	-1.5	639.9
MSEL	MERISEL INC	6.4	-15.4	279.4
MIPS	MIPS COMPUTER SYSTEMS INC	3.7	-8.9	271.1
MS	MORGAN STANLEY GROUP INC	334.7	-4156.9	4247.6
NLN	NEW LINE CINEMA CORP	3.9	-4.0	212.5
NTM	NUTMEG INDUSTRIES INC	2.0	-1.5	200.5
ODP	OFFICE DEPOT INC	6.2	-8.1	1358.1
PWJ	PAINE WEBBER GROUP	27.9	-522.3	916.6
QHRI	QUANTUM HEALTH RESOURCES INC	1.2	-5.2	303.5
BQR	QUICK & REILLY GROUP INC	12.6	-2.6	260.2
RHR	ROHR INC	24.1	-102.6	353.0
RVAC	ROYAL APPLIANCE MFG CO	11.7	-5.4	564.0
SB	SALOMON INC	298.8	-382.0	3375.2
SQNT	SEQUENT COMPUTER SYSTEMS INC	10.3	-4.0	359.6

Exhibit 5–4   (*continued*)

Ticker	Name	Average Earnings	Average Net OCF	Market Value
SPGLA	SPIEGEL INC -CL A	58.2	-19.8	805.7
SPF	STANDARD PACIFIC CP	68.5	-12.5	366.1
SPLS	STAPLES INC	2.0	-6.3	578.8
SSSS	STEWART & STEVENSON SERVICES	22.5	-14.3	820.8
TECD	TECH DATA CORP	5.4	-7.4	282.0
TOL	TOLL BROTHERS INC	15.8	-14.7	421.0
TRMB	TRIMBLE NAVIGATION LTD	1.3	-4.1	230.5
UTVI	UNITED TELEVISION INC	31.4	-7.2	269.6
VLMR	VALUE MERCHANTS INC	3.9	-3.7	259.3
VC	VENCOR INC	1.8	-1.7	529.6
WBB	WEBB (DEL E.) CORP	8.3	-8.5	243.1

cash flows. Cray Research treated its investment in super-computers that are under operating leases and that are expected to be sold in the future as an operating cash flow in 1987, but as an investing cash flow in 1988. Such classification problems may disappear as firms gain familiarity with FAS No. 95.

Furthermore, net operating cash flow measures only the increase in cash that occurred during the period due to ongoing operations of the firm. However, in most cases, if the firm does not reinvest some of the net cash flow generated by operations, the firm gradually shrinks until it finally liquidates. Most firms have to invest in their productive facilities, their distribution channels, or their administrative facilities every period, just to remain competitive. Thus, net operating cash flows almost always understates the cash that owners of a growth company can consume without affecting the economic viability of their firm. This leads us to the concept of free cash flow.

5.5 FREE CASH FLOW

Free cash flow is an intuitive concept; it focuses on the amount of cash that owners of a business can consume without reducing the value of the business. It recognizes that a business has to invest in current and long-term assets in order to continue its operations. Thus, free cash flow focuses on the business's ability to generate cash flows beyond those that are needed to invest in such assets as inventories, plant and equipment, securities of other firms, and so on. *When a firm is able to generate more cash flows from its ongoing operations than is needed to remain in business, the firm has free cash flows.* Such a firm can immediately distribute the free cash flows to its owners through dividends, or retain the free cash flows within the firm for further growth and even greater free cash flows in the future. Thus, a firm with free cash flows may be a good candidate for investment, because these free cash flows will eventually lead to higher security prices.

Exhibit 5–5   Firms with High Growth in Operating Cash Flow During 1983–1990 and Low
Debt (Millions of Dollars)

Ticker Symbol	Name	Growth OCF	Debt/ OCF	Average OCF	Total Debt
ADCT	ADC TELECOMMUNICATIONS INC	14.6	2.6	18.4	47.7
ABT	ABBOTT LABORATORIES	18.6	3.6	758.9	2729.5
AMP	AMP INC	13.9	3.5	323.0	1135.9
ADI	ANALOG DEVICES	16.9	2.7	53.0	144.5
ADM	ARCHER-DANIELS-MIDLAND CO	19.5	4.8	389.6	1876.8
AIND	ARNOLD INDUSTRIES INC	22.3	1.9	19.2	36.5
AUD	AUTOMATIC DATA PROCESSING	14.9	2.5	227.8	565.2
BETZ	BETZ LABORATORIES INC	12.7	3.7	55.8	206.7
BMET	BIOMET INC	118.6	3.9	9.8	37.7
BL	BLAIR CORP	15.7	3.5	18.4	64.5
BOBE	BOB EVANS FARMS	13.9	1.2	37.3	45.4
BVI	BOW VALLEY INDUSTRIES LTD	32.8	3.7	96.2	351.5
BMY	BRISTOL MYERS SQUIBB	18.4	4.3	886.5	3797.0
CPY	CPI CORP	24.3	1.8	37.0	67.0
CZM	CALMAT CO	39.2	3.2	50.4	160.9
CLE	CLAIRE'S STORES INC	28.2	4.8	12.5	60.5
CMY	COMMUNITY PSYCHIATRIC CNTRS	20.5	2.2	40.9	91.1
CPER	CONSOLIDATED PAPERS INC	14.4	1.7	159.1	271.6
CBRL	CRACKER BARREL OLD CTRY STOR	33.9	4.0	11.2	45.2
CYR	CRAY RESEARCH	30.3	2.0	155.6	315.2
ATX.A	CROSS (A.T.) & CO -CL A	15.5	1.6	28.1	45.1
DLX	DELUXE CORP	12.8	1.6	150.8	248.1
DP	DIAGNOSTIC PRODUCTS CORP	38.1	3.0	5.2	15.4
DEC	DIGITAL EQUIPMENT	32.1	3.3	1049.9	3472.9
DOV	DOVER CORP	10.5	4.2	160.9	680.7
ECL	ECOLAB INC	12.1	4.6	101.8	473.4
EC	ENGELHARD CORP	13.0	4.9	124.0	610.2
EBF	ENNIS BUSINESS FORMS	17.6	1.0	16.8	17.4
FSI	FLIGHTSAFETY INTERNATIONAL	13.1	3.1	63.1	197.8
FRK	FLORIDA ROCK INDS	11.6	3.1	43.1	133.3
GCI	GANNETT CO	13.7	4.0	442.0	1763.1
GPS	GAP INC	40.1	3.4	91.1	311.2
GME	GENERAL MOTORS CL E	51.8	4.4	547.7	2383.5
GPC	GENUINE PARTS CO	14.2	2.4	134.2	318.8
GFS.A	GIANT FOOD INC -CL A	15.7	4.8	128.2	619.2
GLT	GLATFELTER (P.H.) CO	16.4	2.8	65.7	186.0
GLX	GLAXO HOLDINGS PLC -ADR	36.1	3.6	788.8	2842.0
HONI	HON INDUSTRIES	24.2	3.6	40.1	145.4
HUN	HUNT MFG	15.5	4.4	12.6	54.8
INTC	INTEL CORP	39.2	4.4	404.7	1784.8
INGR	INTERGRAPH CORP	44.3	4.2	53.2	225.2
INDQA	INTL DAIRY QUEEN -CL A	20.8	4.6	16.9	78.2
IFF	INTL FLAVORS & FRAGRANCES	10.3	2.5	92.4	231.2
JNJ	JOHNSON & JOHNSON	12.3	4.6	1010.7	4606.0

Exhibit 5-5 (*continued*)

Ticker Symbol	Name	Growth OCF	Debt/ OCF	Average OCF	Total Debt
KELYA	KELLY SERVICES INC -CL A	33.9	2.4	45.0	106.0
KBALB	KIMBALL INTERNATIONAL -CL B	15.6	2.2	44.0	98.6
LLY	LILLY (ELI) & CO	11.6	4.0	916.9	3675.3
LIZ	LIZ CLAIBORNE INC	38.0	3.3	82.3	271.4
LUB	LUBY'S CAFETERIAS INC	16.3	1.7	30.8	52.4
MMC	MARSH & MCLENNAN COS	12.8	4.8	277.0	1325.9
MX	MEASUREX CORP	12.3	3.1	31.6	98.8
MRK	MERCK & CO	16.4	3.6	1164.8	4195.4
MLHR	MILLER (HERMAN) INC	15.9	5.0	44.2	219.7
MOLX	MOLEX INC	17.8	1.9	66.3	125.6
3MBEN	MOORE (BENJAMIN) & CO	10.3	2.6	23.7	61.5
MCL	MOORE CORP LTD	10.4	3.1	201.8	628.0
MORR	MORRISON INC	11.2	3.4	41.0	139.5
MYL	MYLAN LABORATORIES	30.9	1.1	14.3	16.3
NLCS	NATIONAL COMPUTER SYS INC	23.2	4.0	31.1	124.5
NSI	NATIONAL SERVICE INDS INC	12.5	3.1	92.5	286.7
NGNA	NEUTROGENA CORP	30.2	3.0	13.7	41.6
NEBS	NEW ENGLAND BUSINESS SVC INC	13.6	1.4	18.9	26.4
NHL	NEWHALL LAND &FARM -LP	28.0	3.8	38.7	148.5
4441B	PALABORA MINING -ADR	13.0	3.5	78.5	278.2
PNS	PANSOPHIC SYSTEMS INC	14.7	2.3	16.5	37.5
PKN	PERKIN-ELMER CORP	13.8	4.0	114.8	462.1
PST	PETRIE STORES CORP	12.1	4.0	63.6	252.8
PHYB	PIONEER HI-BRED INTERNATIONL	31.5	3.8	93.3	356.9
PRE	PREMIER INDUSTRIAL CP	12.7	1.7	39.9	69.5
RBD	RUBBERMAID INC	18.6	3.9	89.8	346.0
RYAN	RYAN'S FAMILY STK HOUSES INC	50.3	2.9	18.5	53.4
SEIC	SEI CORP	21.1	1.5	20.3	31.2
SMLS	SCI-MED LIFE SYSTEMS INC	52.6	2.4	5.9	14.2
SJM	SMUCKER (J.M.) CO	13.7	2.7	23.2	62.2
SREG	STANDARD REGISTER CO	16.4	4.2	33.7	141.1
SYN	SYNTEX CORP	11.8	3.5	291.0	1014.8
TRC	TEJON RANCH CO	16.9	3.7	3.5	12.9
TLAB	TELLABS INC	15.7	3.4	12.3	41.1
TR	TOOTSIE ROLL INDS	13.2	1.9	16.1	29.9
UST	UST INC	20.4	1.0	148.9	148.7
UNRI	UNR INDUSTRIES INC	12.7	4.3	17.8	76.0
UFI	UNIFI INC	19.6	2.7	20.8	55.3
WDFC	WD-40 CO	17.7	0.8	10.2	7.8
WPO	WASHINGTON POST -CL B	17.4	3.3	177.2	591.4
WRE	WASHINGTON REIT	12.8	1.5	11.1	16.3
YELL	YELLOW FREIGHT SYSTEM-DEL	12.7	4.2	155.6	647.1

Unlike net operating cash flow, which is now well defined under FAS No. 95, free cash flow wears many masks and does not have a unique definition. It is known by many names, including raiders' cash flow, surplus cash flow, excess cash flow, distributable cash flow, and disposable cash flow. However, the primary premise behind all these definitions and names is a measure of the maximum cash that is generated during a period and that can be distributed to stockholders of the business enterprise without affecting future growth.

The most common definition of free cash flow, one which is espoused by Standard & Poor's, is pretax income minus capital spending (*The Outlook*, July 20, 1988). The publication writes, "Analysts believe that capital spending should be deducted because almost every business demands a certain minimal level of nondiscretionary plant and equipment spending. This is especially true of capital intensive firms in such fields as auto or steel, where cutbacks in capital spending may hurt productivity."

Surplus cash flow, as defined by many investors, is typically calculated by adding to pretax income the depreciation expense and subtracting capital spending. One money management firm believes that 9–10 times surplus cash flow is a good gauge of private market value. It arrives at this number by determining the price at which companies were being acquired.

Example:

In its 1991 annual report, RJR Nabisco Holding Corp. provides a condensed statement of free cash flow. The definition that RJR Nabisco uses for free cash flow is operating cash flows minus capital expenditures and dividend payments on preferred stock. This definition does not acknowledge that some of the capital expenditures might have been discretionary, or that some of the other cash expenditures on R&D, selling, general and administrative expenses, and even production or purchase of goods might have been discretionary. Thus, definitions of free cash flows other than those used by RJR Nabisco may be warranted.

It is interesting that neither of the above definitions includes a major cash outflow—principal payments on debt. It also excludes other important financing and investing activities such as dividend payments on preferred stock, which are not a tax-deductible item. Unfortunately, there is no simple definition of free cash flow, nor can the analyst simply rearrange a few numbers from the statement of cash flows to come up with an entity's free cash flow. Let us show now a detailed procedure to estimate free cash flows.

5.6 ESTIMATING FREE CASH FLOWS

To estimate free cash flows, one can follow two approaches—the direct and indirect approach—just like the derivation of net cash from operations. Under the direct approach, the cash flow analyst estimates the components of cash flows of operating activities and then estimates the portion of these components that is discretionary in nature. The cash flow analyst also estimates the discretionary components of the firm's major investments in fixed assets.

RJR Nabisco: Consolidated Statements of Free Cash Flow

CONSOLIDATED CONDENSED STATEMENTS OF FREE CASH FLOW* YEARS ENDED DECEMBER 31 RJR NABISCO HOLDINGS CORP. ($ MILLIONS) SEE BOOK 2 FOR CONSOLIDATED FINANCIAL STATEMENTS, RELATED FOOTNOTES AND MANAGEMENT'S DISCUSSION AND ANALYSIS OF FINANCIAL CONDITION AND RESULTS OF OPERATIONS.	1991	1990
INCOME (LOSS) FROM CONTINUING OPERATIONS	$ 368	$ (462)
INTEREST EXPENSE	2,113	3,000
AMORTIZATION OF DEBT ISSUANCE COSTS	104	176
INCOME TAX PROVISION	280	60
DEPRECIATION OF PROPERTY, PLANT AND EQUIPMENT	441	450
AMORTIZATION (PRINCIPALLY INTANGIBLES)	683	680
ACCRETION OF OTHER NONCURRENT LIABILITIES	89	86
EARNINGS BEFORE INTEREST, TAXES, DEPRECIATION AND AMORTIZATION	4,078	3,990
INTEREST PAID	(1,397)	(1,424)
TAXES (PAID) REFUNDED	(368)	32
(INCREASE) DECREASE IN WORKING CAPITAL, EXCLUDING INCOME TAXES AND INTEREST	(392)	379
CAPITAL EXPENDITURES	(459)	(426)
PREFERRED STOCK DIVIDENDS PAID	(205)	—
OTHER, NET	167	151
FREE CASH FLOW	$1,424	$2,702

* Excludes net divestiture proceeds and financing activities.

SOURCE: RJR Nabisco, *Annual Report*, 1991.

Under the indirect approach, the cash flow analyst begins with the change in cash during a period and makes adjustments to that amount for various events that affect free cash flows. Generally, all cash outlays that are not necessary for the firm's continuing operations will be added back to the change in cash, because the firm could have avoided making those payments and still continue its operations. Consequently, free cash flows would have increased had the firm not made those expenditures. Similarly, increases in cash that result from liquidation of fixed assets or from external financing are subtracted from the change in cash, because they do not represent cash flows that were generated by continuing operations of the business or because they represent the gradual liquidation of the firm.

We begin our estimation procedures by using an example. We present the two approaches to the estimation of free cash flows for this firm.

Example:

Hillenbrand Industries, Inc., headquartered in Batesville, Indiana, is a diversified company that consists of six different companies. Among these operating companies we find American Tourister, Batesville Casket, Medeco Security Locks, Hill-Rom electric hospital beds, SSI Medical Services, and a funeral insurance group. Hillenbrand is therefore expected to have stable cash flows because of its diversified lines of business and to have reasonable growth of cash flows due to the relative inelastic demand for its products.

Hillenbrand reports the following results for the year ending on December 1, 1990:

Hillenbrand Industries, Inc.: Statement of Consolidated Income

STATEMENT OF CONSOLIDATED INCOME

Hillenbrand Industries, Inc. and Subsidiaries

(Dollars in thousands except per share data)

Year Ended	December 1, 1990	December 2, 1989	December 3, 1988
Net revenues:			
Industrial	$ 1,067,935	$ 981,104	$ 884,288
Insurance	38,627	19,677	6,497
Total net revenues	1,106,562	1,000,781	890,785
Cost of revenues:			
Industrial	588,894	542,096	479,212
Insurance	14,011	4,069	1,274
Total cost of revenues	602,905	546,165	480,486
Administrative, distribution and selling expenses:			
Industrial	329,705	286,336	256,918
Insurance	26,013	20,617	15,740
General corporate overhead	10,497	13,090	12,765
Total administrative, distribution and selling expenses	366,215	320,043	285,423
Operating profit	137,442	134,573	124,876
Other income (expense), net:			
Interest expense	(15,939)	(17,563)	(17,791)
Investment income, net	9,048	6,030	5,360
Other	(4,211)	(1,674)	707
Income before income taxes	126,340	121,366	113,152
Income taxes	50,662	50,048	46,779
Net income	$ 75,678	$ 71,318	$ 66,373
Earnings per common share	$ 2.05	$ 1.92	$ 1.77
Dividends per common share	$ .55	$ .50	$ .40
Average number of common shares outstanding	36,985,691	37,188,297	37,558,735

SOURCE: Hillenbrand Industries, Inc., *Annual Report*, 1990.

Hillenbrand Industries, Inc.:: Statement of Consolidated Shareholders' Equity

STATEMENT OF CONSOLIDATED SHAREHOLDERS' EQUITY

Hillenbrand Industries, Inc. and Subsidiaries

(Dollars in thousands)	December 1, 1990	December 2, 1989	December 3, 1988
Year Ended			
Common stock	$ 4,442	$ 4,442	$ 4,442
Additional paid-in capital–Beginning of year	1,752	1,470	1,383
Excess of fair market value over cost on reissuance of treasury shares 1990–14,920; 1989–33,733; 1988–40,090	359	282	87
End of year	2,111	1,752	1,470
Retained earnings–Beginning of year (Note 9)	451,702	398,976	347,641
Net income	75,678	71,318	66,373
Dividends	(20,335)	(18,592)	(15,038)
End of year	507,045	451,702	398,976
Unearned restricted stock compensation	(879)	(1,333)	(2,237)
Foreign currency translation adjustment	4,722	2,284	2,013
Treasury stock–Beginning of year	(62,188)	(56,137)	(40,995)
Shares acquired in 1990–517,484; 1989–215,613; 1988–514,400	(19,103)	(6,762)	(15,843)
Reissued	324	711	701
End of year	(80,967)	(62,188)	(56,137)
Total Shareholders' Equity	$436,474	$396,659	$348,527

SOURCE: Hillenbrand Industries, Inc., *Annual Report*, 1990.

Hillenbrand Industries, Inc.: Statement of Consolidated Cash Flows

STATEMENT OF CONSOLIDATED CASH FLOWS

Hillenbrand Industries, Inc. and Subsidiaries

(Dollars in thousands) Year Ended	December 1, 1990	December 2, 1989	December 3, 1988
INDUSTRIAL CASH FLOWS:			
Cash Flow From Operating Activities:			
Net income	$ 76,548	$ 74,407	$ 72,978
Adjustments to reconcile net income to net cash flow from operating activities:			
Depreciation and amortization	93,990	80,959	68,847
Change in noncurrent deferred income taxes	11,231	10,464	7,890
Interest imputed on earn-out accruals	4,291	5,283	4,806
Change in:			
Trade accounts receivable	(9,986)	(27,701)	(38,952)
Inventories	(13,322)	(17,763)	(11,455)
Other current assets	(2,753)	(1,070)	5,986
Trade accounts payable	122	435	1,722
Accrued expenses, excluding earn-out accruals	10,517	4,164	(392)
Other, net	6,207	4,729	4,055
Net Cash Flow From Operating Activities	176,845	133,907	115,485
Cash Flow From Investing Activities:			
Capital expenditures:			
Additions to equipment, property and intangibles	(74,458)	(121,326)	(114,733)
Retirements, net	2,568	1,332	3,864
Capitalized earn-out accruals	14,776	50,403	35,390
Net capital expenditures	(57,114)	(69,591)	(75,479)
Contingent earn-out payments	(32,740)	(31,842)	(19,114)
Net Cash Flow From Investing Activities	(89,854)	(101,433)	(94,593)
Cash Flow From Financing Activities:			
Additions to short-term debt	—	225	2,879
Reductions to short-term debt	(1,920)	(270)	(6,000)
Additions to long-term debt	—	1,051	4,587
Reductions to long-term debt	(5,433)	(10,382)	(8,674)
Payment of cash dividends	(20,335)	(18,592)	(15,038)
Treasury stock acquired	(19,103)	(6,762)	(15,843)
Treasury stock reissued	324	711	701
Unearned restricted stock compensation	454	904	983
Sale of certain accounts receivable	6,000	31,000	—
Net Cash Flow From Financing Activities	(40,013)	(2,115)	(36,405)
Total Industrial Cash Flows	46,978	30,359	(15,513)
INSURANCE CASH FLOWS:			
Net income (loss)	(870)	(3,089)	(6,605)
Change in benefit reserves, net	140,044	100,071	55,734
Change in unearned revenues	35,273	30,018	15,918
Change in deferred acquisition costs	(35,767)	(28,400)	(14,214)
Change in investments, net	(149,810)	(99,860)	(57,040)
Other, net	1,953	(8,340)	(690)
Total Insurance Cash Flows	(9,177)	(9,600)	(6,897)
Consolidated Cash Flows	37,801	20,759	(22,410)
Cash and Cash Equivalents			
At Beginning of Year	48,984	28,225	50,635
At End of Year	$ 86,785	$ 48,984	$ 28,225

SOURCE: Hillenbrand Industries, Inc., *Annual Report*, 1990.

Hillenbrand Industries, Inc.: Consolidated Balance Sheet

CONSOLIDATED BALANCE SHEET

Hillenbrand Industries, Inc. and Subsidiaries

(Dollars in thousands)	December 1, 1990	December 2, 1989
ASSETS		
INDUSTRIAL (Note 1)		
Current Assets:		
Cash and cash equivalents	$ 86,785	$ 48,984
Trade accounts receivable, less allowances of $11,191 in 1990 and $7,613 in 1989	185,801	181,815
Inventories	109,551	96,229
Other current assets	17,982	15,229
Total current assets	400,119	342,257
Equipment Leased to Others	234,701	211,590
Less accumulated depreciation	129,829	78,661
Equipment leased to others, net	104,872	132,929
Property	425,641	400,769
Less accumulated depreciation	216,924	195,421
Property, net	208,717	205,348
Other Assets:		
Intangible assets at amortized cost:		
Patents and trademarks	85,804	84,040
Excess of cost over net asset values of acquired companies	5,327	4,159
Other	9,344	9,688
Deferred charges and other assets	19,644	17,780
Total other assets	120,119	115,667
Total Industrial Assets	833,827	796,201
INSURANCE (Note 10)		
Investments	334,927	185,117
Deferred acquisition costs	83,276	47,509
Other	15,686	15,257
Total Insurance Assets	433,889	247,883
Total Assets	$1,267,716	$1,044,084

SOURCE: Hillenbrand Industries, Inc., *Annual Report*, 1990.

Hillenbrand Industries, Inc.: Consolidated Balance Sheet (*continued*)

	December 1, 1990	December 2, 1989
LIABILITIES		
INDUSTRIAL		
Current Liabilities:		
Short-term debt	$ 4,037	$ 5,957
Current portion of long-term debt (Note 3)	5,344	5,456
Trade accounts payable	32,889	32,767
Income taxes (Note 6):		
Payable	17,542	14,680
Deferred	(8,569)	(3,261)
Accrued compensation	29,908	25,548
Accrued other taxes and expenses	102,761	69,024
Total current liabilities	183,912	150,171
Long-Term Debt (Note 3)	108,119	113,440
Other Long-Term Liabilities (Notes 2 and 4)	63,097	96,630
Deferred Income Taxes (Note 6)	63,981	52,750
Total Industrial Liabilities	419,109	412,991
INSURANCE (Note 10)		
Benefit reserves	316,311	176,267
Unearned revenues	86,930	51,657
General liabilities	8,892	6,510
Total Insurance Liabilities	412,133	234,434
Total Liabilities	831,242	647,425
SHAREHOLDERS' EQUITY (Note 4)		
Common stock—without par value:		
Authorized—199,000,000 shares		
Issued—40,161,956 shares in 1990 and 1989	4,442	4,442
Additional paid-in capital	2,111	1,752
Retained earnings (Note 3)	507,045	451,702
Unearned restricted stock compensation	(879)	(1,333)
Foreign currency translation adjustment	4,722	2,284
Treasury stock, at cost: 1990—3,551,278 shares; 1989—3,048,714 shares	(80,967)	(62,188)
Total Shareholders' Equity	436,474	396,659
Total Liabilities and Shareholders' Equity	$1,267,716	$1,044,084

SOURCE: Hillenbrand Industries, Inc., *Annual Report*, 1990.

We begin our discussion by using the direct approach to estimate free cash flows.

Estimation Procedure I:

We first estimate cash that was generated by operations and then subtract from it capital expenditures of the firm.

	1990	1989	1988	1987	1986	1985	1984	1983	1982	1981	1980	1979	1978	1977
Net income	75.7	71.3	66.4	56.1	50.4	32.8	38.4	35.7	30.9	28.7	25.0	25.3	17.2	13.5
Plus depreciation and amortization	94.0	81.0	68.8	54.4	49.3	28.3	23.2	14.4	12.7	9.5	9.4	8.1	6.6	4.1
Operating cash flow—estimate	169.7	152.3	135.2	110.5	99.7	61.1	61.6	50.1	43.6	38.2	34.4	33.4	23.7	17.6
Subtract capital expenditures	−57.1	−69.6	−75.5	−63.4	−69.5	−32.8	−39.8	−18.3	−13.9	−42.3	−18.9	−11.3	−7.0	−9.1
Free cash flow—definition I	112.6	82.7	59.7	47.1	30.2	28.3	21.8	31.8	29.7	-4.1	15.5	22.1	16.7	8.5

Note that this simple definition of free cash flows uses a crude estimate of cash from operations; net income plus depreciation and amortization. This estimate was reasonable as a first approximation when net cash from operating activities was not reported and when the data necessary to make other adjustments to income for noncash events, or nonoperating cash flows, were unavailable. However, now that operating cash flows are routinely disclosed in the statement of cash flows, one can use these figures to estimate free cash flows.

Estimation Procedure II:

	1990	1989	1988	1987
Operating cash flow—reported	176.8	133.9	115.5	125.6
Insurance cash flows—reported	-9.2	-9.6	-6.9	-3.4
Net operating cash flow—reported	167.6	124.3	108.6	122.2
Subtract capital expenditures	-57.1	-69.6	-75.5	-63.4
Free cash flow—definition II	110.5	54.7	33.1	58.8

This estimation is based on reported operating cash flows, which is available only since 1987. Note that because Hillenbrand operates not only in industrial segments but also in insurance, it segregates cash flows from the two types of operations. We aggregate them here. The inclusion of the entire insurance cash flow as an operating cash flow is done pragmatically; there is not enough data in the financial statements to do it properly. Because the insurance segment is a small portion of Hillenbrand's operations, we feel that it would not materially distort our estimates.

The above estimation technique uses net cash flow from operations as reported in accordance with FAS 95. However, in years prior to 1987, cash from operations is not reported according to FAS No. 95, and it has to be estimated using the procedures outlined in Chapter 3. Specifically, we first estimate the individual components of operating cash flows as follows:

	1990	1989	1988	1987	1986	1985	1984	1983	1982	1981	1980	1979	1978	1977
Total receivables	185.8	181.8	185.1	146.2	135.6	132.1	102.3	86.8	89.2	88.9	77.2	69.2	59.1	34.9
Change in receivables	4.0	-3.3	39.0	10.5	3.5	29.8	15.6	-2.5	0.4	11.7	8.0	10.1	24.2	
Sales	1106.6	1000.8	890.8	730.0	647.7	507.6	484.6	432.5	388.6	367.8	326.5	295.0	229.8	
Collections from customers	1102.6	1004.1	851.8	719.4	644.2	477.8	469.0	435.0	388.2	356.1	318.5	284.9	205.5	

Collections from customers are calculated as sales minus the change in accounts receivable. If one assumes that all sales are on credit, then accounts receivable should have increased during the period by the amount of sales. If they increased by a smaller amount, then some of the accounts receivable were collected during the period. The amount collected can be estimated by subtracting the increase in accounts receivable from annual sales. For example, in 1990 sales amounted to $1106.6 million and accounts receivable increased by $4 million. Thus, collections are estimated as $1102.6 million (1106.6 − 4). In 1989, however, accounts receivable actually decreased, indicating that not only did the firm collect all 1989 sales in cash, but it also collected $3.3 million of the accounts receivable that resulted from 1988 sales. Thus, collections in 1989 are estimated as $1004.1 million (1000.8 + 3.3).

Let us now estimate payments to suppliers, employees, and so forth:

	1990	1989	1988	1987	1986	1985	1984	1983	1982	1981	1980	1979	1978	1977
Total inventories	109.6	103.6	84.8	72.8	74.6	75.6	83.2	71.3	72.4	74.9	80.1	69.5	66.3	27.8
Other current assets	18.0	7.8	7.8	14.3	11.7	16.8	16.3	13.9	2.5	2.0	1.7	1.8	2.7	1.5
Accounts payable	32.9	32.8	32.3	30.6	27.7	25.5	17.9	23.3	17.9	22.7	12.2	12.1	8.5	3.3
Accrued expenses	132.7	94.6	91.7	69.9	46.4	38.5	28.3	27.8	23.5	16.2	14.2	12.6	13.3	6.7
Change in the above	-22.1	15.6	-18.1	-25.6	-16.1	-24.9	19.1	0.6	-4.5	-17.2	8.8	-0.6	27.9	
Cost of goods sold	508.9	465.2	411.6	328.5	286.9	274.6	259.2	236.0	214.8	209.1	184.2	160.4	126.2	
SG&A expense	366.2	320.0	285.4	215.9	191.3	134.2	130.6	115.8	101.2	95.9	81.3	72.2	59.7	
Payments to suppliers and employees	853.0	800.8	679.0	518.8	462.1	383.8	408.9	352.4	311.5	287.7	274.3	232.0	213.9	

Payments to suppliers, employees, and the like are calculated as cost of goods sold plus selling and general and administrative expenses. Compustat excludes depreciation and amortization from cost of goods sold, so the sum of these two expenses can be conceived as cash outflows to suppliers and employees. However, one has to add the change in inventories plus the change in prepaid expenses because these represent additional acquisitions of inventory or payments to suppliers and employees due to current operations. We then subtract the change in accounts payable and the change in accrued expenses, because some of the above expenditures may not have been paid during the current period and may actually be paid only in the next period.

	1990	1989	1988	1987	1986	1985	1984	1983	1982	1981	1980	1979	1978
Interest expense	15.9	17.6	17.8	17.3	15.0	7.3	7.2	5.1	5.3	5.1	5.1	5.2	4.1
Nonoperating income (expense)	4.8	4.4	2.8	1.9	1.4	4.1	5.3	6.7	4.2	2.8	1.7	0.5	1.0
Net interest payment	11.1	13.2	15.0	15.4	13.6	3.2	1.9	-1.6	1.2	2.4	3.4	4.7	3.1

Here, additional data about interest payable or receivable or data about interest capitalized are unavailable on the Compustat database for this company. Thus, interest payments are estimated by interest expense minus nonoperating income, which, for the most part, represents interest income.

	1990	1989	1988	1987	1986	1985	1984	1983	1982	1981	1980	1979	1978
Total income taxes	50.7	50.1	46.8	50.7	47.9	28.9	31.4	32.3	27.8	22.3	23.1	24.2	17.0
Subtract deferred tax expense	5.9	11.6	2.7	2.2	5.0	7.5	3.4	5.7	2.3	8.2	0.8	2.8	0.6
Tax payments	44.7	38.4	44.0	48.5	43.0	21.4	28.0	26.6	25.5	14.1	22.3	21.4	16.3

A portion of the tax expense may be deferred into the next period with an associated increase in taxes payable, and another portion into later periods, as reflected by the increase in deferred taxes. Thus, normally, the payment for taxes is calculated as the tax expense minus the change in taxes payable minus the change in deferred taxes. Here we chose to calculate tax payment by subtracting from the tax expense the portion that was deferred, because Hillenbrand included some deferred taxes among current liabilities, and these were included with other current liabilities by Compustat.

We can now estimate the net cash from operating activities:

	1990	1989	1988	1987	1986	1985	1984	1983	1982	1981	1980	1979	1978
Cash from operating activities	193.7	151.6	113.9	136.8	125.5	69.5	30.3	57.6	50.0	52.0	18.4	26.7	-27.7

Cash from operations is calculated as collections from customers minus payments to suppliers, employees, interest, and taxes. Note that this procedure does not include in net operating cash flows any nonrecurring cash flows. Also note that the reported operating cash flows is reasonably close to those estimated here.

We can now estimate free cash flows by subtracting capital expenditures from estimated net operating cash flows:

	1990	1989	1988	1987	1986	1985	1984	1983	1982	1981	1980	1979	1978
Cash from operating activities	193.7	151.6	113.9	136.8	125.5	69.5	30.3	57.6	50.0	52.0	18.4	26.7	-27.7
Subtract capital expenditures	-57.1	-69.6	-75.5	-63.4	-69.5	-32.8	-39.8	-18.3	-13.9	-42.3	-18.9	-11.3	-7.0
Free cash flow	136.6	82.0	38.4	73.4	56.0	36.7	-9.5	39.4	36.1	9.7	-0.5	15.4	-34.8

In the previous calculations, capital expenditures include all investments in PPE, regardless if these capital expenditures were necessary or not. Recall that management has control over the amounts it decides to invest in capital expenditures. Therefore, some of the discretionary capital expenditures might be beyond what is needed to sustain the growth of the firm at its current level. Therefore, the cash flow analyst should attempt to determine the portion of the capital expenditures that is necessary to sustain growth versus the portion that is not needed to sustain that growth or the portion that was not necessary at all. The portion that is not needed for future growth represents free cash flows, because it can be distributed to shareholders without affecting the current level of growth.

Capital Spending

Of all the discretionary expenditures in a business, capital spending is probably the most scrutinized because of its visibility and its nature. The mere size of capital spending (it is usually the largest use of cash on the statement of cash flows), combined with the fact that cash returns on capital spending occur many periods away, force investors to investigate whether an entity's capital expenditures are economically justified.

Forecasting capital spending is difficult because it depends on the economy, on the industry, and on the specific conditions of the firm, particularly on its expected rate of growth. Thus, most of the time it is best left up to management estimates. For cyclical entities, capital expenditures can be as volatile as cash flow. For such entities, especially when liquidity deteriorates, capital expenditures reflect the bare minimum that is needed to sustain the business entity. Still, we must devise a way to estimate that component of capital expenditures that is discretionary and which is not necessary to sustain the current growth rate of the business.

Some security analysts prefer to look at what they consider to be "maintenance" capital spending, that is, capital expenditures that are adequate to keep up the current level of production. This is faulty thinking because it does not take into account future needs that any capital budget should consider. Because capital spending is typically the largest off-P&L spending item, the analysis of capital spending is most important and is the first item to be affected during changes in the economic environment, whether the change is caused by an adverse change in business conditions or by a merger, when only the most important capital spending plans stay on.

One way of estimating the required level of capital expenditures is (in the case of a manufacturing concern like Hillenbrand) to compare the growth of cost of goods sold with the growth of capital expenditures. Presumably, in order to sustain a specific growth rate of cost of goods sold, capital expenditures should grow by approximately the same rate. If we observe a *substantially* higher growth rate of capital expenditures than cost of sales during a reasonable period, it can be assumed that the firm had overinvested in PPE during the period, and this overinvestment represents discretionary capital expenditures that can be considered free cash flows. To show the estimation for Hillenbrand, we use the following procedure.

We first estimate the annual average growth rate in capital expenditures and cost of sales over the most recent three years:

	1990	1989	1988	1987	1986	1985	1984	1983	1982	1981	1980	1979	1978	1977
Capital expenditures	57.1	69.6	75.5	63.4	69.5	32.8	39.8	18.3	13.9	42.3	18.9	11.3	7.0	9.1
3-year growth rate capital expenditures	-3.4	0.0	32.1	16.8	56.1	32.9	-2.0	-1.1	7.2	81.9	27.7			
Cost of goods sold	508.9	465.2	411.6	328.5	286.9	274.6	259.2	236.0	214.8	209.1	184.2	160.4	126.2	78.0
3-year growth rate cost of goods sold	15.7	17.5	14.5	8.2	6.7	8.5	7.4	8.6	10.2	18.3	33.2			
Excess growth of capital expenditures	0.0	0.0	17.6	8.6	49.3	24.4	0.0	0.0	0.0	63.6	0.0			
Discretionary capital expenditures	0.0	0.0	13.3	5.5	34.3	8.0	0.0	0.0	0.0	26.9	0.0			

For example, for 1988 we divide $75.5 by $32.8 to obtain 2.3018. We take the cubic root of 2.3018, which is equal to 1.321, or an average growth rate of 32.1 percent per year. Note that we use the net capital expenditures from the statement of cash flows. This amount includes (for years after 1986) accruals related to an earn-out agreement.

This agreement was made between prior owners of a business that was acquired by Hillenbrand. The agreement provided for future payments to the previous owner if certain performance targets of the acquired business were met. Hillenbrand accrued such contingent payments by including them in capital expenditures, and we have to subtract them (and retirements) to obtain net capital expenditures. We treat the earn-out payments to the former owner as acquisition costs, because the value placed on the acquired business in 1985 was too low.

We follow similar calculations to estimate the growth rate in cost of goods sold. We then subtract the growth rate of cost of goods sold from that of capital expenditures, and substitute zero if the result is negative. If the result is positive, we multiply the excess growth rate of capital expenditures by total capital expenditures that year to obtain an estimate of discretionary capital expenditures for the year.

Note that in 1989 the average growth rate of cost of sales (17.5 percent) is higher than the average growth rate of capital expenditures (0.0 percent). Thus, no capital expenditures are considered discretionary in 1989.[7] However, in 1988 the growth rate of capital expenditures (32.1 percent) exceeds the growth rate of cost of sales (14.5 percent) by 17.6 percent. Thus, discretionary capital expenditures are estimated by multiplying total capital expenditures of $75.5 by 17.6 percent to obtain $13.3. These discretionary capital expenditures will be added to free cash flows in 1988. Based on these estimates of the discretionary expenditures on PPE, we obtain the estimated free cash flows by subtracting total capital expenditures from net operating cash flows and adding back discretionary capital expenditures. This yields:

	1990	1989	1988	1987	1986	1985	1984	1983	1982	1981	1980
Free cash flow	136.6	82.0	51.7	78.8	90.3	44.7	-9.5	39.4	36.1	36.6	-0.5

The procedure that we used to estimate discretionary capital expenditures may seem arbitrary at a first glance. We first estimate the growth rate over four years in capital expenditures and cost of sales. The decision to use four years stems from a balancing of two errors; a longer period may yield unfair comparisons because firms change substantially over time. They branch out to other lines of business or decide to dispose of existing lines of business. However, a shorter period than four years is unlikely to include an entire business cycle. Thus, we focus on four years in our analysis.

---

[7]The astute reader may ask why we should consider some capital expenditures as discretionary (when the growth rate of capital expenditures exceeds that of cost of sales), but when capital expenditures lag behind cost of sales, we do not subtract from operating cash flows an additional amount that is equal to the "required" capital expenditures that were not undertaken. The reason for this seeming inconsistency is that firms can increase productivity due to technological advances and other measures without requiring comparable investments in capital expenditures. Thus, in our calculations we do not "penalize" firms that became more efficient.

We compare the growth rate in capital expenditures with that of cost of goods sold. Ideally, we should have used a physical measure of output to examine the required growth rate of inputs needed to support the growth level of output. However, firms do not provide physical output or input measures, and we have to resort to estimates. We feel that cost of sales is a good measure of growth in output because it comprises all components of product costs. Given the similarity in price increases between inputs and outputs, the growth rates of cost of sales and capital expenditures should be good proxies for growth rates in physical outputs and inputs.

To assess the extent of a bias that is introduced because of this estimated component of discretionary capital expenditures, we examine the relationship between discretionary capital expenditures and market value of firms. We found that, in any given year, only fewer than 20 percent of all firms have positive discretionary capital expenditures. Furthermore, less than 2 percent of all firms had discretionary capital expenditures that exceed 10 percent of market value of equity. Thus, modifications to our procedure are unlikely to affect the estimate of free cash flows in any significant manner.

Can one identify other expenses beyond capital expenditures that are discretionary in nature? An immediate candidate is expenditures made in the daily operations of the firm, where management may expend some cash flows in its operations beyond those needed to sustain the current level of growth. For example, payments for goods that were acquired or produced, payments for selling, general, and administrative expenses, and payments for research and development efforts may be in excess of those that are needed to sustain the current level of growth in sales. Thus, it is important to obtain estimates of discretionary cash outflows for the firm's ongoing operations.

One of the major components of discretionary expenditures is corporate overhead, oftentimes referred to as corporate "fat." Unfortunately, there has been very little attempt to quantify that portion of overhead that represents corporate "fat." In fact, little has been written about corporate overhead at all in textbooks on security analysis and accounting. The current literature has not tied the financial process to the management process, although management consulting firms have long established that corporate overhead for most firms is excessive. For example, whereas corporate overhead represented about 10 percent of total product cost in the beginning of this century, corporate overhead now contributes more than 40 percent to total product costs (see, for example, most articles that discuss activity-based costing in the *Journal of Cost Management*).

Corporate restructuring, which became so prevalent during the 1980s, still has a long way to go according to the measures explained below. Management consultants agree. According to one leading management consultant, "The Eighties were just the tip of the iceberg, and we're going to see dramatic reductions in the Nineties. Corporate America is still as much as 25 percent overstaffed."[8]

The 1990–1991 recession, as well as the lingering effects of the 1980s debt build-up, brought on a frontal attack on corporate cost structure, both in the United States and abroad.

---

[8] R. Henkoff, "Cost Cutting: How to Do It Right," *Fortune*, April 9, 1990.

Companies including IBM, Digital Equipment, United Technologies, Colgate-Palmolive, and Hitachi were just some of the more visible companies that took a hard look at their corporate "fat" and decided it was too high in relation to their rate of growth and expected rate of growth. The marketplace rewarded these companies as the announcements were made.

Example:

The Wall Street Journal published the following news item on September 12, 1991:

"AMR, in a Sharp Reversal, Curbs Outlays

While the cutbacks ($500 million) represent only about 4 percent of American's capital spending, they signal a major strategic shift for the nation's major airline. . . . Now it's going to try to control costs. . . . News of the strategy shift sent the stock of the Ft. Worth, Texas company higher; AMR was quoted at $59 a share, up $3.125."

On the same date AMR announced its cutbacks, Mr. Robert Stempel, chairman of the General Motors Corporation, said that automotive companies must adopt "lean" production methods. This could mean using about half the traditional factory space and about one-tenth of the inventories. Lean organizations achieved dramatically higher quality and productivity and more efficient and faster product development, with a payoff in lower costs and the ability to bring out different models faster, at lower volumes, and with higher quality. (*Financial Times*, September 12, 1991)

Currently, security analysts are taught to compare various expenses as a percentage of current sales over five- to ten-year periods to get an idea if such expenses are out of line. Such analysis is incorrect even if judged in comparison with its industry, because it is really the growth rate and projected growth rate that should determine the level of many expenses and expense ratios.

Management consultants are well known for studying an entity's productive and administrative processes to determine how cutbacks could be accomplished while maintaining the same or improved level of production. Continuous Process Improvement (CPI) techniques in research and development have added to better quality control and better products, which, in turn, serve to reduce corporate waste.

In order to consider the appropriateness of the level of overhead, it is first necessary to examine the unit growth rate of the entity. Unit growth, rather than dollar growth (revenues), should ideally be examined because dollar growth includes price changes. For example, if prices double with no change in unit growth (e.g., in an inflationary spiral), one should not consider it suitable for the entity to double its selling expenses. The entity's unit growth should also be compared with the industry's unit growth, if possible. This can be done by deflating the firm's cost of sales by the deflator for the industry. If discretionary expenditures grow at a rate in excess of the growth rate for sales over a four-year period, especially if discretionary expenditures growth is greater than that for the industry, it is assumed those expenditures are too high.

The amount of overspending on overhead is directly related to the unit growth rate of the entity and it should be compared to its expenditures on nondiscretionary items. It is important to consider the special case of examining high-unit growth industries such as technology. When the growth rate of these industries slows down due to unavoidable competitive pressures or market saturation, comparing unit growth to expenditures over a long time horizon—even four years—can certainly give the impression that the company has much corporate fat. This occurs because the long-term growth rate in expenses remains high, while current sales grow at a much lower rate. These companies must quickly reduce their discretionary expenditures to match their new, lower, long-term unit growth rate.

Although the term *corporate fat* has a negative connotation, every company, like every living being, has and needs some. The question all but the smallest companies ask is: How much corporate fat is justified under the specific circumstances? Basically, corporate fat represents overspending. Overspending is most often found in the areas of selling, general and administrative (SG&A) expenses, cost of goods sold (COGS) (in which both material expense and labor expenses may be included), and research and development (R&D). Thus, we focus on these items to estimate discretionary cash outflows on the continuing operations of a firm. This can be done using the following procedure.

We first retrieve the estimated collections from customers and payments to suppliers and employees from the computations above. We then calculate the average three-year growth rate of collections from customers and payments to suppliers. We now assume that 20 percent of the excess of growth rate in payments to suppliers over collections from customers represent discretionary expenditures that should be added to free cash flows.

Hillenbrand Industries, Inc.

	1990	1989	1988	1987	1986	1985	1984	1983	1982	1981	1980	1979	1978
Collections from customers	1102.6	1004.1	851.8	719.4	644.2	477.8	469.0	435.0	388.2	356.1	318.5	284.9	205.5
3-year growth rate collections	15.3	15.9	21.3	15.3	14.0	7.2	9.6	11.0	10.9	20.1			
Payments to suppliers and employees	853.0	800.8	679.0	518.8	462.1	383.8	408.9	352.4	311.5	287.7	274.3	232.0	213.9
3-year growth rate payments	18.0	20.1	20.9	8.3	9.5	7.2	12.4	8.7	10.3	10.4			
Excess growth of payments	2.7	4.2	0.0	0.0	0.0	0.0	2.8	0.0	0.0	0.0			
Discretionary payments to suppliers	4.7	6.7	0.0	0.0	0.0	0.0	2.3	0.0	0.0	0.0			

Note that in 1989 the average growth rate of payments to suppliers and employees exceeds the average growth rate of collections from customers by 4.2 percent (20.1 − 15.9). Multiplying this excess by total payments to suppliers and employees of $800.8 and then again by 20 percent yields $6.7 of discretionary cash flows that were spent on excessive payments to suppliers and employees. The decision to use 20 percent of the excess is based on the observation that most corporate cost reduction programs can cut 20 percent from the excess of discretionary spending without impairing the progress or development of the firm. Although the correct amount of corporate fat must be determined on a case-by-case basis, we have found over the years that when public firms restructure their operations, they are able to trim about 20 percent from what we defined as overspending without affecting future growth.[9] Thus, we assume that not all excess payments to suppliers and employees can be considered discretionary, and to be conservative, we classify only 20 percent of these amounts as discretionary cash flows.

Although it seems that our approach is arbitrary, we believe that the data support our estimation procedure. We checked the distribution of what we termed discretionary payments to suppliers and employees in the entire population of Compustat firms (live ones and those on the Research Compustat database). Only about 15–20 percent of all firms had any excess discretionary payments to suppliers and employees in any given year. When we compared the magnitude of these discretionary cash flows with total sales of the firm, we found that fewer than 3 percent of the firms in any given year had any excess discretionary cash flows that exceeded 10 percent of total sales. Thus, errors in our estimates would probably not affect the ranking of firms in terms of their free cash flows in a significant manner. Even if we used other percentages or other approaches to estimate the discretionary components of these expenditures, we would probably have obtained similar results to those obtained in our estimation procedure.

Thus, we add only 20 percent of the excess that we conservatively term discretionary cash expenditures to the prior estimate of free cash flows and get:

	1990	1989	1988	1987	1986	1985	1984	1983	1982	1981
Free cash flow direct method	141.3	88.7	51.7	78.8	90.3	44.8	-7.2	39.4	36.1	36.6

Our estimates of free cash flows were focused on a single year. However, firms may have fluctuations in their free cash flows from one year to another due to shifts in economic and business conditions. Therefore, it may be more instructive to focus on averages for the most recent years. Using the above estimates, we obtain the following four-year average free cash flows:

	1990	1989	1988	1987	1986	1985	1984	1983	1982	1981
4-year average free cash flow	90.1	77.4	66.4	51.7	41.8	28.3	26.2	37.3	36.3	36.6

Note that Hillenbrand's average free cash flow is consistently positive and growing for recent years. This is to be expected given the diversified nature of Hillenbrand's

---

[9] In two closely dated announcements, Tenneco Inc. announced plans to cut a third of its corporate staff to improve performance (10/20/91), and United Technologies Corp. announced reductions of corporate staff by 25 percent (October 1991). The magnitude of these cost reductions is typical to firms in similar stages of restructuring. It indicates that the level of corporate overhead that can be reduced without affecting growth tends to be around 20 percent to 30 percent of the excess of these expenses above the growth rate of the firm.

operations and the relatively inelastic demand for its products. We can compare the behavior of Hillenbrand's average free cash flow with the market value of the firm. However, because of the differing magnitudes of the two numbers, we divide the market value of Hillenbrand by 20, and describe our estimates in Figure 5–1.

As can be seen in the graph, the market value and the average free cash flow dovetail each other well. Thus, it may be tempting to select firms into a portfolio based upon the relationship between market value and average free cash flow. We provide results on this investment approach in Chapter 7.

An Alternative Procedure

An alternative procedure is to estimate the free cash flows in an "indirect" way by a process of tracing the changes in cash during the period. This approach is based on the following rationale: Consider the sources-uses of cash identity,

$$\text{OCF} + \text{NetDebt} + \text{NetEquity} = \text{Div} + \text{Invest} + \text{ChangeCash},$$

Figure 5–1   Hillenbrand Industries: Market Value and Free Cash Flow

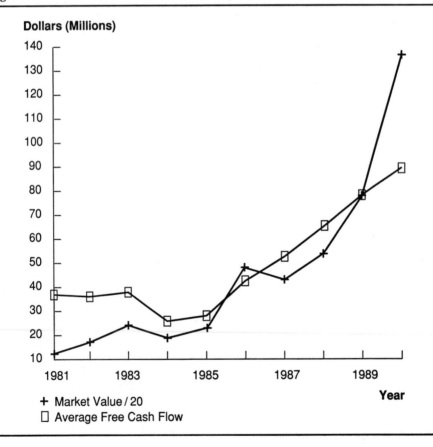

where OCF is the net cash flow from operating activities, NetDebt and NetEquity are the net cash provided by issuance of debt or equity, respectively, Div represents cash dividends paid by the firm, Invest represents cash investments in capital expenditures and such investments, and ChangeCash is the change in cash balance from the beginning to the end of the period. Simple algebraic manipulations yield:

$$OCF - Invest = ChangeCash + Div - NetDebt - NetEquity.$$

On the lefthand side of the equation, we have traditional definitions of free cash flows, that is, net operating cash flows minus net investments during the period—mostly in capital expenditures. By now, we know that some of the investments in capital expenditures can be considered discretionary. Let us denote discretionary investments by DiscInv and nondiscretionary investments by NonDiscInv. Similarly, some of the cash outlays, such as payments to employees and suppliers, R&D, and so forth, may be discretionary. Let us denote these discretionary cash outflows by DiscOCF and the nondiscretionary cash from operations by NonOCF. The equation can be written as,

$$(NonOCF - DiscOCF) - (NonDiscInv + DiscInv)$$
$$= ChangeCash + Div - NetDebt - NetEquity.$$

Simple manipulations yield,

$$NonOCF - NonDiscInv$$
$$= ChangeCash + Div - NetDebt - NetEquity + DiscInv + DiscOCF.$$

The lefthand side of this equation now contains the free cash flow as we defined it above—the cash generated by ongoing operations of the business during the period in excess of necessary investments in capital expenditures and other *necessary* expenditures. Note that this represents free cash flows because net operating cash flows now include cash receipts from operations in excess of necessary cash outflows for generating these cash receipts during the period, and in excess of investments that are intended to maintain the ability to generate these cash receipts in the future. Obviously, the excess cash receipts can be distributed to shareholders without affecting the growth of the business.

The righthand side of the equation shows an alternative way of estimating free cash flows from operations. Instead of directly estimating cash receipts minus necessary cash flows, one begins with the change in cash during the period and makes adjustments to it as portrayed on the righthand side of the equation. For example, decreases in cash due to financing events, such as payment of dividends or retirement of debt, are added back to the change in cash. Similarly, decreases in cash due to discretionary capital expenditures or other investing activities beyond those needed to sustain the growth of the firm are added back to the change in cash. Decreases in cash due to operating expenses beyond those that are needed to sustain the growth of the firm are also added back to the change in cash because they represent discretionary expenditures. Using similar logic, increases in cash due to disinvesting events such as the sale of PPE, or increases of cash due to financing events such as the issuance of common stock, are subtracted from the change in cash. This procedure yields another estimate of free cash flow, but it uses an "indirect" method to estimate the free cash flow. Let us illustrate this approach as it applies to Hillenbrand.

Example:

Hillenbrand Industries, Inc.: Yearly Change in Cash and Equivalents

	1990	1989	1988	1987	1986	1985	1984	1983	1982	1981
Cash and equivalents	37.8	20.8	-22.4	17.4	27.4	-4.7	-38.6	11.4	32.4	0.4

Add to the net change in cash and cash equivalents all financing cash outflows, because they do not represent free cash flows from *operating* activities:

	1990	1989	1988	1987	1986	1985	1984	1983	1982	1981
Cash dividends	20.3	18.6	15.0	13.4	10.9	10.5	10.0	8.8	8.0	7.2
Stock repurchases	19.1	6.8	15.8	23.9	7.1	0.0	9.5	3.3	0.0	0.0
Reduction L.T.D.	5.4	10.4	8.7	11.6	68.1	8.6	7.0	3.4	0.1	0.0

Cash dividends will be added back to the net change in cash because they represent cash that is returned to stockholders. They are not needed to sustain the growth of the firm's business, that is, they are free cash flows. Stock repurchases are similar to dividends; they represent cash flows that are not needed for the continuing growth of current operations and are used to buy out some shareholders. Finally, the reduction of long-term debt is a disfinancing cash flow, which does not affect free cash flow. Thus, it is added back to the change in cash in order to derive the free cash flow that is generated from operating activities.

	1990	1989	1988	1987	1986	1985	1984	1983	1982	1981	1980	1979	1978	1977
Capital expenditures	57.1	69.6	75.5	63.4	69.5	32.8	39.8	18.3	13.9	42.3	18.9	11.3	7.0	9.1
3-year growth rate capital expenditures	-3.4	0.0	32.1	16.8	56.1	32.9	-2.0	-1.1	7.2	81.9	27.7			
Cost of goods sold	508.9	465.2	411.6	328.5	286.9	274.6	259.2	236.0	214.8	209.1	184.2	160.4	126.2	78.0
3-year growth rate cost of goods sold	15.7	17.5	14.5	8.2	6.7	8.5	7.4	8.6	10.2	18.3	33.2			
Excess growth of capital expenditures	0.0	0.0	17.6	8.6	49.3	24.4	0.0	0.0	0.0	63.6	0.0			
Discretionary capital expenditures	0.0	0.0	13.3	5.5	34.3	8.0	0.0	0.0	0.0	26.9	0.0			

Discretionary capital expenditures are estimated by the excess of the three-year growth in capital expenditures over cost of goods sold times the level of capital expenditures for that year. A similar approach is followed for R&D expenditures; we compare the three-year growth rate of R&D expenditures to the three-year growth rate of cost of goods sold. When the growth rate of R&D expenditures exceeds that of the cost of goods sold, we multiply the difference by the current R&D expenditures. The result represents discretionary R&D expenditures.

	1990	1989	1988	1987	1986	1985	1984	1983	1982	1981
Current R&D expenditures	23.8	21.7	18.3	10.8	10.5	6.1	5.8	4.1	3.4	2.4
3-year growth rate R&D (%)	30.0	27.4	44.2	22.9	36.9	22.1	35.1			
3-year growth rate COGS (%)	15.7	17.5	14.5	8.2	6.7	8.5	7.4			
Excess growth of R&D (%)	14.3	9.9	29.7	14.6	30.2	13.5	27.7			
Discretionary R&D expenditures	3.4	2.1	5.4	1.6	3.2	0.8	1.6			

We proceed to estimate discretionary cash flows in the firm's expenditures on cost of goods sold and on selling, general, and administrative expenses. Here we provide a slightly different approach than the one we used for discretionary payments to suppliers and employees under the direct method. The results we get by using this slightly different approach are similar to those we obtained above. The estimation process here is to compare the ratio of cost of goods sold (or selling expenses) to sales with the long-run ratio (average of the most recent four years). If the ratio exceeds the long-run average ratio, some of these expenditures are considered discretionary and 20 percent of the excess is multiplied by current sales to determine the amount of discretionary cash flows:

	1990	1989	1988	1987	1986	1985	1984	1983	1982	1981
COGS percent of sales	46.0	46.5	46.2	45.3	44.8	54.1	53.5	54.6	55.3	56.8
4-year average COGS percent of sales	46.0	45.7	47.6	49.4	51.7	54.4	55.0	55.8	55.7	55.7
Sales	1106.6	1000.8	890.8	724.6	641.1	507.6	484.6	432.5	388.6	367.8
Excess COGS	0.0	7.9	0.0	0.0	0.0	0.0	0.0	0.0	0.0	4.4
20 percent of difference— discretionary COGS	0.0	1.6	0.0	0.0	0.0	0.0	0.0	0.0	0.0	0.9

In 1989, cost of goods sold as a proportion of sales was 46.5 percent, whereas the four-year average of this ratio was 45.7 percent. Thus, in 1989 Hillenbrand spent more on costs of purchases and production of inventories than in the prior four years, indicating that there is a potential of overspending on cost of goods sold that amounted to $7.9 million [(46.5 percent − 45.7 percent) × 1000.8]. Because we assume that only 20 percent of this overspending on COGS is discretionary, we multiply 7.9 by 20 percent to obtain $1.6 million of discretionary expenditures on COGS.

Similarly, for selling, general, and administrative (SGA) expenses:

	1990	1989	1988	1987	1986	1985	1984	1983	1982	1981
SGA percent of sales	33.1	32.0	32.0	29.8	29.8	26.4	26.9	26.8	26.0	26.1
4-year average SGA percent of sales	31.7	30.9	29.5	28.3	27.5	26.5	26.5	25.9	25.4	25.4
Sales	1106.6	1000.8	890.8	724.6	641.1	507.6	484.6	432.5	388.6	367.8
Excess SGA	15.1	10.7	22.4	11.2	15.0	0.0	2.4	3.6	2.6	2.6
20 percent of difference— discretionary SGA	3.0	2.1	4.5	2.2	3.0	0.0	0.5	0.7	0.5	0.5

In 1985, the ratio of selling, general, and administrative expenses to sales was below its four-year average (26.4 percent as compared to 26.5 percent). Thus, no overspending is evident, nor do we assume that there are any discretionary expenditures on SGA expenses for that year. However, in 1990 we estimate the discretionary expenditures on SGA expenses as 3.0, using the same steps as those above for cost of goods sold.

At this point, we can assess total corporate fat as discretionary capital expenditures plus discretionary R&D expenditures and discretionary COGS and SGA. These items represent corporate fat, or additions to free cash flows, because they are not required to sustain the current growth of the firm. Furthermore, we can examine total corporate fat for the largest firms on the NYSE. Such an analysis was conducted by Systematic Financial Management Inc. on January 4, 1990, and is incorporated here.

Company	Corporate "Fat" (millions of dollars)
IBM	$679
Mobil	670
Am Tele.	495
General Motors	490
Bellsouth	382
Amoco	347
Philip Morris	269
General Electric	263
G.T.E.	79

Every company has at least some corporate fat, especially if it is measured in any particular year. This is because, in any single year, the entity can find itself spending too heavily in such areas as capital spending, research, labor, or cost of sales. But, generally, corporate fat represents overspending and it can be quantified!

The table above shows that our largest companies spent excessively in 1989, beyond what was required to maintain their growth rates. However, with the 1990 recession, these companies found a financial cushion to cut expenses.

We now need to subtract from the change in cash those items that increase cash but that represent investing or financing cash inflows:

	1990	1989	1988	1987	1986	1985	1984	1983	1982	1981
Sale of PPE	0.0	0.0	0.0	0.0	0.0	0.0	0.0	0.0	0.0	0.0
Investing activities— other	0.0	0.0	0.0	0.0	0.0	0.0	0.0	0.0	0.0	0.0
Sale of investments loss	0.0	0.0	0.0	0.0	0.0	0.0	0.0	0.0	0.0	0.0
Sale of common and preferred	0.3	0.7	0.7	2.8	0.0	0.0	0.0	0.0	0.0	0.0
Sale of investments	0.0	0.0	0.0	0.0	3.2	2.4	2.7	0.0	0.0	0.0
Increase L.T.D.	0.0	1.1	4.6	3.9	76.0	66.4	22.2	0.1	0.1	0.4
Changes in current debt	-1.9	0.0	-3.1	7.9	-27.2	30.2	3.2	0.0	0.0	0.0
Financing activities— other	6.5	31.9	1.0	-3.2	0.0	0.0	0.0	0.0	0.0	0.0
Extraordinary items	0.0	0.0	0.0	0.0	0.0	0.0	0.0	0.0	0.0	0.0

The proceeds from the sale of PPE would be subtracted from the change in cash, because this increase in the cash balance is not due to operations but is due to disinvesting activity. Similarly, the increase in cash during the period that is due to issuance of common stock or preferred stock ($0.3 million in 1990) is a financing cash inflow and does not affect free cash flows from operating activities. Thus, it is subtracted from the change in cash when estimating free cash flows from operating activities. The increases in long-term debt, current debt, and other financing activities represent increases in cash that are caused by financing activities and not by operating activities, and are therefore subtracted from the change in cash when estimating the free cash flows from operating activities.

After adding and subtracting the relevant figures from the above schedule, we get:

	1990	1989	1988	1987	1986	1985	1984	1983	1982	1981
Net free cash flow— indirect method	116.9	73.8	48.5	96.9	75.6	40.5	-2.9	35.9	67.8	8.6

Notice that the estimated free cash flows are reasonably close to those obtained under the direct method above for every year:

	1990	1989	1988	1987	1986	1985	1984	1983	1982	1981
Net free cash flow—indirect method	116.9	73.8	48.5	96.9	75.6	40.5	-2.9	35.9	67.8	8.6
Free cash flow—direct method	141.3	88.7	51.7	78.8	90.3	44.8	-7.2	39.4	36.1	36.6

As explained earlier, the cash flow analyst should not concentrate on free cash flows from one year alone and should examine the four-year average of free cash flows from operating activities:

	1990	1989	1988	1987	1986	1985	1984	1983
4-year average FCF—direct	90.1	77.4	66.4	51.7	41.8	28.3	26.2	37.3
4-year average FCF—indirect	84.0	73.7	65.4	52.5	37.3	35.3	27.4	37.4

As we saw earlier using the direct approach, Hillenbrand has had consistently positive and growing average free cash flows in recent years, due, presumably, to its nature of operations and lines of business.

Let us now show another example of a firm that generated positive free cash flows from its operations in recent years but that operates in the service sector of the economy.

Example:

Ecolab, Inc. is a leading worldwide developer and marketer of premium institutional and residential services such as cleaning and lawn care. It is considered to be a firm with stable growth.

To estimate the free cash flows, we follow the steps outlined previously for Hillenbrand using the direct approach. We begin by estimating the components of operating cash flows:

	1990	1989	1988	1987	1986	1985	1984	1983	1982	1981
Trade receivables	134.90	167.14	161.56	144.00	133.76	116.96	112.71	94.53	103.61	100.56
Change in receivables	-32.24	5.58	17.56	10.24	16.80	4.25	18.18	-9.08	3.05	
Net sales	1389.99	1305.63	1211.89	1020.15	812.92	726.94	704.02	659.41	670.25	
Collections	1422.22	1300.05	1194.33	1009.92	796.12	722.69	685.84	668.49	667.20	

Ecolab, Inc.: Consolidated Statement of Income

ECOLAB INC.

CONSOLIDATED
STATEMENT OF
INCOME

Year ended December 31 (thousands, except per share)	1989	1988	1987
Net Sales	$1,305,629	$1,211,893	$1,020,155
Cost of Sales	650,126	599,661	482,409
Selling, General and Administrative	562,867	503,306	394,791
Nonrecurring	47,478		31,441
Operating Income	45,158	108,926	111,514
Interest Expense, Net	31,364	30,782	21,506
Income from Continuing Operations Before Income Taxes	13,794	78,144	90,008
Provision for Income Taxes	10,647	33,999	48,330
Income from Continuing Operations	3,147	44,145	41,678
Income from Discontinued Operations			100,063
Net Income	$ 3,147	$ 44,145	$ 141,741
Income Per Share			
Continuing operations	$.10	$1.63	$1.56
Discontinued operations			3.74
Net income	$.10	$1.63	$5.30
Average Common Shares Outstanding	27,399	27,067	26,765

SOURCE: Ecolab, Inc., *Annual Report*, 1989.

Ecolab, Inc.: Consolidated Balance Sheet

ECOLAB INC.

CONSOLIDATED
BALANCE
SHEET

December 31 (thousands, except per share)	1989	1988	1987
Assets Cash and cash equivalents	$ **122,323**	$ 18,867	$ 48,977
Accounts receivable, net	**167,138**	161,558	143,997
Inventories	**95,416**	91,042	89,892
Other current assets	**15,469**	14,902	17,563
Current Assets	**400,346**	286,369	300,429
Property, Plant and Equipment, Net	**274,050**	268,674	257,239
Intangible and Other Assets, Net	**368,483**	388,255	401,230
Total Assets	**$1,042,879**	$943,298	$958,898
Liabilities Short-term debt	$ **44,001**	$ 42,829	$ 61,700
and Accounts payable	**78,735**	61,133	66,618
Shareholders' Compensation and benefits	**43,051**	39,275	31,234
Equity Income taxes	**2,686**	15,871	39,397
Other current liabilities	**88,830**	69,691	88,101
Current Liabilities	**257,303**	228,799	287,050
Long-Term Debt	**224,990**	253,726	254,381
Other Noncurrent	**44,950**	27,505	23,250
Series A Cumulative Convertible Preferred Stock	**110,000**		
Shareholders' Equity (common stock, par value $1.00 per share; shares outstanding: 1989–27,062; 1988–27,355; 1987–26,740)	**405,636**	433,268	394,217
Total Liabilities and Shareholders' Equity	**$1,042,879**	$943,298	$958,898

SOURCE: Ecolab, Inc., *Annual Report*, 1989.

As before, we estimate collections from customers by subtracting the change in accounts receivable from sales.

	1990	1989	1988	1987	1986	1985	1984	1983	1982	1981
Total inventories	75.98	95.42	91.04	89.89	65.76	67.32	63.11	59.72	66.24	73.06
Other current assets	10.66	15.47	14.90	17.56	5.05	5.00	6.34	13.26	4.14	3.06
Accounts payable	63.47	78.73	61.13	66.62	45.89	39.09	41.03	30.41	25.98	38.96
Other current liabilities	123.71	131.88	108.97	119.33	59.07	63.38	57.86	56.24	46.78	34.47
Change in the above	-0.81	-35.58	14.34	-44.35	-4.00	-0.71	-15.78	-11.28	-5.08	
Cost of goods sold	590.19	577.29	531.99	428.86	378.18	283.01	277.07	275.75	292.71	
SG&A expense	599.16	562.87	503.31	394.79	329.72	345.46	337.03	301.53	293.83	
Payments to suppliers and employees	1188.53	1104.58	1049.64	779.31	703.90	627.76	598.32	566.00	581.46	

Ecolab, Inc.: Consolidated Statement of Cash Flows

ECOLAB INC.

CONSOLIDATED
STATEMENT OF
CASH FLOWS

Year ended December 31 (thousands)	1989	1988	1987
Operating Activities			
Income from continuing operations	$ 3,147	$ 44,145	$ 41,678
Adjustments to reconcile income to net cash provided:			
Depreciation	53,398	48,343	38,181
Amortization	21,853	21,564	17,909
Deferred income taxes	(16,280)	581	(1,593)
Other	5,698	4,091	(2,972)
Income and other from discontinued operations			5,193
Changes in operating assets and liabilities:			
Accounts receivable	(6,295)	(16,567)	(3,249)
Inventories	(5,165)	(58)	(10,073)
Other assets	(682)	2,461	(6,112)
Accounts payable	17,929	(5,607)	8,712
Other liabilities	40,973	8,499	51,684
Cash provided by operating activities	114,576	107,452	139,358
Investing Activities			
Capital expenditures	(61,973)	(65,818)	(56,477)
Property disposals	1,704	6,242	6,296
Other, net	(7,292)	(8,242)	(10,257)
Consumer divestiture		(41,507)	198,098
Business acquisitions			(418,327)
Cash used for investing activities	(67,561)	(109,325)	(280,667)
Financing Activities			
Notes payable	7,848	(18,571)	(7,488)
Long-term debt additions	476	25,254	538,656
Long-term debt reductions	(34,572)	(20,231)	(380,026)
Convertible preferred stock issued	110,000		
Reacquired shares	(11,491)	(695)	(8,711)
Dividends	(18,008)	(17,398)	(16,184)
Other, net	2,631	3,407	6,964
Cash provided by (used for) financing activities	56,884	(28,234)	133,211
Effect of exchange rate changes on cash	(443)	(3)	689
Increase (Decrease) in Cash and Cash Equivalents	103,456	(30,110)	(7,409)
Cash and Cash Equivalents, at beginning of year	18,867	48,977	56,386
Cash and Cash Equivalents, at end of year	$122,323	$ 18,867	$ 48,977

SOURCE: Ecolab, Inc., *Annual Report*, 1989.

Ecolab, Inc.: Consolidated Statement of Shareholders' Equity

ECOLAB INC.

CONSOLIDATED STATEMENT OF SHAREHOLDERS' EQUITY

(thousands)	Common Stock	Additional Paid-in Capital	Retained Earnings	Deferred Compen-sation	Cumulative Translation	Treasury Stock	Total
Balance December 31, 1986	$27,195	$52,095	$204,826	$(4,146)	$(6,181)	$(19,671)	$254,118
1987 Net income			141,741				141,741
Common stock dividends			(16,184)				(16,184)
Employee stock options exercised		3,276	(2,994)			6,717	6,999
Employee stock awards		162	9	(1,081)		875	(35)
Conversion of debentures	467	9,505					9,972
Reacquired shares	(40)		(968)			(7,703)	(8,711)
Amortization				1,376			1,376
Translation adjustments					4,941		4,941
Balance December 31, 1987	27,622	65,038	326,430	(3,851)	(1,240)	(19,782)	394,217
1988 Net income			44,145				44,145
Common stock dividends			(17,398)				(17,398)
Employee stock options exercised		185	(399)			3,334	3,120
Employee stock awards		72	91	(1,446)		1,177	(106)
Conversion of debentures	452	6,832					7,284
Reacquired shares						(695)	(695)
Amortization				1,520			1,520
Translation adjustments					1,181		1,181
Balance December 31, 1988	28,074	72,127	352,869	(3,777)	(59)	(15,966)	433,268
1989 Net income			3,147				3,147
Common stock dividends			(18,008)				(18,008)
Preferred stock dividends			(429)				(429)
Employee stock options exercised		462	(1,194)			2,875	2,143
Employee stock awards		153	433	(2,046)		1,844	384
Conversion of debentures	5	73					78
Reacquired shares						(13,566)	(13,566)
Amortization				1,404			1,404
Translation adjustments					(2,785)		(2,785)
Balance December 31, 1989	$28,079	$72,815	$336,818	$(4,419)	$(2,844)	$(24,813)	$405,636

	1989		1988		1987	
Year ended December 31	Common Stock	Treasury Stock	Common Stock	Treasury Stock	Common Stock	Treasury Stock
Common Stock Activity Employee stock options exercised		125,773		145,656		287,880
Employee stock awards		81,445		48,399		30,184
Conversion of debentures	4,809		452,308		466,792	
Reacquired shares		(505,535)		(31,521)	(39,780)	(345,183)
Shares outstanding, end of year	28,079,218	(1,017,489)	28,074,409	(719,172)	27,622,101	(881,706)

SOURCE: Ecolab, Inc., *Annual Report*, 1989.

Payments to suppliers and employees are estimated by cost of goods sold (excluding depreciation) plus selling, general, and administrative expenses. To this we add other expenditures such as increases in inventories and other current assets. However, we subtract those expenditures that were made on credit and not yet paid for by subtracting the changes in accounts payable and other current liabilities (excluding, of course, the changes in short-term debt).

	1990	1989	1988	1987	1986	1985	1984	1983	1982
Interest expense	33.53	35.39	34.34	27.07	8.85	10.52	9.92	15.08	18.31
Interest income	5.46	4.02	3.56	5.56	6.12	7.76	5.45	4.79	5.91
Interest payment, net	28.07	31.36	30.78	21.51	2.73	2.76	4.47	10.29	12.39

As before, interest payment is estimated by the interest expense minus interest income, because more detailed information about interest payable or receivable is not available.

	1990	1989	1988	1987	1986	1985	1984	1983	1982	1981
Income tax refund	0.00	0.00	0.00	0.00	0.00	0.00	0.00	21.51	0.00	0.00
Income taxes payable	11.58	2.69	15.87	39.40	5.71	5.59	7.62	0.00	9.18	0.00
Deferred taxes and ITC	0.00	0.00	0.00	0.00	9.80	10.89	11.09	11.70	11.41	11.98
Change in above	8.90	-13.18	-23.53	23.88	-0.96	-2.23	28.52	-30.41	8.62	
Total income taxes	39.67	10.65	34.00	48.33	28.60	26.57	23.68	14.42	16.69	
Tax payment	30.77	23.83	57.52	24.45	29.57	28.81	-4.84	44.83	8.07	

The tax payment is estimated by subtracting the changes in the tax liabilities from the tax expense on the balance sheet and adding the change in tax receivable.

	1990	1989	1988	1987	1986	1985	1984	1983	1982
Cash from operations	174.85	140.28	56.39	184.66	59.92	63.36	87.89	47.38	65.28

Cash from operations is estimated by collections from customers, minus payments to suppliers and employees, minus payments for interest, and minus payments for taxes. Note that in the last eight years Ecolab shows a consistent pattern of positive cash flows from operating activities. Furthermore, the fluctuations in these cash flows are not very wide.

Let us now estimate free cash flows by first estimating discretionary capital expenditures and discretionary payments to suppliers and employees.

	1990	1989	1988	1987	1986	1985	1984	1983	1982	1981
Capital expenditures	64.19	61.97	65.82	56.48	29.55	27.44	43.46	31.74	41.84	45.37
Net sales	1389.99	1305.63	1211.89	1020.15	812.92	726.94	704.02	659.41	670.25	628.64
Average 3-year growth rate capital expenditures	4.36	28.00	33.87	9.13	-2.35	-13.12	-1.42			
Average 3-year growth rate sales	10.86	17.11	18.57	13.16	7.23	2.74	3.85			
Excess capital expenditures rate	0.00	10.89	15.29	0.00	0.00	0.00	0.00			
Discretionary capital expenditures	0.00	6.75	10.07	0.00	0.00	0.00	0.00			

Discretionary capital expenditures are estimated by multiplying the excess of the growth rate in capital expenditures over the growth rate in sales by the current level of capital expenditures.

	1990	1989	1988	1987	1986	1985	1984	1983	1982
Collections	1422.22	1300.05	1194.33	1009.92	796.12	722.69	685.84	668.49	667.20
Payments to suppliers and employees	1188.53	1104.58	1049.64	779.31	703.90	627.76	598.32	566.00	581.46
Average 3-year growth rate collections	12.09	17.76	18.23	13.77	6.00	2.70			
Average 3-year growth rate payments	15.11	16.21	18.69	9.21	7.54	2.59			
Excess growth rate payments over collections	3.02	0.00	0.46	0.00	1.54	0.00			
Discretionary payments to suppliers	7.17	0.00	0.97	0.00	2.17	0.00			

Discretionary payments to suppliers and employees are estimated by multiplying the excess of the growth rate in such payments over the growth rate of collections from customers by the current level of payments to suppliers and employees.

To estimate free cash flow, we now subtract current capital expenditures from the cash generated by operating activities and add the discretionary capital expenditures and discretionary payments to suppliers and employees.

	1990	1989	1988	1987	1986	1985
Free cash flow—direct approach	117.84	85.05	1.60	128.18	32.54	35.93

As before, it is more instructive to examine the average free cash flow over four years than the free cash flow in any individual year:

	1990	1989	1988	1987	1986	1985
Average free cash flow—4 years	83.17	61.84	49.56	65.55	34.23	35.93

Note that, like Hillenbrand, Ecolab shows a consistent pattern of positive average free cash flows over the period 1985–1990. Furthermore, the amounts of the average free cash flows are reasonably close to each other, so that the firm not only shows a consistent pattern of free cash flows, it also shows a stable pattern of free cash flows.

One should note that Ecolab's financial statements report relatively high levels of nonrecurring charges of $47.5 million in 1989 and $31.4 million in 1987. These charges were included to derive net cash flows from operating activities (using the indirect approach) on the statement of cash flows. However, they are excluded from our estimates of operating cash flows and free cash flows because they represent items that are not expected to recur in the future. In any single year, such differences may be material. However, when one averages the cash flows over four years, such nonrecurring items are spread over four years if the indirect approach is used to estimate free cash flows, and the resulting differences are not significant.

An immediate question that comes to mind is whether Ecolab's security price reflects these consistent and stable free cash flows. To answer this question, let us examine the market value of Ecolab at the end of 1989 and estimate the multiple of the average free cash flow at that time. The market value of Ecolab at the end of calendar 1989, which is also the end of its fiscal year, was $771.3 million. This amount compares to a four-year average free cash flow at the end of 1989 of $61.8 million. Thus, the multiple as of the end of 1989 is about 12.5 times free cash flows ($771.3/ $61.8). This is a relatively low multiple, as compared with 21.5, which was the average for the S&P Industrials at the end of 1989. Thus, it indicates that, on the basis of free cash flows, the firm was a good candidate for investment, because the implicit rate of return was about 8 percent (100:12.5), with a 14.5 percent growth rate of free cash flows over the prior five years. This relatively high rate of return does not include future growth opportunities as a result of the free cash flows, which may be further reinvested in the business. Indeed, if an investor waited until after Ecolab's financial statements were disclosed and invested in Ecolab's stock on April 1, 1990, the investor would have realized a rate of return on the investment of 42.8 percent over the following 12 months. This translates to a return of 13.8 percent in excess of the average return earned on a portfolio of stocks with the same market value at the beginning of 1989. Therefore, Ecolab's stock outperformed its counterparts (in terms of size) by a substantial amount.

Let us now show an example of a firm that had a consistent pattern of negative cash flows in recent years.

Example:

Toys "R" Us, Inc. reports the following results for the year ending on January 28, 1990:
We first estimate the individual components of operating cash flows as shown on page 199. Collections from customers are calculated as sales minus the change in accounts receivable. If one assumes that all sales are on credit, then accounts receivable should have increased during the period by the amount of sales. If they increased by a smaller amount, then some of the accounts receivable were collected during the period. The amount collected can be estimated by subtracting the increase in accounts receivable from annual sales. For example, in 1988 sales amounted to $4,000.19 million and accounts receivable increased by $5.89 million. Thus, collections are estimated as $3,994.30 million ($4,000.19 - $5.89). In 1989, however, accounts receivable actually decreased, indicating that not only did the firm collect all 1989 sales in cash,

Toys "R" Us, Inc.: Consolidated Statements of Earnings

Toys "R" Us, Inc. and Subsidiaries
CONSOLIDATED STATEMENTS OF STOCKHOLDERS' EQUITY

(In thousands except per share information)			Year Ended
	January 28 1990	January 29 1989	January 31 1988
Net sales..	$ 4,787,830	$ 4,000,192	$ 3,136,568
Costs and expenses:			
Cost of sales	3,309,653	2,766,543	2,157,017
Selling, advertising, general and administrative............................	866,399	736,329	584,120
Depreciation and amortization...	65,839	54,564	43,716
Interest expense	44,309	25,812	13,849
Interest and other income	(12,050)	(11,880)	(8,056)
	4,274,150	3,571,368	2,790,646
Earnings before taxes on income	513,680	428,824	345,922
Taxes on income..	192,600	160,800	142,000
Net earnings	$ 321,080	$ 268,024	$ 203,922
Net earnings per share	$ 1.64	$ 1.36	$ 1.04

SOURCE: Toys "R" Us, Inc., *Annual Report*, 1989.

	1989	1988	1987	1986	1985	1984	1983	1982	1981	1980	1979
Accounts receivable	53.10	68.03	62.14	37.50	25.97	23.41	17.91	17.51	14.52	28.26	15.07
Change in accounts receivable	-14.93	5.89	24.64	11.53	2.56	5.50	0.40	2.99	-13.74	13.19	
Sales	4787.83	4000.19	3136.57	2444.90	1976.13	1701.70	1319.64	1041.73	783.28	597.33	
Collections	4802.76	3994.30	3111.93	2433.37	1973.57	1696.20	1319.24	1038.74	797.02	584.14	

it also collected $14.93 million of the accounts receivable that resulted from 1988 sales. Therefore, collections in 1989 are estimated as $4802.76 million ($4,787.83 + $14.93). Let us now estimate payments to suppliers, employees, and the like:

	1989	1988	1987	1986	1985	1984	1983	1982	1981	1980	1979
Inventory	1230.39	931.12	772.83	528.94	413.49	397.91	264.19	191.95	140.66	103.12	93.19
Prepaid expenses	13.96	10.82	5.05	3.57	3.25	2.03	1.54	0.70	4.01	1.86	1.93
Accounts payable	517.90	505.37	403.10	305.70	248.98	250.12	184.50	82.28	65.74	66.77	33.04
Accrued expenses	279.10	239.39	167.28	118.26	93.66	100.48	79.28	66.01	47.05	30.74	30.04
Change in the above	250.17	-10.32	98.95	34.45	24.76	47.39	-42.41	12.48	24.41	-24.57	
Cost of goods sold	3309.65	2766.54	2157.02	1668.21	1322.94	1138.86	881.26	705.26	522.81	409.89	
SG&A expenses	866.40	736.33	584.12	458.53	408.44	344.24	254.45	206.38	166.93	131.43	
Payments to suppliers	4426.22	3492.55	2840.09	2161.19	1756.14	1530.49	1093.30	924.12	714.15	516.75	

Toys "R" Us, Inc.: Consolidated Balance Sheets

Toys "R" Us, Inc. and Subsidiaries

CONSOLIDATED BALANCE SHEETS

(In thousands)		Year Ended
	January 28 1990	January 29 1989
ASSETS Current Assets:		
Cash and short-term investments	$ 40,895	$ 122,912
Accounts and other receivables	53,098	68,030
Merchandise inventories	1,230,394	931,120
Prepaid expenses	13,965	10,822
Total Current Assets	1,338,352	1,132,884
Property and Equipment:		
Real estate, net	1,141,690	951,788
Other, net	553,104	436,264
Leased property under capital leases, net	8,180	8,910
Total Property and Equipment	1,702,974	1,396,962
Other Assets	33,362	25,114
	$ 3,074,688	$ 2,554,960
LIABILITIES AND STOCKHOLDERS' EQUITY Current Liabilities:		
Short-term notes payable to banks	$ 205,513	$ 76,133
Accounts payable	517,903	505,370
Accrued expenses, taxes and other liabilities	280,517	240,928
Income taxes	96,033	55,839
Total Current Liabilities	1,099,966	878,270
Deferred Income Taxes	96,391	78,819
Long-Term Debt	159,518	159,888
Obligations Under Capital Leases	13,467	14,296
Stockholders' Equity:		
Common stock	19,797	13,164
Additional paid-in capital	324,616	305,739
Retained earnings	1,436,855	1,122,445
Foreign currency translation adjustment	23,010	28,049
Treasury shares, at cost	(96,973)	(43,407)
Receivable from exercise of stock options	(1,959)	(2,303)
	1,705,346	1,423,687
	$ 3,074,688	$ 2,554,960

SOURCE: Toys "R" Us, Inc., *Annual Report*, 1989.

Toys "R" Us, Inc.: Consolidated Statements of Cash Flows

Toys "R" Us, Inc. and Subsidiaries

CONSOLIDATED STATEMENTS OF CASH FLOWS

(In thousands)			Year Ended
	January 28 1990	January 29 1989	January 31 1988
CASH FLOWS FROM OPERATING ACTIVITIES Net income	$ 321,080	$ 268,024	$ 203,922
Adjustments to reconcile net income to net cash provided by operating activities:			
Depreciation and amortization	65,839	54,564	43,716
Deferred taxes	17,572	25,463	13,035
Change in operating assets and liabilities:			
Accounts and other receivables	14,932	(5,886)	(24,642)
Merchandise inventories	(299,274)	(158,287)	(243,894)
Prepaid expenses and other assets	(11,391)	(14,366)	(2,829)
Accounts payable, accrued expenses and taxes	92,316	158,802	144,364
Total adjustments	(120,006)	60,290	(70,250)
Net cash provided by operating activities	201,074	328,314	133,672
CASH FLOWS FROM INVESTING ACTIVITIES Capital expenditures - net	(371,851)	(327,010)	(314,827)
Other - net	(5,114)	4,463	15,137
Net cash used in investing activities	(376,965)	(322,547)	(299,690)
CASH FLOWS FROM FINANCING ACTIVITIES Short-term borrowings - net	129,380	58,476	17,663
Long-term borrowings	–	693	96,611
Long-term debt repayments	(1,199)	(3,899)	(1,860)
Exercise of stock options	19,861	52,429	15,221
Share repurchase program	(54,168)	(36,550)	–
Net cash provided by financing activities	93,874	71,149	127,635
CASH AND SHORT-TERM INVESTMENTS Increase/(decrease) during year	(82,017)	76,916	(38,383)
Beginning of year	122,912	45,996	84,379
End of year	$ 40,895	$ 122,912	$ 45,996

SUPPLEMENTAL DISCLOSURES OF CASH FLOW INFORMATION

The Company considers all highly liquid investments purchased as part of its daily cash management activities to be short-term investments.

During the years ended January 28, 1990, January 29, 1989 and January 31, 1988, the Company made income tax payments of $116,770, $110,079 and $119,722 and interest payments (net of amounts capitalized) of $44,265, $25,738 and $9,610, respectively.

SOURCE: Toys "R" Us, Inc., *Annual Report*, 1989.

Toys "R" Us: Consolidated Statements of Stockholders' Equity

Toys "R" Us, Inc. and Subsidiaries
CONSOLIDATED STATEMENTS OF STOCKHOLDERS' EQUITY

(In thousands)	Shares
Balance, February 1, 1987	127,111
Net earnings for the year	—
Exercise of stock options	3,420
Tax benefit from exercise of stock options	—
Repayment of stock option loans	—
Foreign currency translation adjustment	—
Balance, January 31, 1988	130,531
Net earnings for the year	—
Share repurchase program	—
Exercise of stock options	1,106
Tax benefit from exercise of stock options	—
Foreign currency translation adjustment	—
Balance, January 29, 1989	131,637
Net earnings for the year	—
Three-for-two stock split effected in the form	
of a 50% stock dividend payable May 26, 1989	65,948
Share repurchase program	—
Exercise of stock options	389
Tax benefit from exercise of stock options	—
Repayment of stock option loans	—
Foreign currency translation adjustment	—
Balance, January 28, 1990	197,974

Common stock Issued		Common stock in Treasury		Additional paid-in capital	Retained earnings	Foreign currency translation adjustments	Receivable from exercise of stock options	Total
Amount	Shares	Amount						
$ 12,711	(2,591)	$ (5,571)		$ 239,721	$ 650,499	$ 8,449	$ (4,768)	$ 901,041
—	—	—		—	203,922	—	—	203,922
342	(9)	(358)		7,739	—	—	(1,313)	6,410
—	—	—		5,033	—	—	—	5,033
—	—	—		—	—	—	3,778	3,778
—	—	—		—	—	15,137	—	15,137
13,053	(2,600)	(5,929)		252,493	854,421	23,586	(2,303)	1,135,321
—	—	—		—	268,024	—	—	268,024
—	(983)	(36,550)		—	—	—	—	(36,550)
111	(25)	(928)		15,593	—	—	—	14,776
—	—	—		37,653	—	—	—	37,653
—	—	—		—	—	4,463	—	4,463
13,164	(3,608)	(43,407)		305,739	1,122,445	28,049	(2,303)	1,423,687
—	—	—		—	321,080	—	—	321,080
6,595	(2,382)	—		—	(6,670)	—	—	(75)
—	(1,426)	(54,168)		—	—	—	—	(54,168)
38	469	602		12,155	—	—	—	12,795
—	—	—		6,722	—	—	—	6,722
—	—	—		—	—	—	344	344
—	—	—		—	—	(5,039)	—	(5,039)
$ 19,797	(6,947)	$ (96,973)		$ 324,616	$ 1,436,855	$ 23,010	$ (1,959)	$ 1,705,346

SOURCE: Toys "R" Us, *Annual Report, 1989.*

Payments to suppliers and employees are calculated as cost of goods sold plus selling, general, and administrative expenses. Compustat excludes depreciation and amortization from cost of goods sold, so the sum of these two expenses can be conceived as cash outflows to suppliers and employees. However, one has to add the change in inventories plus the change in prepaid expenses because these represent additional acquisitions of inventory or payments to suppliers and employees due to current operations. We then subtract the change in accounts payable and the change in accrued expenses because some of the above expenditures may not have been paid during the current period and may actually be paid only in the next period.

	1989	1988	1987	1986	1985	1984	1983	1982	1981	1980
Interest expense	52.79	32.93	21.95	14.04	11.13	6.78	3.94	5.86	5.78	3.61
Interest income	0.00	0.00	8.06	7.23	8.09	10.97	10.14	9.57	11.65	5.00
Interest payment, net	52.79	32.93	13.89	6.81	3.04	-4.19	-6.20	-3.71	-5.87	-1.39

Here, additional data about interest payable or receivable, or data about interest capitalized, are unavailable. Thus, interest payments are estimated by interest expense minus interest income.

	1989	1988	1987	1986	1985	1984	1983	1982	1981	1980	1979
Taxes payable	96.03	55.84	71.00	73.06	52.00	44.20	33.17	36.95	30.85	18.11	3.83
Deferred taxes	96.39	78.82	53.36	40.32	26.14	16.47	8.71	8.54	5.41	3.94	0.00
Change in tax liability	57.76	10.30	10.98	35.24	17.47	18.79	-3.61	9.23	14.21	18.22	
Tax expense	192.60	160.80	142.00	132.00	100.00	94.75	85.92	60.16	45.20	23.57	
Tax payment	134.84	150.50	131.02	96.76	82.53	75.96	89.53	50.93	30.99	5.35	

A portion of the tax expense may be deferred into the next period with an associated increase in taxes payable, and another portion into later periods, as reflected by the increase in deferred taxes. So, the payment for taxes is calculated as the tax expense minus the change in taxes payable and minus the change in deferred taxes.

We can now estimate the net cash from operating activities:

	1989	1988	1987	1986	1985	1984	1983	1982	1981	1980
Cash from operations	188.91	318.32	126.93	168.61	131.86	93.94	142.61	67.40	57.75	63.43

Cash from operations is calculated as collections from customers minus payments to suppliers, employees, interest, and taxes. Note that this procedure does not include in operating cash flows any nonrecurring cash flows.

We now estimate the annual average growth rate in capital expenditures over the most recent three years:

	1989	1988	1987	1986	1985	1984	1983	1982	1981	1980
Capital expenditures		371.85	327.01	314.83	259.39	221.79	166.16	97.09	68.14	69.40	38.51
Average 3-year growth capital expenditures	12.76	13.82	23.74	38.76	48.20	33.78	36.10			

For example, for 1989 we divide $371.85 by $259.39 to obtain 1.4336. We take the cubic root of 1.4336, which is equal to 1.1276, or an average growth rate of 12.76 percent. We follow similar calculations for sales:

	1989	1988	1987	1986	1985	1984	1983	1982	1981	1980
Sales		4787.83	4000.19	3136.57	2444.90	1976.13	1701.70	1319.64	1041.73	783.28	597.33
Average 3-year growth sales	25.11	26.50	22.61	22.82	23.79	29.52	30.24			

We now subtract the growth rate of sales from that of capital expenditures and substitute zero if the result is negative. If the result is positive, we multiply the excess growth rate of capital expenditures above the growth rate of sales by the total capital expenditures that year to obtain an estimate of discretionary capital expenditures for that year:

	1989	1988	1987	1986	1985	1984	1983
Discretionary capital expenditures	0.00	0.00	3.57	41.34	54.14	7.08	5.69

In 1989 the average growth rate of sales, 25.11 percent, is higher than the average growth rate of capital expenditures (12.76 percent). Thus, no capital expenditures are considered as discretionary in 1989. However, in 1986 the growth rate of capital expenditures (38.76 percent) exceeds the growth rate of sales (22.82 percent) by 15.94 percent. Thus, discretionary capital expenditures are estimated by multiplying total capital expenditures in 1986 of $259.39 by 15.94 percent to obtain $41.34. These discretionary capital expenditures will be added to free cash flows in 1986. Using these estimates of the discretionary expenditures on PPE, we obtain the estimated free cash flows by subtracting total capital expenditures from net operating cash flows and adding back discretionary capital expenditures and other discretionary expenditures and fat. As before, we estimate the latter by using the following procedure.

We first retrieve the estimated collections from customers and payments to suppliers and employees from the previous computations. We then calculate the average 3-year growth rate of collections from customers and payments to suppliers. We now assume that 20 percent of the excess of growth rate in payments to suppliers and collections from customers represents discretionary expenditures that should be added to free cash flows.

	1989	1988	1987	1986	1985	1984	1983	1982	1981	1980
Collections	4802.76	3994.30	3111.93	2433.37	1973.57	1696.20	1319.24	1038.74	797.02	584.14
Payments to suppliers	4426.22	3492.55	2840.09	2161.19	1756.14	1530.49	1093.30	924.12	714.15	516.75
Average growth collections	25.44	26.49	22.42	22.64	23.86	28.63	31.20			
Average growth payments	26.99	25.76	22.89	25.50	23.86	28.93	28.38			
Discretionary payments	13.77	0.00	2.65	12.38	0.03	0.92	0.00			

Note that in 1989 the average growth rate of payments to suppliers and employees exceeds the average growth rate of collections from customers by 1.55 percent (26.99 − 25.44). Multiplying this excess by total payments to suppliers and employees of $4426.22, and then again by 20 percent, yields $13.77 of discretionary cash flows that were spent on excessive payments to suppliers and employees. This yields an estimated free cash flow of:

	1989	1988	1987	1986	1985	1984	1983
Free cash flow	-169.17	-8.69	-181.68	-37.06	-35.76	-64.22	51.21

Our estimates of free cash flows were focused on a single year. However, firms may have fluctuations in their free cash flows from one year to another due to shifts in economic and business conditions. So, it might be more instructive to focus on averages for the most recent years. Based on the above estimates, we obtain the following four-year average free cash flows:

	1989	1988	1987	1986	1985	1984	1983
Free cash flow 4-year average	-99.15	-65.80	-79.68	-21.46	-16.26	-6.51	51.21

The average free cash flow of Toys "R" Us is consistently negative for the most recent six years, which is due to the high expansion rate of the firm. Normally, it is expected that a firm will be able to generate free cash flows from its operations rather than have to finance these negative free cash flows. If a firm shows a consistent pattern of negative free cash flows, it must continuously find sources of funds for its operations, mostly through borrowing or issuance of additional equity. A firm like Toys "R" Us, which experienced a high growth rate in both sales and operating cash flows, and which is perceived by the financial community as a firm with a high future growth rate in operating cash flow, may, in fact, have little trouble raising additional capital for expansion.[10] In the long run, a firm that consistently generates negative free cash flows, if it cannot continually raise new capital, will shrink to the point that it has to liquidate or cease to exist.

---

[10]This is indeed what Toys "R" Us was able to do in recent years. It issued additional debt and additional equity to finance new store openings.

Let us now use the indirect approach to estimate free cash flows.

	1989	1988	1987	1986	1985	1984	1983	1982	1981	1980
Change in cash and equivalents	-82.0	76.9	-38.4	-51.8	-79.1	-20.6	101.3	11.1	47.2	31.7

Add to the net change in cash and cash equivalents all financing cash outflows because they do not represent free cash flows from *operating* activities:

	1989	1988	1987	1986	1985	1984	1983	1982	1981	1980
Cash dividends	0.0	0.0	0.0	0.0	0.0	0.0	0.0	0.0	0.0	0.0
Stock purchases	54.2	36.5	0.0	0.0	0.0	0.0	0.0	0.0	0.0	0.0
Reduction L.T.D.	1.2	3.9	1.9	2.0	3.8	2.9	2.1	52.3	3.1	2.7

Cash dividends will be added back to the net change in cash because they represent cash that is returned to stockholders and are not used to sustain the growth of the firm's business, that is, they are free cash flows. Stock repurchases are similar to dividends; they represent cash flows that are not needed for the continuing growth of current operations and are used to buy out some shareholders. Finally, the reduction of long-term debt is a disfinancing cash flow, which does not affect free cash flow. Thus, it is added back to the change in cash in order to derive the free cash flow that is generated from operating activities.

We now estimate discretionary capital expenditures as we did before, using the direct approach of estimating free cash flows:

	1989	1988	1987	1986	1985	1984	1983
3-year growth rate capital expenditures	12.8	13.8	23.7	38.8	48.2	33.8	36.1
3-year growth rate sales	25.1	26.5	22.6	22.8	23.8	29.5	30.2
Current capital expenditures	371.9	327.0	314.8	259.4	221.8	166.2	97.1
Discretionary capital expenditures	0.0	0.0	3.6	41.3	54.1	7.1	5.7

Discretionary capital expenditures are estimated by the excess of the three-year growth in capital expenditures over sales times the level of capital expenditures for that year.

We proceed to estimate discretionary cash flows in the firm's expenditures on cost of goods sold and on selling, general, and administrative expenses. The estimation process is to compare the ratio of cost of goods sold (or selling expenses) to sales with the long-run ratio (average of the most recent four years). If the ratio exceeds the long-run average ratio, some of these expenditures are considered discretionary, and 20 percent of the excess is multiplied by current sales to determine the amount of discretionary cash flows:

	1989	1988	1987	1986	1985	1984	1983	1982	1981	1980
COGS percent of sales	69.1	69.2	68.8	68.2	66.9	66.9	66.8	67.7	66.7	68.6
4-year average COGS percent of sales	68.8	68.3	67.7	67.2	67.1	67.0	67.5	67.4	67.3	68.3
Sales	4787.8	4000.2	3136.6	2444.9	1976.1	1701.7	1319.6	1041.7	783.3	597.3
Excess COGS	14.6	35.3	33.0	24.7	0.0	0.0	0.0	2.9	0.0	1.8
20 percent of difference (discretionary COGS)	2.9	7.1	6.6	4.9	0.0	0.0	0.0	0.6	0.0	0.4

In 1989, cost of goods sold as a proportion of sales was 69.1 percent, whereas the four-year average of this ratio was 68.8 percent. Thus, in 1989 Toys "R" Us spent more on costs of purchases and production of inventories than in the prior four years, indicating that there is a potential of overspending on cost of goods sold that amounted to $14.6 million [(69.1% − 68.8%) × 4787.8]. Because we assume that only 20 percent of this overspending on COGS is discretionary, we multiply 14.6 by 20 percent to obtain $2.9 million of discretionary expenditures on COGS.

Similarly, for selling, general, and administrative (SGA) expenses we find:

	1989	1988	1987	1986	1985	1984	1983	1982	1981	1980
SGA percent of sales	18.1	18.4	18.6	18.8	20.7	20.2	19.3	19.8	21.3	22.0
4-year average SGA percent of sales	18.5	19.1	19.6	19.7	20.0	20.2	20.6	21.1	21.2	20.5
Sales	4787.8	4000.2	3136.6	2444.9	1976.1	1701.7	1319.6	1041.7	783.3	597.3
Excess SGA	0.0	0.0	0.0	0.0	13.3	1.2	0.0	0.0	0.7	8.9
20 percent of difference (discretionary SGA)	0.0	0.0	0.0	0.0	2.7	0.2	0.0	0.0	0.1	1.8

In 1989 the ratio of selling, general, and administrative expenses to sales was below its four-year average (18.1 percent as compared to 18.5 percent). Therefore, no overspending is evident, nor do we assume that there are any discretionary expenditures on SGA expenses. However, in 1985 we estimate the discretionary expenditures on SGA expenses as 2.7, using the same steps as those used for cost of goods sold.

We now add two more items that represent cash outflows from investing or financing events and that do not, therefore, affect free cash flows from operating activities:

	1989	1988	1987	1986	1985	1984	1983	1982	1981	1980
Change in capitalized leases	-0.7	-3.5	-1.0	-1.0	-1.2	-0.8	-0.8	-1.2	-0.9	-0.3
Investing activities—other	-5.1	-4.1	13.8	0.0	0.0	0.0	0.0	0.0	0.0	0.0

In 1989 there is a decrease in liabilities due to capitalized leases. These liabilities are created when Toys "R" Us enters leasing agreements that provide it with *de-facto* ownership of the leased assets. The firms then increase fixed assets and capitalized lease liabilities by the same amount (usually the present value of future payments on the lease). When payments are made on the lease, a portion is attributed to interest expense and the remainder to a decrease of the principal (the capitalized lease liability). In 1989 the capitalized lease liability decreased by $700,000, indicating that there was a cash outflow of $700,000 in excess of the interest expense on the capital lease. This represents a reduction of cash due to a financing event and it is added back to the change in cash when estimating free cash flow from operating activities.[11] Cash outflows on other investing activities are considered discretionary investing cash outflows and are added back to the change in cash when we estimate free cash flows from operating activities.

Similarly, we need to subtract from the change in cash those items that increase cash, but that represent investing or financing cash inflows:

	1989	1988	1987	1986	1985	1984	1983	1982	1981	1980
Sale of PPE	0.0	0.0	0.0	0.0	0.0	2.0	1.8	4.4	4.1	6.7
Sale of common and preferred	19.9	52.4	15.2	25.0	16.1	8.4	44.0	53.5	0.0	0.0
Increase L.T. debt	0.0	0.7	96.6	0.0	2.5	36.1	15.1	6.2	50.0	9.0
Changes in current debt	129.4	58.5	17.7	-1.1	-19.1	20.1	0.0	0.0	0.0	0.0
Financing activities—other	0.0	0.0	0.0	0.0	0.0	0.0	0.0	0.0	0.0	0.0
Extraordinary items	0.0	0.0	0.0	0.0	0.0	0.0	0.0	0.0	0.0	0.0

The proceeds from the sale of PPE in 1984 of $2.0 million are subtracted from the change in cash, because this increase in the cash balance is not due to operations but is due to disinvesting activity. Similarly, the increase in cash during the period, due to exercising of stock options, amounted to $19.9 million in 1989. This increase is a financing cash inflow and does not affect free cash flows from operating activities. Thus, it is subtracted from the change in cash when estimating free cash flows from operating activities. The increases in long-term debt, current debt, and other financing activities represent increases in cash that are caused by financing activities and not by operating activities and are, therefore, subtracted from the change in cash when estimating the free cash flows from operating activities.

After adding and subtracting the relevant figures from the above schedules, we find:

	1989	1988	1987	1986	1985	1984	1983
Net free cash flow	-167.1	20.5	-168.7	-26.4	-16.7	-76.1	49.0

Note that the estimated free cash flows are reasonably close to that obtained under the direct method above for every year:

---

[11]To the extent that capitalized lease obligations are included in short- and long-term debt, there is no need to adjust for them as we did here.

	1989	1988	1987	1986	1985	1984	1983
Free cash flow—indirect approach	-167.1	20.5	-168.7	-26.4	-16.7	-76.1	49.0
Free cash flow—direct approach	-169.2	-8.7	-181.7	-37.1	-35.8	-64.2	51.2

As explained earlier, the cash flow analyst should not concentrate on free cash flows from one year alone and should examine the four-year average of free cash flows from operating activities:

	1989	1988	1987	1986	1985	1984	1983
4-year average FCF—direct	-99.2	-65.8	-79.7	-21.5	-16.3	-6.5	51.2
4-year average FCF—indirect	-85.4	-47.8	-72.0	-17.6	-14.6	-13.6	49.0

Using the direct approach, Toys "R" Us has consistent negative average free cash flows in the most recent years, presumably due to its rapid expansion. It should be mentioned that Toys "R" Us has shown excellent growth in its operating cash flow. Over a reasonable period, the negative free cash flows activities can be financed by additional equity or debt issuances. However, at some point in time, the firm should begin to generate positive free cash flows from its operations or face the chance that investors and lenders might not continue to finance its operations. This may occur if its rate of growth in operating cash flow considerably slows or declines.

A question that needs to be addressed is whether the market ever rewards firms with negative free cash flows. A cursory look into our Toys "R" Us example indicates that, indeed, the market may reward firms with negative cash flows. Figure 5–2 shows the behavior of stock prices for the firm over the last eight years. It is clear that the stock price showed an increasing trend over the past eight years, although Toys "R" Us was a negative free cash flow generator over that period. In general, investors may desire to own stocks in a firm that proved to be a net borrower of cash if its operating cash flows grew at a high rate, and if there was a high probability that this high growth would continue to be the reason for negative free cash flows. Also, investors in such a firm probably perceive that it is the expansion of the firm that causes negative free cash flows, and without that expansion, the firm can generate positive free cash flows. Chapter 7 is devoted to portfolio selection rules and back-testing of a strategy that are based on investment in firms with low free cash flows multiples.

Figures 5–3 and 5–4 show the relationship between free cash flows and market values for Toys "R" Us and for Ecolab. As can be seen, the market value of Toys "R" Us continued to increase, although its free cash flows decreased, presumably because investors expected the firm to continue its high growth rate and were sufficiently confident that the firm would find the required financing sources. Thus, there is not much of a positive correlation between market value and free cash flow for Toys "R"

Figure 5-2   Toys "R" Us, Inc. Stock Price Trends

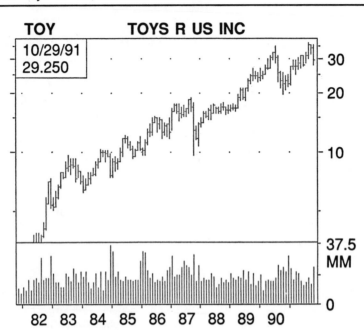

Us. However, this correlation is easily evident for Ecolab. This correlation gives us an indication that identification of firms with consistent free cash flows that are underpriced may exhibit abnormal returns.

An alternative criterion for investment is the recovery rate, or the relationship between operating or free cash flows and total assets of the business. This represents a "rate of return" on assets that are deployed in the business. Such an analysis was conducted by Systematic Financial Management Inc. on September 12, 1989, and is reproduced on page 212. Note that the table is based on operating cash flows as a proportion of total assets, but also includes free cash flows as a percentage of market value of firms. Note also the superior excess returns enjoyed by these firms.

Finally, we provide a list of the largest free cash flow generators for 1990.

Stability of Free Cash Flows

An important element in the analysis of free cash flows is not only the average free cash flow over the most recent four years (and the rate of growth in free cash flows), but also the stability of free cash flows. Firms that are subject to great fluctuations in free cash flows may be less desirable candidates for investors who are risk-averse. Thus, the cash flow analyst should measure not only the average cash flow, but also the variability of free cash flows during the available years. This can be done by "eye-balling" the free cash flows for the investment candidates, say, over a ten-year period, or it can be done

Figure 5–3   Toys "R" Us: Free Cash Flow and Market Value

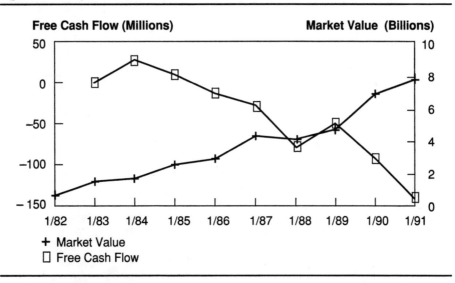

Figure 5–4   Ecolab, Inc.: Free Cash Flow and Market Value

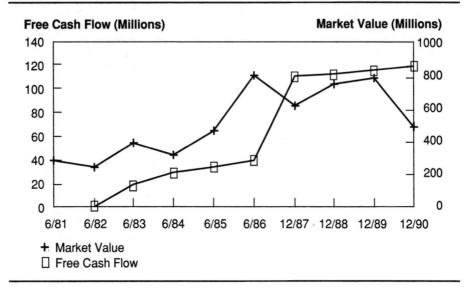

"Recovery Rate" Leaders

	12 mos. O.C.F./ assets	F.C.F./ market value	O.C.F./ assets (LFY)	4-yr. av. O.C.F./ assets	Market value $ mil.	52-wk. pr. percent change vs. 500
Adobe Systems	0.37	0.89	0.42	1.80	504.2	-6.9
Battle Mtn. Gold	0.29	3.32	0.34	0.69	935.1	-30.0
Buffets Inc.	0.29	3.21	0.33	0.62	149.6	59.2
Compuchem Corp.	0.42	0.65	0.45	0.60	67.7	69.1
Datakey Inc.	0.52	0.65	0.35	0.77	21.8	-21.2
Disney (Walt) Co.	0.31	1.37	0.35	0.51	13416.4	32.4
Georgia Gulf Corp.	0.51	10.70	0.42	0.61	976.6	-6.4
Glaxo Holdings PLC	0.29	4.60	0.33	0.56	16935.1	9.0
King World Production	0.32	4.57	0.79	0.98	727.7	16.9
Micron Technology	0.30	1.01	0.34	0.85	579.4	-37.8
PSE Inc.	0.31	9.63	0.47	0.62	64.1	6.3
Pacificare Health Sys.	0.37	5.55	0.41	0.77	178.6	177.7
Price (T. Rowe) Assoc.	0.33	5.32	0.31	0.50	333.2	13.8
Reuters Holdings PLC	0.30	2.52	0.31	0.48	5516.1	11.9
Sbarro Inc.	0.31	0.86	0.33	0.67	301.5	43.9
Southern Mineral Corp.	0.49	3.11	0.48	0.57	16.1	0.5
Total System Services	0.29	1.03	0.32	0.48	400.8	-6.3
Average	0.38	3.47	0.44	0.71	2419.1	19.5

O.C.F. = Operating Cash Flow
F.C.F. = Free Cash Flow
One of the best measures of corporate performance is the "recovery rate," the relationship between funds provided by operations (O.C.F.) and funds invested in the business (assets). The recovery rate can be considered an index of management's ability to deploy effectively (and earn a good return on) corporate assets. The companies listed above have the highest and most consistent recovery rates, as well as positive free cash flow (F.C.F.).

SOURCE: Cash Flow Investors Inc., Fort Lee, NJ.

by the construction of an index, such as the four-year average free cash flow divided by the standard deviation of annual free cash flows. Let us illustrate this index by focusing on the three firms we analyzed in this chapter.

Example:

We first provide estimated free cash flows and four-year averages for the three firms.

Hillenbrand Industries

Free cash flow—direct method	141.3	88.7	51.7	78.8	90.3	44.8	-7.2	39.4	36.1	36.6
4-year average free cash flow	90.1	77.4	66.4	51.7	41.8	28.3	26.2	37.3	36.3	36.6

Largest Cash Flow Generators— 1990

Operating Cash Flow	$000	Free Cash Flow*	$000
1 EXXON	13,634	1 GENERAL ELECTRIC	$5,867
2 GENERAL ELECTRIC	10,247	2 EXXON	4,621
3 IBM	7,472	3 PHILIP MORRIS	4,402
4 FORD MOTOR	7,413	4 AMERICAN TEL	2,729
5 GENERAL MOTORS	6,782	5 BRISTOL MEYERS	2,360
6 AMERICAN TEL & TEL	5,463	6 AMOCO	2,113
7 PHILIP MORRIS	5,385	7 IBM	1,981
8 SEARS ROEBUCK	5,352	8 BOEING	1,958
9 DUPONT	5,146	9 ITT	1,892
10 AMOCO	4,888	10 CHEVRON	1,815
11 AMERICAN EXPRESS	4,741	11 MERK	1,710
12 CHEVRON	4,727	12 AMER. HOME PROD.	1,618
13 BELLSOUTH	4,526	13 S.W. BELL	1,597
14 MOBIL	4,421	14 DOW CHEMICAL	1,516
		15 BELL ATLANTIC	1,475

*Free cash flow is the maximum amount of cash the entity could distribute while still allowing for growth in the firm.

Ecolab

Free cash flow— direct method	117.8	85.1	1.6	128.2	32.5	35.9	44.4
4-year average free cash flow	83.2	61.8	49.6	60.3	37.6	40.2	44.4

Toys "R" Us

Free cash flow— direct method	− 168.4	− 8.7	− 181.6	− 37.1	− 35.8	− 64.2	51.2
4-year average free cash flow	− 99.0	− 65.8	− 79.7	− 21.5	− 16.3	− 6.5	51.2

We can now calculate the standard deviation of annual free cash flows during all available periods and then divide the most recent four-year average free cash flow by the standard deviation of free cash flows. Let us compare the results for the three firms in the following table:

	Standard Deviation	Index
Hillenbrand	38.8	2.3
Ecolab	43.9	1.9
Toys "R" Us	78.0	-1.3

The index for Hillenbrand is calculated by dividing the current four-year average of free cash flow, 90.1, by the estimated standard deviation of 38.8 to obtain 2.3. This shows that for each unit of variability (the standard deviation of annual free cash flows), Hillenbrand recently earned 2.3 units of average free cash flows. The higher the index, the more favorable the investment candidate is, because the stability of free cash flows for the same level of four-year average free cash flow is greater.

We can create such an index or other similar measures to rank all securities that we consider for investment. Whereas the above index was based on a linear relationship between the average free cash flow and the standard deviation, other measures of the relationship can be used, depending on the investor's preferences.

CHAPTER 6

Financial Structure and
Free Cash Flows

6.1 INTRODUCTION

The decade of the eighties will be remembered for the wave of acquisitions and leverage buyouts that were facilitated by the ease of debt issuance. Many firms issued high-yield debt, "junk bonds" as they became known, that promised investors a high return but that had very little security in terms of the firm's assets. These junk bonds were supposed to be paid off by the firm's cash flows or through sales of some business segments that were not focal to the firm. The underlying business rationale for investing in high-yield bonds was that the acquired firms had steady cash flows (or at least adequate operating cash flow to cover debt payments), that the chance of default on these corporate bonds was extremely small, and that the acquisitions that were consummated using the junk bonds were made at attractive prices to the acquirers.

With hindsight, it is easy to see that, in too many instances, none of these three assumptions had been correct: firms ran into cash flow difficulties so that debt payments could not be met from operating cash flows, the actual default rate turned out to be much higher than was initially perceived, and the acquisition prices (including the hefty investment banking fees) were just too high in many cases. Still, there is a very important lesson that can be learned from these transactions—the importance of the relationship among free cash flows, corporate debt, and financial structure *for all firms*. In this chapter, we discuss how the financial structure of a firm is related to the concept of free cash flows.

6.2 FINANCIAL STRUCTURE OF A FIRM

Most publicly held companies are financed by a mixture of internal and external capital. Internal capital consists of all financial instruments that, in effect, provide holders with an equity position in the firm. Examples of such instruments are common stocks, convertible instruments such as preferred stocks and bonds that, for all practical purposes, can be considered as already converted into common stock, stock warrants, stock rights, and so on. External capital can be defined as all financial obligations to outsiders who are not likely to become equity holders in the firm. Examples of such obligations are short-term debt owed to banks and bonds that will not be readily converted to common stock. Other examples of external capital are obligations of the firm under leases, pension and other postretirement benefits to employees, guarantees made by the firm, and other off-balance-sheet liabilities.

Traditional finance theories show that a firm has an "optimal" financial structure, that is, an optimal balance between internal and external capital.[1] The optimal capital structure is derived from theoretical models that balance costs and benefits for each form of financing. Certain benefits and costs are associated with external capital. For example, it is well known that interest payments on debt are tax deductible, whereas dividend payments to preferred and common stockholders are not deductible to the firm and are taxable to shareholders. Thus, a firm has a clear incentive to raise external capital. However, external capital dilutes the control of equity holders because the firm is subject to greater scrutiny by creditors. Also, if at any period the firm's cash flows are insufficient to service its debt, the firm may be forced into bankruptcy or reorganization, and equity holders will be exposed to additional costs (including the issuance of additional equity). In bankruptcy or reorganization, the firm may be forced to sell assets it prefers to own. Thus, there are also costs or risks associated with external capital.

Other financial theories suggest that entrepreneurs have incentives to issue shares in their firms to the public, in effect raising more internal capital when they consider current stock prices too high. They issue additional shares of the firm to the public and enjoy the benefits of cash infusion into the firm that is not justified by future cash flows. Conversely, when owners of firms repurchase stock in their firms, it is likely that they consider the firm's price too low as compared with future cash flows. Therefore, they repurchase the firm's stock, which, in effect, leads to the reduction of internal capital. Note that this explanation is based on the notion that entrepreneurs have more information about their firms than the public at large, that is, that information asymmetries exist between current and future equityholders.[2]

Such information asymmetries, as well as other conflicts of interest, may also exist between stock- and bondholders. For example, stockholders may wish to invest in projects that are too risky for bondholders. These projects may have a negative net present value because of the high risk associated with the project, but are, nevertheless,

---

[1]Miller and Modigliani (*Journal of Business*, 1961) show that it does not matter how a firm finances itself. Ross (*Bell Journal of Economics*, 1977) and Leland and Pyle (*Journal of Finance*, 1977) show that an optimal financial structure exists because of signalling costs. Lewellen (*Journal of Finance*, 1975) and Galai and Masulis (*Journal of Financial Economics*, 1984) show that an optimal financial structure exists because of bankruptcy costs.

[2]Smith (*Journal of Financial Economics*, 1986) provides a review of the literature. Mikkelson and Partch (*Journal of Financial Economics*, 1986) and Eckbo (*Journal of Financial Economics*, 1986) show the negative effects on stock prices when firms issue debt. Masulis and Korwar (*Journal of Financial Economics*, 1986) and Asquith and Mullins (*Journal of Financial Economics*, 1986) provide evidence of negative reactions to announcements of stock issuances, whereas Dann (*Journal of Financial Economics*, 1981) and Vermaelen (*Journal of Financial Economics*, 1981) provide evidence of positive stock reactions to announcements of stock repurchases. Livnat and Zarowin (*Journal of Accounting and Economics*, 1990) provide evidence that is consistent with the effects of financing events as described in the statement of cash flows on security prices.

adopted by owners because they are not left with the risk of an entire loss of capital as are creditors. On the other hand, they stand to gain immensely if cash flows in the future turn out to be larger than expected.[3]

One common characteristic of all these theories is that the financial structure of a firm does not usually lie in either of the extreme cases, that is, firms are not all-equity firms, nor are they all-debt firms. Firms have a mixture of internal and external capital. Another common characteristic of these theories is that firms are not at their optimal capital structure all the time. Instead, firms continuously make adjustments to their financial structure in an attempt to react to changing economic and market conditions, so that they can reach their new optimal financial structure. Thus, we should observe that firms adjust their capital structure in almost every period, as can, indeed, be verified from any casual examination of financing cash flows of firms.

Can one predict how adjustments to the financial structure of a firm should be related to operating and free cash flows? To answer this question, recall that one of the major disadvantages of external capital is the expected cost of bankruptcy and reorganization to stockholders. These expected costs relate, of course, to the likelihood of financial difficulties for the firm; the higher the likelihood of financial difficulties is, the greater the expected bankruptcy costs are, and the more "costly" external financing becomes. An immediate variable to consider for the likelihood of financial difficulties is the stability of operating and free cash flows. The more stable operating and free cash flows are, the lower the probability of financial difficulties and bankruptcy are. Thus, firms with stable operating and free cash flows are expected to be characterized by higher financial leverage than are their counterparts, where financial leverage can be measured by the relative proportion of debt as compared to equity. Such firms are also more likely to be increasing external capital at the expense of internal capital.

Similarly, firms that exhibit volatile operating cash flows, or firms that are characterized by negative free cash flows, are expected to have lower financial leverage, and, on the average, are expected to show decreases in debt and increases in equity financing.

Cash flow analysis can provide worthwhile clues of impending financial risk and return; it has been all too common to find an entity that has been reporting healthy operating gains, yet, because it had been such a heavy user of cash, has found itself unprepared to operate during a business downturn.

Example:

Todd Shipyards appeared to be a healthy company when its earnings were considered. This was not the case when viewed from a free cash flow perspective.

---

[3]Others argue that bondholders may actually fare better than stockholders in case of bankruptcy or reorganization, so that stockholders have an incentive to invest in less risky projects than are optimal for the firm.

Todd Shipyards

Year	Net Income (Millions)	Free Cash Flow (Millions)	Market Value (Millions)
1983	$ 30.17	$ 32.4	$141.1
1984	21.87	(12.4)	134.6
1985	18.88	(1.2)	133.6
1986	(2.34)	(35.7)	116.4
1987	(58.29)	(19.0)	86.0
1988	(20.50)	(72.2)	8.4

The contrast between Todd Shipyard's net income and free cash flow is dramatic. Free cash flow turned negative almost four years before the company filed for bankruptcy. Even when Todd had negative free cash flow for three consecutive years, the company still had a very high market capitalization, indicating that investors were paying scant attention to the terrible state of Todd's free cash flow.

Using the common, but incorrect, definition of net income plus depreciation and deferred taxes gave the impression that Todd was not the poor cash flow entity we saw above. This common definition did not indicate the company was a bankruptcy candidate until shortly before it entered Chapter 11.

Using the most common, but incorrect, definition of free cash flow of deducting capital spending from net income, depreciation, and deferred taxes slightly improved the real picture. However, during 1985, the company reported a profit to shareholders of almost $40 million and a naive definition of free cash flow of $28 million.

Todd Shipyards

Year	Free Cash Flow (Millions)	Net Income plus Depreciation plus Deferred Taxes (Millions)	Net Income plus Deferred Depreciation plus Taxes minus Capital Expenditures (Millions)
1983	$ 32.4	$ 51.52	$ (12.8)
1984	(12.4)	44.55	(.6)
1985	(1.2)	39.55	27.81
1986	(35.7)	8.37	(47.57)
1987	(19.0)	(92.80)	(104.56)
1988	(72.2)	(16.20)	(19.60)

When low-growth firms have large and stable free cash flows, we expect these firms to be able to reduce debt and/or repurchase stock. The reason is that firms with large free cash flows can divert them to the retirement of debt or to the repurchase of equity without affecting future growth. Recall that the definition of free cash flows is that proper investments are made to ensure the normal growth of the firm. Thus, free cash flows represent either growth opportunities beyond expected growth, or, if excellent growth opportunities are unavailable, they represent cash that can be used to retire unnecessary debt or unnecessary equity. So, firms with good free cash flow profiles are expected to reduce debt on the average or to reduce equity. We can use these relationships to identify firms that are good candidates for investment purposes, as we describe in the next chapter.

We now discuss several specific areas of the financial structure and their relationship to free cash flows.

6.3 FINANCIAL LEVERAGE AND DEBT COVERAGE

Financial leverage may be defined as the proportion of total debt to total capitalization of a firm. A firm is considered highly levered when the ratio of debt to total capitalization is high. A firm is unlevered when it has no debt in its capital structure. For most practical applications, debt can be defined as total debt, including lease obligations and any off-balance-sheet liabilities such as unfunded pension and other postretirement benefits. Short-term debt must also be included in total debt because many companies have short-term loans that take advantage of favorable short-term interest rates to finance longer-term projects. Also, some companies have large "balloon" payments due within a year, so one should include in a firm's total debt short- as well as long-term debt and any off-balance-sheet liabilities. Total capitalization includes debt plus total stockholders' equity, where the latter is measured by either market value of equity or by accounting book value of equity.

Traditional finance thinking views financial leverage as increasing a firm's risk; if operating cash flows at any period are lower than debt payments, the firm has to liquidate some assets or increase its capitalization just to continue its operations. Thus, the more levered a firm is, the riskier it becomes. At the same time, debt has a desirable benefit, because interest payments on debt are tax deductible, whereas dividend payments are not. Finance theory suggests that there exists an optimal combination of debt and equity for each firm, known as the optimal financial structure. Firms can continuously change their financial structure by issuing debt or equity so that the optimal level of financial leverage will be attained. Generally, it is argued that the greater the volatility of operating and free cash flows is, the lower the financial leverage should be. Conversely, the greater the stability of operating or free cash flows is, the more levered a firm can become.

Example:

It is not unusual for financially weak brokerage firms to borrow at the parent level and then send the cash to the broker–dealer where it counts as capital. In the industry, it is known as double-leveraging.

The Securities and Exchange Commission regulates the industry and is in charge of setting capital requirements—how much equity and capital the firm must have invested in the business. The SEC also allows short-term debt to be counted as part of capital.

Because loans are counted as part of capital, Drexel Burnham Lambert, even when it was rapidly heading toward bankruptcy, was able to claim it was exceeding federal capital requirements. In fact, just before Drexel entered bankruptcy, it stated it had almost $300 million more in capital than was required by the SEC. However, much of the capital was in the form of loans from its parent, Drexel Burnham Lambert Group, Inc., which was financing itself with short-term loans. Soon afterwards, Drexel's house of cards collapsed when the SEC and the New York Stock Exchange refused to allow Drexel's brokerage unit to reduce its capital by repaying loans from its parent (*New York Times*).

Traditional measures of a firm's ability to pay interest on its debt include the debt coverage ratio, measured by earnings before taxes plus interest, divided by interest expense. The greater this ratio is, the easier it is for the firm to meet interest payments. While this ratio measures the short-term ability of a firm to service its debt, *it totally ignores the firm's ability to reduce its financial leverage*. For example, the firm might generate enough operating cash flows to sustain its current level of growth and to cover existing interest payments. However, it might not have any free cash flows that it can use to retire old debt. Consequently, it may be exposed to a greater financial risk than a firm that generates free cash flows. We, therefore, suggest an additional measure of a firm's financial risk—the relationship between total debt and free cash flows.

To assess the firm's freedom to attain its desired financial structure, we focus on the ratio of total debt to free cash flows. As we have seen in the previous chapter, it is more meaningful to focus on average free cash flows during the most recent four years. Thus, we propose an examination of the following ratio for firms that are likely candidates for investment decisions:

$$\frac{\text{Total Debt}}{\text{Average Free Cash Flow}}$$

The greater this ratio is, the greater the financial risk of the firm. The lower this ratio is, the lower the financial risk of a firm. Ideally, one would like to invest in firms that are able to generate free cash flows in a consistent manner but that are also subject to a lower debt burden. Such firms have the ability to make large capital investments if they find good investment opportunities, because they can use their free cash flows or because they can increase their debt.

Example:

During 1987, The Phillips-Van Heusen Corporation acquired G. H. Bass & Co. for $79 million and repurchased $168.6 million through a Dutch tender auction. As reflected on the statement of cash flows, Phillips has been undergoing a series of financial transactions to help spread out the debt payments taken on as a result of the business transactions, initially financed with short-term debt.

As is evident from the 1989 statement of cash flows, Phillips has not been generating an adequate amount of free cash flow, when taking into account other investing activities, to help pay down its leverage. In 1989, to aid cash flow, Phillips sold businesses for $10.1 million in cash.

Reviewing Phillips long-term debt footnote, the company reports the following principal debt payments due over the next five years.

Phillips-Van Heusen: Schedule of Principal Payments

1990	$12.9 million
1991	$10.1
1992	$14.2
1993	$15.9
1994	$12.9

It seems quite evident by reviewing the past three years' statement of cash flows that Phillips is unlikely to be able to generate sufficient funds to service the principal unless its business improved. Subtracting the $8.7 million of operating cash flow from discontinued operations during 1987, and averaging over the three years 1987–1989, yields an average operating cash flow of $10.5 million. Phillips must add to and improve its existing capital base, which has been growing by about 30 percent over the last 4 years and about 12 percent over the past 8 years.

Reviewing Phillips's balance sheet indicates it could draw down some inventory, thus providing cash. But, given the large growth rate in revenues during the past 4 and 8 years of about 13 percent and 7 percent, respectively, it is doubtful inventories could be dramatically reduced.

Example:

In its "Heard on the Street" column, *The Wall Street Journal* published an analysis of Trizec on September 23, 1991. According to the analysis, Trizec, a Canadian firm that has real-estate investments, saw its debt downgraded due to cash flow difficulties. Apparently, the cash flows that Trizec and its largest subsidiary, Bramalea, generated from operations were insufficient to cover debt payments. Thus, the firm needed to use additional debt to hold onto its properties.

As is well accepted in finance theories, it is useful to consider not only the ratio of total debt to average free cash flows, but also the volatility of free cash flows. The volatility of free cash flows is a measure of an operating risk of a firm; the more volatile free cash flows are, the greater the operating risk of the firm is. The ratio of total debt to average free cash flow is a measure of financial risk; the higher this ratio is, the greater the financial risk of a firm. Other measures of stock risk, such as the systematic risk, Beta, or the total variability of stock returns, were shown to consist of financial and operating risks. Similarly, we can cast these two risks in terms of the volatility of free cash flows (operating risk), and the ratio of total debt to average free cash flows (financial risk).

Figure 6–1 portrays the two dimensions of risk. In the figure, we show the risk profile of a hypothetical Firm X. We can make comparisons of the risk profiles of other firms to this firm. Naturally, most people will prefer firms with lower risks than firms with higher risks. Thus, firms with risk profiles that fall into region C would certainly be superior to Firm X, because they have both a lower operating risk and a lower financial risk. Firms that fall into region B are strictly inferior to Firm X, because both dimensions of risk are greater than those of Firm X. The selection of a preferred firm

FIGURE 6–1   Financial Risk and Operating Risk

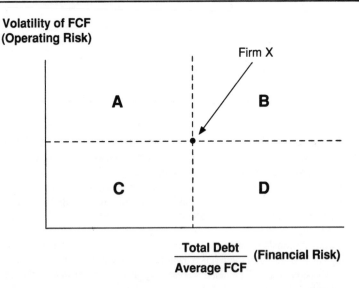

Region A   Firms with lower financial risk but greater operating risk
Region B   Firms with *both* greater operating *and* financial risk
Region C   Firms with *both* lower operating *and* financial risk
Region D   Firms with lower operating risk and greater financial risk

in regions A and D depends on the decision maker and the decision maker's relative tolerance for each of the two measures. Individuals who can more easily tolerate financial risk than operating risk may prefer firms that fall into region D over Firm X, because firms in that region have lower operating risk. The converse is true for region A.

As mentioned in the previous chapter, the cash flow analyst should always examine the behavior of free cash flows in the most recent four- and eight-year period to assess how the firm was able to overcome downturns in the economy, and how stable its free cash flows are. The cash flow analyst should also examine the instances in which a firm has negative free cash flows. In most cases, investments in firms with several years of free cash flows are only justified if the investor is willing to absorb a higher operating risk.

6.4 DEBT, CAPITAL SPENDING, AND FREE CASH FLOWS

Charles Exley, the former Chairman of the NCR Corporation, now a subsidiary of AT&T, always believed technology companies do not make good LBO candidates because they need growing amounts of research budgets to stay competitive. This can be generalized to entities that cannot make the necessary cutbacks to capital spending and other discretionary cash outlays, which are also not suitable candidates for LBOs because high leverage impairs potential growth opportunities. When such entities get away from what they should be doing—making better products—and move toward being financially motivated companies, their operating cash flows suffer as they are overtaken by competitors.

We examined Chairman Exley's belief that a high rate of R&D and capital spending is important for future growth, with a subsequent positive spillover into the stock price. To test this hypothesis, we investigated the performance of entities that have had positive growth rates in free cash flows, because it was assumed these entities had the wherewithal to increase their spending on research and new capital. In fact, these entities also had the credit facilities to undergo such spending, but for one reason or another decided not to place such funds in those two areas.

We looked at the eight-year period from 1982 to 1990 —a rather unique period— because it encompassed the longest peacetime expansion. In order to be included in the "leveraged group," the entity would need to have a minimum market capitalization of $50 million and either have a growth rate in R&D spending or capital spending of less than 3 percent per year over the period. Additionally, to be included in the leveraged group, the growth rate in total debt must have been greater than 12 percent per year over the eight-year period. We then compared this group versus the S&P Industrials. This comparison is made in Exhibit 6–1.

The leveraged group has had a slightly higher growth rate of free cash flow than that of the S&P. However, the far greater growth rate in debt made that group, as perceived by investors, to be a far riskier investment. To that end, the leveraged group had a total return of slightly more than a third of the S&P. It would take the leveraged group almost 17 years to repay its total debt versus just 6.3 years for the S&P.

The lack of investment has already taken a toll on operating cash flow and book earnings. The entities have been able to continue a positive growth rate in free cash flow through cutbacks in expenditures that the marketplace felt were vital to the health of the firm. Of course, an entity can only continue to sacrifice spending on necessary plans and R&D for a finite period, before the effect on operating cash flow is also felt on free cash flow. The managers of the enterprise can only "squeeze the lemon" so hard for so long before it runs dry.

Even for the S&P, leverage has shown a steady rate of growth, indicating that the assumption of debt is not necessarily detrimental to the entity's financial health, nor does the marketplace necessarily shun such enterprises. However, if the rate of growth in financial leverage is greater than the long-term growth of free cash flows, especially when it sacrifices necessary expenditures, the market takes notice.

One might be tempted to believe the entities in the leveraged group would be comprised of unknowns. This is untrue. The leveraged group includes such companies as Avon Products, Borden, Coca-Cola, General Motors, ITT, IBM, Litton, Safeway, Unisys, Westinghouse, and Xerox.

IBM, for instance, has had a growth rate in its capital spending of negative 2.2 percent per year, while its growth rate of short-term and long-term debt has increased by 21.8 percent per year! Needless to say, its stock price, having risen at an annual rate of 3.1 percent per year including dividends, has performed dramatically short of the

Exhibit 6–1 When Leverage Comes at the Future's Expense: A Study of the Current Business Expansion

	8-Year Growth Rate in R&D	8-Year Growth Rate in Capital Spending	7-Year Growth Operating Cash Flow	5-Year Price Change	5-Year Earnings per Share Growth	Market Value $ Million	7-Year Growth Free Cash Flow	Debt/Equity (%)	4/85–4/90 Total Return	Years for Free Cash Flow to Repay Debt
Leveraged Group	-1.3	-2.2	1.3	23.0	7.6	391.6	7.9	96.5	43.9	16.7
S&P Industrials	10.1	8.3	9.5	92.8	11.6	398.0	6.8	53.9	124.2	6.3

Positive free-cash-producing entities that have had less than 3 percent annual rate of growth in either capital spending or research, when combined with an annual growth in leverage of greater than 12 percent, have had miserable stock price performance. Although the free cash flow of this group has grown at a rate slightly in excess of the S&P Industrials, the far greater growth in leverage results in a much more risky investment. In fact, it would take the leveraged group almost 17 years to repay its total debt versus 6.3 years for the S&P Industrials, with leverage also having a negative effect on operating cash flow and earnings growth. The moral: Leverage is O.K., as witnessed by the returns on the S&P, but not when it comes at the future's expense—even for excess cash generators.

S&P. Perhaps if the management of IBM was spending more time making operating efficiencies in its factories, its free cash flow would have been higher and there would have been less need for the increase in debt. As Exhibit 6–2 illustrates, IBM's capital spending in 1989 rebounded, but only back to its 1982 level.

Summing up this section, we find that free cash flows and debt are interrelated because firms cannot neglect improving operations and making proper investments without sacrificing future operating and free cash flows. Even if such firms resort to external debt in the short run because it is initially less costly due to tax deductibility of interest payments, free cash flows in the future could be hurt by larger interest payments. Thus, firms should probably pay less attention to financial management and more attention to management of operations and future growth. Apparently, the market is able to distinguish among firms along these dimensions and, in the long run, penalizes firms that underinvest in future growth and assume too much leverage.

We now describe in detail some additional liabilities that should be explicitly considered as part of total debt.

6.5 LEASES

The accounting profession distinguishes between two major types of leases—capital leases and operating leases. Assets under capital leases are recorded as assets on the balance sheet with offsetting liabilities (usually denoted ''capital lease obligations'') among the long-term liabilities. Assets under operating leases are not shown on the balance sheet as assets, nor are there any liabilities that are created due to these leases. Disclosure of information about operating leases is done only through a footnote to the

Exhibit 6–2   IBM

Year	Current Debt	New Debt	Debt Retired	Capital Expenditures
90	7602.0	4676.0	3683.0	6509.0
89	5892.0	6471.0	2768.0	6414.0
88	4862.0	4540.0	3007.0	5390.0
87	1629.0	408.0	719.0	4304.0
86	1410.0	1059.0	845.0	4620.0
85	1293.0	1614.0	928.0	6430.0
84	834.0	1363.0	768.0	5473.0
83	532.0	174.0	351.0	4930.0
82	529.0	480.0	298.0	6685.0
81	773.0	751.0	181.0	6845.0
80	591.0	604.0	94.0	6592.0
79	932.7	1449.5	145.7	5991.0
78	241.5	74.1	44.4	4045.5
77	172.4	22.7	42.1	3394.7
76	115.9	24.8	44.8	2518.2

financial statements and not on the balance sheet itself, hence the name off-balance-sheet liability. Accounting and disclosure requirements for leases are covered primarily by FAS No. 13 (1976) and later FASB pronouncements that served to interpret FAS No. 13 or slightly modify it.

The distinction between operating and capital leases is mainly through several tests that are intended to examine whether the benefits and risks of ownership were, in fact, transferred from the lessor to the lessee. If they were, the lease is classified as a capital lease and an asset with an offsetting liability is included on the balance sheet. Otherwise, the lease is classified as an operating lease and the information is reported in a footnote. There are four general tests for the classification of leases as capital or operating leases. If any of these tests is satisfied, the lease is classified as a capital lease:

1. The title to the asset is transferred to the lessee at the end of the lease term.
2. The lease agreement contains an option to purchase the asset at the end of the lease term by paying a "bargain" price (i.e., below-market price).
3. The lease term is for more than 75 percent of the remaining economic useful life of the leased asset.
4. The present value of payments under the lease exceeds 90 percent of the asset's market value at the inception of the lease agreement.

The accounting standard prevents firms from applying tests (3) and (4) when the leased asset is at the last 25 percent of its remaining economic life.

Note that test (1) indicates that, at the end of the lease term, ownership of the asset is transferred to the lessee. Thus, we view the lease agreement as an installment sale, where the lessee agrees to purchase the leased asset through a series of payments, but with official transfer of legal title occurring at the end of the lease term instead of at the beginning of the lease term. Similarly, test (2) ensures that a reasonable lessee will exercise the bargain purchase option and will, in effect, purchase the asset. Therefore, as with test (1), we view the lease as an installment sale and immediately show the asset and the liability on the balance sheet. In principle, we treat the lease as a compound transaction where the leased asset is purchased by the lessee and where the lessor provides the lessee with a loan that is equivalent to the value of the asset.

The leased asset under a capital lease is included among the fixed assets of the firm and is subject to the same depreciation methods as the firm's other fixed assets. The loan is included among the long-term liabilities of the firm, with the current portion included among current liabilities. Note that at the inception of the lease the asset and the liability are identical and are equal to the present value of the lease payments. However, at any other period, the asset is depreciated using the firm's depreciation methods, whereas the liability is treated as any other long term debt, that is, it is carried on the balance sheet using the effective interest rate method. Under that method, the effective interest rate implicit in the lease (at the inception of the lease) is used to discount future payments on the lease. Thus, the liability "capitalized lease obligations" will usually not represent the market value of these liabilities. The market value of these obligations can be determined by using the market interest rate at the time the calculation is made, whereas capitalized lease obligations are calculated using the rate in effect at the inception of the lease. The two will deviate from each other because of economic conditions, Federal Reserve Bank policy, and so forth.[4]

Test (3) ensures that most of the remaining benefits from the asset (75 percent) will be reaped by the lessee, making the lessee the *de-facto* owner of the asset. Similarly, the lessee in test (4) makes payments under the lease that, in current values, are sufficient to purchase more than 90 percent of the asset. Thus, under test (4), we treat the lease as if it represented an outright sale of the asset. Note that both tests (3) and (4) are not applicable at the end of the asset's life, because we want to ensure that the lessee will enjoy most of the economic benefits of the leased asset.

These tests are very restrictive; they guarantee that the lessee becomes the *de-facto* owner of the asset. However, there is really no theoretical reason for classifying any lease agreement as an operating lease. Theoretically, the promise to make any lease payments in the future should be treated as a liability, regardless of whether the leased asset is *de-facto* purchased or not. Similarly, the right to obtain benefits from using the leased asset in the future should be construed as an existing asset, regardless of whether the leased asset is *de-facto* owned by the lessee or not. Thus, conceptually, one should probably record in the financial statements all assets under leases, no matter if they are capital or operating leases.

For our purposes, to estimate total debt of a firm, we need to estimate the present value of future payments under operating leases, because the present value of capitalized lease obligations is already included in the long-term debt of the firm. We, therefore, add the present value of payments under operating leases to long-term debt of the firm. To do that, we use information that is available in the footnotes to the financial statements.

Example:

H&R Block Inc. helps customers with tax matters, provides computer services, and offers temporary help services. In 1991, more than 40 percent of total revenues came from the latter two segments.

In its 1989 financial statements, H&R Block Inc. disclosed the following information about its commitments, where data were provided on operating leases:

"Substantially all of the Company's operations are conducted in leased premises. Most of the operating leases are for a one-year period with renewal options of one to three years and provide for fixed monthly rentals. Lease commitments at April 30, 1989, for fiscal 1990, 1991, 1992, 1993 and 1994 aggregated $40,335,000, $29,271,000, $18,020,000, $9,275,000 and $5,461,000, respectively, with no significant commitments extending beyond that period of time. The Company's rent expense for the years 1989, 1988, and 1987 aggregated $45,448,000, $40,661,000 and $38,243,000, respectively."

---

[4]This treatment is not unique to capitalized lease obligations. All long-term debt of the firm is carried at the present value of future payments on the debt, using the interest rate in existence at the time the debt was issued. Thus, the market value of the debt will be different from the accounting value of debt.

The footnote provides information about actual rent expense for operating leases in 1989, 1988, and 1987, the years for which income statements are presented. Also, the firm reports estimated rent expense under its operating leases for 1990, and onwards for the next four years. According to these estimates, rent expense for 1990 is estimated to be $40,335,000. Note, however, that this figure is substantially lower than the actual rent expense for 1989, and it is about the same as the actual rent expense incurred in 1988. Is it possible that the firm expects to lease fewer premises? Is the firm expected to shrink its operations or renegotiate its current leases? Note also that after 1990 the forecasted rent expense drastically drops to levels substantially below the actual rent expense in the most recent years. What can cause this phenomenon?

The firm reports in this footnote its actual rent expense for the years 1987–1989. It also reports *current* commitments under leases *in force* for periods beyond fiscal 1989. The firm estimates only payments on those leases that will remain in force beyond the current period. Because most of its leases are for short periods, that is, for one year, a large portion of those leases that are expected to be renewed is not included in the forecasted rent expense for future years because H&R Block does not have firm commitments to renew those leases. However, it is very likely that H&R Block will incur a greater rent expense in the future, because it is expected to grow. To verify this, we provide in Exhibit 6–3 the actual rent expense in 1990 and 1991, the years for which we had financial statements when this book was written. As can be seen from the exhibit, rent expense in 1990 and 1991 actually exceeded rent expense in 1989 and was substantially greater than that forecasted by the firm in 1989.

To forecast the level of future rent expenses more accurately, we use Exhibit 6–3 to demonstrate a simplistic prediction rule. The actual rent expense for the current year is multiplied by one plus the actual growth rate in actual rent expense over the most recent three years. For example, to forecast rent expense for 1990, we first estimate the growth rate of the actual rent expense from 1987 to 1989 by finding the squared root of the rent expense in 1989 divided by that of 1987. This yields about 9 percent (square root of 45.448 / 38.243 minus 1). We now multiply the actual rent expense in 1989 by 1.09 to obtain the forecasted rent expense in the first column marked "forecast," $45,545,000. The estimate for 1991, based on the same data and estimation procedure, is simply $45,545,000 times 1.09, or $54,010,000. The estimates for the next three years follow suit. Notice that these estimates are much closer to actual rent expense incurred in 1990 and 1991 than those forecasted by the firm. The actual rent expenses in 1990 and 1991 were reported by the firm as $52,541,000 and $58,348,000, respectively. This estimation procedure yields a good estimate for 1991 too, when data for 1988 through 1990 are used for forecasts. Thus, to estimate future cash outflows needed for rent payments, the analyst is better-off with forecasts that are based on current levels of rent payments than on forecasts based on leases still in force beyond the current year.

To estimate the effect of capitalizing the operating leases, we discount the forecasted rent expenses in the next five years by using three assumptions about discount rates, 10 percent, 8 percent, and 12 percent. These estimates are provided in the exhibit. Note that the estimated present value of rent payments under these operating leases, *using the forecasted figures by the firm*, yields a liability of about $80 million. This is compared with total debt of the firm (current and noncurrent) at the end of 1989, which amounted to about $212 million. Thus, had we added the off-balance-sheet liability that was created by operating leases to total debt of the firm, total debt would have increased by about 40 percent, as reported at the bottom of the exhibit. The increase would have been much more pronounced had we used our forecast of future payments under operating leases, 105 percent.

Exhibit 6–3   H&R Block—Rent Expense under Operating Leases

	1989	Forecast	1990	Forecast	1991	Forecast
1987	**38.243**					
1988	**40.661**		**40.661**			
1989	**45.448**		**45.448**		**45.448**	
1990	40.335	45.545	**52.541**		**52.541**	
1991	29.271	54.010	42.752	59.725	**58.348**	
1992	18.020	58.879	31.094	67.892	46.350	66.112
1993	9.275	64.186	18.865	77.175	30.850	74.910
1994	5.461	69.972	10.350	87.728	18.607	84.878
1995			5.657	99.724	10.740	96.172
1996					2.659	108.969
PV 10%	84.124	221.201	89.318	290.228	90.599	319.129
PV 8%	87.281	233.720	92.677	307.125	93.840	337.668
PV 12%	81.167	209.697	86.175	274.720	87.556	302.111
Total debt	211.500		245.500		228.500	
Percent increase in total debt (PV 10%)	39.775	104.587	36.382	118.219	39.649	139.662

Notes:
1. Bold figures represent actual rent expense under operating leases as reported by the firm.
2. Figures under the bold numbers are predicted future rent expense as forecasted by the firm.
3. Figures in the forecast column represent predictions of rent expense that are based on the current known rent expense, multiplied by the growth rate of rent expense over the prior two years.
4. Total debt is reported current debt plus reported long-term debt (including capitalized lease obligations when applicable).
5. The percent increase in total debt is found by the reported total debt plus the present value of rent payments under operating leases, divided by the reported total debt.

Thus, one should examine the off-balance-sheet liability created by operating leases that are not capitalized or incorporated on the balance sheet.

Example:

Vulcan Materials Company is the nation's foremost producer of construction aggregates and a leading chemicals manufacturer.

In its 1988 financial statements, Vulcan reported both capital and operating leases. Unfortunately, Vulcan reported the actual rent expense incurred in 1986 through 1988 only for capital and operating leases combined. However, it listed forecasted rent payments under capital and operating leases separately for each of the following five years, and for all other years thereafter. These forecasts are based on leases that are in force at the time financial statements are prepared, and are an understatement of actual future rent expense, as explained in the example above.

The data for Vulcan are provided in Exhibit 6–4. Vulcan reports the present value of all capital leases at the end of 1988 at $5.813 million, with interest implicit in the future rent payments evaluated at $2.5 million. The exhibit shows that if we discount all future payments under capital leases using a 10 percent discount rate, and assuming that all payments beyond 1993 are made at the end of 1994, the present value of these payments

Exhibit 6–4   Vulcan Materials— 1988

	Total	Capital	Operating	Actual	Forecast
1986	**3.881**				
1987	**6.042**				
1988	**8.966**				
1989	6.937	0.929	6.008	**10.156**	11.509
1990	5.833	0.930	4.903	**12.265**	14.242
1991	5.360	0.924	4.436		16.880
1992	6.050	2.219	3.831		19.565
1993	4.246	0.838	3.408		22.227
Thereafter	15.162	2.473	12.689		24.901
Total	43.588	8.313	35.275		109.323
Interest — capital leases		2.500			
Present value of capital leases		5.813			
Present value assuming 10%	30.481	5.739	24.742		76.134
Total debt	66.100				
Percent increase in total debt			37.431		106.498

Notes:
1. Figures in bold represent actual rent expense reported by the firm.
2. The firm reports both capital and operating leases. The present value of capitalized lease obligations, as reported by the firm in the 1988 financial statements, is 5.813.
3. Total debt is reported current and long-term debt.
4. The percent increase in total debt is found by the present value of operating leases divided by total debt.
5. The forecast is found by the current total rent expense plus the average increase in rent expense over the most recent three years.

is $5.739. Thus, assuming a discount rate of 10 percent and condensing all payments after 1993 into 1994 seem to provide a good estimate of the liability for capital leases.

We use the same assumptions to estimate the present value of operating leases using the forecasts reported by Vulcan. This yields an additional liability of $24.742 that should be added to the total debt of the firm. The increase in total debt due to this additional off-balance-sheet liability is about 37 percent. Because the forecasted rent payments under both capital and operating leases are understated, we forecast total rent payments by adding the total current rent expense to the average increase in total rent expense over the most recent three years. When we discount these total payments to the present, we obtain a total (capital and operating) liability of $76.134 million. Thus, if we subtract the $5.813 that is already included on the balance sheet, total debt would have increased by about 106 percent if we added the present value of operating leases as forecasted by us to the total debt of the firm. Again, we see that operating leases can add a substantial amount to the total debt of the firm.

Vulcan reports on its balance sheet capitalized lease obligations (the liability) of $5.813 million, of which $5.418 million are included in long-term obligations and $.395 in current liabilities. In the footnote that provides additional information on the property, plant, and equipment, Vulcan reports that the original cost of assets under capital leases is $10.434 million, and amortization on these assets is $8.023 million. Therefore, the carrying value of the assets under capital leases is $2.411, whereas the liability for these assets is $5.813 million. The two figures are identical only at the inception of the lease or at its termination. At other times, the assets and liabilities for capital leases are expected to be different, because the assets are amortized using the normal depreciation policy of the firm. The liability is amortized using the effective interest method and is dependent on the actual pattern of cash payments on the lease.

Exhibit 6–5 provides a list of firms with lease obligations that exceed total debt of the firm.

6.6 UNFUNDED PENSION AND OTHER POSTRETIREMENT OBLIGATIONS

Most entities in the United States have plans that promise employees various post-retirement benefits, most notably pension and health-care benefits. It is important to study and understand the entity's postretirement liabilities in any cash flow and credit analysis. We shall describe in this section some of those postretirement benefits, their accounting description, and their effects on debt.

There are two general types of pension plans that firms use—defined benefit and defined contribution plans. Defined benefit plans promise employees specific monetary payments that will be made to them (or their remaining spouses) upon retirement. The firm has the responsibility to make sure that funds will be available to pay for those future benefits. Defined contribution plans set the specific contribution that the employer currently has to make to the plan. The employees are paid from funds that are available when they retire. Under defined benefit plans, the employer bears the risk of a shortfall in funds if the employee reaches retirement and the plan has insufficient assets to make the required payments.Thus, the employer will, in this case, be called upon to supplement payments by the funds, such that the employee will receive all the promised benefits. Under defined contribution plans, the employer discharges all responsibility as soon as the necessary contributions are forwarded to the plan. Any risk of shortfall in funds is borne by the employee.

Typically, firms will set up a separate entity, the pension fund, which will be jointly administered by employees and management of the firm. Employer contributions to the fund (called *funding*) will increase the assets of the pension fund. Fund assets are also invested (in governmental and corporate bonds, equities, real estate, etc.) and the return on these investments will increase fund assets. Fund assets decrease because of payments to current retirees and expenses in managing the fund. Pension plans are subject to the provisions of the Employee Retirement Security Act of 1974, known by its abbreviation ERISA.

Defined contribution plans pose very little accounting problem. When employees earn the right to the contribution by the employer, the employer accrues the obligation as a current liability. Funding (payment) of the contribution to the fund discharges this obligation. The employer is not legally concerned with the value of the assets in the fund or with making additional payments to existing and future retirees. Fund managers are hired to maximize the returns on the plan assets. An example for a defined contribution plan is one in which the employer transfers a specified percentage of the

Exhibit 6-5   Additional Liability Due to Operating Leases— 1990

Ticker	Firm	P.V. Operating Lease Obligation	Total Debt	Percent Increase in Total Debt	Market Value (Millions of Dollars)
ABF	AIRBORNE FREIGHT CORP	164.4	132.9	1.24	$ 473.7
ALK	ALASKA AIRGROUP INC	395.3	343.1	1.15	275.4
ACV	ALBERTO-CULVER CO -CL B	73.6	65.8	1.12	667.1
ABS	ALBERTSON'S INC	190.0	179.0	1.06	4937.7
AAL	ALEXANDER & ALEXANDER	279.5	192.7	1.45	800.7
AMH	AMDAHL CORP	102.1	55.8	1.83	1606.4
AAPL	APPLE COMPUTER INC	315.9	122.6	2.58	6512.8
AUD	AUTOMATIC DATA PROCESSING	205.0	55.0	3.73	5373.6
BV	BLOCKBUSTER ENMNT CORP	244.2	173.8	1.41	1845.5
BG	BROWN GROUP INC	196.4	189.2	1.04	461.5
BCF	BURLINGTON COAT FACTORY WRHS	101.5	96.2	1.06	310.3
CC	CIRCUIT CITY STORES INC	182.7	109.4	1.67	1054.3
COMR	COMAIR HOLDINGS INC	98.9	55.2	1.79	148.0
CNS	CONSOLIDATED STORES CORP	76.9	51.3	1.50	458.1
CNM	CONTINENTAL MEDICAL SYSTEMS	123.1	92.7	1.33	527.3
DAL	DELTA AIR LINES INC	2775.9	2137.6	1.30	3377.9
DEC	DIGITAL EQUIPMENT	805.4	173.3	4.65	7259.3
DEMP	DRUG EMPORIUM INC	82.2	61.3	1.34	95.1
DNB	DUN & BRADSTREET CORP	613.8	239.2	2.57	8725.4
EBS	EDISON BROTHERS STORES	319.8	188.2	1.70	752.3
FCA	FABRI-CENTERS OF AMERICA	88.5	52.1	1.70	374.0
FLR	FLUOR CORP	231.7	71.9	3.22	3622.2
GME	GENERAL MOTORS CL E	503.7	447.7	1.13	5501.4
HAL	HALLIBURTON CO	206.0	195.7	1.05	3688.1
HKT	HONG KONG TELECOM LTD -ADR	135.2	60.5	2.24	11152.8
IPG	INTERPUBLIC GROUP OF COS	348.7	260.5	1.34	1894.2
IYCOY	ITO YOKADO CO LTD -ADR	1307.7	806.9	1.62	14831.0
LTD	LIMITED INC	1239.3	540.4	2.29	8444.3
MMC	MARSH & MCLENNAN COS	509.6	386.5	1.32	5370.9
MES	MELVILLE CORP	1328.6	400.2	3.32	4593.2
MEYR	MEYER (FRED) INC	364.4	251.2	1.45	513.6
MIKE	MICHAELS STORES INC	78.6	54.8	1.43	140.2
MCL	MOORE CORP LTD	136.1	104.4	1.30	2442.7
NFC	NFC PLC -ADR	396.2	189.8	2.09	2045.3
ORCL	ORACLE SYSTEMS CORP	221.4	198.1	1.12	2044.5
PST	PETRIE STORES CORP	262.2	125.0	2.10	1092.7
PIR	PIER 1 IMPORTS INC-DEL	309.2	212.5	1.45	324.9
PCO	PITTSTON CO	190.7	118.8	1.60	639.1
RTRSY	REUTERS HOLDING PLC -ADR	277.3	71.9	3.85	7139.6
RSTOB	ROSES STORES -CL B	149.1	118.4	1.26	130.2
ROST	ROSS STORES INC	195.7	57.6	3.40	356.9
SHW	SHERWIN-WILLIAMS CO	144.3	141.2	1.02	2013.0
SPLS	STAPLES INC	93.1	80.1	1.16	346.9
TJX	TJX COS INC-NEW	323.4	315.2	1.03	1064.2
UAL	UAL CORP	2543.6	1785.0	1.42	3158.6
USR	U S SHOE CORP	557.8	274.2	2.03	554.3
VEN	VENTURE STORES INC	96.5	94.1	1.02	332.2
WIN	WINN-DIXIE STORES INC	653.2	99.9	6.54	2863.4
Z	WOOLWORTH CORP	1337.6	299.0	4.47	3717.4
	Median	231.7	141.2	1.45	1606.4

employee's current compensation to a fund designated by the employee. Usually, these contributions are not taxable until they are drawn from the fund.

Defined benefit plans, on the other hand, pose great difficulties from an accounting point of view. Here, the employer retains the responsibility for the specified future benefits until the employee or the employee's survivors are no longer eligible for those benefits. Until all future payments are made, the employer is liable for the benefits. The major accounting issues are how to estimate the value of this liability and how it should be recorded in the financial statements. The major concern for the cash flow analyst is the effect of the liability on cash flows and long-term solvency of the firm.

Initially, firms reported no liability for pension obligations and included in the income statement an expense that was equal to the actual payment to existing retirees during the accounting period. This practice was stopped by APB Opinion No. 8, which required firms to estimate their liability to employees and disclose in a footnote to the financial statements some information about the liability. To better understand the nature of the liability and the associated accounting disclosure, let us use the following example.

Example:

This is a hypothetical example, although many firms have most of the features seen here.

The pension plan is a defined benefit plan. It promises that employees who reach retirement age (65 years old) will receive, for each year of service, annual compensation that is equal to 2 percent of their average annual salary with the firm during the five-year period prior to retirement. Thus, an employee who worked for the firm for 30 years is entitled to 60 percent of the average annual salary prior to retirement. These benefits continue until the employee dies, at which point only 50 percent of these benefits will be paid to the surviving spouse. The plan has other restrictions. For example, employees who leave the firm before they spend at least five years with the firm are not eligible for any pension benefits. Employees who remain with the firm for more than 5 years, but for less than 10 years, will get only 50 percent of their pension benefits when they reach retirement age, even though they are no longer employed by the firm. After 10 years, employees are eligible to 100 percent of the earned pension benefits when they reach retirement age, even if they are no longer employed by the firm.

Several factors affect the estimation of the firm's liability under the above plan. First, the firm has to consider the current age of employees, so that it would know how many years are left before pension benefits have to be made. Second, the firm has to estimate the life expectancy of the employees and their spouses. This is important in estimating how long the pension benefits should be paid. Third, the firm should estimate the turnover rate of employees, because it is *not* necessary to accrue any pension obligation for those employees who will not remain with the firm for at least five years, and they must accrue only 50 percent of the benefits for those employees who will remain with the firm between five and ten years. The firm should then estimate the average annual salary of the employee upon which pension benefits will be based.[5] Finally,

---

[5]In some pension plans, payments received from Social Security reduce payments to employees. In such cases, it is also important to determine the future level of payments from the Social Security system.

these future payments should be discounted to the present in order to estimate the current value of the pension obligation. The estimated liability is called "actuarial present value of pension benefits," because actuarial assumptions are made in estimating future payments under the plan.

Typically, when firms initiate pension plans, or when firms make amendments to existing pension plans (e.g., increasing the rate of compensation from 1.5 percent to 2 percent for each year of service), the benefits are applied retroactively to employees who were eligible for these benefits at the time of the plan adoption or amendment. Thus, in addition to the continuous accumulation of pension benefits for current services by employees, firms may be liable to pay pension benefits to employees for past and prior services. These lump-sum additions to the pension liability may be spread over future periods by amortizing the liability for prior services over the remaining time until employees retire.

As explained above, the firm makes contributions to the pension fund, and fund assets are invested further to yield greater assets in the future. Thus, at any point in time, the pension plan will have a liability for future pension benefits and assets from which this liability can be paid in the future. When the liability exceeds the assets in the fund, we describe the fund as "underfunded," and, conversely, as "overfunded" when assets exceed the liability.

The funding status of the plan can change every year for several reasons. The firm might increase contributions to the plan or investments might yield a rate of return beyond that which was initially expected. However, the funding status can also change because of "actuarial gains and losses" that are caused by changes in the actuarial assumptions that underlie the estimated liability. For example, when the turnover rate of employees increases above prior expectations, the pension liability decreases because fewer employees will reach the point at which benefits "vest," that is, the point at which benefits will have to be paid even if the employee leaves the firm before retirement.[6] Another example is when employees die at a younger age than that assumed by the plan's actuary. This reduces the future benefits and also the current liability of the firm, thus producing an actuarial gain. Such actuarial gains and losses are not incorporated into income in the year they occur. Instead, they are amortized over several years.

APB Opinion No. 8 (1968) required firms to estimate their pension liability using an acceptable actuarial method and to include in the pension expense an amortization of prior service costs. It also required firms to disclose in a footnote to the financial statements the unfunded vested benefit obligation and the pension expense for the period. Unfunded vested benefits are equal to the actuarial present value of pension obligations that will be paid regardless of whether employees remain with the firm, minus fund assets that are available for payments to employees. Firms also disclosed the unfunded prior service cost due to SEC disclosure requirements.

---

[6]Note that for pension liability one cannot necessarily use the rule-of-thumb that increases in liabilities are economically bad for the firm and decreases are necessarily beneficial to the firm. For example, an increase in the turnover rate will decrease the pension liability, but the increase in the turnover rate also means that the firm loses skilled and trained employees. Thus, the economic loss from the higher turnover ratio may actually exceed the economic benefits from reduced pension payments in the future.

In 1976, the FASB made some changes to these accounting and disclosure requirements. First, fund assets had to be disclosed using the fair market value of those assets, and not at their accounting carrying cost. This usually tended to increase the value of fund assets because equity and real-estate investments were typically understated when historical cost values were used. Second, the FASB required additional disclosure about pension plans in a footnote to the financial statements. Among these disclosure requirements, firms had to supply information about the actuarial present value of their vested and nonvested pension benefits. Firms also had to supply information about the fair market values of pension plan assets, about discount rates used in the estimation of the liability, and the expected rate of return on pension plan investments. Still, no liabilities or assets were incorporated into the financial statements by these pronouncements.

In 1985, the FASB issued FAS No. 87, which imposed new accounting and disclosure requirements. FAS No. 87 required for the first time the recording of a pension liability on the balance sheet if certain conditions (to be described later) are met. It also broadened the amount of disclosure in the footnotes to the financial statements. The standard became effective in 1987, although some firms chose to adopt the standard earlier. Let us examine some of the major changes this standard imposed.

Probably the largest effect of this standard is the requirement to use the "projected benefit obligations" instead of the "accumulated benefit obligations" in some tests employed by the standard and in disclosure of the liability. The difference between projected and accumulated benefits relates to the forecast of future salary increases. Recall that a pension plan usually has a formula for pension benefits that is based on the average salary at some point close to retirement. Naturally, the longer an employee's service with the firm is, the more likely it is that he or she will have a higher salary due to promotions and salary increases as a result of inflation. Thus, in estimating the actuarial present value of *projected* benefit obligations, the actuary takes into account expected future salary increases. However, to estimate the actuarial present value of *accumulated* pension benefits, the actuary uses current salary levels. The difference between the two measures is substantial; for the average firm future salaries increase the actuarial present value of the liability by about 20 percent–40 percent.

The second major change in FAS No. 87 is the requirement to accrue a liability *on the balance sheet* that is equal to the excess of the actuarial present value of *accumulated* pension benefits over plan assets. Therefore, if a firm's actuarial present value of accumulated pension benefit is larger than the value of plan assets to satisfy this liability, the difference is shown as a liability on the balance sheet. This requirement is effective for firms with large shortfalls in their pension plans.

The third major change in FAS No. 87 is the treatment of the "transition amount." At the adoption of the standard, the difference between the actuarial present value of *projected* pension benefits and the plan assets is considered the transition amount. This difference is amortized over the average remaining service of employees or fifteen years. Note that if the plan is overfunded at the adoption of FAS No. 87, the transition amount is an asset that is incorporated into the balance sheet (through the amortization) over a period of time. The converse is true if the plan is underfunded at the adoption of FAS No. 87, where a liability will be incorporated into the balance sheet over the amortization period.

FAS No. 87 also required firms to disclose information in a footnote to the financial statements, some of which is just a carryover of past FASB pronouncements, but most of which is new and broadened information. The required information is generally of three types: (1) information about plan assets and liabilities, whether incorporated on the balance sheet or not, (2) information that provides additional details about the pension expense for the period, and (3) information about the pension plan, funding policy, and assumptions used to estimate the liability. We provide next a description of these information items.

The new standard requires firms to disclose information about the actuarial present value of accumulated pension benefits and the actuarial present value of projected pension benefits. Because the old disclosure requirements are still in effect, the pension liability is broken down into vested and nonvested benefits. The footnote also discloses the fair market value of pension plan assets, so one can immediately determine if the pension plan is over- or underfunded. The standard also requires firms to reconcile the funding status, that is, the amount of over- or under-funding with the pension plan assets/liabilities that were not yet recognized and incorporated on the balance sheet. For example, the transition amount is likely to appear for most firms in the late 1980s and beginning of the 1990s, because it is amortized over a period of about 15 years. The firm is likely to disclose those unamortized actuarial gains/losses that are not yet incorporated on the balance sheet. The firm is also likely to include such items as prior period pension costs that are not yet incorporated into the balance sheet.

Example:

Times Mirror Company is a media and information company principally engaged in newspaper, book, magazine, and other publishing, and cable and broadcast television. Among its newspapers are the *Los Angeles Times* and *Newsday*.

Times Mirror reports in a footnote to its 1990 financial statements the following information (in millions of dollars):

	1990	*1989*
Actuarial present value of benefit obligations:		
Vested benefits	512.6	458.1
Nonvested	8.7	8.4
Accumulated benefit obligations	521.3	466.5
Projected benefit obligations	693.2	607.6
Plan assets at fair value	853.1	894.7
Excess of plan assets over projected benefit obligations	159.9	287.1
Unrecognized net loss from past experience different from that assumed	227.1	78.8
Prior service cost not yet amortized	5.9	3.6
Unrecognized net asset being amortized over 13–15 years	(176.4)	(198.0)
Other	9.4	15.1
Prepaid pension cost	225.8	186.6

First note that the plan in 1990 is overfunded; the plan assets exceed the projected benefit obligations by $159.9 million. Also note that the projected benefit obligation exceeds the accumulated benefit obligation by about $172 million, or about one-third of the accumulated pension benefit obligations. Thus, the incorporation of future salary increases into the estimation of the liability greatly affects the liability.

Times Mirror incorporated on the balance sheet an asset—prepaid pension cost—that, at 12/31/90, amounted to $225.8 million. However, as of that date, plan assets exceeded the obligation only by $159.9 million, as disclosed above. To reconcile the two figures, the firm reports four items. The first is the transition amount that was an asset whose portion has not yet been incorporated on the balance sheet—$176.4 million. This amount, together with the amount that was already incorporated on the balance sheet as an asset, $225.8 million, represent total pension assets in excess of liabilities as of 12/31/91, or $402.2 million (176.4 + 225.8). Unfortunately, the firm had experienced net actuarial losses, of which the portion that had not been amortized as of 12/31/90 is $227.1 million. Thus, the net pension assets in excess of liabilities are reduced to $175.1 (402.2 − 227.1). Furthermore, there existed on 12/31/90 prior period costs of $5.9 that had not been amortized, which further reduced the net assets over liabilities to $169.2 million (175.1 − 5.9). Other adjustments in the amount of $9.4 million reduced the net pension assets in excess of liabilities to $159.8 million (169.2 − 9.4). This is, indeed, the amount by which the plan assets actually exceed the projected benefit obligation as of 12/31/90 (except for a rounding-off error).

Example:

In a footnote to its 1989 financial statements, Ecolab reports the following information about its pension assets and liabilities (in millions of dollars):

	1989	1988
Actuarial present value of:		
Vested benefit obligation	61.9	49.9
Nonvested benefit obligation	6.4	7.1
Accumulated benefit obligation	68.3	57.0
Effect of projected future salary increases	18.6	13.1
Projected benefit obligation	86.9	70.1
Plan assets at fair value	82.0	73.5
Plan assets (less than) in excess of the projected benefit obligation	(4.9)	3.4
Unrecognized net loss and prior service cost	16.8	10.0
Unrecognized net transition asset	(21.7)	(22.7)
Unfunded accrued pension expense	9.8	9.2

Note that Ecolab's pension plan was overfunded by $3.4 million on 12/31/88, but underfunded by $4.9 million on 12/31/89. It is easily verified that the effect of future salary increases on the estimated liability increased the accumulated pension benefit by more than

20 percent. On the balance sheet, Ecolab has accrued pension liabilities of $9.8 million in 1989, and $9.2 million in 1988. To reconcile the amount recorded on the balance sheet as a liability and the net liabilities over assets of $4.9 million in 1989, the firm reports two additional items. First is the unamortized actuarial net losses and prior service cost, which amounted to $16.8 million in 1989. Thus, total liabilities in excess of assets should have been $26.6 million (9.8 + 16.8). However, the firm also reports an unamortized transition asset that was $21.7 million on 12/31/89. Thus, the net liability as of that date, that is, the amount of underfunding, is $4.9 million, as reported above.

The standard requires firms to disclose information about the major components of the pension expense for the accounting period. The first component is the normal service cost for the period. This represents the additional pension benefits that employees earned during the period, simply because they spend one additional year of service with the firm. Recall that the pension plan has a formula that provides pension benefits according to the number of service years with the firm. Thus, this additional year entitles employees to greater pension benefits and the actuarial present value of those additional benefits is the normal service cost.

The second component of the pension expense is the interest expense. This component represents the fact that the balance of the pension liability at the beginning of the year has come one year closer to maturity. As is true of debt, when a loan is one year closer to maturity, its present value increases, and the increase in the present value of the loan from the beginning of the year to its end represents interest expense. Similarly, because the actuarial present value of the pension liability that existed at the beginning of the year is larger at the end of the year, the increase in the present value is considered interest expense and is shown as the second component of the pension expense for the year.

The third component of the pension expense—the rate of return on pension plan assets—is actually a pension revenue in most cases. As a mirror image of the interest expense on the pension plan liability at the beginning of the year, the return on plan assets represents the "interest revenue" on assets that existed at the beginning of the year. Recall that in most cases the pension plan will have assets in the fund at the beginning of the period. These assets are supposed to offset the liability that exists at the beginning of the period. Just as we recognize the increase in the present value of the liability over the year as interest expense, we should recognize the increase in plan assets due to good investments during that same year as revenue.

The final component of the pension expense in the footnote to the financial statements is the amortization of various amounts. Among these amounts that need to be amortized and included in the pension expense are items such as actuarial gains and losses, which are incorporated into the balance sheet over a period of time.[7] Other items that will be amortized are prior service costs due to amendments of the plan and the transition amount. As a matter of fact, most of the firms that had a large overfunding at the time they adopted FAS No. 87, which meant that they also had a large transition

---

[7]FAS No. 87 allowed firms to amortize actuarial gains and losses only if they exceed a certain minimum amount. This is the "corridor" approach adopted by this standard.

asset, reduced pension expense that year because of the amortization of the transition asset. Let us review examples of disclosure of the components of pension expense.

Example:

In its note to the 1990 financial statements, Times Mirror reports the following information about the components of pension expense (in millions of dollars):

	1990	*1989*
Service cost—benefits earned during the period	39.5	29.2
Interest cost on projected benefit obligation	51.1	44.7
Return on plan assets	(89.8)	(79.9)
Net amortization and deferral	(18.9)	(20.8)
Net periodic pension expense (income)	(18.2)	(26.8)

Note that Times Mirror not only did not show an expense on its defined benefits pension plans, but it actually showed income on its pension plans under defined benefits. The reason for this is that the firm showed a high return on its assets, $89.8 million, whereas the increase in the value of the pension obligation at the beginning of the year was only $51.1 million. Thus, the firm had an excess income of $38.7 million (89.8 − 51.1) to offset pension costs of $39.5 million for the year. In addition, the firm had an amortization and deferral amount that also *decreased* the expense by $18.9 million, with a net result of income on pension plan of $18.2 million. A large portion of the $18.9 million that were amortized during the year is due to the amortization of the transition amount. Indeed, if we go back to the data previously provided on Times Mirror pension assets and liabilities, we can see that the transition amount decreased from $198.0 million on 12/31/89 to $176.4 million on 12/31/90. Thus, the transition amount alone contributed about $21.6 million (198.0 − 176.4) to a decrease of the current pension expense. Obviously, the firm amortized some costs as well because the net amortization figure was only $18.9 million.

Example:

In a footnote to its 1989 financial statements, Ecolab reports the following information about its components of pension expense (in millions of dollars):

	1989	*1988*
Service cost—employee benefits earned during the year	3.9	3.3
Interest cost on projected benefit obligation	6.4	5.6
Actual return on plan assets	(9.8)	(9.5)
Net amortization and deferral	1.5	1.7
U.S. pension plan expense	2.0	1.1

Note that, unlike Times Mirror, Ecolab reports an expense from its pension plan in 1988 and 1989. Also note that, although the return on plan assets in both years exceeded the interest cost component, the net amortization and deferral figure *increased* the expense by $1.5 million. This figure represents amortization of losses and prior service costs, because, as we saw before, the transition amount was an asset and not a liability.

The last type of information that is disclosed in the footnote on pensions is about assumptions made to estimate the pension liability, description of the pension plans and pension formulas, and the funding policy of the firm. For example, the firm will disclose discount rates, the rate of return on plan assets, and the rate at which salaries are expected to grow in the future. Interestingly enough, most firms assume that the rate of return on plan assets and the rate used to discount the pension liability are higher than the rate at which salaries are expected to grow.

The firm usually describes its pension plans in general terms such as who is eligible for participation in the plan, the major elements of the plan formula, and any other plans that are not standard U.S. plans. Thus, information is separately provided about foreign pension plans and about multiemployer plans within the United States. (Multiemployer plans are plans that are common to all employees of a particular union, regardless of the specific employer. All employers in the union are responsible for pension liabilities and assets). The firm will also describe its funding policy, that is, what contributions are expected to be made every year.

Example:

In its first footnote about significant accounting policies, Times Mirror states:
"The company has defined benefit pension plans and various other contributory and noncontributory retirement plans covering substantially all employees. In general, benefits under the defined benefit plans are based on years of service and the employee's compensation during the last five years of employment. In determining net periodic pension income, unrecognized net gains or losses that are amortizable and prior service costs are amortized on a straight-line basis over 10 years. The defined benefit plans are funded on a current basis in accordance with the Employee Retirement Income Security Act of 1974....The majority of the Company's defined benefit plans are overfunded, and funding has not generally been required for several years."

Times Mirror also reports the following information about the assumed rates in the estimation of the liability:

	1990	*1989*
Discount rate	8.25%	8.25%
Rate of increase in compensation levels	6.25%	6.25%
Expected long-term rate of return on assets	10.0%	10.0%

It should be noted that the firm states that it did not contribute to the pension funds in 1990 because the plans were highly overfunded. Thus, there was no cash outflow from the firm to the fund. Also, the firm expects the rate of return on plan assets to be 10 percent, although the discount rate is assumed to be only 8.25 percent. Furthermore, employees should expect salary increases of only 6.25 percent.

Let us now check whether the interest expense component and the rate of return component of the pension expense are consistent with the assumed discount rate and the rate of return on plan assets. Recall that the projected benefit obligation as of 12/31/89 was reported by Times Mirror as $607.578 million and plan assets as of that date were $894.658 million. Multiplying the projected benefit obligation at the beginning of 1990 by the discount rate of 8.25 percent yields $50.125 million (607.578 x 0.0825), which is very close to the reported interest cost component of $51.014 million for 1990. Similarly, the expected rate of return on plan assets can be estimated as $89.466 million (894.658 x 10 percent), which is close to the reported return on plan assets of $89.871 million in 1990.

Example:

Ecolab reports the following information in the footnotes to its 1989 financial statements:
"The Company has a defined benefit pension plan covering substantially all of its U.S. employees, except ChemLawn. Plan benefits are based on years of service and average compensation during the last years of employment. Various international subsidiaries also have defined benefit pension plans. . . . The company's policy is to fund pension costs currently to the extent deductible for income tax purposes. U.S. pension plan assets consist primarily of equity and fixed income securities. Effective July 1, 1989 the company amended its U.S. pension plan to change the formula for pension benefits and to provide a more rapid vesting schedule. The plan amendments resulted in a $6 million increase in the December 31, 1989, projected benefit obligation. The impact on the 1989 pension expense was not material."

The firm reports the following assumed rates:

Discount rate for service and interest cost	9.0%	9.0%	9.0%
Projected salary increases, weighted average	5.6%	5.6%	5.6%
Expected return on assets	9.0%	8.5%	8.5%
Discount rate for year-end benefit obligations	8.5%	9.0%	9.0%

When we multiply the projected benefit obligation at the beginning of the year, which is reported by Ecolab as $70.143 million on 12/31/88, by the assumed discount rate of 9.0 percent, we get $6.313 million. This is very close to the interest cost component of the pension expense of $6.439 million for 1989. However, when we multiply plan assets at the beginning of 1989, which were reported by the firm as $73.546 million on 12/31/88, by the assumed long-term return on assets of 9 percent, we get an expected return on assets of $6.619 million. Note that Ecolab reported *actual* return on assets of $9.820 million, far exceeding the expected long-term rate of return on assets. Most of the difference between the actual and the expected return on assets is included in the net amortization and deferral. It should also be noted that the assumed rate of increases in salaries is substantially below the discount rate or the expected rate of return on assets.

What are the implications of pension plan liabilities and assets to total debt and free cash flows? The easy answer is that a firm could have an underfunded pension plan and the liability that is recorded on the balance sheet (if one is recorded at all) might be smaller than the projected benefit obligation. In such cases, the cash flow analyst should add to total debt the difference between the present value of projected benefit obligations and the pension liability that is incorporated on the balance sheet. This additional liability is an off-balance-sheet liability, as are operating leases.

Example:

Bally Manufacturing Corp. operates in three lines of business. It operates casino hotels in Atlantic City and Las Vegas, more than 300 fitness centers, and it produces instant ticket lottery games and lottery machines.

In a footnote to its 1989 financial statements, Bally reports the following information about its pension plans' funding status (in millions of dollars):

	1989	1988
Actuarial present value of benefit obligations:		
Vested benefits	35.489	30.615
Nonvested benefits	.890	1.996
Accumulated benefit obligations	36.379	32.611
Effect of projected salary increases	4.781	7.882
Projected benefit obligations	41.160	40.493
Fair value of plan assets	10.817	9.593
Projected benefit obligations in excess of plan assets	30.343	30.900
Unrecognized transition obligations	(3.687)	(7.168)
Other	1.484	(1.127)
Accrued pension liability recognized in the consolidated balance sheet	28.140	22.605

Bally's pension plan is underfunded. The underfunding in 1989 amounts to $30.343 million, of which $28.140 million is incorporated on the balance sheet as a liability. Thus, the cash flow analyst should increase total debt of the firm by the difference, or $2.203 million (30.343 − 28.140). The equivalent amount in 1988 is substantially greater, $8.295 million (30.900 − 22.605). However, this addition is not material to Bally's total debt that reached about $2.4 billion during these years.

Example:

We saw before that Ecolab's plan was underfunded by $4.861 million as of 12/31/89. However, the firm had already incorporated on the balance sheet a liability of $9.777 on the same date. Thus, the cash flow analyst can, in this case, *reduce* total debt by the difference, or $4.916 million (9.777 − 4.861). In effect, total debt is *smaller* after making the adjustment for the current value of the pension liability.

In some cases, the pension plan is overfunded to such a degree that the plan actually has more assets than are incorporated on the balance sheet. In these cases, the cash flow analyst could increase net assets of the firm and net equity by the difference between these two amounts. The difference represents additional assets that will save future cash inflows into the plan.

Example:

National Service Industries Inc. operates in seven industries, but derives most of its revenues and cash flows from three core businesses—lighting equipment, textile rental, and specialty chemicals.

In its 1990 financial statements, National Service Industries reports a projected benefit obligation of $49.325 million as of 6/30/1990 and plan assets of $73.780 million on that date for its plans that are overfunded. Thus, for these overfunded pension plans, assets are reported at $24.455 million. The firm reports that it had incorporated on the balance sheet an asset in the amount of $7.652 as of 8/31/90.[8] Thus, net assets due to this plan should increase by the difference, or $16.803 million (24.455 − 7.652).

The firm also reports information about plans that are underfunded. For these plans, the actuarial present value of projected benefit obligations amounted to $15.464 million, whereas plan assets on that date were only $10.765 million. Thus, these plans were underfunded by $4.699 million. The firm reports that the liability that is incorporated on the balance sheet for these plans was only $3.806, so that the total debt of the firm should *increase* by $0.893 million (4.699 − 3.806). For convenience, one can probably net the increase in net assets with the increase in total debt.

Example:

As we saw before for Times Mirror, its overfunding on 12/31/90 was $159.867 million. However, the firm had already incorporated on the balance sheet a prepaid pension asset of $225.776 million as of 12/31/90. Thus, the cash flow analyst should *reduce* the net assets of the firm as well as its equity by the difference in these two amounts, or $65.909 million (225.776 − 159.867).

The cash flow analyst should also attempt to evaluate cash flow that the firm will fund to its pension plan and compare it with the pension expense. Any discrepancies should be added to free cash flows if the expense is greater than the cash outflow, or subtracted from free cash flows if the cash outflow is greater. In most cases, however, the firm provides only very general information about its funding policy, which does not allow the cash flow analyst to make an adequate assessment of contributions to the pension plan. Thus, the cash flow analyst can, in most instances, assume that the pension expense is equal to the cash outflow to the plan and the only adjustment will be to total debt of the firm.

Exhibit 6–6 shows the effects of the additional liability due to pension obligations for a sample of firms with large underfunded pension plans.

---

[8]According to FAS No. 87, the actuarial estimates and the balance sheet date should be no more than three months apart. Earlier, firms could have made the actuarial estimation on any day during the year.

Exhibit 6-6   Additional Liability Due to Pensions—1990

Ticker	Firm	Additional Pension Liability	Total Debt	Percent Increase in Total Debt	Market Value (Millions of Dollars)
ADCT	ADC TELECOMMUNICATIONS INC	2.7	6.6	0.41	$ 345.8
AA	ALUMINUM CO OF AMERICA	357.6	1487.9	0.24	5432.1
BEC	BECKMAN INSTRUMENTS INC	24.8	94.6	0.26	549.7
BS	BETHLEHEM STEEL CORP	298.4	663.8	0.45	1161.5
BA	BOEING CO	364.0	315.0	1.16	17151.0
BAB	BRITISH AIRWAYS PLC -ADR	806.1	3094.8	0.26	2524.8
CCC	CALGON CARBON CORP	4.5	11.4	0.39	804.1
CMFB	CHEMICAL FABRICS CORP	1.1	2.6	0.41	96.0
ACCOB	COORS (ADOLPH) -CL B	40.8	110.0	0.37	711.1
CRD.B	CRAWFORD & CO -CL B	6.8	30.4	0.22	936.1
CNP.A	CROWN CENTRAL PETROL -CL A	9.0	2.6	3.47	242.1
DSCP	DATASCOPE CORP	0.7	1.8	0.41	416.5
DAL	DELTA AIR LINES INC	586.9	2137.6	0.27	3377.9
DYA	DYNAMICS CORP OF AMER	0.8	4.0	0.21	50.9
FKM	FLUKE (JOHN) MFG CO	2.1	1.3	1.58	132.2
GCO	GENESCO INC	13.1	39.0	0.34	122.7
GPC	GENUINE PARTS CO	32.3	43.1	0.75	3355.1
GLK	GREAT LAKES CHEMICAL CORP	82.6	136.8	0.60	3381.0
HKT	HONG KONG TELECOM LTD -ADR	54.7	60.5	0.90	11152.8
HRL	HORMEL (GEO. A.) & CO	17.8	26.3	0.68	1535.0
LTEK	LIFE TECHNOLOGIES INC	1.9	4.1	0.45	255.3
MDP	MEREDITH CORP	8.3	0.2	33.94	446.1
NBB	NBB BANCORP INC	0.3	0.8	0.32	105.9
GOSHA	OSHKOSH B'GOSH INC -CL A	4.4	9.2	0.48	510.5
PESC	POOL ENERGY SERVICES CO	0.8	0.1	12.58	96.3
3RVTL	ROSEVILLE TELEPHONE CO	6.7	9.9	0.67	304.1
SHLM	SCHULMAN (A.) INC	2.2	7.0	0.32	797.5
SMF	SMART & FINAL INC	2.5	3.2	0.78	140.5
TBP	TAB PRODUCTS	1.4	0.5	3.11	73.5
UTVI	UNITED TELEVISION INC	2.4	0.2	10.58	281.3
VOD	VODAFONE GROUP PLC -ADR	3.1	13.7	0.23	6450.0
WLA	WARNER-LAMBERT CO	112.0	537.1	0.21	9947.5
WS	WEIRTON STEEL CORP	91.5	398.9	0.23	75.8
WMRK	WESTMARK INTERNATIONAL INC	4.5	8.0	0.56	498.3
WDHD	WOODHEAD INDUSTRIES INC	0.4	0.2	2.64	51.0
	Median	6.7	9.9	0.45	498.3

Exhibit 6-7 provides another example in which we adjust total debt to include both additional debt due to operating leases and to pensions. To show the importance of these items, we selected an extreme example, Delta Airlines Inc., which has a significant liability due to operating leases.

As can be seen in Exhibit 6-7, when one uses 10 percent to discount payments under capital leases, the capitalized amount, $144.1 million, is remarkably close to the capitalized obligation reported by Delta. When we capitalize the payments under operating leases net of sublease revenues, we obtain an additional liability of $5.87 billion, which increases total debt of $1.4207 billion by about 413.2 percent.

Exhibit 6–7   Delta Airlines 1990 (Millions of Dollars)

		Capital Leases	Operating Leases	Subleases	Net Operating Leases
1988			435.3		
1989			536.2		
1990			545.5		
1991		24.4	533.9	6.0	527.9
1992		24.7	533.1	6.0	527.1
1993		19.7	523.4	5.9	517.5
1994		20.6	515.5	5.5	510.0
1995		18.3	512.9	5.2	507.7
Thereafter		108.6	6984.8	72.1	6912.7
Total		216.3	9603.6	100.7	9502.9
Interest—capital leases		69.6			
Present value of capital leases		146.8			
Present value assuming 10 percent		144.1			5870.0
Total debt	1420.7				
Increase in total debt (%)—leases					413.2
Projected benefit obligation	3904.1				
Plan assets (FMV)	3521.5				
Net pension obligation	382.6				
Accrued pension costs (liability)	21.7				
Additional pension liability	360.9				
Increase in total debt (%)—pensions					25.4
Increase in total debt (%), total					438.6

When we examine the footnote on pensions, we find that Delta has an underfunding of about $382.6 million, whereas the liability that has been incorporated on the balance sheet at the end of 1990 is only $21.7 million. Thus, additional liability due to pensions in the amount of $360.9 million should be included in total debt. This increases the reported total debt by about 25.4 percent. Together with operating leases, and before considering the effects of other postretirement benefits, total debt increases by 438.6 percent! This shows the importance of considering off-balance-sheet liabilities.

6.7 PENSION PLAN SURPLUS OR DEFICIENCY

The growth in corporate unfunded pension liabilities has brought on a visible awareness, especially by unions and union members, employees, Congress, and investment bankers of the potential risk that these long-term liabilities could not be met. Prior to the 1970s, a detailed analysis of an entity's pension plan was usually not undertaken until after a merger. With the enormous growth in the pension liability and the effects on cash flows, that situation changed considerably. Now, due to the potentially large impact of contributions to the pension plan on cash flows, the pension liability is closely examined by potential buyers, investors, and creditors.

Several entities with positive operating and free cash flows have chosen to file for bankruptcy protection to avoid large pension payments.

Example:

LTV Corporation, a large steelmaker, bought Republic Steel for $712 million in stock and assumed about $800 million in debt. What it ignored was Republic's large unfunded pension liability, which at the time of LTV's bankruptcy petition had been paying close to $250 million a year on its $2 billion unfunded liability. LTV's management transferred the entire pension obligation to the U.S. government's Pension Benefit Guarantee Corporation (PBGC), the government's sponsored and administered program that insures the private pension system. Because the PBGC became liable for the LTV pension payments of about $250 million annually, LTV could use those funds to modernize. LTV was further able to improve its free cash flow by renegotiating onerous union agreements and contracts for iron ore and coal. It was further relieved from paying the $16 per person annual insurance premium the PBGC charged for ongoing pension plans. While the PBGC continued to foot the pension obligation, LTV recorded in 1988 an operating cash flow of $410 million on $1.4 billion in revenues.[9] At the same time, the financial position of the PBGC deteriorated considerably, and, in essence, there was no guarantee that this plan could have undertaken payments for another large pension plan that defaulted on its obligations. Eventually, to free itself from bankruptcy status, LTV negotiated a solution for its pension obligation.

For firms with overfunded pension plans, that is, plans in which pension assets exceed pension obligations, there is a temptation to terminate the pension plan, settle existing obligations, and use the excess assets in the firm. This, of course, may be viewed as "hidden" free cash flows, which get recognized with a formal action by the firm.

Example:

In 1989, Alexander and Alexander Inc. purchased annuity contracts for $37.4 million to settle the accumulated benefit obligations to certain retirees and recorded a pretax gain of $15.7 million. The company recognized the gain as a reduction of its 1989 pension expense.

It should be noted that not all net pension assets can be taken over by the firm. During the LBO era of the 1980s, the pension plan, once perceived to be a cost center for the firm, began to be considered a profit center because the investments of the pension plan yielded higher returns than were expected. A careful examination of the surplus of assets in the pension fund revealed, however, that only a small portion could have been immediately utilized by the firm.

Example:

When speculation spread that USX was a candidate for a hostile takeover, many security analysts and financial reporters pointed to the seemingly large surplus of pension assets in

---

[9]See Sarah Smith, "The Joys of Bankruptcy," *Corporate Finance Magazine*, April 1990, for a thorough review of the LTV case.

the fund. Presumably, the acquired firm could have reverted cash back from the pension plan to pay down debt that was used to acquire USX. The same argument was raised by security analysts in 1989 when investor Harold Simmons acquired a large stake in Lockheed Corp.

However, the large surplus that seemed to exist when security analysts simply subtracted pension liabilities from the fair market value of pension assets at year end was drastically reduced in reality. What analysts ignored were:

1. Taxes on the gains in the pension assets, including a 15 percent excise tax.

2. The rates on Guaranteed Insurance Contracts (GICs) were lower than the discount rates assumed by the pension plan at that time. Thus, to satisfy the pension obligations, more assets would have been needed to be invested in low yielding GIC's.

3. For Lockheed, the U.S. government would be entitled to most of the surplus because the Pentagon funded the plan.

It is vital that investors have a thorough understanding of the magnitude of the pension plan's liabilities that are assumed as a result of a business combination. Oftentimes, due to the haste with which many deals are put together, the acquiring company is not fully aware of the full extent of the liabilities it is assuming. Other entities are more than happy to sell divisions because of the enormity of their pension fund liabilities and the future negative impact on cash flows of funding those liabilities.

The wording in a purchase agreement concerning the meaning of a particular liability can be so vague that not all parties can later agree on what was meant when the initial agreement was signed. For example, Banner Industries charged Pepsi-Cola that it dumped a large liability in its lap when Banner purchased its trucking subsidiary.

If the acquiring entity continues the plan of the acquired entity, it assumes a liability for that portion of the plan's vested liability that is not funded (the unfunded vested liability) up to 30 percent of the acquiring entity's net worth. The vested liability is the actuarial present value of benefits that must be paid even if current employees leave the company. In addition, the acquiring company may assume other liabilities. Nonvested benefits, or benefits that will become vested if the employee stays under the employment of the company, may be assumed, with the possibility that such liabilities will be substantial. If the acquired entity has been a publicly held firm, information about vested and nonvested benefits are included in the pension footnote to the annual report. More typically, the acquiring entity elects to terminate the acquired entity's plan, preferring to meld the new employees into its own plan with appropriate credits given for length of service.

Liabilities under a multiemployer pension plan must be evaluated by the analyst because of the penalties associated with withdrawal. Severe withdrawal penalties can be imposed on the acquirer if it decided to terminate a pension plan. The extent of outstanding claims must also be reviewed, including other postretirement benefits such as life insurance or catastrophic claims. It is therefore important to learn of the annual (cash) pension expense from the company if it is not well specified. However, as we argued above, very few firms reveal the annual contribution to the pension plan.

6.8 LIABILITIES FOR POSTRETIREMENT BENEFITS OTHER THAN PENSIONS

In November of 1984, the FASB issued FAS No. 81, which required firms to disclose information about postretirement health-care and life insurance benefits. Under that standard, firms were to disclose the cost of health-care and/or life insurance benefits to retirees, their dependents, or survivors. If such costs to retirees could not have been separated from costs to current employees, such total costs were required to be disclosed as well as the number of active employees and the number of retirees covered by the plan. A general description of the plan, covered employees, and benefits was also required.

Example:

Brush Wellman Inc. is a leading international supplier of high-performance engineered materials. It is a fully integrated source of beryllium, beryllium alloys, and beryllia ceramic. It also supplies specialty metal systems and precious metal products.

In a note to its 1990 financial statements, Brush Wellman states:

"In addition to providing pension benefits, the Company provides health care and life insurance benefits for certain retired employees. The costs for these benefits are charged to expense as paid or accrued, and amounted to $803,000 in 1990; $1,044,000 in 1989; and $906,000 in 1988. In connection with operations discontinued in 1985, the Company retained certain obligations for these employees' postretirement medical benefits. At December 31, 1990 and 1989, $4,600,000 and $5,200,000 respectively, relating to such medical benefits were included in Other Long-Term Liabilities."

To get an idea about the magnitude of these benefits, Brush Wellman's total expenses in 1990, excluding taxes and interest, were about $270 million. Thus, the expenses on the two items to current retirees seem small (only $0.8 million in 1990). However, note that the firm also discloses the magnitude of its obligation for medical benefits to employees in discontinued operations, which amounted to about $4.6 million in 1990. Again, to put it in its proper perspective, total liabilities of Brush Wellman as of 12/31/90 were about $123 million, with long-term liabilities about $60 million. Thus, the postretirement medical liability to those employees seems significant in relation to both total debt and certainly for long-term debt. It is tempting to speculate that, had the firm also accounted for future postretirement benefits to its *current* employees, total liabilities would have been significantly increased.

In December 1990, the FASB issued FAS No. 106, which deals with accounting for postretirement benefits other than pensions. Under FAS No. 106, firms will have to accrue postretirement benefits expected to be paid to *active* employees, their beneficiaries, or their covered dependents for services that the active employees provide today. Thus, instead of showing in the financial statements an expense for *current payments to retirees*, firms will have to also include an expense that is equal to the actuarial present value of additional benefits that *current active employees* earned during the period. In addition, footnote information will provide data about the liability associated with these benefits, as well as assets that were set aside to discharge the liability.

The requirements of FAS No. 106 are similar to those of FAS No. 87 for pension benefits, but with proper modifications. Similar to FAS No. 87, a transition amount is created and is either included immediately in income as the effect of an accounting change or it can be spread over 20 years (or the average remaining service period of active plan participants). Because most firms had not provided any funds to offset this liability, they will have to set a transition liability, which will either substantially reduce net income in the period of adoption or affect future income over a long period of time. Similarly, total debt of the firm will be materially affected if the transition liability (with future adjustments due to additional services and reductions due to contributions) will be added to the firm's existing liabilities.

Example:

In a press release issued in September 1991, General Electric announced it had decided to adopt FAS No. 106 in the third quarter of 1991. GE writes that "the new accounting will be applied by the Company on a 'catch up' basis rather than prospectively and will result in a one-time, after-tax charge to net earnings of approximately $1.8 billion, less than 10 percent of GE's equity."

To place the expected decline of 1991 GE's earnings in perspective, note that GE's total earnings for 1990 were $4.303 billion and 1991's first quarter earnings were initially reported as $999 million.

Indeed, in its 1990 financial statements, GE provided the following data about post-retirement benefits:

"GE and its affiliates sponsor a number of plans providing retiree health and life insurance benefits. GE's aggregate cost for the principal plans, which cover substantially all employees in the United States, was $249 million in 1990, $283 million in 1989 and $302 million in 1988.

Generally, employees who retire after qualifying for optional early retirement under the GE plan are eligible to participate in retiree health and life insurance plans. Health benefits for eligible retirees under age 65 and eligible dependents are included in costs as covered expenses are actually incurred except for certain accruals provided in connection with business acquisitions and dispositions. For eligible retirees and spouses over age 65, the present value of future health benefits is funded or accrued and is included in costs in the year the retiree becomes eligible for benefits. The present value of future life insurance benefits for eligible retirees is funded and is included in costs in the year of retirement.

Most retirees outside the United States are covered by government programs, and GE's cost is not significant.

In December 1990, The Financial Accounting Standards Board issued FAS No. 106 — 'Employers' Accounting for Postretirement Benefits Other than Pensions,' establishing accounting principles for retiree health and life insurance plans. At January 1, 1991, GE had obligations for postretirement benefits other than pensions estimated at $4.2 billion while related assets in trust and cost accruals totaled $1.5 billion. SFAS No. 106 must be adopted by 1993 either by amortizing this net transition obligation (about $2.7 billion) over 20 years or by charging it immediately to operations; earlier adoption is encouraged."

As can be seen from GE's 1990 footnote, postretirement payments for health and life insurance benefits were about $249 million in 1990. The transition amount at the end of 1990 was estimated as $2.7 billion, before applicable taxes. Thus, adopting FAS No. 106 at the beginning of 1991 would have increased total liabilities by $2.7 billion, or about 2 percent (total liabilities amounted to about $131 billion at the beginning of 1991). They also reduced stockholders' equity, which amounted to about $22 billion at the beginning of

1991, by the net of the tax effect of the accounting change, or $1.8 billion. Thus, the change had a substantial impact on GE's financial statements.

It should be noted that, within a month of GE's announcement of this large expense to its 1991 financial statements, Westinghouse Electric also announced a $1.68 billion pretax charge to earnings due to problems at its credit unit. Westinghouse announced plans to cut 3.4 percent of its work force in an effort to reduce future cash outflows. Westinghouse's stock price declined more than 10 percent after the announcement, whereas GE's stock price was largely unaffected by its announcement of the charge against earnings because of the adoption of FAS No. 106. The difference in the market reaction can probably be attributed to expectations about future cash flows. GE's postretirement liability was known by the market and the adoption of FAS No. 106 had no cash flow effect. Westinghouse's announcement may have taken the market by surprise because the problems at its credit subsidiary may have been greater than expected by market participants.

To understand the provisions of FAS No. 106, let us initially assume that it relates only to health-care benefits that are paid after retirement. Suppose that the plan promises health-care benefits to all employees who attain age 55 while in service, and only if they have at least 10 years of service with the firm. Suppose we wanted to determine the obligation for an employee who is 45 years old, who has been with the firm for 13 years, and who is expected to remain employed by the firm until retirement at the age of 65. The employee is expected to live until the age of 75, and health-care benefits are assumed to be $1,500 during the first year after retirement and to increase by 8 percent each year. For simplicity, assume that the employee is single and that all benefits are paid at the end of the year. The firm assumes a discount rate of 9 percent for the postretirement benefits. Exhibit 6–8 contains the calculation of the future claims, the present value of these claims at four different ages, and the amount of the expected benefit obligation and the accumulated benefit obligation up to that age.

The first step in estimating the obligation is to determine the expected payments after retirement age, that is, at ages 66 through 75. We then discount the obligation to the present, when the employee is at age 45 (or 50, 55, and 56, in the other columns of the exhibit). The discounting is done by using the assumed rate of 9 percent. At the current age, 45, the present value of these future postretirement costs is $2,357. This is the actuarial present value of *expected* benefit obligations. It is the actuarial present value because we have to make actuarial assumptions about life expectancy, length of service, marital status, and so forth. However, note that at present the employee is not yet fully eligible for the postretirement benefits. The employee will only become fully eligible at the age of 55, and then only if he or she is still employed by the firm. Thus, the employee has not yet attained the date of *full eligibility*.

FAS No. 106 attributes postretirement benefits to years of service in an equal manner. Thus, at the age of 45, with 13 years of service, the employee has 10 more years to attain the full eligibility age of 55. FAS No. 106 requires recognition of the portion of the obligation that the employee accumulated to date using the number of years of service to date divided by the total expected number of years until the employee becomes fully eligible. At the age of 45, this yields 13/(13 + 10), and at the age of 50, the ratio increases to 18/23. Thus, the actuarial present value of the *accumulated* benefit obligation at the age of 45 is 13/23 of the *expected* benefit obligation, or $1,332. Similarly, at the age of 50, the accumulated benefit obligation is valued at

Exhibit 6-8   Estimation of Expected and Accumulated Benefit Obligation

	Age	Future Cost	Present Value at Age			
			45	50	55	56
	66	1500	246	378	581	634
	67	1620	243	374	576	628
	68	1750	241	371	571	622
	69	1890	239	368	565	616
	70	2041	237	364	560	611
	71	2204	234	361	555	605
	72	2380	232	357	550	600
	73	2571	230	354	545	594
	74	2776	228	351	540	589
	75	2999	226	348	535	583
Total benefits		21730	2357	3626	5579	6081
Actuarial present value—expected benefits			2357	3626	5579	6081
Years from hiring date			13	18	23	24
Years until full eligibility			10	5	0	0
Ratio of accumulated services			13/23	18/23	23/23	23/23
Actuarial present value—accumulated benefits			1332	2838	5579	6081

18/23 of the expected benefit obligation, or $2,838. However, at the age of 55, the employee becomes fully eligible and the accumulated and expected benefit obligations are identical, $5,579. From then on, the actuarial present value of the two benefit obligations is identical.

Note that from the age of 55 to the age of 56, the actuarial present value of the accumulated benefit obligation increased by $502 (6,081 − 5,579). This increase represents the interest cost component of the expense and is equal to 9 percent of the accumulated benefit at the age of 55, $5,579. This seems intuitively reasonable, because, at the age of 55, the employee is fully eligible and an additional year of service does not add any new postretirement benefits. The only change is that the obligation's maturity is one year shorter at the age of 56 than at the age of 55, which represents the interest expense component, as we saw for pension benefits. However, before age 55, the increase in the liability is comprised of both an interest expense and a service cost component, because some of the postretirement benefits are attributed to that year's services.

FAS No. 106 requires firms to estimate the actuarial present value of the accumulated postretirement benefits at the date of adoption of the new accounting rule and subtract from it any assets that were set aside for satisfying this liability. This difference is called the *transition amount* and can be treated in one of two ways. The first approach is to immediately include the offset to the transition amount in income as the effect of a change in an accounting principle, that is, placing it after extraordinary items and just before net income on the income statement. The second approach is the delayed recognition approach in which the transition amount is amortized into income over 20 years or the average remaining service years of active employees.

The FASB requires the adoption of the standard for fiscal years beginning after December 15, 1992 for public U.S. firms. Thus, firms will have to adopt the standard in their 1993 financial statements at the latest. Unlike pension plans, postretirement plans are largely unfunded and typically highly underfunded, so the transition amount is likely to be a liability for most firms, with an offsetting expense in the financial statements. Whether a firm will choose to immediately recognize the expense or delay its recognition will depend on the firm's earnings status and its expectations about future earnings. If earnings for the year are very high or very low, the firm may choose to immediately incorporate earnings into income. If earnings in the future are expected to be high, the firm may delay the incorporation of the expense into earnings of future years. Also, firms have some flexibility in adopting the standard earlier (before 1993) or later in their financial statements. It is expected that more successful firms will adopt the standard earlier to signal that they are in a better position.

Regardless of the date and method of adoption, there is no effect on cash flows. The only cash flow effects are the firm's payments to current retirees and contributions to a fund that will make future payments to retirees. These cash outflows are unlikely to change because of the adoption of the standard. Indeed, in its press release announcing the adoption of FAS No. 106 in its 1991 financial statements, General Electric writes:

> There will be no cash flow impact from the charge to earnings, and the Company has been informed by both Moody's and Standard & Poors that the adjustment will have no impact on GE's triple-A debt ratings.

Thus, credit rating agencies behave as if they were aware of this liability even prior to its incorporation into a footnote or the balance sheet itself. Because it has no cash flow effects, it is only an accounting change and is likely to have very little effect on stock prices.

Other disclosure requirements of FAS No. 106 parallel those of FAS No. 87 for pensions. For example, a firm is required to disclose the amount of the net periodic postretirement cost, showing separately the service cost component, the interest cost component, the actual return on plan assets for the period, amortization of the transition amount, and other amortization and deferrals. A firm is also required to provide information about assets and liabilities such as the fair value of plan assets, the actuarial present value of the accumulated benefit obligation (identifying separately the portion attributable to retirees, other fully eligible employees, and other active plan participants), unrecognized prior service cost, unrecognized net gain or loss, unrecognized transition amount, and the amount included on the balance sheet (whether an asset or a liability).

A firm is also required to disclose information about the terms of the plans, the participants, the assumed rates (including health-care cost trend rate), the effects of a one-percentage-point increase in the assumed health-care cost trend rates, and the type of assets held to discharge postretirement obligations. Because of their similarity to pension benefits, we will not expand the discussion of these items here.

Some firms have begun to take steps to prepare for the adoption of FAS No. 106 even before the standard is issued. For these firms, the effects on income or on the balance sheet due to the formal adoption of FAS No. 106 are likely to be small.

Example:

In a footnote to its 1990 financial statements, Vulcan Materials Inc. includes the following paragraphs:

"In addition to pension benefits, the Company provides certain health care benefits and life insurance for some retired employees. Substantially all of the Company's salaried employees and, where applicable, hourly employees may become eligible for those benefits if they reach at least age 55 and meet certain service requirements while working for the Company. Generally, company-provided health care benefits terminate when covered individuals become eligible for Medicare benefits or reach age 65, whichever first occurs.

Effective January 1, 1989, the Company changed to the accrual method of accounting for the aforementioned postretirement benefits based on actually determined costs to be accrued over the period from the date of hire to the full eligibility of employees who are expected to qualify for benefits. In the first quarter of 1989, the Company recorded the full amount of its estimated accumulated postretirement benefit obligation, which represents the present value of the estimated future benefits payable to current retirees and a pro rata portion of estimated benefits payable to active employees after retirement period. The pretax charge to 1989 earnings was $15,331,000 with a net earnings effect of $9,562,000 ($.23 per share). The latter amounts were reflected as cumulative effects of the accounting change in the consolidated statement of earnings.

The cost of providing postretirement benefits under the new accrual method amounted to $2,985,000 in 1990 and $2,549,000 in 1989. In prior years the Company recognized the cost of providing the postretirement benefits by expensing the contributions when made. The amount included in expense for 1988 under the previous method approximated $629,000. If the 1990 and the 1989 costs had been determined under the previous method, the amounts recognized would have been $1,157,000 and $1,064,000, respectively.

In December 1990 the Financial Accounting Standards Board issued Statement No. 106, *Employer's Accounting for Postretirement Benefits Other than Pensions*, which requires the use of an accrual method. The method adopted earlier by the Company, as described above, is substantially in compliance with the new standard. The Company expects to modify its methodology in 1991 to fully comply with FAS No. 106. No significant effect on earnings is expected as a result of this modification.

The Company funds the postretirement benefits plan each year through contributions to a trust fund for health care benefits and through payments of premiums to providers of life insurance. All assets of the plan relate to life insurance and are composed of reserves held by the insurer."

As indicated by Vulcan Materials, the firm has already adopted FAS No. 106 in substance and it expects no significant effects from the complete adherence to the standard in 1991. Probably, the only major change for the firm will be the additional disclosure that is required by the new standard. In terms of annual expense, postretirement benefits expenses more than doubled under the new standard as opposed to the old "pay-as-you-go" method. This is likely to be accentuated for firms that have not yet attempted to switch to accrual of the liability.

What are the implications for the cash flow analyst? As stated above, the direct effects of the standard on cash flows are likely to be minimal. However, firms may go through some steps to decrease future cash payments to retirees. For example, American Airlines wants its work force to pay a monthly fee to prepay future health benefits. Ralston Purina introduced an ESOP instead of its retiree medical plan. Other firms either discontinue such benefits to new employees or ask their employees to share in the costs of these postretirement benefits. Other firms begin funding additional amounts beyond the current contributions to cover payments to current retirees. Thus,

Ecolab: Postretirement Health-Care Benefits

NOTES TO CONSOLIDATED FINANCIAL STATEMENTS
ECOLAB INC.

7. Retirement Plans

Pension Plans

The company has a noncontributory defined benefit pension plan covering substantially all of its U.S. employees, except ChemLawn. Plan benefits are based on years of service and average compensation during the final years of employment. Various international subsidiaries also have defined benefit pension plans. Pension expense included the following components:

(thousands)	1991	1990	1989
Service cost-employee benefits earned during the year	$ 5,379	$ 4,630	$ 3,885
Interest cost on projected benefit obligation	8,161	7,245	6,439
Actual return on plan assets	(12,224)	5,545	(9,820)
Net amortization and deferral	3,556	(14,032)	1,516
U.S. pension expense	4,872	3,388	2,020
International pension expense	802	921	1,035
Total pension expense	$ 5,674	$ 4,309	$ 3,055

The funded status of the U.S. pension plan was:

December 31 (thousands)	1991	1990	1989
Actuarial present value of:			
Vested benefit obligation	$ 75,413	$ 67,100	$ 61,864
Non-vested benefit obligation	6,291	6,157	6,429
Accumulated benefit obligation	81,704	73,257	68,293
Effect of projected future salary increases	32,126	24,452	18,594
Projected benefit obligation	113,830	97,709	86,887
Plan assets at fair value	91,971	76,724	82,026
Plan assets (less than) the projected benefit obligation	(21,859)	(20,985)	(4,861)
Unrecognized net loss and prior service cost	33,243	31,792	16,831
Unrecognized net transition asset	(18,941)	(20,344)	(21,747)
Unfunded accrued pension expense	$ (7,557)	$ (9,537)	$ (9,777)

The company's policy is to fund pension costs currently to the extent deductible for income tax purposes. U.S. pension plan assets consist primarily of equity and fixed income securities. International pension benefit obligations and plan assets were not significant.

U.S. pension plan assumptions, in addition to projections for employee turnover and retirement ages, were:

	1991	1990	1989
Discount rate for service and interest cost	8.5 %	8.5%	9.0%
Projected salary increases, weighted average	5.6	5.6	5.6
Expected return on assets	9.0	9.0	9.0
Discount rate for year-end benefit obligations	8.25%	8.5%	8.5%

Postretirement Health Care Benefits

Effective January 1, 1991, the company adopted the provisions of Statement of Financial Accounting Standards No. 106, "Employers' Accounting for Postretirement Benefits Other Than Pensions" (FAS 106). The company provides defined benefit postretirement health care benefits to substantially all U.S. employees, except ChemLawn. The plan is contributory based on years of service and family status, with retiree contributions adjusted annually.

The company elected to record immediately the net transition obligation of $40,000,000, and the related deferred income tax benefit of $15,440,000, resulting in a one-time charge to results of operations of $24,560,000 for the cumulative effect of the change in accounting principle.

Adoption of FAS 106 increased 1991 pre-tax expense by $4,800,000 ($2,947,000 after-tax, or $0.11 per common share). The company previously recognized the estimated costs of these benefits on a modified accrual basis; pre-tax expense under the prior method was $1,771,000 in 1990 and $1,936,000 in 1989.

Employees outside the U.S. are generally covered under government sponsored programs and the cost for providing benefits under company plans was not material.

Postretirement health care benefit expense was:

(thousands)	1991
Service cost–benefits attributed to service during the period	$ 3,181
Interest cost on accumulated postretirement benefit obligation	3,828
Actual return on plan assets	(356)
Net amortization and deferral	56
Total expense	$ 6,709

Ecolab: Postretirement Health-Care Benefits (*continued*)

NOTES TO CONSOLIDATED FINANCIAL STATEMENTS

ECOLAB INC.

7. Retirement Plans *(continued)*

The funded status of the postretirement health care plan was:

December 31 (thousands)	1991
Actuarial present value of accumulated postretirement benefit obligation for:	
Retirees	$ 14,406
Fully eligible active participants	7,543
Other active participants	30,606
Total	52,555
Plan assets at fair value	6,235
Plan assets (less than) accumulated postretirement benefit obligation	(46,320)
Unrecognized net (gain)	(56)
Unfunded accrued postretirement health care benefits	$(46,376)

For measurement purposes, 16 percent (for pre-age 65 retirees) and 12 percent (for post-age 65 retirees) annual rates of increase in the per capita cost of covered health care were assumed for 1992. The rates were assumed to decrease gradually to 7 percent and 6 percent, respectively, at 2001 and remain at those levels thereafter. The health care cost trend rate assumption has a significant effect on the amounts reported. To illustrate, increasing the assumed health care cost trend rate by 1 percentage point in each year would increase the accumulated postretirement benefit obligation as of year-end 1991 by approximately $9,000,000 and 1991 expense by approximately $1,500,000.

The discount rate used in determining the accumulated postretirement benefit obligation and the expected long-term rate of return on plan assets were consistent with those of the U.S. pension plan.

Savings Plan

The company provides a 401(k) savings plan for all U.S. employees. Employee contributions of not more than 6 percent of eligible compensation are matched 50 percent by the company. The company's contribution is invested in Ecolab common stock and for continuing operations amounted to $3,550,000 in 1991, $3,402,000 in 1990 and $3,073,000 in 1989.

8. Research Expenditures

Research expenditures for continuing operations which related to the development of new products and processes, including significant improvements and refinements to existing products, were $17,435,000 in 1991, $17,432,000 in 1990 and $15,050,000 in 1989.

9. Rentals and Leases

Rental expense for continuing operations under all operating leases was $28,870,000 in 1991, $32,098,000 in 1990 and $28,676,000 in 1989. As of December 31, 1991, future minimum payments under operating leases with noncancelable terms in excess of one year were:

(thousands)	
1992	$ 10,911
1993	6,422
1994	4,482
1995	2,904
1996	2,556
Thereafter	710
Total	$ 27,985

10. Stock Incentive Plan

The company's Stock Incentive Plan provides for grants of stock options, stock awards and stock appreciation rights. Common shares available for grant as of December 31 were 465,266 for 1991, 46,812 for 1990 and 501,804 for 1989.

Options may be granted to purchase shares of the company's stock at not less than fair market value at the date of grant. Options become exercisable over periods up to six years from date of grant and expire within ten years and three months from date of grant. Stock option transactions were:

Shares	1991	1990	1989
Granted	226,000	492,310	268,600
Exercised	(123,830)	(80,182)	(125,773)
Canceled	(68,600)	(91,468)	(41,532)
December 31:			
Outstanding	1,753,781	1,720,211	1,399,551
Exercisable	897,521	781,901	655,058

Average price per share	1991	1990	1989
Granted	$ 28.61	$ 26.77	$ 28.18
Exercised	16.90	14.28	13.36
Canceled	26.00	26.16	26.48
December 31:			
Outstanding	24.82	23.80	22.37
Exercisable	$ 22.29	$ 20.81	$ 18.77

SOURCE: Ecolab, *Annual Report*, 1991.

Ecolab: Statement of Cash Flows

CONSOLIDATED STATEMENT OF CASH FLOWS			
ECOLAB INC.			
Year ended December 31 (thousands)	1991	1990	1989
Operating Activities			
Net income (loss)	$(243,577)	$ 53,716	$ 3,147
Adjustments:			
Discontinued ChemLawn operations	274,693	4,408	29,379
Cumulative effect of the change in accounting for postretirement health care benefits	24,560		
Income from continuing operations	55,676	58,124	32,526
Adjustments to reconcile income from continuing operations to cash provided:			
Depreciation	43,565	49,855	42,984
Amortization	11,416	10,585	9,659
Deferred income taxes	(3,360)	2,853	(4,881)
Equity in earnings of joint venture, net of royalties received	(1,976)		
Other	(2,157)	1,355	5,505
Changes in operating assets and liabilities:			
Accounts receivable, net	(5,740)	(3,006)	(2,785)
Inventories	(707)	7,739	(3,035)
Other assets	(3,755)	287	480
Accounts payable	6,288	711	13,197
Other liabilities	15,372	227	21,889
Cash provided by (used for) discontinued ChemLawn operations	7,666	17,455	(963)
Cash provided by operating activities	122,288	146,185	114,576
Investing Activities			
Capital expenditures	(51,966)	(57,146)	(53,431)
Property disposals	474	2,145	1,125
Investment in joint venture and Henkel businesses	(131,535)		
Investments in securities	(4,915)	(15,397)	(951)
Other, net	426	(22,549)	(6,341)
Discontinued ChemLawn operations	(5,288)	(10,116)	(11,601)
Cash (used for) investing activities	(192,804)	(103,063)	(71,199)
Financing Activities			
Notes payable	(1,783)	1,055	7,848
Long-term debt additions	185,000		476
Long-term debt reductions	(34,265)	(15,711)	(34,572)
Convertible preferred stock issued			110,000
Reacquired shares	(2,433)	(104,442)	(11,491)
Dividends	(22,027)	(24,387)	(18,008)
Other, net	2,092	768	2,631
Cash provided by (used for) financing activities	126,584	(142,717)	56,884
Effect of exchange rate changes on cash	324	603	(443)
Increase (Decrease) in Cash and Cash Equivalents	56,392	(98,992)	99,818
Cash and Cash Equivalents, at beginning of year	21,227	120,219	20,401
Cash and Cash Equivalents, at end of year	$ 77,619	$ 21,227	$ 120,219

Bracketed amounts indicate a use of cash.

SOURCE: Ecolab, *Annual Report*, 1991.

the direct cash flow effects are likely to be insignificant, although the indirect effects are likely to be more beneficial to future cash flows than would have otherwise been the case.

The cash flow analyst should, however, remove the effect of the amortization of the transition amount, or the catch-up adjustment due to the new standard, from earnings, because it represents a noncash expense just like depreciation. The cash flow analyst should also add the difference between the net obligation (excess benefits over assets) and the amount incorporated in the balance sheet to total debt. Just as for pensions, this amount represents an additional off-balance-sheet liability that should be incorporated as total debt.

Example:

Ecolab Inc. decided to adopt FAS No. 106 in its 1991 financial statements. As can be seen from its Notes to Consolidated Financial Statements, which detail its footnote on the adoption of FAS No. 106, the pretax expense in 1991 more than tripled by the standard and the net effect on the income statement was to reduce net earnings by $24.6 million. However, the adoption of the standard had no effect on cash flows in 1991 as can be seen in the Statement of Cash Flows. In 1991, Ecolab added the cumulative effect of the change of $24.56 million to the net loss for the period to derive the net cash flows from operations, because the adoption reduced earnings but not cash flows. Note that, consistent with what we saw in Chapter 5, Ecolab had a similar level of net operating cash flows in 1991 to those in prior years, although its income substantially decreased due to the expected loss on the discontinued operations of ChemLawn.

6.9 CONTINGENT LIABILITIES

Another potential off-balance-sheet liability can be found in contingent liabilities. These liabilities are obligations that occurred before the end of the period covered by the financial statements, but whose effect on the financial statements is not clearly determinable. The FASB postulated in FAS No. 5 three degrees of uncertainty— probable, reasonably possible, and remote. The firm must set a liability for expected obligation if it is probable that a liability has been incurred *and* the amount of the liability can be reasonably estimated. For example, when a firm distributes coupons that can be redeemed with purchases of future merchandise, a contingent liability exists and must be accrued. In such a case, it is probable that some coupons will be presented in the future. Furthermore, the firm can reasonably forecast what percentage of the coupons will be presented by the due date. Thus, a liability is accrued on the balance sheet with an offsetting charge against income.

FAS No. 5 specifies that if a contingent liability is probable, but the amount cannot be reasonably estimated, or if the likelihood that a loss occurred is only reasonably possible, a footnote disclosure is necessary. Thus, most legal proceedings against a firm are disclosed in a footnote on contingencies, because the firm either deems their chances of success to be less than probable, or because the firm cannot reasonably estimate the extent of the liability.

The cash flow analyst should closely examine the footnote on contingencies to determine if any events occurred that may affect cash flows in the future, although they had not been given accounting recognition in the financial statements.

Example:

In footnotes to its 1991 financial statements, Kennametal reports the following:

"In 1991, a trial court awarded $7.1 million in damages, plus attorneys' fees in an amount not yet determined, to GTE Products Corporation (GTE) in a patent infringement suit filed against the company in the Federal District Court for the Western District of Virginia. The suit involved an infringement of a GTE patent on certain styles of carbide cutter bits used in the road planning industry. Kennametal is currently appealing the decision.

In connection with this litigation, the company recorded a pretax charge to earnings in fiscal 1991 totalling $6.4 million, or $0.36 per share after tax. While the outcome of the appeal cannot be predicted at this time, management believes that the ultimate resolution of the litigation will not have a material adverse effect on the financial position of the company."

Note that in the above litigation, a loss contingency is probable, and the amount is measurable reasonably well, due to the court's award. Thus, Kennametal recorded a liability on its financial statements, although it still plans to pursue the decision in court. However, Kennametal also reports other litigation that is still pending in its 1991 financial statements:

"In the ordinary course of business, there have been various legal proceedings brought against the company, including certain product liability cases. Since 1984, the company, along with varying numbers of other parties, has been named as a codefendant in numerous complaints which allege that former or existing employees of competitors and customers suffered personal injury as a result of exposure to certain metallurgical substances or other materials during their employment. The involvement of many of the defendants, including the company, is based on assertions that these defendants sold metallurgical materials or other products to the plaintiffs' former or existing employers.

Damages are sought jointly and severally from all defendants, with certain of the complaints seeking both compensatory and punitive damages and others seeking compensatory damages only. The company is vigorously defending these cases and, to date, a significant number of these cases have been either dismissed or settled for a nominal amount. All such dismissed or settled cases have been resolved without a finding of liability of the company. It is management's opinion, based on its evaluation and discussions with outside counsel, that the company has viable defenses to the remaining complaints and that, in any event, this litigation will not have a material adverse effect on the financial position of the company."

The second footnote discloses information about litigation concerning product liability. In this case, the firm had not set up a liability and was merely reporting the fact in a footnote to the financial statements. These liabilities may have a material effect on future cash flows if any of the product liability suits is successful in court. This is well known in the tobacco industry, where investors pay close attention to court cases regarding product liability.

Example:

Scimed Life Systems Inc. disclosed on 9/25/91 that it expected three lawsuits against it due to patent infringement. In reaction to this announcement, the stock price of Scimed dropped 30 percent, although second quarter earnings were up about 70 percent due to a large increase in sales. The lawsuits against the firm were for the segments with the greatest growth, and, theoretically, all the products of the firm were subject to a risk of litigation.

6.10 CONVERTIBLE BONDS

Convertible bonds have the characteristics of straight-debt bonds plus an additional option to purchase a specified number of shares at a fixed price. Thus, the convertible bondholder enjoys a fixed interest payment until the bond reaches maturity, and, at the same time, the bondholder enjoys the option to partake in the capital appreciation of the stock. If the stock of the firm increases in value to a point above the fixed price implicit in the convertible bond, then the convertible bondholder is likely to exercise its option and convert the bond to common stock. In such cases, the convertible bonds should be viewed as equity rather than debt of the firm. However, when the firm's stock sells below the exercise price implicit in the conversion option, the holder is unlikely to convert the bond to common stock and the bond should be considered as part of total debt.

Example:

Hercules has convertible bonds outstanding with a maturity date of 06/30/1999. These bonds pay 6.5 percent interest rate, and as of 8/30/91, every $1,000 bond could have been converted to 28.571 shares of common stock with a common stock price of $40.375, whereas the price of the bond on the same date was $1,140. Assuming the bond was converted to common stock, a bondholder can receive 28.571 common shares, which could be sold in the market place for $1,154 (28.571 x $40.375). Thus, it pays for a bondholder to convert the bonds into common stock, and the bonds should be considered common stock.

Example:

NBI, a company in Chapter 11 bankruptcy, has convertible bonds with coupon rate of 8.25 percent, which will mature on 11/15/2007. The bonds were traded at a price of $137.50 for each $1,000 par value on 8/30/91. On that date, each bond could be converted to 22.727 common shares, which had a market price of $0.141 per share on 8/30/91. Thus, if a bondholder would have converted the bond into common stocks and sold the proceeds immediately, the proceeds from the sale of the common stocks would have been only $3.20 (22.727 × $0.141). Therefore, a bondholder is unlikely to convert the bond into common stock at that time and the convertible bond should be considered debt, not common stock.

6.11 DEFERRED TAXES

Most firms include among the long-term liabilities on their balance sheets a liability for future tax payments, or deferred taxes. This liability has attracted the attention of investors, creditors, managers, and accountants for a long time. At issue is the difference between the tax expense reported in the financial statements and the actual tax payment to the tax authorities. The two are not the same because of different treatments of items for tax and for financial reporting purposes. Some differences are permanent, that is, they are not expected to result in offsetting differences in the future, whereas others are timing or temporary differences.

A firm may depreciate an asset using a straight-line depreciation method for financial reporting purposes and accelerated depreciation schedule for tax purposes. The firm enjoys lower tax payments in the beginning of the asset's life, but greater tax payments toward the latter part of the asset's life. Because the entire amount to be depreciated (the asset original cost) is the same regardless of the depreciation method, the difference between the depreciation for tax and financial reporting purposes is nothing but a timing or temporary difference. However, amortization of goodwill is a financial reporting expense that is not deductible for tax purposes. Thus, a permanent difference exists between the tax expense on the financial statements and on the tax return.

The accounting profession requires firms to record a liability for timing or temporary differences, using the assumption that the situation will be reversed in the future and larger tax payments will be due in the future. Thus, the firm creates a liability on its books for future tax payments. Such a tax liability is not required for permanent differences, presumably because they are not going to be reversed in the future.

Opponents of the deferred tax liability argue that, in reality, firms have a large build up of deferred taxes that will never be paid to the government. They argue that as long as the firm keeps growing and as long as additional temporary differences are obtained, deferred taxes will continue to grow. This is empirically verified by observing the steady growth of the deferred tax liability on most firms' financial statements over the last two decades. Furthermore, the deferred tax liability is never discounted to the present, unlike most other long-term liabilities of the firm. Indeed, this issue has only recently been resolved by the FASB, which issued FAS No. 96 that deals with accounting for income taxes. The effective date of the new standard was deferred with the issuance of FAS No. 100, which deferred it again with FAS No. 103. FAS No. 109 was issued in December 1991, which will become effective in 1993.

Because the cash flow effects of deferred taxes are extremely difficult to ascertain, we recommend that the cash flow analyst *not* include deferred taxes among long-term liabilities of the firm when considering total debt of the firm.

6.12 SUMMARY

In this chapter, we examined the relationship between capital structure of the firm and the firm's ability to generate consistent operating and free cash flows. We showed that firms with stable and large free cash flows are likely to be better off, because they can use these free cash flows to reduce debt, repurchase stock, or take advantage of investment opportunities. Firms with volatile cash flows that issue too much debt are exposed to a greater financial risk.

We also proposed a ratio to measure the firm's ability to retire debt without affecting its growth opportunities—the ratio of total debt to average free cash flows. The higher this ratio is, the less able a firm is to repay its debt without impairing its future growth. The lower this ratio is, the more able the firm is to retire its debt, withstand adverse business conditions, maintain or increase dividends, and repurchase common stock.

However, to apply this ratio properly, the cash flow analyst should consider what constitutes total debt of the firm. We show that certain liabilities are not included on the balance sheet such as operating leases, pensions, other postretirement benefits, contingencies, and so on. In contradistinction, some liabilities that are included on the balance sheet should be excluded from total debt because they represent equity, such as convertible bonds that are likely to be converted, or when there is too much uncertainty about the nature and timing of the liability, such as for deferred taxes.

The next chapter will show how the cash flow analyst can use the relationship between financial structure and free cash flows for portfolio selection.

CHAPTER 7

Free Cash Flow and Portfolio Selection

7.1 INTRODUCTION

In the previous chapters we discussed the differences between operating income, operating cash flows, and free cash flows. We illustrated the derivations of these three measures, reviewed their effects on the financial structure of the firm, and discussed their potential usefulness for portfolio selection. The purpose of this chapter is to compare the performance of portfolios that is based on these three measures, or, to be more precise, on price multiples of earnings, net operating cash flows, and free cash flows.

In this chapter, we describe investment strategies that are based not only on price multiples but on other investment considerations, such as the relationship between debt and free cash flows. We provide results of back-testing these investment strategies, and show the superiority of using free cash flows for investment purposes. In addition, we show the performance of a live portfolio by using an investment strategy that was based on free cash flows.

It is important to provide results on live portfolios as well as results of back-tests of the investment strategies. Superior performance of a live portfolio is stronger evidence about the success of an investment strategy than back-tests of the same strategy. In back-tests of a strategy, many biases may inadvertently be introduced into the study by the researcher. For example, the researcher may not be properly controlling for survivorship bias, timing of information disclosure, missing data, restated data, and so on. Thus, one should attach more credence to evidence about the performance of a live portfolio than the performance of portfolios in back-tests of a strategy. However, back-tests are useful in proving that the portfolio was indeed selected according to a specified strategy. For a live portfolio, the portfolio manager may actually use other decision rules in buying or selling securities that are not explicitly stated in the stipulated strategy. Back-tests ensure that such additional decision rules do not become part of the investment strategy. Therefore, it is useful to report results that are based on back-tests of the investment strategy, as well as results that are based on a live portfolio. We now provide results about both strategies.

7.2 BACK-TESTS OF A P/E STRATEGY

Basu (*Journal of Finance*, 1977) has shown that an investment strategy that is based on P/E ratios can outperform the market index. In particular, Basu showed that portfolios that have a "long" position in securities with low P/E ratios and a "short" position in securities with high P/E ratios consistently obtain excess returns for many years. These excess returns can be earned even after adjusting for transaction costs and dividend yields. Other researchers claim that Basu's results were due to the fact that firms with extreme high or low P/E ratios tended to be small capitalization stocks. Indeed, Keim (*Journal of Financial Economics*, 1981) and Reiganum (*Journal of Financial Economics*, 1981) showed that portfolios of small capitalization firms yielded better returns than the market as a whole. As a reaction to this research, several mutual funds that specialized in small firms became substantially more attractive to investors. However, with the dramatic stock market fall of October 1987, it became evident that these small firms were subject to another dimension of risk—the low level of liquidity that prevents investors from fast or easy liquidation of a position in these securities.

Basu (*Journal of Financial Economics*, 1983) has shown that the P/E effect is independent of the small capitalization effect and that it exists for large firms as well as for small firms. Thus, it seems that an investment strategy that is based on buying firms with low P/E ratios and short selling firms with high P/E ratios may provide excess returns to investors. The rationale behind such an investment strategy is that the P/E ratio may be perceived as the number of years that it would take for the investment in a firm (the price) to be paid back through earnings of the firm. The longer it takes to recapture the original investment, the worse off the investor is. However, one should note that the P/E ratio serves as an indication of a payback period only if one assumes that earnings are equivalent to free cash flows, and only if earnings are expected to remain at the same level. Indeed, some high P/E ratios are justified if the firm's cash flows are expected to grow at higher rates in the future than current rates. Also, the market price presumably adjusts for differential effects on earnings of various accounting methods (Beaver and Dukes, *The Accounting Review*, 1973). In recent years, money managers who based their investment decisions solely on P/E ratios have had an inferior performance.

We back-tested an investment strategy that is based on P/E ratios. To make sure that we did not introduce any survivorship bias into the back-tests, we included in the sample all firms that were available for investment, regardless if they survived at the time the study was conducted. Specifically, firms were selected to the study from the universe of stocks covered by Standard & Poor's Compustat Annual Industrial File, as well as the Compustat Research File. To ensure that the P/E ratio would include the most recent information at the time, we restricted ourselves to firms that had a December fiscal year end. For these firms, we assumed that all financial statement information was available within the first four months of the year. This restriction is intended to reduce the information bias that may be introduced in back-testing. Specifically, one may be using information that was not yet available at the time portfolios are assumed to be formed. For example, if we allowed all firms to be used for the P/E portfolios, we may have sorted firms according to P/E ratios that were based on earnings that were not yet known on the portfolio formation date, because the firm's fiscal year end occurred subsequent to the portfolio formation date. Thus, we formed portfolios on April and held these portfolios until the following April, but included only December fiscal year end firms.

We further restricted our analysis to firms with a market capitalization of at least $50 million as of the portfolio selection date, because we wanted to retain in our portfolios only firms that guaranteed reasonable liquidity in their stock trading. The performance of these portfolios was compared to the performance of the S&P 500 during the same time period.

We repeated the process of portfolio selection for all years from 1980 through 1989. To illustrate the portfolio selection, we ranked all firms that had December fiscal year end in 1980 according to their P/E ratios as of April 1981. At the end of April 1981, the earnings for 1980 are already available, and the price at the end of April 1981 is used to calculate the P/E ratio as of the end of April 1981. We omitted from our analysis firms that had negative earnings because their P/E ratios are ill-defined. We then segregated all firms into ten portfolios according to their P/E ratio and assumed that we held the portfolio until April 1982. We then repeated the process using the P/E ratios as of the end of April 1982, and so on, for all years until April 1990, when we used 1989 earnings and April 1990 prices to calculate the P/E ratios.

The results of this investment strategy are available in Exhibit 7-1. As can be seen in the exhibit, the first decile in the period 5/81–4/82, which had about 107 firms (because the total number of firms was 1,077), had a median P/E ratio of 22.08. The median annual return on this portfolio was -24.7 percent, whereas the return on the S&P 500 Composite Index for the same period was -7.31 percent. Thus, this portfolio considerably underperformed the S&P 500 index. Further examination indicates that the ninth and tenth deciles, with median P/E ratios of 5.85 and 4.91, respectively, had median returns that were positive and amounted to 14.4 percent and 3.9 percent, respectively. Therefore, the investment strategy of buying low P/E firms and selling short high P/E firms seems to be profitable in 1981–1982. Note that although the first and tenth deciles had lower median market capitalization than other deciles, the differences were not that great. So, the assignment of firms to the first or tenth decile is not strictly based on size and most likely is based on the P/E ratio, too.

Further examination of Exhibit 7-1 shows that from 5/82–4/83, while the tenth decile had slightly outperformed the S&P 500 index, the first decile had also outperformed the S&P 500 index. Thus, a strategy of selling short the firms in the first decile and holding long firms in the tenth decile would not have been profitable in 5/82–4/83. This strategy would have been profitable in 5/83–4/84 and 5/84–4/85, but not in any other years. As a matter of fact, the data in the exhibit show that in only four out of ten years did the tenth portfolio of low P/E stocks outperform the S&P 500 index. However, in eight of the ten years, the first portfolio of high P/E stocks underperformed the S&P 500 index, so that shorting this portfolio could have yielded superior returns. Given the greater transaction costs associated with short selling, as well as the greater risk associated with short selling, it seems the investment strategy that is based

Exhibit 7-1 Results of Investments Based on Price/Earning Ratios

PE Portfolio	5/81–4/82			5/82–4/83			5/83–4/84			5/84–4/85		
	P/E	Annual Return	Market Value	P/E	Annual Return	Market Value	P/E	Annual Return	Market Value	P/E	Annual Return	Market Value
First decile Median	22.08	-24.70	220.0	21.21	51.79	162.6	29.48	-13.21	182.0	26.71	-5.03	200.7
Second decile Median	15.10	-22.56	377.0	13.21	55.83	239.4	21.25	-4.20	317.4	18.76	7.55	210.4
Third decile Median	12.33	-16.44	488.7	10.40	41.35	327.5	17.27	-3.61	251.3	15.37	8.98	283.8
Fourth decile Median	10.30	-10.08	386.0	8.87	46.57	286.2	14.71	-1.04	294.4	13.35	15.12	360.6
Fifth decile Median	9.06	-10.98	375.4	7.65	38.87	338.4	12.77	3.14	302.7	11.68	19.28	226.1
Sixth decile Median	7.95	-11.31	412.4	6.92	47.91	419.4	10.79	3.93	378.9	10.17	18.20	331.9
Seventh decile Median	7.24	-7.94	277.4	6.30	39.69	239.4	9.21	9.80	309.6	8.96	24.33	276.3
Eighth decile Median	6.55	-1.05	327.7	5.73	38.96	258.8	7.92	8.43	406.4	7.91	36.88	261.1
Ninth decile Median	5.85	14.40	522.5	5.10	43.85	262.6	7.04	9.48	313.0	6.86	40.40	263.6
Tenth decile Median	4.91	3.90	161.2	4.22	52.76	193.8	5.96	9.05	229.8	5.39	45.54	422.0
Overall Median	8.47	-9.58	329.9	7.28	44.83	263.2	11.99	1.62	294.4	10.92	21.87	276.9
S&P 500 Composite	8.96	-7.31		7.58	48.95		13.01	1.66		11.41	17.63	
Number of firms	1077.00			1137.00			1171.00			1261.00		

continued

Exhibit 7-1 *(continued)*

PE Portfolio	5/85–4/86 P/E	5/85–4/86 Annual Return	5/85–4/86 Market Value	5/86–4/87 P/E	5/86–4/87 Annual Return	5/86–4/87 Market Value	5/87–4/88 P/E	5/87–4/88 Annual Return	5/87–4/88 Market Value	5/88–4/89 P/E	5/88–4/89 Annual Return	5/88–4/89 Market Value
First decile Median	26.56	19.37	214.6	31.43	15.14	230.8	31.88	-4.93	319.5	30.62	8.34	221.4
Second decile Median	18.27	33.65	322.3	23.44	9.74	413.2	23.62	-9.17	421.1	21.38	7.18	499.5
Third decile Median	14.89	27.32	275.3	19.62	11.15	300.3	19.94	-1.99	478.2	17.86	10.23	308.9
Fourth decile Median	12.84	35.92	291.3	17.04	12.99	449.9	17.61	-4.43	502.5	15.44	14.44	490.9
Fifth decile Median	11.27	32.38	359.7	15.07	11.70	360.6	15.50	-1.33	346.2	13.71	16.80	358.7
Sixth decile Median	10.16	40.99	354.5	13.50	7.25	297.5	13.94	-0.61	233.2	12.27	12.16	470.9
Seventh decile Median	9.33	40.54	299.3	12.10	8.55	485.3	12.47	-7.50	315.5	11.03	15.53	352.0
Eighth decile Median	8.44	39.90	349.9	11.00	9.59	424.7	10.95	0.06	499.7	9.91	13.74	516.1
Ninth decile Median	7.67	44.56	387.0	9.68	12.82	520.3	9.64	-1.99	612.2	8.60	17.58	464.5
Tenth decile Median	5.91	37.05	414.2	7.26	9.31	386.3	6.72	-17.99	355.2	5.72	20.00	287.6
Overall Median	10.73	36.59	322.3	14.17	10.57	366.7	14.76	-4.05	398.4	12.96	13.66	373.5
S&P 500 Composite	10.81	36.19		16.12	26.53		19.92	-6.44		14.93	22.78	
Number of firms		1331.00			1285.00			1230.00			1315.00	

266

Exhibit 7-1 *(continued)*

PE Portfolio	5/89–4/90			5/90–4/91		
	P/E	Annual Return	Market Value	P/E	Annual Return	Market Value
First decile Median	28.75	2.18	236.4	29.05	-2.79	335.6
Second decile Median	20.39	1.34	441.5	20.95	15.94	382.9
Third decile Median	16.78	4.61	511.8	17.08	10.98	437.2
Fourth decile Median	14.89	-0.64	489.6	14.88	8.61	480.7
Fifth decile Median	13.13	7.41	370.9	12.81	13.47	516.9
Sixth decile Median	11.46	3.80	370.1	11.27	13.56	315.7
Seventh decile Median	10.33	6.31	578.3	10.19	14.93	524.6
Eighth decile Median	9.36	2.41	541.8	8.95	14.07	368.7
Ninth decile Median	7.95	-0.50	658.3	7.74	12.12	629.0
Tenth decile Median	5.82	-7.57	352.4	5.54	5.70	402.1
Overall Median	12.27	2.23	442.8	11.97	10.90	427.0
S&P 500 Composite	13.04	10.44		14.46	17.57	
Number of firms	1350.00			1287.00		

on P/E ratios might not be worthwhile for many investors.[1] Figures 7-1 and 7-2 show the performance of the portfolios with the lowest and the highest P/E ratios. It is easily seen from the two figures that an investment strategy that is based only on buying low P/E stocks would have underperformed the market in recent years. The portfolio of high P/E ratios underperformed the market, but was riskier because it required short selling. Thus, it is useful to examine other investment strategies.

Figure 7-1   Performance of Portfolios with High P/E Ratios (May–April)

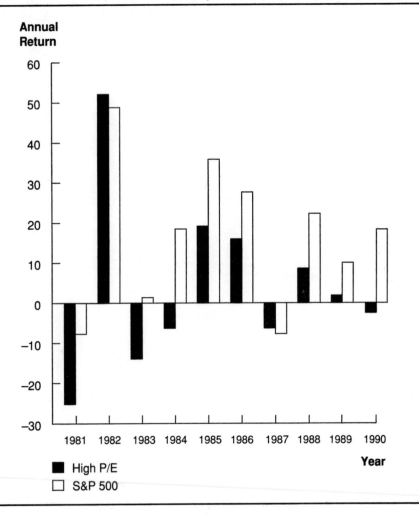

---

[1]Since shorted stock must be borrowed, a short-seller of an illiquid stock may be confronted with having to constantly buy back stock, or even not be able to short in the first place if the stock cannot be borrowed.

7.3 BACK-TESTS OF NET OPERATING CASH FLOW MULTIPLES

The investment strategy that is based on P/E ratios assumed that one wants to invest in firms with low P/E ratios because these firms have shorter investment recapture periods. As we explained earlier, this is true if one assumes that earnings and free cash flows are very close to each other and that such cash flows will grow at least at the same rate in the future. As an alternative to P/E ratios, one can use the net operating cash flow multiple, which can be defined as market value of equity divided by the net operating cash flow. This multiple uses as the denominator the net cash flow generated by operations, or, if one wishes to abstract from an extreme observation

Figure 7-2   Performance of Portfolios with Low P/E Ratios (May–April)

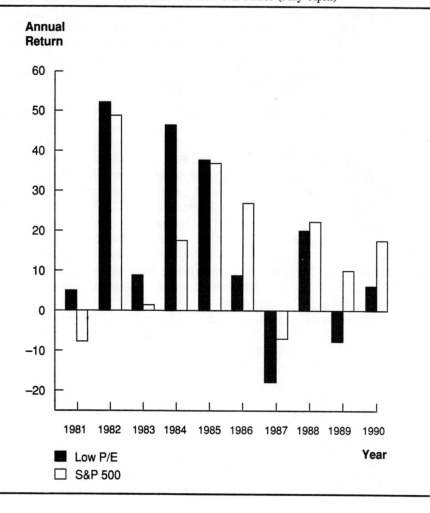

in a particular year, the average cash flow generated from operations over the most recent four years.

The net operating cash flow multiple can be more useful than the P/E ratio for several reasons. The P/E ratio is affected by accounting methods that underlie the earnings computation in general and the earnings-per-share computations in particular. Net operating cash flows, on the other hand, are free from many of the assumptions that underlie earnings and is less influenced by managerial selection of accounting methods. Net operating cash flow is probably a better measure of cash flow returned on the investment in the business than is earnings. Moreover, by averaging net operating cash flows over the most recent four years, we get a better measure of expected net cash flows in the future.

Example:

Tandy Corp. reports in its 1991 statement of cash flows a sale of customer receivables that contributed about $350 million to net operating cash flows, which totaled about $617 million in 1991. (Net operating cash flows were $58 million in 1990 and $353 million in 1989.) The sale increased operating cash flows, thereby producing an artificially low net operating cash flow multiple for 1991. Thus, an averaging of cash flows over four years may abstract from temporary increases in operating cash flows.

To examine the performance of the net operating cash flow multiple for investment in securities, we again formed portfolios, this time according to the net operating cash flow multiples. We first estimated the components of operating cash flows for all firms during the period 1977–1989 and obtained an estimate of net operating cash flows. We then defined the net operating cash flow multiple as the current market value of equity divided by the four-year average net operating cash flows. For example, we used the average net operating cash flows during the four years 1977–1980, together with the market value of equity at the end of April 1981, to form ten portfolios according to the net operating cash flow multiple. As before, we restricted our selection to firms with December fiscal year end, and to firms that had positive average net operating cash flows. The performance of each of the portfolios is measured by the median return on the portfolio and is compared to the performance of the S&P 500 index. It is expected that portfolios based on low net operating cash flow multiples will outperform the market, whereas portfolios based on high net operating cash flow multiples will underperform the S&P 500 index. The results for portfolios based on the net operating cash flow multiples are reported in Exhibit 7-2.

As can be seen in Exhibit 7-2, for the period 5/81–4/82 the returns on the high net operating cash flow multiples are indeed much worse than the return on the S&P 500 index. However, the returns on the portfolios with low net operating cash flow multiples, that is, the portfolios marked by ninth and tenth deciles did not generate returns in 5/81–4/82 that were superior to the S&P 500 index. As with the P/E portfolios, the extreme portfolios have lower market capitalization, although it is more emphasized for the low net operating cash flows multiples. Note that the number of observations drops, as compared to portfolios based on P/E ratios. This is to be

Exhibit 7–2   Results of Investments Based on Operating Cash Flow Multiples

OCF Portfolio	5/81–4/82			5/82–4/83			5/83–4/84			5/84–4/85		
	OCF Multiple	Annual Return	Market Value	OCF Multiple	Annual Return	Market Value	OCF Multiple	Annual Return	Market Value	OCF Multiple	Annual Return	Market Value
First decile Median	28.6	-30.51	321.9	27.0	40.07	192.4	29.2	-6.37	335.0	28.6	-2.38	233.1
Second decile Median	21.1	-28.89	241.1	19.5	51.13	195.0	19.1	-11.26	243.4	19.9	12.91	161.7
Third decile Median	17.0	-19.31	384.4	15.2	36.52	430.1	14.9	-2.54	470.9	15.8	20.68	448.1
Fourth decile Median	14.0	-19.84	356.2	13.2	43.16	195.3	12.5	-0.14	276.3	13.3	12.96	257.3
Fifth decile Median	11.1	-21.62	284.5	11.3	47.73	234.1	10.6	-1.62	373.9	11.3	14.78	271.1
Sixth decile Median	9.4	-13.09	447.7	9.4	50.22	302.2	9.0	0.08	261.7	9.8	9.19	271.1
Seventh decile Median	8.1	-11.10	431.8	8.2	47.47	316.3	8.1	-1.91	295.7	8.4	15.90	413.2
Eighth decile Median	6.9	-11.14	357.0	7.2	53.20	321.4	7.1	-3.22	525.8	7.2	7.00	463.3
Ninth decile Median	6.1	-8.94	327.9	6.2	56.39	302.7	6.3	4.38	350.8	6.4	7.57	365.5
Tenth decile Median	5.4	-12.76	283.6	5.4	58.30	338.3	5.3	3.67	295.9	5.5	12.31	374.7
Overall Median	10.3	-15.76	344.3	10.6	47.85	274.2	9.7	-2.14	316.5	10.5	10.88	305.4
S&P 500 Composite		-7.31			48.95			1.66			17.63	
Number of firms	628			549			604			716		

continued

Exhibit 7-2 *(continued)*

OCF Portfolio	5/85–4/86 OCF Multiple	Annual Return	Market Value	5/86–4/87 OCF Multiple	Annual Return	Market Value	5/87–4/88 OCF Multiple	Annual Return	Market Value	5/88–4/89 OCF Multiple	Annual Return	Market Value
First decile Median	27.0	28.23	164.3	28.9	8.09	271.9	31.0	-6.87	317.9	28.8	7.35	278.1
Second decile Median	18.8	34.49	223.0	21.1	10.01	242.2	22.9	-3.35	243.6	20.9	10.89	359.1
Third decile Median	15.1	31.79	429.8	17.4	14.68	462.1	18.3	-5.21	320.1	16.8	7.83	382.4
Fourth decile Median	12.4	36.29	267.0	14.5	18.82	218.3	15.5	-7.39	255.2	14.0	12.01	726.2
Fifth decile Median	10.7	29.44	275.3	12.2	15.59	296.3	12.6	-5.96	445.8	11.8	15.43	364.1
Sixth decile Median	9.2	38.97	247.2	10.6	12.67	350.8	10.8	4.51	527.2	10.4	7.26	407.5
Seventh decile Median	8.1	37.81	330.2	9.0	19.88	320.4	9.4	-2.94	426.5	8.9	10.49	466.4
Eighth decile Median	7.2	39.59	514.0	7.8	14.59	330.7	8.0	-0.82	339.3	7.7	14.97	385.0
Ninth decile Median	6.3	35.05	490.4	6.8	18.23	580.2	6.8	-9.91	410.8	6.5	14.47	383.6
Tenth decile Median	5.5	30.39	457.8	5.5	28.27	544.6	5.7	-3.33	737.9	5.6	12.50	364.2
Overall Median	9.9	34.76	314.8	11.3	16.26	335.8	11.6	-4.00	382.8	11.1	11.85	386.6
S&P 500 Composite		36.19			26.53			-6.44			22.78	
Number of firms		685			758			762			721	

Exhibit 7-2 *(continued)*

OCF Porfolio	5/89–4/90			5/90–4/91		
	OCF *Multiple*	Annual *Return*	Market *Value*	OCF *Multiple*	Annual *Return*	Market *Value*
First decile Median	30.0	-0.50	278.4	31.1	-0.50	285.3
Second decile Median	21.4	0.96	431.0	22.1	10.36	270.4
Third decile Median	17.5	12.80	355.0	17.7	9.79	445.0
Fourth decile Median	14.7	5.08	429.2	14.9	7.92	382.8
Fifth decile Median	12.4	-0.30	562.7	12.9	4.84	306.1
Sixth decile Median	10.8	2.42	517.3	11.1	6.61	656.9
Seventh decile Median	9.3	3.53	558.8	9.5	13.41	327.8
Eighth decile Median	7.9	-3.45	645.8	8.0	5.16	368.1
Ninth decile Median	6.7	1.61	730.1	6.9	7.66	590.9
Tenth decile Median	5.6	-1.02	418.7	5.7	10.95	862.8
Overall Median	11.7	1.60	463.2	11.9	7.67	434.8
S&P 500 Composite		10.44			17.57	
Number of firms		732			765	

Figure 7-3   Portfolios with High Operating Cash Flow Multiples (May–April)

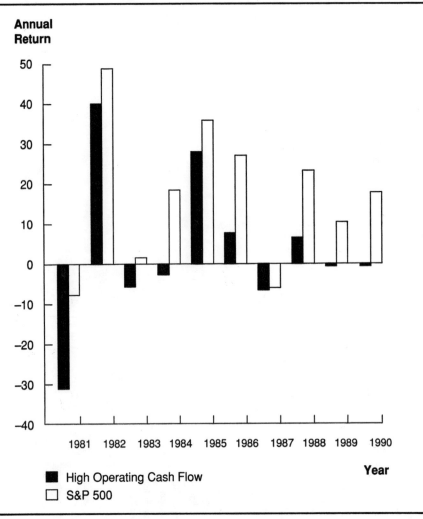

expected given the more stringent data requirements for calculation of the average net operating cash flows.

Further examination of Exhibit 7-2 shows that the low net operating cash flow multiple portfolio, the tenth decile, outperformed the S&P 500 index in 5/82–4/83, 5/83–4/84, 5/86–4/87, and 5/87–4/88. This represents four out of ten years for which we conducted our analysis—not a very impressive record. Further note that in the most recent period, the tenth portfolio consistently underperformed the S&P 500. Thus, the net operating cash flow multiple cannot be used to select firms for long positions in a portfolio that will outperform the market. However, note that the portfolio with high net operating cash flow multiples, the first decile, provided returns that were lower than the returns on the S&P 500 index in all ten years covered in this study. The results for

Figure 7-4 Portfolios with Low Operating Cash Flow Multiples (May–April)

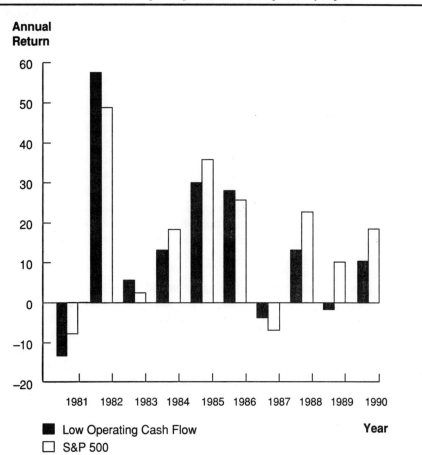

the portfolios with extremely low and high net operating cash flow multiples are portrayed in Figures 7-3 and 7-4. As seen from the figures, a portfolio that is based on short positions in high multiples can yield results that outperform the S&P 500 index. Whether such a strategy is desirable depends, to a great extent, on the investor's preferences. However, the performance of the portfolio with low net operating cash flow multiples cannot be justified in the time period studied.

7.4 LOW DEBT FIRMS WITH LOW NET OPERATING CASH FLOW MULTIPLES

As we saw in Chapter 6, one criterion that may be used to screen firms into or out of portfolios is the extent of their financial leverage. For example, one may desire to hold long positions in firms that have low net operating cash flow multiples, because such firms are more likely to have greater capital appreciation. In addition, one can impose another investment criterion that will, in effect, reduce the financial risk of such firms through the requirement of low financial leverage. To assess whether a firm has low *de-facto* leverage, we can use the debt multiple, which is calculated as *total* debt divided by the four-year average of net operating cash flows. This criterion will assess the extent to which a firm can repay its debt principal out of the cash it generates from operating activities.

To evaluate the performance of an investment strategy that takes into account not only the net operating cash flow multiple but also the debt multiple, we follow these steps. As before, we restrict ourselves to firms that had positive average net operating cash flows and a December fiscal year end. We further require that the debt multiple, that is, total debt divided by average net operating cash flows, will be less than ten. This criterion focuses on firms that could have paid off their principal debt from net operating cash flows within ten years, assuming one does not reinvest these operating cash flows. We then classify firms into portfolios according to their net operating cash flow multiples. However, due to the decrease in the number of firms that have lower debt multiples than ten, we use only five portfolios. The performance of these portfolios is described in Exhibit 7-3.

As can be seen in Exhibit 7-3, during the period 5/81–4/82 the portfolio of firms with low net operating cash flow multiples and low debt, denoted by the fifth quintile in the exhibit, underperformed the S&P 500 index. This portfolio consisted of firms that were probably a little smaller in terms of market capitalization and had slightly higher debt multiples than other firms in our analysis. Further examination of the exhibit shows that this portfolio outperformed the S&P 500 index in only three of the ten years analyzed. Thus, consistent with our prior results, we cannot use the net operating cash flow multiple to select firms for long positions in stocks.

Consistent with our prior findings, the portfolio of firms that had high net operating cash flow multiples and low debt multiples underperformed the S&P 500 index in nine of the ten years studied here. This strategy could be used to select firms into portfolios that hold short positions. This, of course, depends on the risk preferences of the investors. Once again, we portray the performance of the two extreme portfolios in Figures 7-5 and 7-6.

7.5 PERFORMANCE OF A PORTFOLIO BASED ON CASH FLOW MULTIPLES

The investment strategy we recommend is based on market valuation using free cash flow multiples. Recall that free cash flows represent the amount of cash that stockholders can receive without hampering future growth of the firm at its current rate of growth. Thus, a multiple that is based on free cash flows measures more accurately the investment-recapture period. The free cash flow multiple has an additional advantage; it is free from the selection of accounting methods and from managerial decisions about dividends.

The model that we use here to justify the free cash flow multiple is a simple extension of the dividend discount model, with a minor modification; instead of

Exhibit 7-3 Results of Investments Based on Operating Cash Flow Multiples and Low Levels of Debt

OCF Portfolio Low Debt	5/81–4/82				5/82–4/83				5/83–4/84			
	OCF Multiple	Annual Return	Market Value	Debt Multiple	OCF Multiple	Annual Return	Market Value	Debt Multiple	OCF Multiple	Annual Return	Market Value	Debt Multiple
First quintile Median	22.9	-26.98	402.5	4.6	19.3	45.65	286.1	3.7	20.7	-10.71	394.4	3.7
Second quintile Median	14.2	-19.80	352.4	4.4	12.7	41.98	237.6	3.5	13.1	0.39	338.8	3.4
Third quintile Median	9.6	-13.41	423.8	4.4	9.3	46.93	318.1	3.7	9.5	-0.76	309.1	4.3
Fourth quintile Median	7.2	-10.45	405.3	4.9	7.3	52.48	343.7	4.7	7.3	-0.91	395.7	3.8
Fifth quintile Median	5.7	-9.53	360.7	5.1	5.7	52.73	355.5	4.6	5.9	3.67	350.4	4.7
Overall Median	9.6	-15.18	383.2	4.8	9.3	48.00	318.3	4.2	9.5	-1.51	377.6	3.9
S&P 500 Composite		-7.31				48.95				1.66		
Number of firms			499				416				469	

OCF Portfolio Low Debt	5/84–4/85				5/85–4/86				5/86–4/87			
	OCF Multiple	Annual Return	Market Value	Debt Multiple	OCF Multiple	Annual Return	Market Value	Debt Multiple	OCF Multiple	Annual Return	Market Value	Debt Multiple
First quintile Median	22.2	11.71	255.5	3.6	20.7	29.45	244.9	3.2	22.3	13.48	283.1	3.4
Second quintile Median	13.5	18.66	309.8	3.4	12.7	37.25	426.9	3.0	14.7	17.46	321.1	3.5
Third quintile Median	9.9	14.97	373.5	3.7	9.5	41.68	286.2	3.7	10.9	15.03	327.9	3.8
Fourth quintile Median	7.5	9.90	368.1	3.7	7.4	40.95	496.3	4.5	8.2	25.00	746.2	4.4
Fifth quintile Median	5.8	7.91	419.8	4.4	5.8	35.35	518.8	3.7	5.9	20.33	596.0	4.7
Overall Median	9.9	13.02	348.5	3.8	9.5	36.70	411.6	3.8	11.0	17.20	398.2	4.0
S&P 500 Composite		17.63				36.19				26.53		
Number of firms			573				532				563	

continued

Exhibit 7-3 (continued)

5/87–4/88

OCF Portfolio Low Debt	OCF Multiple	Annual Return	Market Value	Debt Multiple
First quintile Median	23.9	-5.08	465.0	3.4
Second quintile Median	15.4	-7.58	292.4	4.0
Third quintile Median	10.8	-0.39	570.3	4.5
Fourth quintile Median	8.2	-1.91	432.7	4.1
Fifth quintile Median	6.2	-4.79	549.1	5.2
Overall Median	10.8	-3.32	433.7	4.3
S&P 500 Composite		-6.44		
Number of firms			561	

5/88–4/89

OCF Portfolio Low Debt	OCF Multiple	Annual Return	Market Value	Debt Multiple
First quintile Median	22.4	5.75	497.4	3.3
Second quintile Median	13.8	11.48	716.7	4.5
Third quintile Median	10.2	9.09	487.7	4.8
Fourth quintile Median	7.9	10.39	420.5	4.5
Fifth quintile Median	5.9	14.44	561.4	5.3
Overall Median	10.2	10.86	534.6	4.4
S&P 500 Composite		22.78		
Number of firms			522	

5/89–4/90

OCF Portfolio Low Debt	OCF Multiple	Annual Return	Market Value	Debt Multiple
First quintile Median	21.5	8.20	347.5	3.8
Second quintile Median	14.4	5.45	646.0	4.2
Third quintile Median	10.8	1.54	651.3	4.6
Fourth quintile Median	8.0	-1.12	784.8	4.6
Fifth quintile Median	6.1	0.73	511.1	4.7
Overall Median	10.8	3.15	587.8	4.4
S&P 500 Composite		10.44		
Number of firms			—	

5/90–4/91

OCF Portfolio Low Debt	OCF Multiple	Annual Return	Market Value	Debt Multiple
First quintile Median	22.8	13.61	569.7	3.8
Second quintile Median	15.4	13.52	540.8	4.0
Third quintile Median	11.2	6.50	634.5	4.4
Fourth quintile Median	8.3	10.19	434.8	4.9
Fifth quintile Median	6.2	11.54	946.8	4.9
Overall Median	11.2	10.35	617.9	4.4
S&P 500 Composite		17.57		
Number of firms			—	

Figure 7-5   Portfolios with High Operating Cash Flow Multiples and Low Debt (May–April)

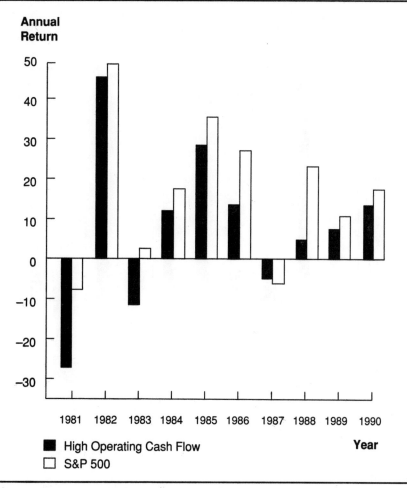

dividends, we use free cash flows as the variable of interest. This makes sense because management has discretion over the amount of cash that it decides to distribute. However, management has almost no discretion over free cash flows as we defined it before. Similarly, when a firm pays no dividend, the dividend discount model will show a value of zero for the stock, unless some arbitrary number is substituted for dividend (such as earnings times an assumed payout ratio). For our simple model, there is no need to worry about the dividend policy of the firm.

Let us define the variables that we use in the analysis:

V_t = The value of the firm at the end of period t. We assume that period 0 is the current period.

FCF_t = The free cash flow generated during period t. For simplicity we assume that the free cash flow is generated at the end of period t.

Figure 7-6   Portfolios with Low Operating Cash Flow Multiples and Low Debt (May–April)

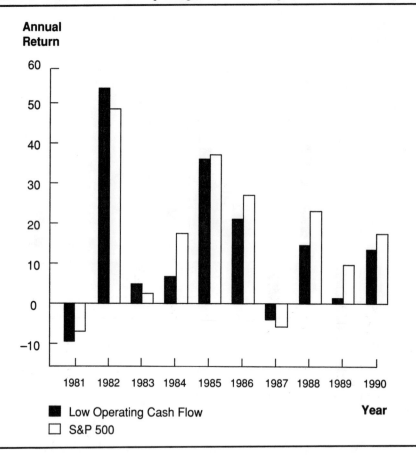

k = The required rate of return on the security of the firm. The required rate of return is assumed constant across periods.

r = The growth rate of free cash flows from period to period. This rate is assumed constant across periods, i.e., free cash flows grow by a rate of r every period.

M = The free cash flow multiple, that is, V_t/FCF_t.

The current market value of the firm is equal to the present value of the free cash flow in the next period and the market value at the end of the next period. Formally,

$$V_0 = \frac{FCF_1}{1 + k} + \frac{V_1}{1 + k} \tag{7-1}$$

Substituting for V_1 in the above equation the present value of the free cash flow in period two, FCF_2, plus the value at the end of period 2, V_2, we get,

$$V_0 = \frac{FCF_1}{1 + k} + \frac{FCF_2}{(1 + k)^2} + \frac{V_2}{(1 + k)^2} . \tag{7-2}$$

Similar substitutions for all future values of the firm yield,

$$V_0 = \frac{FCF_1}{1 + k} + \frac{FCF_2}{(1 + k)^2} + \frac{FCF_3}{(1 + k)^3} + \ldots \tag{7-3}$$

Assuming that free cash flows grow at a constant rate, r, we get the following series:

$$V_0 = \frac{FCF_0 (1 + r)}{(1 + k)} + \frac{FCF_0 (1 + r)^2}{(1 + k)^2} + \frac{FCF_0 (1 + r)^3}{(1 + k)^3} + \ldots \tag{7-4}$$

Using the formula for a sum of a geometric series and assuming that k is larger than r, we get,

$$V_0 = FCF_0 \sum_{t=1}^{\infty} \left[\frac{(1 + r)}{(1 + k)} \right]^t = FCF_0 \frac{(1 + r)}{(1 + k)} \frac{1}{\left[1 - \frac{(1 + r)}{(1 + k)} \right]} . \tag{7-5}$$

After some simplifications, this yields,

$$V_0 = FCF_0 \frac{(1 + r)}{(k - r)} . \tag{7-6}$$

Thus, we get the following free cash flow multiple:

$$M = \frac{V_0}{FCF_0} = \frac{(1 + r)}{(k - r)} . \tag{7-7}$$

We can discover the theoretical multiple for combinations of the growth rate of free cash flows, r, and the difference between the required rate of return and the growth rate of free cash flows, $k - r$. Exhibit 7-4 illustrates the theoretical multiple for several such combinations.

As seen in the exhibit, the free cash flow multiple is very sensitive to the difference between the required rate of return and the assumed growth rate of free cash flows. For example, when the required rate of return, k, exceeds the growth rate of free cash flows, r, by more than 6 percent, it is unlikely that the free cash flow multiple will exceed 20. For a security with a 15 percent cost of capital and a 5 percent growth rate of free cash flows, the theoretical free cash flow multiple from the table should be 10.50 ($r = 0.05$ and $k - r = 0.10$).

To apply the above model, one needs to estimate the current free cash flow, FCF_0, the required rate of return, k, and the expected growth rate of free cash flows, r. We estimate the current free cash flow by the four-year average of free cash flows, as explained in Chapter 5. However, we do not attempt to estimate the required rate of return and the growth rate of free cash flows for each firm. Instead, we require that firms we select into the portfolio have a maximum free cash flow multiple of 20. This seems intuitively appealing if one assumes a spread of at least 5 percentage points between the required rate of return and the growth rate of free cash flows, as seen in Exhibit 7-4.

One limitation of this model is that it does not seem to address the problem of firms with negative free cash flows. There are several ways to apply the valuation model for firms with negative free cash flows. The most obvious way is to focus on firms with positive average free cash flows in the most recent four years. Thus, even if a firm had a negative free cash flow in any particular year, the model is applicable so long as the average free cash flow is positive. Another approach is to estimate the growth rate in *future* free cash flows and estimate the next period's free cash flows. Recall that the model uses *future* cash flows for valuation, and not past cash flows. Past cash flows are useful only when they help us predict future free cash flows. Finally, one can "impute" positive free cash flows by examining firms in the same industry that are similar in composition to the firm under analysis.

Sample Selection

To select firms for the portfolio, we restrict ourselves to firms with December fiscal year end, which had the necessary data to calculate free cash flows during the period 1977–1989. The restriction to December fiscal year-end firms is intended to make sure

Exhibit 7-4   Theoretical Free Cash Flow Multiples for Several Combinations of r and $k-r$.

Growth Rate FCF $(-r)$	The excess of cost of capital over the growth rate in FCF $(k - r)$									
	0.01	*0.02*	*0.03*	*0.04*	*0.05*	*0.06*	*0.07*	*0.08*	*0.09*	*0.10*
0.01	101.00	50.50	33.67	25.25	20.20	16.83	14.43	12.63	11.22	10.10
0.02	102.00	51.00	34.00	25.50	20.40	17.00	14.57	12.75	11.33	10.20
0.03	103.00	51.50	34.33	25.75	20.60	17.17	14.71	12.88	11.44	10.30
0.04	104.00	52.00	34.67	26.00	20.80	17.33	14.86	13.00	11.56	10.40
0.05	105.00	52.50	35.00	26.25	21.00	17.50	15.00	13.13	11.67	10.50
0.06	106.00	53.00	35.33	26.50	21.20	17.67	15.14	13.25	11.78	10.60
0.07	107.00	53.50	35.67	26.75	21.40	17.83	15.29	13.38	11.89	10.70
0.08	108.00	54.00	36.00	27.00	21.60	18.00	15.43	13.50	12.00	10.80
0.09	109.00	54.50	36.33	27.25	21.80	18.17	15.57	13.63	12.11	10.90
0.10	110.00	55.00	36.67	27.50	22.00	18.33	15.71	13.75	12.22	11.00
0.11	111.00	55.50	37.00	27.75	22.20	18.50	15.86	13.88	12.33	11.10
0.12	112.00	56.00	37.33	28.00	22.40	18.67	16.00	14.00	12.44	11.20
0.13	113.00	56.50	37.67	28.25	22.60	18.83	16.14	14.13	12.56	11.30
0.14	114.00	57.00	38.00	28.50	22.80	19.00	16.29	14.25	12.67	11.40

that data necessary to estimate free cash flows were indeed available to market participants at the portfolio formation date (April 30 of the next year). We began the selection process by estimating the average free cash flows over the most recent four years for each of our firms. We then divided the market value of equity by the average free cash flows. We restricted our portfolio to firms that had positive average free cash flows and that had free cash flow multiples below 20, which we believe represents a fair valuation, based on Exhibit 7-4 and the average free cash flow multiple for the S&P 500. We further deleted firms that had debt multiples above ten, where the debt multiple is found by dividing total debt by the average free cash flows. This restriction is intended to select firms that not only have low free cash flow multiples, but can also easily repay the principal of their debt within ten years from their excess cash flows. Finally, we required that the four-year and eight-year growth rate of free cash flows be positive. It is important to exclude firms that cannot maintain their levels of free cash flows or are cannibalizing their assets or operations to produce free cash flows. Recall that one of the investment criterion we postulated is the consistency of free cash flows. This can be examined through the growth rates in free cash flows.

Exhibit 7-5 contains information about the performance of this investment portfolio. The number of stocks that pass the investment criteria in any particular year is very small, about 20 to 60 stocks. These securities are not small, as can be seen from the median market value in the various years. Thus, the excess returns on this portfolio are not due to additional risk assumed by small size firms.

Figure 7-7 portrays the performance of the portfolio as compared to the S&P 500 index. As can be seen from the figure and the exhibit, the portfolio of low free cash flow multiples and low debt multiples outperformed the S&P 500 in nine of the ten years that we studied. Further note that the portfolio is particularly helpful during years

Exhibit 7-5   Results of Investments Based on Low Free Cash Flow Multiples and Low Debt

Year	Number of Firms	Annual Return	S&P 500 Return	Market Value	FCF Multiple
5/81–4/82	22	4.27	-7.31	694.1	14.1
5/82–4/83	23	59.90	48.95	512.9	12.9
5/83–4/84	46	6.24	1.66	780.0	13.2
5/84–4/85	62	27.34	17.63	770.4	12.6
5/85–4/86	37	40.69	36.19	1871.6	14.2
5/86–4/87	21	23.39	26.53	972.9	14.1
5/87–4/88	22	4.01	-6.44	1474.5	13.5
5/88–4/89	20	24.90	22.78	2758.5	15.0
5/89–4-90	24	11.85	10.44	2528.9	13.5
5/90–4/91	27	17.67	17.57	5971.9	15.0

Figure 7-7   Portfolios with Low Free Cash Flow Multiples and Low Debt (May–April)

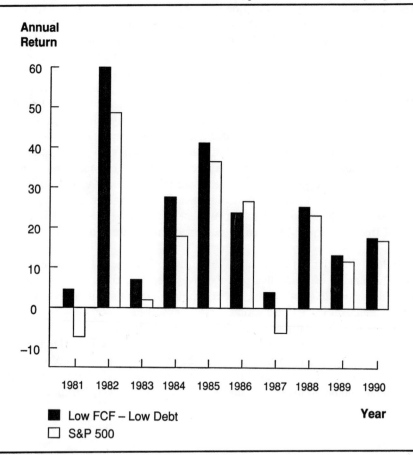

in which the market as a whole declines, as is evidenced for the periods 5/81–4/82 and 5/87–4/88. In both of these periods, the portfolio of low free cash flow multiples yielded positive returns, exceeding the market significantly.

The preceding results indicate the usefulness of the free cash flows in portfolio selection.

7.6 PERFORMANCE OF A LIVE PORTFOLIO

The discussion in the previous sections of this chapter revolved around an investment strategy that is implemented by back-testing the strategy. However, what seems to work well in back-testing may not work when implemented on a live portfolio. Sometimes the researcher is not careful enough to eliminate all possible biases that are inherent in an *ex-post* analysis. Furthermore, in reality, portfolio managers make decisions in a manner that cannot be entirely captured by any investment strategy. For example, our investment strategy called for portfolio formation once a year and holding the securities in a portfolio for an entire year. Our investment strategy also assumed that we invest an equal amount in each security in the portfolio. In reality, portfolio managers hold different proportions of the portfolio in each of the individual securities. They also examine the performance of securities in the portfolio throughout the year, purchasing additional securities or selling securities according to their market conditions. Another difference between back-tests and a live portfolio relates to the effects that trades have on market prices. When a large block of securities is traded, the effect on the market price may be such that the transaction cannot be implemented at the price that is assumed in the back-test of the model. Thus, it is impossible to design a back-test of an investment strategy that will replicate real-life decisions by a professional money manager. We therefore provide evidence about the performance of a live portfolio that is selected according to the concept of free cash flows.

Systematic Financial Management, Inc., which managed about $500 million at the time of publication of this book, and of which co-author Kenneth Hackel is the president, has managed portfolios that are based on the free cash flow concept stipulated throughout this book. To be included in Systematic's portfolio, a firm must have a market capitalization of at least $200 million. It has to have a low free cash flow multiple, usually below 20. The free cash flow multiple is defined as the current market value of the common equity divided by the average free cash flows over the most recent four years. The firm usually has total debt that is less than 40 percent of its net worth. The firm generally has a low debt multiple, that is, total debt divided by the average free cash flows is less than five. Finally, the firm must exhibit strong growth rates in operating and free cash flows over the most recent four and eight years and show consistent free cash flows over a long horizon that will include at least one business cycle.

Exhibit 7-6 reports the results of a composite of Systematic's fully discretionary portfolios since the beginning of 1981. Note that, unlike the data presented before in the back-tests, data here refer to actual quarters or calendar years. In our back-tests, we wanted to avoid using information that was not available to market participants at the time portfolios were formed. Thus, we selected to the back-test portfolio only firms with December fiscal year end and formed the portfolios at the beginning of April each year. Here we report the results of live portfolios, which include actual securities in the portfolio and the return on this portfolio for the calendar quarter or year. We also portray the results of this portfolio in Figure 7-8.

As can be seen in the exhibit and the figure, the live portfolio outperforms the S&P 500 index in seven out of the ten years presented. Its total performance since inception is superior to the S&P 500, as seen from the mountain chart in Figure 7-9 and the accumulated value of a $100 investment in Exhibit 7-6. Note that the live portfolio usually outperforms the S&P 500 index in quarters when the market is down. This indicates that firms with solid records of free cash flows do not suffer as much from market declines. This is why Systematic is viewed as a conservative equity manager by pension sponsor consultants.

Exhibit 7-6 Performance Record Equity Portfolio

Quarter/Year	SFM Equity Portfolio	SFM Dollar Value	S&P 500	S&P 500 Dollar Value
4/80	—	100.0	—	100.0
1/81	8.7%	108.7	1.4%	101.4
2/81	8.2%	117.6	-2.3%	99.1
3/81	-11.1%	104.5	-10.3%	88.9
4/81	14.9%	120.1	6.9%	95.1
Year 1981	20.1%		-4.9%	
1/82	0.1%	120.2	-7.2%	88.3
2/82	2.1%	122.7	-0.6%	87.8
3/82	14.6%	140.6	11.5%	97.9
4/82	14.0%	160.3	18.2%	115.6
Year 1982	33.5%		21.6%	
1/83	13.6%	182.1	10.0%	127.2
2/83	12.6%	205.0	11.1%	141.3
3/83	1.5%	208.1	-0.1%	141.2
4/83	0.0%	208.1	0.4%	141.7
Year 1983	29.8%		22.5%	
1/84	-1.9%	204.1	-2.4%	138.3
2/84	-3.1%	197.8	-2.6%	134.7
3/84	6.5%	210.7	9.7%	147.8
4/84	5.1%	221.4	1.9%	150.6
Year 1984	6.4%		6.3%	
1/85	14.5%	253.5	9.2%	164.5
2/85	4.2%	264.1	7.4%	176.7
3/85	-2.2%	258.3	-4.1%	169.5
4/85	14.4%	295.5	17.2%	198.7
Year 1985	33.5%		31.8%	
1/86	11.1%	328.3	14.1%	226.7
2/86	2.0%	334.9	5.9%	240.1
3/86	-1.6%	329.5	-7.0%	223.3
4/86	2.3%	337.1	5.6%	235.7
Year 1986	14.1%		18.6%	
1/87	17.5%	396.1	21.4%	286.1
2/87	1.0%	400.1	5.0%	300.4
3/87	6.5%	426.1	6.6%	320.2
4/87	-17.3%	352.4	-22.6%	247.9
Year 1987	4.5%		5.2%	
1/88	17.5%	414.1	5.7%	262.0
2/88	6.6%	441.4	6.6%	279.3
3/88	1.5%	448.0	0.4%	280.4
4/88	1.5%	454.7	3.0%	288.8
Year 1988	29.0%		16.5%	
1/89	4.9%	477.0	7.1%	309.3
2/89	9.0%	519.9	8.7%	336.2
3/89	10.5%	574.5	10.7%	372.2
4/89	0.0%	574.5	2.1%	380.0
Year 1989	26.3%		31.6%	
1/90	-2.0%	563.0	-3.0%	368.6
2/90	5.6%	594.5	6.3%	391.8
3/90	-13.1%	516.6	-13.7%	338.1
4/90	13.4%	585.8	8.9%	368.2
Year 1990	2.0%		-3.1%	
1/91	15.9%	678.9	14.5%	421.6
2/91	1.5%	689.1	-0.2%	420.8
3/91	3.6%	713.9	5.2%	442.7

Annual Performance Summary Percent As of September 30, 1991

Year-to-Date				
(9 Months)	21.9%		20.2%	
1 Year	38.2%		30.9%	
3 Years	16.8%		16.4%	
5 Years	16.7%		14.7%	
7 Years	19.0%		17.0%	
10 Years	21.2%		17.4%	
Since inception				
(10 3/4 years)	20.1%		14.8%	

Figure 7-8   Live Portfolios with Low Free Cash Flow Multiples and Low Debt
(January–December)

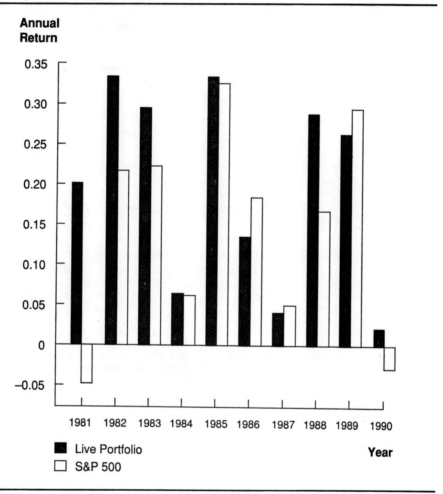

Figure 7-9   Systematic Financial Management, Inc. Mountain Chart Performance Comparison

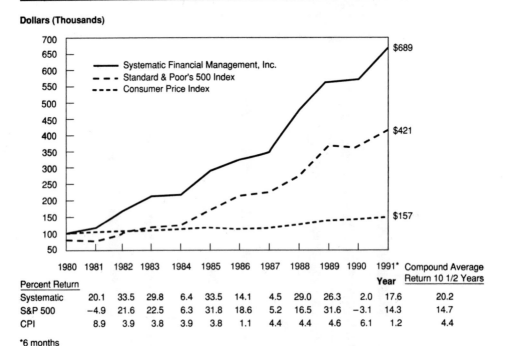

Dollars (Thousands)

Percent Return	1980	1981	1982	1983	1984	1985	1986	1987	1988	1989	1990	1991* Year	Compound Average Return 10 1/2 Years
Systematic	20.1	33.5	29.8	6.4	33.5	14.1	4.5	29.0	26.3	2.0	17.6		20.2
S&P 500	-4.9	21.6	22.5	6.3	31.8	18.6	5.2	16.5	31.6	-3.1	14.3		14.7
CPI	8.9	3.9	3.8	3.9	3.8	1.1	4.4	4.4	4.6	6.1	1.2		4.4

*6 months

The chart shows that a $100,000 investment achieving the same rate of return as a composite of Systematic Financial Management's accounts beginning on January 1, 1981 would have increased to a value of $689,000 on June 30, 1991. Over the same period, the value of a $100,000 investment that achieved a return equal to that of the Standard & Poor's 500 Index (S&P 500) or equal to the rate of increase in the Consumer Price Index (CPI) would have increased to $421,000 and $157,000 respectively. The CPI is used as a measure of inflation.

Systematic's performance information includes reinvestment of all income and gains and is determined on a time-weighted average. Results for the S&P 500 have been adjusted to reflect the reinvestment of dividends and income, but do not reflect transaction costs.

Beginning with 1991, Systematic has deducted its average advisory fee rate of 0.75% in determining performance results. Advisory fees were not deducted for periods prior to 1991, except for 1981. Advisory fees vary among accounts, and certain brokers charge a flat "wrap fee", which includes the advisory fee and all brokerage commissions. While Systematic has deducted all brokerage commissions for accounts which are not subject to wrap fees, Systematic has deducted wrap fees only to the extent of Systematic's average advisory fee rate. Please contact Systematic if you would like information as to what Systematic's performance data would reflect if your advisory fee rate were applied in calculating such data.

Systematic's performance results were compiled each quarter from a composite of fully discretionary accounts in which no extraordinary client withdrawals or contributions were made. Prior to the formation of Systematic in 1983, these accounts were managed by Kenneth S. Hackel, founder and President of Systematic, using Systematic's investment philosophy.

No implication is intended, and no inference should be drawn, that accounts will achieve similar investment performance in the future.

7.7 SUMMARY

The results we presented in this chapter show quite unambiguously that if one wants to identify securities for a "long" position, one cannot use low P/E ratios or low net operating cash flow multiples. These measures were useful in identifying firms for long positions in the beginning of the 1980s. Toward the end of the 1980s and the beginning of the 1990s, these investment strategies do not seem to outperform the market.

In contrast, investment strategies that are based on low free cash flow multiples, together with low debt restrictions and consistent ability to generate operating and free cash flow, yield returns that outperform the market. This is validated by back-tests of the model as well as by the performance of a live portfolio. Thus, the importance of free cash flows for portfolio selection is established by this evidence.

Index